Methodological Cognitivism

Riccardo Viale

Methodological Cognitivism

Vol. 1: Mind, Rationality, and Society

Springer

Prof. Riccardo Viale
Rosselli Foundation,
Torino,
Italy

The volume has been made possible with the support of Fondazione Rosselli, Turin (ITA)

Some of the chapters have been translated from Italian into English by Lucinda Byatt, Edinburgh and Deborah M. Craig, London (Geolink s.a.s., Turin)

ISBN 978-3-642-24742-2 e-ISBN 978-3-642-24743-9
DOI 10.1007/978-3-642-24743-9
Springer Heidelberg Dordrecht London New York

Library of Congress Control Number: 2012937032

Printed on acid-free paper

Springer is part of Springer Science+Business Media (www.springer.com)

In memory of my father
To Tancredi, Vittoria and Lucia

Foreword

When Massimo Egidi, Robin Marris and I collaborated with Herbert Simon in 1992 on the publication by Elgar of the book "Economics, Bounded Rationality and the Cognitive Revolution", the contribution of cognitive sciences to the theory of social rationality, and in general to the development of social sciences, was absolutely marginal and contested in Europe and in the United States. Cognitive sciences were seen with suspicion by sociologists, economists, political scientists, anthropologists and even philosophers. I had already experienced this type of hostility from the philosophical world directly a few years earlier, in Oxford in 1984. When I proposed the outline for my doctorate thesis in the Philosophy of Science, I had to overcome a great deal of hostility and disparagement on the part of my supervisor towards the issue of the *cognitive theory of science*. In Europe, in particular, the neopositivist culture still prevailed, maintaining a clear separation between the context of discovery and justification, an opinion strenuously sustained even by a non-neopositivist like Sir Karl Popper. Methodological rationality could not be analysed empirically because of the risk of falling prey to the mortal sin of naturalistic fallacy. The naturalistic revolution of W.O. Quine and the contribution of philosophers like Steven Stich or Alvin Goldman were not represented in the philosophy of science. Even Larry Laudan, who had considered the problem of the empirical-historical evaluation and justification of methodological rationality, was not part of the mainstream of the philosophy of science and was underestimated in Europe. My work in Oxford and my subsequent work at the L. Bocconi University of Milan, where I began to teach Logic and Epistemology as part of the course in Economic and Social Disciplines (DES) in 1987, provided the basis for my book "*Metodo e Società nella Scienza*", which was published in 1991, soon after Ronald Giere published his "*Explaining Science*" in 1988. Both set out to propose a naturalistic approach to the philosophy of science. Mine also argued in favour of the explanatory supremacy of the cognitive approach over the social approach in the study of the dynamics of conceptual change in the scientific community. This book is both a synthesis of my work on the *cognitive theory of science* (which will be the subject of the second volume) and the start of two working programmes, one in the epistemology and methodology of social sciences designed to overcome the intentionalism and rationalism inherent in the current Methodological Individualism, and the other designed to develop the cognitive foundations of social rationality, with particular reference to the economic context.

Where the first programme is concerned, the contemporary references were Raymond Boudon and Jon Elster. I introduced the term *Methodological Cognitivism* for the first time in 1994, to define the proposal of an individualistic methodology of social sciences, that based its theory of action on a causal model of the mind-action relationship. To develop this programme, I had to analyse a number of issues related to the philosophy of mind, the epistemology of causality, the methodology of social sciences and the cognitive models of reasoning and decision-making. In the years between 1997 and 2001, some of these issues were refined at the meetings of the Scientific Network of the European Science Foundation "Human Reasoning and Decision Making", particularly the encounters at the Sorbonne, Paris IV and the College de France. My recent work on methodological cognitivism, which developed in the direction of neurocognitive social sciences and the theory of mirror neurons in particular, was triggered by a theory of the strong identity between the mind and the brain.

My work on the cognitive theory of rationality, particularly in an economic context, evolved in parallel in that same period, from 1987 on. From the 1988 seminar with Herbert Simon at the Rosselli Foundation in Turin, until the conference on "Cognitive Economics" at the Bocconi University in Milan in 1996, the subsequent creation of the magazine *Mind & Society* in 2000 and, after Simon's death, the foundation of the Herbert Simon Society in 2008, numerous initiatives have enabled me to develop Simon's programme. The term "Cognitive Economics", which I coined at the conference in 1996 and subsequently returned to in the publication of the proceedings *Cognitive Economics* (1997), underlines an "extreme" attempt to overcome the epistemological bottlenecks of experimental economics and the scientific bottlenecks of behavioural economics. Only a reformulation of the theory of economic action according to the best models of neurocognitive sciences can stimulate positive economics and its realistic and empirical goals.

And finally, we come to the empirical work undertaken with Dan Osherson from 1995 on the inductive models of reasoning based on categories. This work was undertaken in Italy, but also in Vietnam at the University of Ho Chi Min City, and in New Delhi at the Indian Institute of Technology, and it allowed us to study the effects of the membership of different cultural or social groups on inductive reasoning among adults and children, and in particular the application of the "difference principle" and the Bayesian model. These studies of cognitive anthropology also contributed to the debate taking place in the scientific community, between supporters of relativism and of epistemological and cognitive universalism, and between those on innate bases or the cultural bases of the inferential capabilities of the human brain.

I have had the good fortune to develop some of these considerations at the Bocconi University in Milan, at Milan Bicocca University and at the Scuola Superiore di Pubblica Amministrazione in Rome, where I taught, and during periods spent at foreign universities such as Oxford, Aix en Provence, Fribourg, Rice-Houston, California-Santa Barbara and Columbia.

This volume of selected papers is divided into three parts to reflect the division into the three areas of study described above.

A second volume will be published in 2012. It will contain selected papers on cognitive theory of science, social epistemology, tacit knowledge and knowledge transfer. In any case both volumes are characterized by a common denominator: the *Methodological Cognitivism* as the new methodological tool to analyze the social action.

"Mind, Rationality, and Society" is the first book of Selected Papers, *"Methodological Cognitivism"*. Most of the chapters are modified versions of earlier publications. In this regard, I wish to first thank Laura Gilardi, without whose punctilious and professional editorial assistance I would not have been able to complete the work.

My main scientific debt is to Herbert Simon, who has been a constant benchmark for my work over the years.

Among those who are no longer with us, I am particularly indebted to Norberto Bobbio, who taught me to see new horizons in the relationship between the philosophy of science and human sciences. I must also mention Kathy Wilkes for her important comments on the philosophy of mind, and Martin Hollis for his considerations on the theory of rationality.

My encounter with Sir Karl Popper marked an important moment in my development; his intellectual reference has been fundamental throughout the years.

I am grateful to Giulio Giorello, Angelo Petroni, Dario Antiseri, Diego Marconi and Massimo Egidi for having introduced me to the issues that I have developed in the past years.

I would like to mention with particular gratitude the study and research undertaken in Oxford with William Newton Smith, and in Milan and Houston with Dan Osherson.

I am grateful to the following for their discussions and critical comments on my work over the years (in casual order and with many omissions): William Herbert Newton Smith, Dan Osherson, Raymond Boudon, Massimo Egidi, Giulio Giorello, Dan Sperber, Giovanni Dosi, Paolo Legrenzi, Vittorio Girotto, Rino Rumiati, Diego Marconi, Achille Varzi, Angelo Petroni, Dario Antiseri, Guido Martinotti, Denis Hilton, Steven Lukes, Luciano Gallino, Simona Morini, Laura Macchi, Jonathan Evans, Phil Johnson Laird, Margaret Boden, Giacomo Rizzolatti, Corrado Sinigaglia, Alvin Goldman, Rom Harre, Richard Nelson, Henry Etzkowitz, Loet Leyersdorff, Jon Elster, Domenico Parisi, Pietro Terna, Donato Masciandaro, Umberto Filotto, Raffaele Caterina, Margherita Balconi, Nicolao Bonini, Fabio del Missier, Davide Pietroni, Colin Blakemore, Elisabetta Galeotti and Bas Van Fraassen.

A special thank you to the editorial board of *Sistemi Intelligenti* since 1992 for the interesting critical discussions of many of the issues dealt with in this book.

My thanks also go to the Model Based Reasoning group and above all to Lorenzo Magnani, Ronald Giere, Nancy Nersessian and Paul Thagard, for the interesting periodical study meetings organised.

I owe a great deal for the work done to the collaboration of Andrea Cerroni, Davide Diamantini and Andrea Pozzali. I would also like to thank the Logic and

Epistemology classes of the course in Economic and Social Disciplines (DES) at Bocconi University in Milan between 1987 and 1999 for the shrewd critical observations and analyses presented in their dissertations and degree theses.

Many of the issues examined in this volume have been discussed at seminars or developed in research organised by the Rosselli Foundation in Turin from 1988 to 2008. For this reason, I would like to thank all those people who have made these important meetings and research possible, first and foremost Daniela Italia, Anna Mereu, Laura Gilardi.

A final thank you goes to Barbara Fess of Springer for her patience and for the interest she has always shown in the publication of my work.

And finally, this book would have been impossible without my wife's help, support, and advices.

New York, September 2011 Riccardo Viale

Contents

Introduction

1

The volume is divided into three parts and 14 chapters. The Introduction will be based, mainly, on parts of the various chapters of the volume.

Part I "*Cognitive Rationality and Society*" deals with the philosophical justification of *methodological cognitivism.*

The first chapter of the Part I "*Psychologism and Anti-Psychologism*" is dedicated to a short historical excursus on the fortunes and misfortunes of psychologism in methodology of social science. A number of key positions will be illustrated, without any desire for historical completeness but with the aim of establishing the premises for the arguments developed later in the book. The chapter starts with a question of John Stuart Mill: "*Are human actions subject to invariable laws like all other natural events? Are they really ruled by the constant of causality that underlies every scientific theory of successive phenomena?*" (Mill, 1st edition 1843; 8th edition 1956; Italian translation 1968, VI, I, § 1, p. 827). Mill answer that empirical generalizations are possible about society. They are generalization of some aspects of social life. However they derive their truth from causal laws, of which they are the consequence. If we are familiar with those laws, we know the limits of the derived generalizations; instead, if we have not yet justified the empirical generalization – if it is based on observation alone – then there is no guarantee in applying it out with the limits of time, place and circumstance in which the observations were made. Causal laws that can justify empirical generalisations must refer to the human mind. In other words, the laws of ethology, derived deductively from the laws of psychology, should allow us to explain the different characters of social or national contexts in the presence of different starting condition. But are the fundamental laws of psychology that constitute the causal barycentre of social explanation.

Mill's position was either neglected or criticised by later contributions to scientific methodology. These were marked by a generalised antipsychologism expressed by authors whose theses were radically divergent on other essential methodological questions. Marx, Weber, Menger, L. von Mises, Popper, von Hayek, Watkins, Boudon, Elster all share a stringent criticism of Mill's psychologism and, more in general, of the thesis concerning the reduction of social action to causal mechanisms

R. Viale, *Methodological Cognitivism*,

DOI 10.1007/978-3-642-24743-9_1,

of the human mind. It is significant that Popper takes Marx as one of the main objects of his critical analysis, but he finds himself in complete agreement with his antipsychologism and with the Marx's famous maxim: "It is not men's conscience that determines their being, but, on the contrary, their social being that determines their conscience" (Marx, Italian translation 1971, p. 5). According to Popper "The error of psychologism consists in claiming that methodological individualism in the field of social sciences entails the need to reduce all social phenomena and all social regularities to psychological phenomena and psychological laws" (Popper, 5th edition 1966; Italian translation 1974, vol. II, p. 131).

What kind of methodological individualism is justified by psychologism. Regarding the epistemic dimension only the *non-reductionist* option seems justified. What can be explained is only the particular social event (that is considered a linguistic fiction without any real content) and the explanation is based on laws and the starting conditions of individuals and their properties (therefore it cannot be considered an explanatory reduction of social events to laws and facts about individuals). This variation of Epistemic Individualism has no substantive ontological implications relating to what we propose as laws on individuals and their properties. The possibility of social laws is implicitly denied because the ontological existence of social phenomena is rejected. It is not assumed, however, which type of entity and individual properties are important for the explanation. The entities might be everything related to individual action. At the ontological level psychologism does not include *physical atomism* which seeks to explain social events on the basis of the physical and behavioural properties of single individuals. On the contrary, psychologism can be interpreted as a form of *psychological atomism* that intends to trace social events back to the individual's mental properties. Psychological atomism supports that only acceptable explanations of mental states are those accomplished by empirical science, by knowledge on human psychology and that the only relevant facts for individualistic explanation are the mental ones.

While the main stream of MI was antipsychologist until the recent past, from the 70s onwards the Millian tradition started to put forward new interpreters. For example Homans' thesis is that the explanation of social events by psychological propositions cannot be proved philosophically. It is a matter of empirical investigation and analysis. He states that all social phenomena can be analysed without residue into the actions of individuals. And since methodological individualism entails psychologism, all sociological facts can be explained by the use of psychological propositions.

The final paragraph of the chapter drafts the outline of an hypothesis, which I dub *methodological cognitivism*. It can be regarded as an evolution of methodological individualism given that it appears to neutralise some of its epistemological and methodological difficulties and is more firmly rooted in the fabric of scientific knowledge, which is now more widely accredited in the study of social action, that is cognitive science. The epistemological reasons for choosing cognitive science as a source of models to give scientific content to our individualist hypothesis are the following.

Causality. Cognitive science, in all its variants, includes the search for compatibility of mental states and processes with their brain substratum. This physicality of mental activity meets the requisite for continuity and spatial and temporal contiguity that is typical of all causal relations. The type of explanation of action offered by cognitive science is of a constituent nature in that it aims to identify the intimate causal mechanisms responsible for behavioural output.

Empirical nature. Cognitive science gives considerable importance to empirical research for the construction and checking of hypotheses. In experimental research, in the form of tests and in computer simulation, it is possible to make an independent determination of the starting conditions and the falsification of the hypothesis.

Irrationality. Cognitive science satisfies the principle of symmetry. Not only so-called rational behaviours but also irrational ones are explained by the same type of hypothesis.

Theoretical support. Cognitive science is not alone, instead it has or tries to have the theoretical support of some of the most accredited hypotheses of the scientific community. The search for this link is shown by the current debate on whether an overly strong characterisation of cognitive activity in linguistic terms is compatible or not with evolutionary theory, in view to the evolutionary delay with which language appeared. There are also significant links with Shannon's information theory, with Wiener's cybernetics, with Turing's and von Neumann's mathematical and computational models, and with the predominant theories of neurochemistry, neurobiology, neurophysiology and neuropathology. Support for cognitive science could also be found in the opposite direction. The importance of language and of inferential activity in moulding social relations is beyond doubt. The relationship is clearly biunique, but the constraints and limits with which the mind elaborates and filters return input from social relations are fundamental to explain the role of social factors in individual action. These constraints show a certain degree of regularity, which allows generalisations to be drawn that are useful, also at a predictive level, and which can provide support for compatible so-called *social theories*. One need only think of the potential importance of the decision-making heuristics in relation to economic theory, or of the theory of mental models in relation to the sociology of knowledge.

The second chapter "*The Mind-Society Problem*" deals with the relationship between mental and social phenomena. Often the "problem" is mediated by concepts like individual action or decision. In other cases the problem is implicit or even hidden. Nevertheless, every methodology of social sciences must, sooner or later, "cross the street" that connects mind and society. In the same way as the parallel mind-body problem, the mind-society problem concerns a number of variegated fundamental philosophical questions. These are metaphysical when they deal with the existence of one or more ontological levels of reality between mind and society; with the efficacy of social causation as distinct from individual mental causation; with the feature of social properties as second order properties compared to the first order mental properties; and so on. They are epistemological when they privilege the problem of explanation and representation. There are two strong critiques to the tentative reduction of social phenomena to mental mechanisms. The first and most powerful critique is what we might call the "hermeneutic surrender". The second can be termed the "holistic illusion".

In its most radical version the first critique claims that every individual action is so full of subjective social meaning that it can never be explained objectively, but only interpreted as we do for paintings and poems. The champion of this approach is Charles Taylor (1985) and the methodological model is Max Weber's concept of *verstehen* (1949). This affirms that there are no general laws that allow us to predict or explain the social action, nor we can hope to discover them. We can divide this position in two claims: (a) the interpretation of social action is not made according to general laws; (b) the meaning of social action is not reducible to general natural facts of the human mind.

If we fully accept the first claim – that there are no explanatory generalizations in social sciences – the most coherent conclusion is that it would be impossible even to describe the external behaviour of the social actors. In fact every description implies a certain amount of general categorization expressed by concepts being used in the description. Moreover, many of the behavioural concepts imply some kind of general psychological hypothesis. Lastly, the use of general psychological hypotheses is unavoidable if, as prescribed in the *verstehen* methodology, we want to understand the mental states of the agent. How can the hermeneutic social scientist infer the agent's mental state from a knowledge of his behaviour and of the social and cultural context? By applying some general hypothesis regarding the relationships between his beliefs, desires and actions. Namely, by applying a general theory that we usually call *common sense* or *folk psychology*.

Concerning the second claim the meaning of a social action is not reducible to general facts of the human mind because, according to hermeneutics, mental properties are not reducible to physical properties. Therefore they cannot be explained by laws referring directly to the properties of aggregate physical entities. The properties of mind are different from the properties of brain (property dualism). If hermeneutics implicitly supports the previous concept of mind, it therefore entails the impossibility to make an appeal to any form of causal explanation of social action. In fact, causality is a property of matter and can refer only to relations between events in the physical world. Moreover, if the thesis of completeness of physics is correct, any causal relation at any level of aggregation of reality should be reducible to an explanation at an inferior level. Any claim of causal relation at a given level can be accepted if a causal explanation is available based on the properties of entities at the underlying level of aggregation of nature. It seems that property dualism cannot allow this kind of causal explanation. If we want to establish a causal picture of the relations between mind and action we must avoid having to rely on any kind of property dualism. Only a strong identity theory between mental and neural properties can let us work out causal models that try to explain the mechanisms of individual action. It is obvious that some methodologies of social sciences like hermeneutics do not share either the premises and the conclusion of this argument. There is an alternative solution. As affirmed by

Kim (1998), the identity between mental properties and neural properties does not imply the elimination of the mental dimension. Even if the claim of identity is that the causal role is played exclusively by the neural realizers of the mind and there is no autonomous and separate mental causation, it is possible to preserve the property dimension of the mind for practical reasons. The mental property will be considered second order property of the neural first order property, that is a property of having a property in the neural base with given causal potentials (functional reduction).

There are two different research programme linked to these alternative options. Strong identity theory seems to incline towards the eliminative option, represented by computational neuroscience. On the contrary the second functionalist reduction is coherent with most of research in cognitive psychology. The first programme tries to derive psychological concepts starting from neural phenomena, while the second starts from the mental level of rules and representations and tries to find the neural counterparts. In other words, one is bottom-up and the other is top-down. Only scientific research will prove if our mental activity is merely a distributed pattern of neural activation or if it has to be modelled as the neural embodiment of syntactic rules processing representations. Actually, current cognitive psychology, which attempts to discover the syntactic rules or procedures that process representations without overly resorting to folk psychology, has provided the best generalizations to explain social action to date.

The second critique is towards the *holistic illusion*. Theories are still present in the methodologies of social sciences that support an autonomous and separate level of social phenomena. Structuralism and social functionalism are two examples. The first consideration is that if we want to reduce something, the reducible phenomenon must be real. And the separate ontology of social phenomena is, in my opinion, more dubious than that of water compared to its molecular structure. If this is true, concepts and language about social phenomena are only, and not always, useful elliptical metaphor referring to group of individuals and the explanations of social phenomena are the explanations of the behaviour of these groups of individuals. As in the previous eliminative programme about mind-brain identity, there is no reduction but only the elimination of one non-existent level by the other. The social dimension is quite dubious even from a conceptual point of view. Often the social concepts only have an *intensional* life, in other words they only live in the heads of social scientists and they lack any *extensional* reference. In other cases their extension is definable only with reference to individuals and their behaviour. Teleological social *functionalist* explanations can always be interpreted causally as individual actions reinforced by positive feedback from the environment to the mental representations and decision-making processes of the agent. Another holistic remark tries to show that social phenomena are emergent and are not reducible to individual cognition. For example, unintended consequences of action or social learning cannot be explained in terms of cognitive mechanisms of action. At first glance these phenomena seem to have something that goes beyond individual cognition. In the chapter it will be shown that this is not the case.

The third chapter "*Cognition and Rationality of Beliefs in Social Sciences*" analyzes one side of rationality neglected by neoclassical economy, that of the rationality of beliefs. The theoretical focus has mainly been concentrated over the past few years in analyzing the side of the *formal rationality* of preferences. One question comes naturally to mind: why have researchers concentrated mainly on the formal aspects of rationality, and on preferences in particular, neglecting to analyze the *substantial aspects of rationality*, in particular the extremely important question of beliefs? The most probable response might arise from the fact that the theoretical elaboration of the concept of rationality has above all been provided by economists, who are clearly interested mainly in the formal relationship between preferences and consumer choice, and only secondarily in the question of contents and the foundation of beliefs and expectations.

Economists have introduced two key meanings for rationality. There is a *broader definition of rationality*. It is felt that an actor acts rationally, for example, when he has a utility function whose arguments are defined as alternative uses of the resources with which he is endowed. The quantity of these resources are seen as constraints to the possible choices available to the decision-maker, so that rational behaviour consists, in terms of solving a problem of bounded maximisation, in determining the whole panoply of resources to dedicate to each of the possible uses. The second definition of rationality is a *narrow* one, which has replaced the broader definition in many descriptive contexts. Rationality is seen as the maximisation of expected utility, which is instead based on strong *a priori* psychological assumptions. It assumes preferences as being given and coherent, a corpus of beliefs corresponding to a true description of the world, and an unlimited decisional power for the decision-maker. Therefore, there is no need to draw a distinction between the real world and the decision-maker's perception of it, given that he has a true representation of the world. Contrary to these assumptions, if instead we accept the empirically confirmed finding on the limited capacity of knowledge and the computational power of the human decision-maker, then we must distinguish between the real world and the representations of it formed by the decision-maker. In other words, we must elaborate an empirical theory of the cognitive processes that lead to the decision. This will therefore include the perception, representation and memorization of beliefs in the world and the deductive and probabilistic reasoning on the factual base it produces. This is what Simon defines as *procedural rationality*. The neoclassical economic approach to rationality has instead hampered the development of effective methods to investigate the processes through which selected aspects of reality are perceived, or how a representation of the situation of choice is formed or how inferential processes are responsible for particular conclusions based on the previous representation. It is clear from various examples given by Simon (1986, pp. 29–38) that many explanations of neoclassical economics taken with the ad hoc addition of auxiliary assumptions could have been reached using the postulate of limited procedural rationality without the assumption of the maximisation of utility. For example, the neoclassical theory, with or without resorting to the assumption of rational expectations, cannot explain the phenomenon of the economic cycle without resorting to auxiliary irrational assumptions, like that of *monetary illusion*, which clearly correspond to a deviation from objective rationality.

At this point we could characterise the rationality model in three successive stages, each featuring a specific type of rationality. The informative process gives the agent a range of more or less accurate evidential data (*perceptive rationality*), which are represented and memorised (*rationality of beliefs*); using logical and probabilistic forms of reasoning, the decisional process infers the possible action from the information (*decisional rationality*); and the implementation processes transform, with more or less accurate results, the potential action into real action (*rationality of action*). Decisional rationality can, in turn, be broken down into two main forms of rationality: *cognitive rationality*, linked to processing the available data in order to define the agent's expectations about himself and the surrounding environment, and *instrumental rationality*, which, based on these expectations, tries to select the most appropriate action. Perceptive and decisional rationality correspond to Simon's procedural rationality.

To my way of thinking, Simon's normative solution is too biased towards instrumental rationality and fails to focus sufficiently on the problem of rationality of beliefs, the accuracy of representing the world (and also of representing the problem of choice) which forms the information base for heuristic inference. This inference will be more or less effective depending on whether the representation of reality is more or less correct, more or less significant and not banal. The rationality of representing informative inputs presents problems of an epistemological nature which are still far from being resolved using a cognitive and simulative approach. An epistemological solution to these problems might be the *internalist* that sustains that the rationality and reliability of our belief formation processes is guaranteed *a priori* by ourselves and that no empirical and experimental study would be able to question the rationality of these processes. If anything, they could only describe them. Quine's naturalization program of epistemology (1985) moves in this direction. Instead of asking how we ought to go about forming our beliefs, we should ask how do we actually go about it.

Perception is a central theme of this program. One of the standard approaches in the psychology of perception is based on pattern recognition. People recognize the presentation of a particular object as an example of a certain pattern. Perception output implies a classification of the stimulus. Perception is ultimately made up of two kinds of elaboration: bottom-up elaboration, in which information flows from small perceptive inputs to larger units made up of those inputs, and top-down elaboration, in which background beliefs influence the interpretation of the most elementary perceptive units. For example visual control of action is mediated by cortical pathways that are different from those involved in visual control of the perception. In other words, when we merely see an object, such as chair, we process differently that if we intend also to pick up the object. Usually we perceive the object holistically. But if we intend to act on them, we perceive them more analytically so that we can act in an effective way (Ganel and Goodale 2003). Moreover, a trade-off phenomenon between rapidity and reliability of perception is evident. Strong emotions, such as desires and fears, generally related to primary needs, lead to an improvement in perception rapidity to the detriment of reliability.

The corpus of beliefs, the factual foundation of rationality, depends on memory. The first consideration to make concerns which database is used in the inference. Various experiments, as well as everyday observation, clearly show that the factual database used often corresponds only to a part of the beliefs available in long-term memory and useful for inferences (Sternberg 2009). People cannot gain access to a significant part of their knowledge and consequently the resulting inferences are generally wrong. Sometimes the individual cannot connect all elements, useful for inference, existing in his memory. Associated to memory we find the irrational phenomenon of perseverance in the belief, carefully studied by Nisbett and Ross (1980). People are inclined to preserve a belief even after it has been proved false by new evidential data. There is also another characteristic of memory which goes against the rational principle of revision of beliefs in the face of new informational data. According to psychologists, long-term memory is not a blackboard from which propositions can be wiped out on the basis of new evidence. On the contrary, there seems to be no real loss of informational material from memory unless as a result of physical damage. Every piece of information memorised, and every belief acquired, is stored in memory and cannot be erased even after it has been proved false. If information cannot be erased from memory, it will contain contradictions and time structures.

Therefore how can we establish a sound rationality of beliefs that is the factual premise of our decision, if the memory and perception generate so many biases and distortions? The principal condition of rationality of beliefs is that the factual base, the corpus of beliefs, is founded, and corresponds, as reliably as possible, to the real world. Any particular method of gathering information yields putative results because of its own peculiarities, its biases and distortions. *Triangulation*, that is using multiple procedures, methods or assumptions to get at the same putative object, trait, or regularity serves to correct such biases in order to know the real properties of the phenomenon being studied. Truth as correspondence to reality can be well expressed by the following metaphor used by Alvin Goldman (1986): unlike the metaphor of truth as a mirror of pre categorized nature, truth can be seen as a garment that is tailor-made to fit reality using a variety of instruments. The styles, and also the categories, produced by man, may vary and differ, what is important is that they achieve the result of "clothing" reality. Triangulation would entail using all the decision-maker's cognitive, heuristic and methodological resources, critically and cross-referenced, in line with the techniques identified by cognitive science. They would be used to construct a corpus of beliefs, a factual base that has a reliability and likelihood that has been produced and verified independently by different cognitive processes.

Chapter 4 "*Brain, Mind, and Social Action*" deals with how the brain research can contribute to the methodology of social sciences.

One of the most important concerns of contemporary philosophy of social sciences is the relationship between the researcher and human behavior, specifically the modality employed by the social researcher to understand or predict the actions of a social agent through the identification or simulation of her mental states. Cognitive identification and simulation is the necessary premise to understand an action and generalize it into an ideal-type representing aggregate social behavior or a social phenomenon.

In studying social action, the researcher tries to reconstruct the mental process that led or could lead the agent to act in a certain way. There are various candidates for her mindreading, which may be conducted with one of three main methods: through simulation by the researcher of the target's mental states; through theoretical inference of the target's mental states based on a folk psychology theory; through inference of the target's mental states based on a specialist scientific theory. Through mindreading, the researcher aims to identify the mental states directly responsible for an action. So his attention will focus largely on propositional attitudes like beliefs, desires, decisions, plans, hopes. Mindreading of these mental states typically takes place at conscious level with a certain degree of willpower (Goldman 2006, p. 147). The reader may interrupt, slow down or speed up the reading. He can decide which mental states to include in or exclude from the reading process. He has a partially clear conscious idea of the various steps in the reading process. In the relationship between mindreader and target, however, the target's mental states are also read at another level. This level corresponds to emotional empathy (or with a new term *mindfeeling)* reading of sensations like feelings and pain and of emotions like disgust and anger. The characteristics of this low-level mindreading (Goldman 2006) differ from those of the first type of mindreading. It is an automatic reading, independent of the will. The reading is often not conscious, although subsequently it may become so when we become aware of its effect. We cannot govern the process.

What principle does the researcher adopt when mindreading and processing the target's choice of action? In trying to make sense of his target, the attributor "will try for a theory that finds him consistent, a believer of truths, and a lover of the good" (Davidson 1980, p. 253). According to Davidson and Dennett, mindreading is possible if the mental states are identified on the basis of a priori normative principles. Without such principles, reconstruction of the reasons for the target's action is impossible. Likewise, some contributions from social psychology (Hamilton and Sherman 1996) and pragmatics of language (Grice 1989) highlight attributors' tendency to adopt principles of consistency, wholeness of information and truth in understanding or predicting others' actions. In contrast to normative a priori attribution we have the possibility of an empirical a posteriori attribution, which aims during the mindreading process to identify the principles governing mental state attribution and action prediction. Quine despaired of the possibility that we can infer the specific content of the mental states of a target. The only way is to bootstrap from our mental states and to proceed by empathetic imaginative projection (McGee 2005). To do this, the social attributor must avoid projecting his own normative principles and concentrate on the target's life, history, reference context and empirical data, using this inductive knowledge and active imagination to attribute a posteriori the principles used by the target.

In conducting empirical research, the social scientist, like every other scientist, is however generally conditioned by the theories of his field and his background knowledge. According to Theory Theory (TT) (Premack and Woodruff 1978), attribution of other people's mental states is possible only through construction and development of a theory. Our mental states and others' mental states are unobservables empirically linked, in the first case, with sensorial input and, in the second, with external behavior and action, and consequently any attribution is of a theoretical nature. On the basis of these theoretical entities, beginning in infancy we build our theoretical assumptions on third person's mental activity and first person's mental activity. Thus, every time we mindread a target, we apply a "Hempel model" where our theory, generally a more or less complex version of folk psychology, represents the major premise of the explanans. By analogy this deductive hypothetical activity also takes place in social research. In order to identify the causes of a social agent's action, the mindreading on the various individuals will be guided deductively by the folk theory and its concepts. The mindreading will lead to the development of the scientific hypothesis under investigation.

As Goldman has convincingly shown (2006), various experimental cognitive and neuroscientific findings appear to diminish the theoretical importance of TT in mental attribution. One of the cornerstones of TT, the theoretical aspect of mental states, has been questioned by a series of studies on first person attribution. There is asymmetry between the access to third person and first person mental states. The access to first person mental states resembles the visual perception. The representation of mental types is direct 'perception-like recognition process in which a given occurring token is mapped into mental category selected from a relatively smallish number of types' (Goldman 2006, p. 253). The representation of mental content instead utilizes the redeployment (and in the case of visual format the translation from visual code to belief code) of the content already present in mind to produce the content assignment contained in the metarepresentation. (Goldman 2006, p. 254). This model of introspective self-attribution supporting a strong asymmetry between first person and third person attribution seems to be supported by neuroscientific data. Furthermore, social researchers know that self-reflection is the source of the main intuitions regarding an hypothesis as well as its first test-bed. If the researcher is free to simulate the relationship between mental states and action directly in his own mind without reference to a folk theory, he will have a better chance to catch genuine features of the causes of the social action. A reliable mindreading of the target's mental states requires the researcher to put aside his theoretical models and idiosyncratic positions and simulate those of the target without distortions. The greater the match between the two states, the greater the cognitive value of mindreading. As we have seen, TT rejects the possibility of theory-free reading. Simulation theory, on the other hand, regards it as one of its distinguishing characteristics. This is not to say there are no egocentric tendencies nor that the mental state content is that of the target. Specifically, there appears to be evidence that mindreading in everyday life has a tendency to make egocentric attributions with regard to knowledge, preferences, feelings. Behavioral economics offers extensive literature on this point. In attributing propositional content, the attributor necessarily takes his personal conceptual and ontological constructs as a basis. Even if the way he builds the representation and derives the inference tends to correspond with that of the target, the building blocks are those of the mindreader. In any case the neuroscience findings seem to indicate that a specific area of the brain is responsible for self-perspective inhibition, a vital function if the mindreader is to quarantine his egocentric projective tendencies. When the mindreader is a social scientist, a double effort is required: to quarantine egocentrism and to inhibit the interpretative role of the scientist's professional knowledge, in particular of the social theory for which he is performing the mindreading. The scientist may be unable to achieve this dual inhibition by himself and may require external aids to conduct a critique of his personal viewpoint in order to quarantine it. This could take the form of intersubjective comparisons with other researchers or, better still, with non-experts using the three-step mindreading procedure proposed by Goldman (2006, p. 170).

The main approaches in social sciences favor mindreading at the level of propositional attitudes. Understanding or predicting an action requires mindreading of the mental states – beliefs, desires and intentions – responsible for the action. This is achieved through conscious, intentional metarepresentation of the target's mental states by the attributor. Forms of automatic, unconscious reading of intentional mental states are not contemplated nor does reading of emotions and sensation play an important part. This is the thesis shared by the normative approaches in social sciences and advocated by TT. Recent neuroscientific research, however, appears to show otherwise. Recent studies on a human cortical network composed of the rostral part of the inferior parietal lobule and the caudal sector of the inferior frontal gyrus plus the adjacent part of the premotor cortex (Rizzolatti et al. 2001) found a type of neuron, the *mirror neuron*, that seems to intermediate automatic unconscious attribution of intentional content to a third person observed in action.

When we see *transitive* hand/arm gestures (involving an object, such as picking up a cup) or *intransitive* hand/arm gestures (not involving an object, such as a dance step), there is an activation of part of the same motor circuits that are recruited when we ourselves perform that action. The mirror neuron system encodes not only the gesture under observation, but also the intention with which it is performed, as demonstrated by recent research by Iacoboni et al. (2005). Additionally, other studies with fMRI found a functional connection between the areas in the mirror neurons, the insula and the emotional areas of the limbic system, in particular the amygdala (Carr et al. 2003). The mirror neurons are activated when we see other people expressing emotions as if we ourselves were making those facial expressions. The activated neurons also transmit signals, via the insula, to the emotional cerebral centers of the limbic system, so that we ourselves experience what the person we are watching is experiencing (Iacoboni 2008). Both types of attribution are simulative processes, albeit a type of automatic and unconscious embodied simulation.

Should this hypothesis be confirmed by future research, it will have a considerable impact on understanding of social action. Embodied simulation of mirror neuron theory is creating difficulties not only for the normative approach, already undermined by the weakening of TT and the other approaches positing theoretical mindreading, but also for the pure cognitive approach. Cognitive simulative action mindreading often seems to be overridden by automatic, unconscious attribution of intentional content. And this is not just a question of attribution of "a motoric plan" (Gallese and Goldman 1998, p. 498) because the "real attributor does not go back to a distal goal or set of beliefs" (Gallese and Goldman 1998, p. 498), as mirror neuron researchers themselves believed a few years ago. On the contrary, as recent research by Iacoboni et al. (2005) has found, the real attributor does indeed go back to a distal goal or set of beliefs! Moreover, the emphatic resonance might penetrate action understanding in a forceful manner. It might add emotional overtones to the context in which intentional content is automatically attributed to the observed action. The viscero-motor simulation of the emotional expression of the observed subject might enhance the somato-motor simulation of the observed action, providing a better focus on the internal reasons for the action. The hermeneutic approach in social sciences seems to be the only approach to anticipate and be consistent with the results of research on mirror neuron theory embodied simulation, in particular because of the importance it attaches to emotional and affective simulation and to the corporeality of the simulation.

Part II of the volume "*Cognitive Economics*" analyzes the features of *cognitive economics* born trough the application of *methodological cognitivism* to theory of economic action.

The first chapter "*Developing Simon's Bounded Rationality*" analyzes the implications of Simon's bounded rationality theory in economics.

Herbert Simon is the father of the empirically based microeconomics. His economic theory is founded on a new concept of economic rationality. Herbert Simon's contribution to the theory of economic rationality can be characterized by one *pars destruens* and one *part costruens*. The first part is the attack to the neoclassical Olympic rationality. The second is the proposal of an empirically based bounded rationality theory. While the first seems justified theoretically and empirically the second shows some serious flaws.

In science there are two basic ways to control a theoretical hypothesis: (a) indirectly, by upholding the general propositions to which the hypothesis is deductively connected; (b) directly, through the control of factual, singular propositions that can be derived from the hypothesis, in the form of initial conditions. In posing the problem of controlling the theoretical hypothesis of the rational maximizing actor in neoclassical economics we can refer to either way.

To which general propositions is the economic actor hypothesis connected in neoclassical economics? According to Simon (1987, p. 26) this model of rational actor is mainly connected to the following hypotheses:

1. His beliefs about aims and values are given and not liable to change in time and through experience.
2. His beliefs are internally coherent.
3. The agent is capable of an objective description of the world.
4. His abilities to elaborate data to define his expectations, that is, respectively, his probabilistic and deductive reasoning, are not limited.

We could express these properties otherwise by saying that, in the neoclassical economic actor, perceptive rationality and rationality of beliefs – the rationality which is assumed in the representations of informational data – and decisional rationality – the rationality which is assumed in inferential activities which lead from data to decisions – are non-limited (from the point of view of some normative canons). Neoclassical *perceptive rationality* and *rationality of beliefs* presupposes an objective representation of the world, in the form of coherently organized true beliefs. Empirical control of this hypothesis has been effected mainly through cognitive study of perception and memory mechanisms and of the codes of representation of informational data. As I have shown before up to now these controls prove that the representation of informational data is often unreliable and incoherent. Top-down elaboration of perceptive stimuli often tends to add something which was not present in the stimulus itself: some internal constructive process mediates between the entry stimulus and the perceptive result. This can lead to an improvement or to a decline in the reliability and truth of the perception, depending on the kind of perception and on individual mnemonic patterns. Various experiments, as well as everyday observation, clearly show that the factual data base used in inference often corresponds only to a part of the beliefs available in long term memory and useful for inferences. People can't gain access to a significant part of their knowledge and consequently the resulting inferences are generally wrong. Sometimes the individual cannot connect all elements, useful for inference, existing in his memory. People are inclined to preserve a belief even after it has been proved false by new evidence. The reason of this perseverance can be found in the emotional refusal of new beliefs, deemed unsatisfactory, and in the search for factual validation of old beliefs through the retrieval of supporting information from memory. Moreover every piece of information memorized, and every belief acquired, is stored in memory and cannot be erased even after it has been proved false. If information material cannot be erased from memory, it will contain contradictions and time structures.

Serious cognitive constraints to the "Olympian" pretences of neoclassical rationality have also been empirically brought to attention in regard to *decisional rationality*. In elaborating the available data to define expectations about environment and agent and to select, on the basis of these expectations, the most appropriate action, people seem to deviate from the rules underlying the neoclassical rational agent. This is evident in many studies of *probabilistic reasoning*, which have shown that man forms estimates about the likelihood of future events, assigns numbers and percentages, combines probabilities and values in a way which does not conform to the theory of probability. The selection of information deemed relevant for decisional purposes is not carried out through an exhaustive examination at mnemonic level of all relevant information (Tversky and Kahneman 1973). Man tends to select examples of large classes rather than of small ones, even if they are just as relevant in the decisional context (heuristic of availability). Another tendency discovered by Tversky and Kahneman is the propensity to give counter-normative judgements according to the degree to which the salient characteristics of an object or person are representative of or similar to characteristics conceived as peculiar to some category. Some experiments have shown that subjects underestimate the effects of new evidence and that this underestimate is reflected in their evaluation of the subsequent probability, evaluated as lower than predicted by Bayesian theorem. This behaviour has been called conservative by Edwards (1968). On the other hand, subjects have more often been found to ignore completely, in certain situations, previous probability.

A decision is generally elaborated by combining probabilistic and *deductive reasoning*. One implicit logical form which can often be identified in the argument at the basis of inferences is the syllogism. In it premises and conclusion can have various forms, among them universal, particular, probabilistic or hypothetical propositions, so that we can speak of categorical syllogisms, statistical syllogisms and quasi-syllogisms. Empirical results of experiments on syllogistic reasoning have shown very low levels of performance. One of the most important inference rules that has been studied till now is the *modus ponens* of material implication. It rules that given the proposition "if A then B", and given also A, then one can validly infer B. Most people find little difficulty in accepting arguments based on the *modus ponens*, but often have problems with another inference rule known as *modus tollens*. This rule dictates that, given the proposition "if A then B", and given also the fact that B is false, we can infer that A is false. Both these inference rules seem quite obvious, but people find some difficulty in applying them. The difficulty arises from the inability to behave in a way which fits with the correct interpretation of the rules, and from the inclination to draw conclusions which are not justified.

To conclude, empirical control of the propositions at the basis of the model of rational actors in neoclassical economics appears to falsify them. Common man's inferential and decisional performances diverge from the prescriptions of the hypotheses underlying maximizing rationality. This reason alone would be enough to reject the hypothesis itself.

For the sake of methodological completeness one could also control the factual predictions inferred from the model of neoclassical rationality. If the predictions too were falsified by empirical data of an economic kind, one would have another strong argument against preserving the hypothesis of maximizing rationality. There are two main ways of controlling the factual consequences of an economic theory: through observation in artificial experiments or through historical recording in the so-called natural experiments. From a methodological point of view economists are rather doubtful about whether *artificial experiments* can be considered as a reliable testing ground for the rational actor theory. There are three specific constraints for an experiment to be acceptable by economists (Hogarth and Reder 1987, pp. 11–13):

1. Subjects in the experiment must have experience as maximizing actors in the specific market sector.
2. Subjects must be appropriately motivated so that rewards are a progressive function of the correctness of their answers.
3. Experimental settings must correspond with a context in which competition market forces are active.

However, some experiments have been carried out in recent years to reproduce the conditions of choice outlined by economists. Results are contradictory. In some experiments which aimed at reproducing motivational patterns in relation to the correctness of answers, results have been counter-normative. Thaler (1987) and Kahneman and Tversky (1987) have quoted studies in which an inverse relation between incentives and rational behaviour has emerged. Other studies, conducted on experts in experimental realistic settings, have highlighted a proportion of errors analogous to the one of non-expert groups (Eddy 1982). In artificial experiments the possibility of selecting and isolating the most relevant decisional variables allows, in principle, direct control of the maximizing rationality hypothesis. Verifying the rational choice hypothesis in the so-called *natural experiments* is a different matter. Economic science has a pre-eminently deductive nature. Given the general framework of the rational choice hypothesis – in its enlarged version of constrained maximization of the utility function or in the restricted version of maximization of expected utility – economists are interested in extending the applicable domain of the hypothesis. This is achieved through various conventional stratagems, but chiefly through an abundant use of suitable, and often *ad hoc*, auxiliary assumptions, which protect the rational choice hypothesis from falsifications, without increasing the empirical content of the theory.

To conclude, both the control of the general propositions at the basis of the model of rational actor and the control of the factual consequences of this theory seem negative. The successful explanation of the economic behaviour doesn't rely only on the neoclassical theory of rational actor plus the initial conditions but needs the *post hoc* addition of new assumptions. These assumptions, in many cases, have the form of empirical psychological laws about economic decision making. These laws often add empirical content to the theory, therefore their introduction may be considered non *ad hoc* and then accepted. But in many cases they rob the neoclassical theory of rational actor of its predictive primacy. The "maximizing" theory itself becomes an auxiliary assumption that may be substituted by the "satisficing" one without any loss of explicative power. In other cases the *post hoc* assumption, doesn't add any empirical content nor function as a semantic device to define the situation. These are typical *ad hoc* adjustments that show the inadequacy of the theory.

The *pars costruens* of Simon is the proposal of an empirically based bounded rationality theory. The first consideration is to be made on the ontology of the economic actor concept. Does it refer to the general characteristics of the agent, or does it simply single out the functions of the actor who is present in economic contexts? Or, to put it another way, does it describe the real man or only a part of him specialising in economic interaction? If we think back to two of the founding fathers of economic theory, Adam Smith and John Stuart Mill, the difference is clear. In Smith's view (1776), man's self interest conduct, the object of economic study, was not aimed solely at increasing his pecuniary wealth, but rather at sentiments such as honour, ambition, social esteem, love of dominion and so on – themes of psychological study; Mill (1848), instead, saw it as a hypothetical exemplification isolating a select set of the functions, such as the maximisation of wellbeing and the desire for leisure time, which underpin economic behaviour.

Homo oeconomicus is thus an abstraction of only a part of human conduct, not of the whole. This "fictional man" differs from the real man proposed by other authors, such as Neville Keynes (1917), according to whom the economic actor is not an abstraction of a specific part of behaviour, since self-interest and the pursuit of subjective utility are pervasive and predominant over other forms thereof, such as altruism and solidarity. In this conflict, the realistic position would appear to enjoy clear predominance in most of modern and contemporary economics. But the question is: what kind of realism are we referring to? How can the economic actor theory be generated from the characteristics of the real man? One way would be to construct generalised psychological functions that are significant for economic action: this is the realist and empirical way suggested by Hutchinson (1938) and by bounded rationality theory. The other is to use intuition or introspection to separate a limited number of principles which govern the behaviour of the real man, and which characterise him as *homo oeconomicus*. This is the way followed by virtually all economic theory from Senior (1836; 1965) onwards, and the one which characterises the neoclassical global rationality concept. Its aim is to describe the economic agent in terms of a general behavioural principle, that of maximisation and individual utility functions.

What are the implications for Simon's bounded rationality of his sharp realist and empiricist characterisation? Perceptive rationality, rationality of beliefs and decision-making rationality correspond to Simon's *procedural and bounded rationality*. If by perceptive rationality and rationality of beliefs we mean the perceptive and mnemonic modalities of correct and coherent representation of the real world, then we can perform this screening by tacitly introducing two important epistemological and prescriptive principles, that of truth and that of coherence. In my view, it is, above all, the principle of truth or likelihood, in its various forms of correspondence to reality – a veritable labour of Sisyphus in contemporary epistemology - which acts as a conceptual stumbling-block in the way of Simon's programme to reduce the normative theory of procedural rationality to the descriptive theory of perception and decision. To reach his objective, therefore, Simon first has to solve the normative problem of how and why a perceptive, mnemonic data-base is correct, and hence acceptable as a point of departure for our inferences and decisions.

The second problem we encounter is that of the scope of the realism of the rational actor hypothesis. Insofar as Simon's bounded and procedural rationality seeks to be a realistic representation of human cognitive activity, it finds its *raison d'étre* in the hypotheses of scientific psychology. The first question we have to ask is: "what type of psychology?". One initial doubt concerns the code of mental representations, which Simon considers entirely reducible to *list structures*. Are we really sure that propositions and, above all, representations in image-form are built into the long-term memory as list structures? Simon himself has recognised that they cannot represent the images' metrical and spatial continuity properties. As recent neurophysiological research would appear to suggest, the mental image is irreducible and it is produced by the activity of the same structure of the central nervous system as visual perception.

A second, and much more important, doubt regards the type of mental processing. Research in the fields of neuropsychology and artificial intelligence is increasingly reinforcing the thesis that memory, learning and mental activity in general happen not through the manipulation of separate symbols according to explicit rules as in Simon's production systems, but through the parallel processing of distributed representations created by the fusion of many separate experiences.

Finally if decision making often seems determined by causes in our unconscious emotional life, this important dimension of mental activity does not seem to be given the place it deserves in the psychology underlying Simon's bounded rationality concept. Simonian production systems based on rules and explicit symbols seem inadequate as models of unconscious mental life and mental events such as emotion, which seemingly display characteristics of impenetrability and cognitive holism.

The second chapter "*Feasibility and Realism in Cognitive Economics*" faces the key question of how to deal with the empirical anomalies and inadequacies of economics? In summarizing the various methodological solutions, I have attempted to extrapolate two positions. The first is the Popperian position or non-sophisticated falsificationism expressed by authors like Mark Blaug (1980, pp. 160–161). In Blaug's opinion neoclassical economics does not fit the methodological desiderata of an empirical theory. The second position is Friedman's anti-realist "as if" proposal (1953). We may know that our economic theory is false or we do not care about its truth. What is important is that it saves the phenomena, that it makes good predictions. Therefore, faced with the empirical failures of neoclassical economics, we must confront the problem of building a different representation of the economic phenomena which we want to explain and predict. To achieve this goal we must solve the following dilemma: can the descriptive and predictive power of economics be increased by developing and improving the neoclassical theory or, as Blaug maintains, must we abandon the neoclassical postulates and look for an alternative theory?

There are three main philosophical flaws that, in my opinion, condemn neoclassical economics to a barren desert of research with no prospect of development and improvement.

The first is related to the *model of mind* used in economics. This model, which is based on the belief-preference-action triad, seems empirically empty and unfalsifiable. First since the triad belief-desire-action stems from the common sense of everyday life – and in fact the relative psychology is called "commonsense or folk psychology" – the interchangeable and confused use that is made in economics of concepts related to belief and desire is incorrect and goes against the commonsense meaning of the words. For example, the economic use of synonyms for preference words like desire – while it is possible to prefer something that is not desirable – goal – while I might be constrained to follow a certain goal without having preferred it, let alone desired it – want, and so on. Also belief is sometimes exchanged with opportunity and expectation, although there is a clear difference between them: expecting that something might happen, or having an opportunity to do something does not imply believing in either. In addition, according to commonsense psychology, the mental machine responsible for economic action is impressive for its poverty. How can we limit the causal variables of action only to belief and preference? We know from personal experience how many other factors are involved in decision and action.

Second, during the past 20 years there has been a great debate among those specializing in philosophy of the mind and psychology about the empirical adequacy of folk psychology (L). Folk psychology cannot be controlled empirically because every control presupposes the truth of L. This result conceals another serious drawback: the tautological dimension of L. Every description of human action according to L is equivalent to a repetition of the event to be described. We cannot describe an action without reference to the beliefs and desires that contain the action and we cannot describe the belief without reference to the desires and actions.

Third, another strong criticism of the model of action based on belief and preference is that it is a theoretical fiction that does not correspond to any natural kind, and it cannot be reduced or supported by any other accepted scientific theory.

Therefore, the mental machinery responsible for economic action must be enriched far beyond the folk concepts of belief and preference. Cognitive science and, in particular, cognitive psychology have developed many different empirical generalizations and laws that can give a richer and more accurate representation of the reality of the mental life, and in particular its reasoning and decision-making.

Even if this model of mind were valid there is a second flaw that impedes the improvement of neoclassical economics: this is a *theory of rationality* built in an *a priori* way and justified by an old-fashioned rationalistic epistemology. As pointed out by Hausman and McPherson (1993, reprinted in Hausman ed. 1994, pp. 256–259), the normativity of the theory of rationality has created a powerful rhetorical argument for neoclassical economists which can be summarized as follows: since the positive theory of actual choice is also a normative theory of rational choice, it gives us one strong reason to accept and save the positive theory. I do not want to highlight the empirical refutations of this claim: the markets are full of systematic failures and of pervasive, crystallized, irrational behaviour. We may say that the market floats on irrationalities. What I want to point out is that this argument relies on old-fashioned epistemology, as it is the case of neo-positivism, which justifies rationality in an *a priori* way. The failures of the neo-positivist programme, and also other *a priori* attempts, were mainly the result of two reasons, one linked to conceptual difficulties and inadequacies and the other to the unfeasibility of these prescriptions when applied to the reality, in the case of both scientific decision-making and social behaviour.

On the contrary, a theory of rationality that aims not to fall in the previous errors should follow a naturalistic approach that can be represented by a common criterion of theory choice and on three alternative methods of theory generation. The *criterion of theory choice* is called the "*feasibility criterion*" (Goldman 1993) and states that every standard of rationality can be accepted if it fits the feasibility of this standard by the cognitive constraints of the human mind. For example, with regard to perceptive rationality – namely, the data base for reasoning – standards like the logical consistency of our set of beliefs – in other words, rational beliefs which do not entail any contradiction – are clearly unfeasible for the cognitive limitations of the structure of long-term memory. Similarly, the limited possibility of computation of the human mind does not match the normative principles of reasoning for rational decision-making. As regards the alternative *criteria of theory generation,* they all are *a posteriori*, but in different ways: the first supports a cognitive theory of rationality, that is a generalization of the cognitive mechanisms of how we judge and choose or, at a meta-level, of how we justify our judgements and choices (Stich 1990); the second is based on Goodman's (1965) concepts of reflective equilibrium, that is on generalizations of the pre-analytical intuitions of people or experts about what might be justified as a rational judgement and choice; the third, which includes generation and evaluation, is based on the pragmatic adequacy and feedback of rational choice concerning the results that the choice has produced in solving a problem or attaining a particular goal (Stich 1990; Holland et al. 1986; Langley et al. 1987; Gigerenzer, Todd, and the ABC Research Group 1999).

Lastly, even if the first two flaws could be overcome, neoclassical economics subscribes to a *philosophy of science* that is too similar to that of physical science in the past. Nowadays the primacy of theoretical explanations and of goals like coherence and deductive elegance are questionable in physical sciences, but they continue to be popular in economics. This methodological attitude constrains and impedes genuine and bold empirical research. As Rosenberg pointed out (1983, reprinted in Hausman ed. 1994, pp. 378–380), since the nineteenth century economists have been elaborating a theory whose form is identical to the great theoretical breakthroughs made in science from the sixteenth century onwards. The strategy is to view the behaviour economists seek to explain as reflecting forces that always move towards a stable equilibrium, which maximizes or minimizes some theoretically crucial variable. In the case of microeconomics, this crucial variable is utility (or its latter-day surrogates) and the equilibrium is provided by a level of price across all markets that maximizes this variable. This strategy is most impressively exemplified in Newtonian mechanics and in Darwinian theory of natural selection. In Newtonian mechanics the system's behaviour always minimizes or maximizes variables that reflect the state of the system which is mechanically possible, while in Darwinian theory it is the environment that maximizes the fitness of individuals of a species. In Newtonian mechanics attempts to describe the systems under study more completely resulted in the discovery of new planets and new laws, like those of thermodynamics. In biology, the assumption that fitness is maximized led to the discovery of forces not previously recognized to effect genetic variation within a population and led to the discovery of genetic laws that explain the persistence in a population of apparently non-adaptive traits, like sickle-cell anaemia. But what about microeconomics? The success of this strategy in other disciplines may justify the attempts made by economists to make recalcitrant facts about human behaviour and the economic systems humans have constructed fit the economic theory. Moreover, this strategy allows the use of many powerful formal tools, such as differential calculus, topology and differential geometry. But many years of work in the same direction have produced nothing comparable to the physicists' discovery of new planets or new technologies, or the biological understanding of the mechanism of adaptation and heredity. Therefore it is time to question the merit of applying this approach to economics, since it carries all the disadvantages of empirical non-falsifiability without the advantages of the discovery of novel facts and applications.

Chapter 3 "*Economic and Cognitive Rationality in Political Behavior*" aims to analyse the weaknesses of the economic theory of politics and the potential advantages of an alternative, cognitive-type approach which can offer a better explanation of political action.

What is meant by an economic approach to politics, and in particular to democratic politics? We can start by referring to the research tradition led, among others, by Downs (1957). The voter is treated in the same way as an economic actor in a market. In the same way as an economic actor maximises profits by exploiting the available economic resources, so the voter tries to maximise his or her utility or benefits using the resources available to him, above all the right to vote. He is therefore likely to vote for the party that guarantees to form a government whose programme will bring the greatest benefits, or so he believes. On the other hand, parties, too, are maximisers and their benefit are, in this case, the votes. Each party tries to adopt a mode of behaviour that allows it to attract the greatest number of voters to the detriment of its rivals. This model of political democracy has both a normative significance, given that it aims to justify democracy in rational terms, and an empirical significance because it aspires to take account of how modern democratic systems work. This model has ambitions that are respectively *normative* (the rational political actor is one who maximises his benefit) and *explicative* (the political actor is rational because he maximises his benefit). This approach is open to two forms of criticism. The first highlights the formal inconsistency, the paradoxes or the impossibility of justifying the political choices based on individual rationality. The second emphasises the empirical falsifications of the various consequences derived from the model.

In formal criticism the approach based on individual rationality is compared to that of collective rationality leading to the discovery that there is systematic incongruence between the two forms of rationality. Condorcet Paradox shows that is logically impossible, based on individual preferences, to claim to represent the "general will" or, to put it differently, to identify the function of social well-being; that democracy consists of situations of instable equilibrium in which alternating majorities on individual themes are formed and then collapse; that the importance of controlling the areas of interest on the political agenda stimulates the activation of strategies to manipulate the order of priorities and the tactical inclusion of new themes. Kenneth Arrow (1951) clearly identifies a series of conditions that allow a collective decision to be rationally constructed on the basis of individual preferences. By deduction, Arrow demonstrates the impossibility of building a collective decision that can satisfy all the conditions simultaneously. His *impossibility theorem* asserts that, if an aggregation method allows voters to have any preference order, if it meets given conditions and excludes any form of imposition, then it will inevitably result in a non-transitive and inconsistent aggregate of preferences compared to those expressed by individual participants in the process of choice. Another important aspect of political behaviour which cannot be justified by the rational action model is that of participation in the vote. The most significant inconsistence is *Downs' Dilemma* (Downs 1957). What prompts an elector to vote? Evidently individuals vote when the benefits of doing so exceed the costs. However the expected benefit compared to the various rival manifestos does not vary much between one party's manifesto and another, above all in a bipartite system and, moreover, the probability that an individual's vote, among the millions of other votes cast in an election, might be relevant to the results is practically zero. This gives rise to the following paradox: when the probability of obtaining a benefit is little above zero it becomes irrational to vote, and therefore the only rational conduct is to abstain from voting. Hence, democracy cannot be rationally explained using an economic approach to democracy.

The core of the rational theory of political competition from Downs (1957) to Enelow and Hinich (1984) borrows the spatial approach from economic models of competitive equilibrium among enterprises. It is expected that electors will vote for the closest party, namely the one that corresponds to their preferences; that competition will allow a single equilibrium represented by the position of the voter in the middle or at the centre of the field, and that parties can only get as close as possible to this if they want to maximise their probability of winning. Such a simplistic model of maximising economic rationality shows scant success in representing or explaining the complexity of political phenomena. It can claim some empirical success in explaining the decision-making processes of restricted groups, but not in macroprocesses, such as participation, competition between parties and coalition processes (Sartori 1987, pp. 214–253).

The *homo politicus* proposed here does not follow abstract and unrealistic calculations of benefit, but instead elaborates his own decisions in line with the subjective constraints of his cognitive ability, and with the objective constraints of the time available to choose and the complexity of the problem. This has both explicative and normative consequences. It serves to create a research program that appears to be very promising and fertile at an empirical level. In order to control this hypothesis we can consider one of the most successful example of an economic approach to politics: the model offered by Mancur Olson (1965, 1982) about collective action. It occurs when organised groups, whether large or small, act in collusion and apply pressure to improve the well-being of their members. Olsonian collective action highlights two main aspects: the "micro" aspect, namely how collective action is formed, and the "macro" aspect, namely the pressure group's impact on the efficiency of the system. On the first aspect, Olson states that only organisations made up of a small number of members do not need added incentives to motivate their members to take action. Instead, in large organisations this does not happen since increased well-being has to be divided by a considerable number of beneficiaries and, generally speaking, the gain is far less than the cost of action. This is the reason why large organisations (trade unions, for example) have to introduce selective incentives, whether formal or informal, negative or positive, in order to encourage individual participation in collective action, which would otherwise be very weak. Using this individualistic and economic model of collective action, Olson offers the key to interpret many social and institutional phenomena which have been traditionally examined using sociological and holistic type methodological instruments.

In the "micro" part of his study, Olson proposes a social actor model that seems rather unsatisfactory. His social actor is without question an ingenuous caricature of a real social actor. Like a mechanical Pythagorean table, he calculates the individual benefit of the action, dividing global benefit by the number of persons who benefit and subtracting the cost of the action. If the result is positive he acts, otherwise he does not take part. On the contrary in my opinion when evaluating the decision to act, it is important to take account, as comprehensively as possible, of all the "micro" factors that might or might not trigger the action based on the decision-making context. The following are just a selection. The cost of participation in a collective action (industrial action, for example) can be calculated differently depending on the type of involvement. As cognitive scientists and economists who study the psychological phenomena of negotiation processes now know we all have both a certain initial resistance to increasing an "investment" we have mentally set aside for a particular expenditure, and a certain propensity to spend even more just to make the most of an investment, once it has been made. There is an inferential propensity known as *mental budget allocation* that makes us reluctant to spend a certain sum for the first time, but, once it has been allocated, we tend to set aside even more than we might have agreed in the first place. Therefore, the perception of the cost of participating in a social action – for example, supporting industrial action – changes over time, depending on whether the person has been involved for some time or whether she has recently decided to join. Once a supporter has joined, he will not renege on the action even if it has proved costly and seems likely to fail because of another psychological mechanism studied by cognitive science, namely the *regret* or sorrow that would result from abandoning investments or initiatives already loaded with history, projections and scenarios of success, attempted recovery, etc.

Faced with the dilemma of whether or not to act there is also another phenomenon that theoreticians of social action, like Olson, should have examined carefully: the cost of acting. If there is an equal chance of losing, irrespective of whether or not the individual chooses to act, she will feel greater regret if action is taken, since this requires greater justification than not acting and leaving matters as they are. This phenomenon, together with the *mental budget allocation*, allows us, in part, to explain the tendency towards the conservative and non-participatory behaviour of many social categories, such as the newly employed and *newcomers* in general.

The actor's evaluation of the benefit and his or her consequent response changes significantly depending on how the social context of action is presented. For example, a company that wishes to restrict the burden of negotiations should create a "front" of success and gain for the workers' organisation, while the trade union should underline the negative aspects of negotiations in order to motivate its supporters to fight back. Indeed, it is well known that there is a *bias* that makes the decision-maker more conservative in a context of certainty and victory, but emphasizes the propensity for risk in situations of uncertainty and loss. More generally, and as demonstrated by the *framing effect* (see Kahneman and Tversky 1979b), we reach decisions differently depending on how the choices are presented. Our decisions may therefore clash with the forecasts or prescriptions of the expected benefit theory, a key component of the Olsonian model.

The above illustration serves to highlight the cognitive poverty of the Olsonian actor model. Greater sensitivity to these aspects of the decision-maker would have allowed Olson to interpret the dynamics of the various forms of collective action differently. For example, when a worker chooses to take action in order to gain an economic advantage, he does not do so for the overall amount granted to the entire category to which he belongs, but for the local increase in his wage packet. The striking worker focuses on the extra tens of Euros that he will bring home rather than on the hundreds of millions gained by the category, which then have to be divided with a huge number of colleagues in order to obtain his benefit, from which he will subtract the cost of action. This increase will be more or less valuable, namely its marginal benefit will vary depending on the worker's particular starting conditions. For example, it will be very beneficial if he or she has a large family, high expectations of quality of life, previously well-off living standards, good education, etc.; or it will be less beneficial if he or she comes from a backward background, has been unemployed for years, is unmarried, has no educational qualifications, no ambitions and no expectations. The pressure to take collective action depends on these motivations, and also on the clarity and transparency of the result to be achieved.

If consumers cannot put together an effective claim action, this is not necessarily because of the fragmentary nature of their social role in relation to the variety of goods, as Olson affirms, but rather because of the cognitive opacity of the result to be achieved. While a worker fights for a clear result tailored to his needs, such as a pay rise, and consequently manages to engage the motivational and decision-making machine, the consumer is faced with much vaguer and ambiguous objectives. This is also the case for an unemployed person faced with a complex situation (who can change his social condition and by means of what hiring methods?) that is difficult to attain on the basis of "previous probabilities". On the other hand, even if the supposed Olsonian calculation were to exist, it would not provide a convincing explanation for the differences in the propensity to take collective action based on the larger or smaller number of participants. Why would a worker from a company with a small number of employees have more reasons to go on strike for a pay rise than a worker employed by a large company? Indeed, based merely on a rational calculation, the individual benefit (the overall benefit divided by the number of beneficiaries) and the cost of action (strike, picketing, assemblies, etc.) do not vary much in relation to the number of those involved. Instead, the fact that workers belonging to smaller groups appear more motivated to take part is based on other factors, namely on the greater proximity and transparency of the objectives, on greater accessibility to decision-making processes, and on a stronger identification with local trade union leadership, namely on factors that are marginal in Olson's analysis.

Chapter 4 "*Which Mind for Cognitive Economics*?" deals with the model of mind in the theory of action of cognitive economics.

At the basis of economics, like other social sciences, there is always a theory of agent. This identifies the key characteristics of the subjects who, through their actions, give rise to collective social and economic phenomena. Among these, the most important characteristics are those that explain the origin of the agent's behaviour: why (s)he acts in a particular way; how his or her choice is affected by context; what principles guide or characterise his or her decisions? In short, whether explicitly or implicitly, every action refers to a theory of mind. It is this that, with varying degrees of detail and direct involvement, represents the causal variables responsible for generating the action. However, in general, a theory of mind is neither explicitly nor fully described in economics. Above all, what is referred to are summary psychological indications or implicit assumptions inferred from the principles of choice attributed to the agent by the postulates of economic theory.

There is no question that neoclassical economics is the most important economic theory of the last century. In its first phase – from Irving Fisher and Vilfredo Pareto to the late 1930s and the introduction of Paul Samuelson's weak axiom of revealed preferences – it inherited from the marginalist school a psychological representation of the economic agent as the intentional maximiser of his self-interest based on available beliefs. The theory of mind is based on the triad of belief–aim–action which corresponds to common sense psychology or folk psychology. As Egidi (1992) notes, this simplified psychology of the economic agent reflects the cognitive minimalism requested by the aims of neoclassical economics: namely to explain general economic equilibrium. In order to choose the equilibrium price one does not have to pretend that the economic agent has complex gifts of strategic analysis. A parametric capacity is sufficient, in other words an ability to represent the situation as if it were governed by simple, easily foreseeable phenomena. Even the simplified theory of mind of the first phase of neoclassical economics was eliminated in contemporary neoclassical economics (from Samuelson onwards). Instead, we witness the progressive replacement of the traditional maximisation view in favour of the consistency view (Giocoli 2003, p. 7). In place of the mind the new economic agent has the equations of Bayesian decision theory. No psychology is needed to describe it. What matters is the *a priori* and "conventionalist" ascription of the computational capacities able to allow the agent to resolve the equations, in a formally correct manner, which guide his or her decisions. The history of economic thought shows that there was an inverse relationship between the articulated and empirical development of the economic agent's theory of mind and the attribution of rational capacity to the said agent. The greater the demand for rationality, the less the agent's psychological characterisation was developed. This inverse proportionality appears to be a natural consequence of the relationship between reason and mind. Gifts of unlimited reasoning, like those ascribed to the neoclassical economic agent, are not combined with the empirical representation of a mind characterised by cognitive limits and weaknesses. The unlimited reason attributed, *a priori*, to the economic agent compresses and suffocates any space for human psychological expression. This dualism between reason and mind is not a novelty, but instead has deep, philosophical roots. It is linked to a precise tradition that can be seen as the progenitor of the model of rationality that was in vogue in economic science for two centuries.

The results of studies on reasoning, judgment and choice have highlighted the limits of rational activity in the context of economic decision-making. The evidence of bounded rationality has given rise to new models of economic rationality. These have sought to build on the real characteristics, not the *a priori* ones, of economic action, namely on a theory of mind generated empirically. We can describe the main hypotheses that have emerged from cognitive criticism of unbounded rationality by following a criterion linked to two parameters, corresponding to the two blades of Simon's famous scissors of rationality (1990, p. 7): (a) The real constraints of the agent's computational capabilities; (b)The real constraints of the structure of the task environment. The first hypothesis is that of *optimisation under constraints*. The search for information must be limited because the decision-makers only have a finite amount of time, attention and resources available. Stopping rules optimise the research, namely they calculate the costs and benefits of searching for each additional information and stop as soon as costs outweigh the benefits. The second hypothesis is the programme put forward by Tversky and Kahneman (1974) of *heuristics and biases*. These highlighted a series of inferential mechanisms responsible for fallacies (biases) in human reasoning given that they violate some rule of logic or of the calculation of probability. The third hypothesis is Herbert Simon's renowned theory of *bounded rationality* (2000). While, as an empirical theory *par exellence*, it is principally interested in both series of constraints, cognitive and environmental, its central focus is above all on the former, and indeed it is defined as procedural. Furthermore, it remains anchored to an intentionalist-type theory of action that leaves little room for the unconscious and tacit sphere of factors responsible for the action. The most recent hypothesis called programme of *fast and frugal heuristics* set forth by Gigerenzer and the Adaptive Behaviour and Cognition (ABC) research group (1999), is the natural development of Simon's theory. This broadens and extends the Simonian programme with the aim, above all, of identifying those heuristics which seem, on the one hand, to meet the requisites of bounded rationality, namely the limitation of cognitive capacities, and on the other those of *ecological rationality*, namely the ability to adapt inferences to the environment.

What is Bounded Rationality (Simon 1956; Gigerenzer and Selten 2001a)? Simon's metaphor of the pair of scissors is the best representation of the concept and of the connected naturalizing nature of the research program. One blade is the nature of our reasoning and decision making processes with all its limits in computation and time and the other blade is the nature of the environment, with all its complexity. The first blade is characterized by limited features compared to the ideal optimization model. The second is characterized by a changing complex structure. Sometimes the first blade fits with the second and those rational scissors work, but sometimes this does not happen. The rationality, that is the ability of the scissors to cut, is bounded by the fitting of one blade, that is reasoning and decision making, with the other blade, that is the environment. Fitting, in other words, means adaptive choices in a given environment. Bounded rationality is therefore a research program aiming to discover what are the natural specific decision rules that are adaptive in specific different environments. From this point of view the natural decision rules of bounded rationality are the only rules that can be labeled as rational in a prescriptive meaning. Their label of rational is obviously non universal but local to the specific environment or problem space where the rule is adaptive. In other words human beings are often, but not always, bounded rational. Actually sometimes they are also irrational, that is when their choice is not adaptive to the environment because they don't use the specific natural rule of bounded rationality that is suitable for the particular environment. Many are the field of research that can contribute to bounded rationality beyond economics and cognitive psychology.

From an *evolutionary psychology* (EP) perspective (Gaulin and Mc Burney 2003), cognition is not "general purpose," but uses heuristics, or strategies, that generally increase the likelihood of solving problems our ancestors routinely faced. From this point of view EP tries to single out the bounded rationality of our ancestors. For example, humans are far more likely to solve a logic problem that involves the detection of cheating (a common problem given our social nature) than the same logic problem put in purely abstract terms. Since our ancestors did not encounter truly random events, we may be cognitively predisposed to incorrectly identify patterns in random sequences. "Gamblers' Fallacy" is one example of this. Gamblers may falsely believe that they have hit a "lucky streak" even when each outcome is actually random and independent of previous trials. Most people believe that if a fair coin has been flipped nine times and Heads appears each time, that on the tenth flip, there is a greater than 50% chance of getting Tails. Humans find it far easier to make diagnoses or predictions using frequency data than when the same information is presented as probabilities or percentages, presumably because our ancestors lived in relatively small tribes (usually with less that 150 people) where frequency information was more readily available. Evolutionary psychology emphasizes the importance of kin selection and reciprocity in allowing for prosocial traits, such as altruism, to evolve. Like chimps, humans have subtle and flexible social instincts, allowing them to form extended families, lifelong friendships, and political alliances. Lastly EP underlines the evolutionary implications of some emotions (Eldakar et al. 2006; Eldakar and Wilson 2008). Some of them are universal and have a clear evolutionary meaning. For instance disgust has undoubtedly evolved to protect animals from toxins. Fear allowed animals to take flight and escape from predators.

Nowadays the revolution in *developmental psychology* is showing data that can be very useful for the bounded rationality program. We know that infants are endowed with an innate set of principles that allow them to begin to interact with world. Principles of causal attribution; principles that allow them to characterize a living being from an artifact; principles that allow them to assume that external states of affairs may cause mental states and there is a causal chain from perception to beliefs to intentions to actions. Today with the mirror neurons theory we have also a possible neural explanation of mind reading and empathy in children. What can be the relevance for bounded rationality of these hypotheses? One example. One of the most important phenomenon, also affecting scientists, is the confirmation bias that we find already in children. It has been considered a serious classical flaw by psychologists and philosophers of science in the rational image of scientists and humans. What are the suggestions coming from the developmental age? That in many cases the confirmation bias is a successful adaptive choice that allows children, like scientists and folks, to strengthen their theories by building, as Imre Lakatos pointed out, a protective belt of auxiliary hypotheses to make invulnerable the theoretical core. Therefore, in many cases it is bounded rational to commit the so called confirmation bias.

Biological evolution seems to have selected behavioral modules or decision rules. Some of them are bounded rational in given environmental structures whereas others are not. Is *cultural evolution* and social interaction capable of affecting the inherited behavioral patterns? Cultural transmission seems to accumulate and stabilize cultural-evolutionary products that act as effective decision making algorithms, without the individual participants understanding how and why the particular system works. Systems of divination provide interesting examples of how culture provides adaptive solutions (Henrich et al. 2001; Dove 1993). Among the Kantu of Kalimantan, a tribe of Borneo, swidden farmers select a new garden location based both on the type of bird observed there, and the type of call the bird makes after it is first observed. They believe that birds actually supply supernatural information that foretells the future. This randomized selection diversified the types of garden across community members which spreads risk among households. This bounded rational cultural rule, based on superstition, suppresses errors that farmers make in judging the chance of a flood and reduces the chance of catastrophic failures across the entire group, decreasing the probability that many farmers will fail at the same time. The cultural transmission and socio-interactional processes can combine to give rise to adaptive group processes that distribute cognition, knowledge, skill, and labor. Decision making institutions like companies and markets, or governance structures like political systems, or government bodies aggregate information and processing powers distributed among group members in adaptive ways without individual participants necessarily understanding how and why the total system works. According to some authors (Boyd and Richerson 2001), cultural change through conformist and prestige-biased transmission can give rise to a high-level selective process called cultural group selection that can build increasingly adaptive and efficient systems at the group level that involve both distributed cognition and the complex division of labor. It is well known that the bounded rationality approach can also help in understanding the *adaptive emergence of conventions and social norms* (March 1994). Conventions help in solving coordination problems. They can simplify decision making by creating "default choices" and "default choice rules". Moreover, they help communication because it is easier to convey ideas about conventional things. Social norms such as those incorporated into the social roles in family as in labor identified themselves in an interiorized and often automatic set of rules that frees people from evaluating the appropriateness of their behavior and permit them to direct attention to other matters.

It is recognised that an important part of human cognition, responsible for decision-making, exists that cannot be represented by the accumulation of explicit information, the search for cognitive completeness and the conscious application of decision-making rules intentionally selected by the agent (Gigerenzer 2007). It is precisely this awareness that marks out *cognitive economics* in the theory of economic action. Instead of referring to it as a dualism of rationality it is better to represent it as a *Cognitive Double-Mindedness*. This is composed of a first component, which corresponds to the tacit, intuitive activity modulated by context-dependent affective and emotional factors, and of a second component, representing the conscious activity of reasoning, dependent on rules but independent of context. The first component could also be termed the *Intuitive Mind*, and the second the *Reasoning Mind*. Many authors have expressed support for this double hypothesis. Epstein (1994) affirms that there is a coexistence between a system that is holistic, affective and guided by associationistic connections, and one that is analytic, logical and reason orientated. Likewise, Sloman (1996) proposes one system that is associative, and its computations reflect similarity and temporal structure, while the other is rule based, and it operates on symbolic structures and follows explicit computational principles. Even Kahneman (2003) reaffirms the thesis of a two-system cognitive architecture and refers to Stanovich's proposal (1999). The operations of the System 1 are fast, automatic, effortless, associative, and often emotionally charged; those of System 2 are slower, serial, effortful and deliberately controlled and rule-governed. The first system corresponds to intuition and shares many common characteristics with perception, while the second is associated with reasoning. Cognitive economics fully encapsulates this double features of mind. No theory of economic action can be constructed without including the causal role of the factors indicated by the intuitive mind. On the other hand, for years theorists of decision-making using psychological techniques and neural imaging have recognised the intrinsic influence of these components. Damasio (1994) hypothesised that the best decisions need a somatic marker or a gut feeling which allows us to anticipate the pain or the pleasure resulting from the choice. Indeed, the images linked to positive or negative sentiments and emotions often guide decisions. The facility with which these images are represented in the mind gives them an alternative role in decision-making processes to judgments based on formal rules which are intentionally followed (Loewenstein et al. 2001). In this sense, we speak of "*affective heuristics*" (Slovic et al. 2001) as a way of explaining various phenomena.

The fifth chapter "*Epistemological Pluralism and Economics*" tries to analyze the specific epistemological identity of economics compared to the other sciences.

All scientific disciplines have specific characteristics which set them apart from what is not science. However, these characteristics do not constitute a universal epistemology that can forge the unity of science. On the other hand, they do characterise regional or specific epistemologies. If one analyses the various disciplines, from physics and mathematics to musicology, including chemistry, evolutionary biology, epidemiology, archaeology, economics and sociology, one will note that they have an ontology and language of their own.

Where its *ontology* is concerned, science has traditionally been broken down into three categories: *physical-chemical sciences*, *life sciences*, and *human sciences*. The ontology of the objects studied allows different languages to be used to represent them and to theorise. The ontology of particle physics makes it possible to use a formal, quantitative language to describe it. The ontology of life sciences (from molecular biology to histology) permits the use of languages that are symbolic (DNA), figurative (the cell) and verbal (the description of mitogenesis). The ontology of individual and aggregate facts of human history, on the other hand, allows them to be described in a natural and figurative language (rarely quantifiable in statistical terms). The more a science tends to build quantitative natural laws, based on the abstract behaviour of homogeneous object classes, the more it will be theory driven. The more ontological non-homogeneity prevents effective abstraction, the more the theory will depend on the contingent facts noted. From this viewpoint, we can break sciences down into *nomothetic-deductive* and *historical-inductive*. Physics, as a nomothetic and deductive science, starts from theory to deduce facts. History, as an inductive science, starts from facts to induce hypotheses. What sets the former apart from the latter is above all the manner in which concepts such as *time*, *explanation* and *causality* are approached. In physics and in econometrics, laws are dehistoricised outside time. And in physics there is no causality because there can be no timing asymmetry between events (a characteristic of the relationship between cause and effect). On the other hand, time is irreversible for historical sciences, there is timing asymmetry and therefore a causal relationship between antecedent and consequent. The explanation aims to identify the causal relationships between the phenomena and to open the black box of mathematical laws and statistical regularity. Science like economics tries to formalise a historical reality mathematically. Econometric models establish the limits to apply the nomothetic ideal to historical reality. Built on the model of universal physical laws, they are dehistoricised and eliminate the chronological and historical dimension of changes.

The correct standard in experimentation is to control hypotheses that are as non-generic as possible. In physics, chemistry and molecular biology, where ontology allows greater abstraction, represented numerically (in physics), symbolically (in chemistry) and figuratively or verbally (in molecular biology), experimentation can be based on fairly generic hypotheses. In these cases, the experimental control, which by its very nature cannot regard a large number of variables, manages to corroborate or falsify fairly generic hypotheses. In economics and social sciences, where ontology does not allow great abstraction and where potentially significant variables are more numerous, the control must be based on very circumscribed hypotheses.

Only with the work of John Stuart Mill (1836) do we find a clear identification of the epistemological problems that characterised the new discipline of economics. They can basically be divided into three components: (a) *method,* i.e. the definition of how to generate and justify the hypotheses in the economic field; (b) *rationality,* i.e. how the principles at the basis of the action are characterised; (c) *wellbeing*, i.e. what it is right to pursue for the individual and for society.

1. Mills proposes an *a priori* method which overturns the relationship between cause and effect. First of all the individual causes of economic phenomena must be identified. This may be achieved through *introspection* for fundamental principles, such as the desire for wealth or to satisfy present pleasures and the aversion to work. From causal laws we can deduce the economic effects that are then compared with empirical reality. If the effects do not tie up with the phenomena this does not question the primary causal principles, which are considered true, but only our exactness in having taken all the relevant factors or minor and disturbing causes into consideration. Mill's position has been criticised from opposing fronts. Some, from a *realist* position, have accused him of refusing the role of empirical research both in the identification of the theory and in its falsification. On the other hand there are those who challenge his concern with the causal and realistic nature of explicative principles, from an *instrumentalist* position.
2. Rationality that is taken as the basis of the theory of choice in economics in the nineteenth century, right up to modern neoclassical economics, belongs to the rationalist philosophical current. It is Olympic, universal and has the dual normative and descriptive character. The theory is normative to the extent that it defines what type of choice must be made on the basis of specific preferences and rational beliefs. Preferences are rational if they are comprehensive and transitive. Beliefs are rational if they satisfy the axioms of the calculation of probability. Choices are rational if they maximise utility. It is therefore irrational to choose one alternative from various options if another one maximises utility. The theory is descriptive because it states that in reality an economic agent will never choose an alternative from various possibilities if a second one is available that does maximise utility. This theory of rational choice has its roots in Mill's definition of the *homo œconomicus* as man's sphere of action, separate and limited to economic contexts according to the principle of the pursuit of maximum wellbeing. The theory of rationality has been the target of a great deal of criticism. The first comes from contemporary epistemology and regards the prescriptive and *a priori* character of rationality. According to the *internalist* theories of rationality the normative source of reason must stem from man's intuitive and cognitive capabilities. There can be no genesis or justification of the principles of rationality other than what is generated within the human mind. This criticism of the normative aspect is easily linked to criticism of the descriptive component of rationality. As Hutchinson had already pointed out in 1938, the empirical nature of economics cannot regard only the 'protective belt' of auxiliary hypotheses (like those of the type of assets, the function of costs, economic institutions, etc.) that surrounds the principle of maximisation. Even the fundamental assumptions of rationality must have an empirical weight. Herbert Simon's concept of *bounded rationality* (1957; 1982; 2000) starts from this descriptive purpose.

3. Starting from Adam Smith's work, economics have taken the pursuit of individual wellbeing to be the fundamental assumption of his theory of action. From this viewpoint, the descriptive component of the theory of action of contemporary economics has been accused of conforming to an ethic of selfishness. Only individual utility, substantiated by a greater wealth of tangible assets, seems to characterise the choice of the economic player. In fact, this criticism is also extended, and wrongly so, to the normative component of the theory of rationality. This does not seem correct because the normative part of rationality is purely formal, and makes no claims about the content of preferences and choice, but only specifies their logical structure. In fact the egoism or altruism of a choice depends only on the content of preference. As Amartya Sen (1992) maintains, they can be designed to increase one's economic wellbeing or, on the contrary, they can also be designed to promote other people's well-being. One may pursue the maximisation of individual utility by sacrificing oneself for other people instead of only thinking of oneself. Unlike the neoclassical conception that considers the individual to be driven only by egoistic interests, experimental economics has highlighted how the economic agent is also moved by dispositions that focus on other people's social and economic conditions. From the concept of *homo œconomicus* we progressed to one of *homo reciprocans* (Fehr and Gachter 1998).

Experimental economics has been successful in opening new areas of economic research, as in the case of the economics of happiness. Experimental economics has particular epistemological features and problems by comparison with cognitive economics. How can we sum up the differential characteristics of the regional epistemology of experimental economics? One of the accusations made against a certain experimental economics is that of being *neoclassical economics masked* by conventional devices. The experiments would be used to give neoclassical economics an increasingly complicated, intricate protective belt based on ad hoc hypotheses. If experimental economics were to take this direction, it might also generate some interesting data regarding marginal external aspects of economic behaviour, but, as Hutchinson said, it would abandon the attempt to develop circumscribed hypotheses that might converge on a new theory of economic action. One obviously must not think that the new theory could include all economic behaviour. Nor should one think that a general and simplified theory of economic action, like the neoclassical, is still possible. There are various components of economic behaviour that must be developed in addition to a new utility theory that could derive from the development of the prospect theory. Here are some examples: a *theory of learning* necessary to explain how previous successes and mistakes affect decision-making processes, and how information is transformed into cognitive patterns that guide decisions; a *theory of relational assets* or altruism, outside the theory of utility, that is able to model the effect of empathy, of sharing one's actions with others, of sharing common decisions, of the pooling resources etc.; a *theory of time* that is able to explain how we represent time, what are the external factors that influence a different ponderation of time, how the value of time changes in relation to the different propensity to risk (weak will, time discounting, short-sightedness); a *theory of the representation of uncertainty and of risk* that is not based on simplistic mental arithmetic.

Economics is proposed as a *de-historicised science* that tends to create universally valid laws. Experimental economics must not fall into this physicalist error, which is also typical of a large part of cognitive science. On the contrary, it must realise that reasoning and decision-making processes are guided by the pragmatic schemes and semantic structure of knowledge, which has a fundamentally contextual and historical dimension. One strong temptation of experimental economics is that of considering the reasoning and decision-making processes dictated by mental logic as impermeable to factors of context and learning. Instead, as numerous successful theories have highlighted, like Johnson Laird's theory of mental models, Cheng and Holyoak's theory of pragmatic schemes, reasoning and decision-making are guided by our schemes, and by the significance that we give to the external objects and actions on which our learning is based. If this is true, then the historical context must enter deliberately among the initial conditions of every experimental setting.

The sixth chapter "*Neurocognition and financial behaviour*" introduces an emerging field in economic, that of behavioural finance. It is the result of the collection of many kinds of data coming from experimental, behavioural, cognitive economics and neuroeconomics.

Financial analysts and all "forecasters" generally have an impossible task. As Karl Popper said, while natural science forecasts never have a sure inductive basis and are therefore just conjecture, those regarding society do not even have the minimal coordinates of an inductive basis. Social reality is too complex, there are too many initial conditions to take into consideration and above all, there is never any regularity in the phenomena. So all "forecasters" can do is extrapolate arbitrary regularities from contingent trends and project them into the future. This is what financial analysts do all the time, cloaking their products behind the label of scientific analysis. The forecasts mentioned are the product of this fallacious methodology. But the error is magnified if we consider a recurring bias that forecasters fall into systematically. When they select the data on which to base their projections, they are unconsciously conditioned by what is known as the *anchoring and adjustment heuristic*. This describes the individual's tendency to perform a numerical estimate in two steps. First he anchors himself to some initial value, which is then corrected in the most plausible direction, up or down. This heuristic produces a chain reaction: the saver is anchored to the forecasts of the bank analysts, who are themselves influenced by the news from economic journalists, who are conditioned by the numbers of the analysts of the large merchant banks, which are influenced by the forecasts of the rating agencies or the assessments of international financial institutions, themselves anchored to present and immediately past stock values and prices. What is more, the way the data are presented also has a powerful effect. Tversky and Kahneman (1974) asked two questions about the trend of the Dow-Jones Index which were semantically the same but differed in the manner of their presentation, and obtained different results.

The framing of the second question, which contained numerical information, acted as an anchor which automatically influenced the reply, hooking onto the numbers read. This phenomenon emerges in many financial decisions, like the choice of a form of financing or insurance cover, because most financial and welfare products focus attention on specific threshold values.

As Fyodor Mikhailovich Dostoevsky asked in *The Gambler*, when is the irrational escalation behaviour that takes a gambler to bankruptcy manifested? Towards the end of the evening, when the gambler perceives that the day is closing at a loss and he wants to overturn the result by increasingly risky behaviour. The same attitude was noted in a series of studies of the banking and financial world of Wall Street and other international stock markets. When the Stock Exchange adds up the gains and losses at the end of the day, there will be a greater trend on the part of traders to take risky decisions if negotiations have not gone well during the day. The same also happens when the Stock Market opens the following day; focusing on the losses and overlooking the gains will also generate risky investment behaviour.

The different psychological impact of a loss as opposed to a gain is represented by *prospect* theory (Kahneman and Tversky 1979b). The function of the value of this theory disregards this aversion to loss. The value of this coefficient is equal to 2: in other words, to put it simply, one has to gain approximately 2,000 € to compensate for the annoyance of having lost 1,000. This function of the value, which differs from that of neoclassical economics which presumes a coefficient of 1, explains much economic behaviour that violates the forecasts of economic theory. First of all, it explains the difficulties of negotiation between the purchaser and the buyer (Pietroni and Rumiati 2008): the seller who deprives himself of an asset, values it much higher than his counterpart who purchases it, who must deprive himself of his money. In addition to which, each of the parties perceives the concession made to the other as a loss, thus attributing greater weight to it than to a potential gain.

An aversion to loss also produces the well-known *disposition effect*, i.e. the tendency to sell shares whose prices has risen too soon but to hold on to shares that have lost value. In some analyses by American and Israeli fund managers, we can note a systematic tendency to the disposition effect, which damages their performance. The best managers are those that have shown the greatest ability to realise losses. Is it only aversion to loss that is responsible for this behaviour? No, various studies seem to show that anticipated regret for the loss of possible future earnings prevails, determining the disposition effect. The regret illustrated in the previous example introduces to an increasingly important chapter of economic psychology and behavioural finance: the role of affection and emotion in judgement, choice and decision. For example, affect plays a role in the value function (utility) and the pondering of probabilities. Subjective probabilities are not independent of the affective nature of outcomes. A 1% probability is greater when the outcome has a significant affective component rather than a poor affective component. The subjective perception of probability depends on the affective value that the individual associates with the expected results. Another effect of affect on judgement is linked to the relationship between risk and utility. Generally speaking, in economic theory there is a direct link between the two variables: the more a choice embodies risks, the greater the apparent utility of the outcome. On financial markets, the riskier the share, the greater the premium paid as a result; we can think of the bonds of risky countries like Argentina and Greece compared to those of Germany and the United States. At a psychological level, we tend to apply a trade-off between risk and affective evaluation. For example, when we positively value a share for its past history, for the company's good communicative image, for its pleasant managing director, etc. we are attributing a low risk of negative outcomes to it. Take the effect on investors of adding ".com" to the name of shares, at the peak of the Internet bubble, between June 1998 and July 1999. In a study undertaken a few years ago (Cooper et al. 2001) out of 95 shares analysed, the "dotcom effect" caused their value to increase by an average of 74% in the 10 days following the announcement of the name change. Financial bubbles seem to owe a great deal to the value of the affect component in judgement.

What is surprising after the various financial crisis or the scandals that have involved several industrial giants, is that they have not taken into consideration the explanations and possible remedies that behavioural and cognitive economics has for years been proposing to decision-makers to avoid or attenuate this disaster (Bazerman 2009). Take the case of the LTCM (Long Term Capital Management), a hedge fund created in 1994 which was increasingly successful until its disastrous collapse in 1998. Various emotive and cognitive components, as well as the adoption of an incorrect model, allowed a predicted disaster to occur: hyper security and pathological risk propensity; egocentricity and organisational narcissism; the illusion of control and a confirmation bias; conformism to the flock effect. What is surprising is that the same formula that brought disaster in the case of LTCM – also known as the Black-Scholes case – remained popular until it finally contributed to the great crisis of 2008!

The LTCM disaster highlights a whole range of problems that were later responsible for the 2008 crisis. Some of them are related to the organisational and social *dyscrasia* that underpins risk evaluation and management in financial organisations. Two are particularly important. First of all, at an organisational level, risk managers are actually subordinate to traders. A company's purpose is to make deals, so if we are talking of risks, it tends to undervalue them and to take them. And secondly, there is a cultural subservience to the rating agencies (which continues today). It is a shame that, as numerous cases show, they often make dreadful errors of judgement, and there is a serious problem of a conflict of interest between companies to be rated and rating agencies. Many of the problems of social behaviour in the financial field could be neutralised, at least in part, by standards, rules and laws that induce the saver or finance operator to take care to avoid situations in which it is easy to make errors of judgement. The *libertarian paternalism* of Thaler and Sunstein (2008) tends to gently *nudge* the individual to protect his interests better and to prevent institutional mechanisms, like those of the rating agencies, from damaging the saver.

Today's neuroscientific discoveries are opening up the black box of economic and financial behaviour. It looks as if we will be able to challenge the pessimism shown by Jevons in 1871, when he expressed his scepticism about the possibility of directly measuring the sentiments that determine human behavior. For example the discovery of *mirror neurons* explains one of the most important cognitive functions of economic behaviour that is the attempt to understand what we can expect from other people. In negotiation, competition, cooperation and economic organisation, we act in relation to what we think other people will do. We try to understand what other people are thinking (mindreading) and to enter their way of thinking, in order to predict how they will act. And how do we do this? From the latest research, it appears that we do it by mirroring the significance of other people's behaviour, activating neuronal circuits that are responsible for our behaviour to an equal degree (Rizzolatti and Sinigaglia 2006). This mindreading mechanism lies at the heart of economic thought. The very concept of *equilibrium* demands that agents correctly predict what other people will do. This is made possible both by constructing hypotheses about other people's minds, and by learning processes based on imitation that seem to be caused by the same type of mirror neuron networks.

One of the most important results of this neurocognitive revolution is to have obtained observational proof of the prevalence of the *affective and automatic component* over the *cognitive and controlled component* in psychological activity. This is something that psychologists had maintained for decades, particularly psychoanalysts. But today we have empirical visual proof of this psychic architecture. This discovery has an important falsifying effect on the psychology implicit in the theory of economic rationality, all focused on the conscious and deliberative capacity of the economic operator. As Camerer et al. says (2005) (see Table 1 in Chap. 6 of part II), mental activity can be represented by a diagram with four quadrants related to cognitive and affective variables on one hand and controlled and automatic processes on the other. Each quadrant corresponds to a part of the brain responsible for the specific psychological activity. The controlled cognitive and affective processes (quadrants I and II) are located in particular in the front areas of the brain; the automatic cognitive processes (quadrant III) particularly in the occipital (corresponding to the rear part of the brain), parietal (upper part) and temporal (lateral) areas of the brain. A structure under the cortex, known as the amygdale, seems to be responsible for a conspicuous part of automatic affective processes (quadrant IV).

As neuroeconomics has shown (Camerer et al. 2005), affective components, conveyed by cortical and subcortical structures like the amygdala or the insula, underpin risk behaviour and the perception of trust in one's own actions and those of others. Let us see how. According to some authors, one area that specialises in trust is the *prefrontal cortex* (Brodmann's area 10). Neuroscientific research has analysed the way the brain functions in behavioural experiments that imply the attribution of trust. Above all, they used strategic interaction games in which the decision of one of the two players is influenced by the existence or lack of a relationship built on trust. There are various *trust games*. In them one player may, if he wishes, trust the other, who may reciprocate or defect. The main result common to many of them is the presence of cooperative decisions guided by trust, which are contrary to the rational prescriptions of the theory of the games, according to which a player should not trust and the other should defect. The explanation of this behaviour is the presence in the subjects of rules of *fairness* which prompts them to behave in a manner contrary to their economic utility. The brain areas activated in unfair situations seem to be the *dorsolateral prefrontal cortex*, for cognitive processes like the evaluation of offers, the *insula*, which is associated with negative emotions (like indignation or pain), and the *frontal cingulate gyrus* which has executive functions. Some hormones also seem to play an important role in the mechanisms of trust. In various types of games an increase in oxytocin has been noted in the player who is prompted to stimulate the trust of the other player. This increase occurs when the contact is direct, face-to-face and not mediated by communications technologies. Looking in the eye someone who has cooperated with us also seems to activate the ventral striate areas that generate gratification.

There are various traditional concepts that neuroeconomics questions and redefines, from intertemporal choice to the indirect utility of money, decision-making in a state of risk and uncertainty, and behaviour in the theory of games. One of the strongest criticisms of neuroeconomics is voiced by Gul and Pesendorfer (2005), who accuse it of not providing an exact example of precise empirical application, i.e. in which it is possible that "a parameter of choice – such as the coefficient of aversion to risk or the discount factor – can be observed by visualising brain activity". Camerer et al. (2005) retorts that this is not true and refers to a series of experiments that link parameters of choice to neural processes. This was obtained for the degree of aversion to ambiguity, aversion to loss, the discount rate and many other means of economic choice.

Part III "*Mind, Culture, and Epistemological Universals*" deals with the cognitive dimension of culture and its epistemological implications.

The first chapter "*Subjective Rationality and Cultural Diversity*" faces the problem that even simple beliefs or the most familiar types of behavior that we observe in everyday life can only be explained with difficulty by the two dominant models to which the familiar labels of Homo sociologicus and Homo oeconomicus are attached respectively. Sociological analysis needs a third model, called the rational model in the broad sense (RBS): it takes the form "the subject x had good, though possibly objectively invalid reasons for doing y, since . . ." (Boudon and Viale 2000). According to Simon (1982), the rationality of the subject can be qualified as subjective when the reasons are objectively invalid. When the reasons are objectively valid, we return to the economic model, a particular version of the RBS. The core notion – subjective rationality – of the RBS model is methodologically crucial, because it fills a wide gap between irrational actions ("x had no reasons for doing y, but. . .") and narrowly rational ones ("x had objectively valid reasons for doing y, since. . ."). While this point is not always sufficiently recognized, the findings of modern cognitive psychology confirm the importance of the Weberian postulate that reasons can be objectively ungrounded and still good. In many cases, it is impossible to understand the inferences of subjects placed in a problem-solving situation without this category: their answers are false, yet they are *verstaendlich,* that is they can be explained by the fact that the subjects have good reasons for believing that they are valid. There are many cases of explanations of subjective rationality type even among the fathers of the sociological thought (Boudon and Viale 2000). When Durkheim (1897) tries to explain in his *Suicide* why economic booms appear to be associated with higher suicide rates, he effectively introduces an explanation of the subjective rationality type. Suicide rates appear to be high in the ascending phase of the cycle, contrary to natural expectations, because this is when *anomie* is high. Being in an uncertain situation, Durkheim's economic subjects have good reasons to try to reduce the uncertainty by using the most current method of prediction-extrapolation from the present to the future. In the first part of the ascending phase, before the inflection point, their expectations would tend to be under-optimistic, while in the second part, they would be over-optimistic. At least, this is one way of explaining why Durkheim predicts an increase in disillusionment and consequently in suicide rates in the second part of the ascending phase of the business cycle, but not in the first.

In the same fashion, nobody needs to believe in the Marxian theories of exploitation and surplus value. Nevertheless, it is interesting to see that, when Marx tries to understand why workers accept exploitation, as well as in many of his other analyses, he proposes a subjective-rational interpretation. In order to discover whether they are exploited, the workers should calculate the difference between their salaries and the value of their work. But to determine the value of their work, they would have to master a complex economic theory they are unlikely to be aware of, as well as a series of empirical information to which they do not have access. As they still want to know whether their salaries are fair or not, they turn toward a natural substitute: comparing their salaries to the salaries of individual producers. Suppose then that a craftsman working alone needs the same number of hours to produce one pair of shoes as the baker needs to produce x loaves. If he sells his pair of shoes for the price of x loaves, he will be satisfied. So also will the workers in a shoe factory, suggests Marx. They will tend to consider that the natural fair price of one pair of shoes is x loaves. By doing so, they introduce a bias in their estimation, since an individual producer uses more time to produce a pair of shoes than the average worker in a shoe factory. So they will underestimate the value of their own work, but they will develop this illusion with good reasons. On the whole, according to this analysis, the workers will agree with good reasons to leave to the capitalist the gain resulting from the division of labour without counterpart.

Again, the theory of magic that Durkheim (1912) develops sketchily in *The Elementary Forms of Religious Life* appears to be far removed from the basic methodological principles generally associated with his name. In fact, his theory is very close to Weber's (1922) and it illuminates both the content of the notion of subjective rationality itself and its scientific fruitfulness. According to this theory, one should first take seriously the fact that those who believe in magic have no knowledge of a number of theories that Westerners have developed over the centuries. Secondly, everyday action needs theories, and magic is a theory that provides guidelines for the actor. According to Durkheim, magical theories are applied theories derived more or less directly from religious theories exactly as many of our technical devices are inspired by scientific theories. Of course, these guidelines are not as efficient as those of science. But showing that magic is inefficient requires the mobilization of methods of causal analysis, which were developed by science. Weber (1922, pp. 227–228) wrote that, to the primitive, "the actions of the rainmaker are exactly as magical as the actions of the firemaker." By this aphoristic statement he meant that primitive man has no reasons to introduce the asymmetry between rain and firemaking which we introduce ourselves, precisely because the process by which kinetic energy is transformed into thermal energy is familiar to us. Reciprocally, the primitive man to whom this process is unfamiliar has no reason to see a basic difference between fire and rainmaking.

Weber's and Durkheim's diagnosis of magic parallels some interesting results in cognitive anthropological studies of reasoning and belief formation. Also according to these studies there are no important differences between the civilized mind of Western people and the primitive mind of tribal people. Magical thinking "is an expression of a *universal disinclination* of normal adults to draw correlational lessons from their experience coupled with a *universal inclination* of normal adults to seek symbolic and meaningful connections (resemblances) among objects and events" (Shweder 1977, p. 447). Primitive thinking does not seem different from our way of reasoning because magical thinking, as a practice, is not a mode that distinguishes one culture from another. Resemblance, without probabilistic justification, is a fundamental conceptual tool of the normal reasoner. The universality of resemblance stems from peculiar cognitive constraints of the human mind. In fact, it is well known that chance and probability are non-intuitive concepts, difficult to learn and absent from the thinking of normal adults. It may be too pretentious to use normative models of reasoning as a reference to compare different styles of reasoning among Western and non-Western reasoners. Consequently, it might be preferable and less demanding to make transcultural analyses comparing descriptive models of reasoning. The best approach is to compare reasoning performances to some descriptive model of reasoning, for example the category based induction (induction that relies on category premises) (Osherson et al. 1990). For example Lopez et al. (1997) found a striking difference between Americans and Itzajs Indian of Guatemala with respect to diversity-based reasoning. Americans preferred arguments with more diverse premises. In sharp contrast, the Itzajs did not. The diversity phenomenon seems to be a stable feature in category-based reasoning among Western people and not among far east people and Centre and South American Indians. Actually this kind of induction seems to be an important part of scientific rationality. Newton's theory commands such wide assent because it accurately predicts heterogeneous, diverse phenomena, such as the trajectories of balls thrown into the air, the behavior of gyroscopes, and the orbit of celestial bodies. Most theories in the philosophy of science agree on the importance of the diversity principle in theory choice. And the history of some of the main scientific discoveries confirms the importance of this principle as a guide to scientific change. Nonetheless there are some critical reflections to be made on the empirical differences among Western and non-Western reasoners present in these and other experimental studies. First it seems that the different scientific expertise and knowledge plays the major role in diversity-based reasoning. Therefore within-culture differences in expertise and scientific knowledge may correspond to cross-cultural differences. Culture might be a problem of expertise. Second, the context dependency seems to play a major role in cross-cultural differences. For example in the Itzaj follow-up 4 (Lopez et al. 1997, p. 284) the researchers tested the Itzaj's reasoning about real-world scenarios. The tests were about saving money, inspecting farmland and buying corns. Results show that most of the Itzaj responses on these items were diversification responses, indicating that the Itzaj follow the diversity principle when reasoning about everyday life and problem solving. In conclusion, primitive thinking and modern thinking, non-Western cultures and Western cultures resemble each other much more than is shown by superficial evidence. There is a negative similarity between them in sub-optimal performances compared to normative canons of reasoning. But these canons and the experimental tests that incorporate them are often too abstract and too, computationally, demanding compared to the kind of real problems that human reasoners face in everyday life. Moreover, the cultural differences found in non-Western thinking do not appear to be deeply rooted in the skills of the reasoners. Instead they are motivated by the different kinds of problem solving and pragmatic contexts that shape and drive the reasoning processes. Western education, culture and everyday problem-solving (e.g. the economic decision-making of a customer; the rational choice made by an elector; technical skill in using everyday machines; scientific knowledge in taking care of his own health and the environment; etc.) shape particular kinds of reasoning more inclined to abstractness and pattern recognition. But we can observe the same kind of thinking in non-Western cultures. The difference is that it is less widespread in everyday reasoning, but it is only present in particular tasks (as in the case of the use of abstract star compass by Puluwat and the weaving patterns of Zinacantenan). Moreover Western culture and education teach us to deal with arbitrary problems (e.g. games, puzzles, tests, mathematical and logical problems, etc.), while in more primitive cultures people are trained to deal, mainly, with concrete and real problems linked to survival. This difference may explain their inclination not to assume, hypothetically, the premises of the cognitive tests, but to deal with them in a realistic way. Obviously if this is the case the results of the tests do not stem from different reasoning processes, but from a different understanding and interpretation of the premises.

There are good reasons to explain the different ways of thinking in cultures different from ours. It is very likely that Westerners in the same situation – of education, culture and everyday problem solving – would reason in the same way. There are good reasons for Itzaj Mayans to rely on ecological knowledge in dealing with the premises of category-based induction tests. The presence of good reasons to explain odd way of reasoning in cultures that are different from ours provides strong support for the methodological thesis of RBS (Rational model in Broad Sense). The reconstruction of the good reasons to explain beliefs and actions would have been impossible if the competence of non-Western reasoners had been completely different from ours. Without common inferential principles even the RBS model would not work. We cannot explain any social action without presupposing some common way of reacting to the situations or some common reasoning and decision-making processes. The universality of ways of thinking is, therefore, a necessary condition for any rational explanation of social action.

The second chapter "Biology and *Culture of Human Inference*" introduces the fundamental questions of the biological or cultural bases of human inferential abilities. Looking at children and other cultures it is possible to get some important clues about. In the past philosophers used to put infants and children on the opposite side from science in the spectrum of cognitive rationality. Their supposed cognitive immaturity did not allow them to approach the ideal image of rational beings. Two psychologists Alison Gopnik and Andrew Meltzoff declared, at the end of the introduction to their book: "*Ultimately, our reason for watching and talking to children is the same as Socrates'. The most central questions in cognitive science are questions that only they can answer*" (Gopnik and Meltzoff 1997, p. 9). Infants are endowed with an innate set of principles that allows them to begin to interact with the world. Among these principles, one of the most important allows a causal attribution to relations between physical events. The three main intuitive theories individuated by cognitive science are the theory of physical objects, the theory of biology and the theory of psychology. These theories allow that infants individuate some theory-specific causal mechanisms to explain interactions among the entities in a domain. A child has an intuition of what characterises a living being from an artefact or an object. Between the ages of 2 and 5, the child assumes that external states of affairs may cause mental states and that there is a causal chain from perception to beliefs to intentions to actions. Norms and criteria of theory change and conceptual development in children give a positive representation of the rational attitude of humans. On the contrary, there is a dark side of the coin. Little scientists seem not to satisfy elementary canons of correct inductive reasoning. A general inductive argument is one in which the category in the conclusion properly includes the categories in the premises. For example, one candidate principle of inductive reasoning concerns the diversity of evidence in support of a general hypothesis. It is widely claimed that greater diversity entails greater support. The diversity principle has been the object of psychological investigation. Osherson, Smith, Wilkie, López and Shafir (1990) have discovered that it is one of the phenomena present in category-based induction tasks. American adults seem to support a general or a specific conclusion more when the premises are more different than when they are more similar. On the contrary, studies made by López, Gelman, Gutheil and Smith (1992) and Gutheil and Gelman (1997) among 6- and 9-year-olds show an opposite attitude. Viale and Osherson (2006) argue against the use of the diversity principle as a normative standard of inductive reasoning. The diversity variable is not related in such a simple fashion to argument strength, even at the prescriptive level. If we accept the Bayesian probability theory as a normative account of scientific inference, as most contemporary philosophy of science is doing (Howson and Urbach 1993), we may propose that it is the probability of premises prior to accepting the conclusion that governs its strength (Horwich 1982). Under these conditions argument strength stands in a simple relation to premise-probability. The less probable the premises, the stronger the argument. The premise probability principle (PPP) has better credentials for inductive rationality since it follows from the axioms of probability and a plausible definition of argument strength. The experiments reveal detectable conformity to PPP on the part of young children in different cultures. If these findings are supported and extended by further experimentation, they provide one clear sense in which young children's inductive methodology can be interpreted as properly scientific.

If the studies on biases and errors during developmental age do not generate great concern about the image of human rationality, on the contrary, the enormous amount of empirical evidence collected over the past 40 years on sub-optimal ways of human reasoning and decision-making has provoked great bewilderment. "How can we go to the Moon with so many constant errors of judgement?" was the question asked by a colleague to Nisbett and Ross after having read the proofs of the first eight chapters of their book *Human Inference: Strategies and Shortcomings of Social Judgement* (1980). The image of man that is portrayed in the book is of a person unable to use formal criteria of reasoning and decision-making like those that scientists use in their activity. Man chooses samples that are biased by systematic tendencies; he is not able to assess the co-variation between events; he is biased in the causal attribution; he makes predictions ignoring base rate and regression towards the mean; he tends to confirm the theory instead of falsifying it. When we analyze the cognitive rationality stemming from the cognitive tests on everyday reasoning, one important question concerns the cultural variability of the styles of reasoning. Are cognitive abilities universal or context-dependent? Can we discover common patterns of thinking among different cultures or does each socio-cultural environment shape its system of thought? An answer to this question comes from Nisbett and Masuda (2006), Nisbett, Peng, Choi and Norenzayan (2001) and Nisbett (2003) on the differences between Asian and American thinking. They rely on an impressive number of cognitive tests that try to compare the way of reasoning of North Americans, mainly university students, and East Asians – Korean, Chinese and Japanese – mainly university students. The East Asians and the Americans respond in qualitatively different ways to the same stimulus situation in many different tests. For example, American participants showed large primacy effects in judgements about co-variation, whereas Chinese participants showed none. "Control illusion" increased the degree of co-variation seen and the reported accuracy of Americans but tended to have the opposite effects on Chinese. Koreans were greatly influenced in their causal attribution by the sort of situational information that has no effect for Americans. Koreans showed great hindsight bias effects under conditions where Americans showed none. Finally, Americans responded to contradiction by polarising their beliefs, whereas Chinese responded by moderating their beliefs.

But the crucial thesis of Nisbett et al. (2001) and Nisbett and Masuda (2006) is that the different ways of reasoning are not a contingent and superficial feature, but they are rooted in two completely different systems of thinking, that is, in different metaphysical and epistemological principles that shape the American and East Asian cognition differently. These two different systems of thinking originated causally from two different socio-cultural environments: the old Greek trading society and classical philosophy on one hand and the old Chinese agricultural society and Confucian philosophy on the other.

The first consideration about this anti-universal conception of cognition comes from the supporters of the universal endowment of cognitive abilities. If the innate theories of physics, of biology and of mind are true, then these theories form a common universal cognitive basis for the thought of every human in the world. In my opinion, this position may be consistent with the anti-universal thesis of Nisbett et al. The little scientist hypothesis can explain why. We know that conceptual and theory change in the developmental age does not start from nothing, but from an innate endowment of theory about causality, the physical world and so on. The change towards new theories is triggered by empirical evidence and informative inputs that come from the environment. These evidential and informative inputs obviously are variable in relation to the particular developmental contexts. Therefore, they drive the generation of different theories on how to interpret and understand the world. They are the metaphysical and epistemological theories representing the implicit premises of our reasoning and thinking. In conclusion, it is very likely that such different socio-cultural contexts as the East Asian and American ones are able to lead, in the developmental age, to the generation of different metaphysical and epistemological theories that have a different effect on ways of reasoning.

Another support to the presence of cognitive universals come from the experiments described by Atran, Medin and Ross (2006). It emerges that genetically inherited cognitive universals, represented by "universal taxonomic structures, centred on essence-based generic species", are likely to be present. These innate concepts could have been selected at an evolutionary level in order to represent important and recurrent aspects of nature. These studies confirm the hypothesis that *folk biology* does not come from folk psychology. Children from different cultures relied on the concept of underlying essence and not on the properties of human beings to reason on the properties of animals and plants. Also among the American adults the level of generic species is preferred to make inductions on the distribution of biological properties and for "predicting patterns in the face of uncertainty".

The complexity of networks and social ties in human communities makes the possibility of mind-reading, getting inside other people's minds, an essential tool to detect and track failures to co-operate and to avoid the costs of cheating. This *folk psychology*, termed by some authors the Theory of Mind (ToM), appears to emerge, universally, very early on and can already be found at the age of 9 months when the movement of a human hand is interpreted as intentional (Woodward 1998). As the child learns language, he tends to follow the mother's gaze to understand what is the referent for the word (Baldwin 1991). As Hirschfeld affirms (2006) a ToM milestone in the developmental age "is the capacity to grasp that other people hold beliefs that one knows to be false".

The fundamental level of folk psychology is also manifested in a form of *folk ontological holism* which is found when we attribute intentionality to social aggregates. As Hirschfeld writes (2006) "traffic jams, stampedes, riots, folie a deux (trois ou beaucoup), and other forms of 'groupthink' are aggregate phenomena that are best understood without appeal to individual persons' mental states" but ascribing to them intentions as if they had a mind of their own. According to most authors, this attribution of intentions is parasitic on folk psychology and does not constitute an independent *folk sociology*. Hirschfeld (2006) disputes both the thesis that social understanding is largely concerned with the interactions of individual persons and their mind and the thesis that only individual persons (and other complex living organisms) are genuine intentional agents. The understanding of the social dimension may also occur without understanding other persons' minds as postulated by ToM.

As we have seen above, one of the evolutionary explanations of folk psychology and the capacity for mind-reading represented by ToM is the possibility of foreseeing and intercepting untruthful behaviour that pretends to co-operate. The creation of social networks and organisations and even institutions themselves appear to be fostered by the ability to avoid the social costs of cheating behaviour. According to Goldman (1999), social practices like communication, testimony and argumentation are developed to help the individual pursue the goal of truth in the furthering of knowledge. This goal seems to represent an epistemological universal. Unfortunately, this truthful function of social procedures is not univocal, but, as Sperber affirms (2006), Goldman fails to point out that a "significant proportion of socially acquired beliefs are likely to be false beliefs and this not just as a result of the malfunctioning, but also of the proper functioning of social communication". If we analyze two means of communication, testimony and argumentation, we find that truth was not the evolutionary factor that led to the stabilization of communications. It is the causing of desirable effects on the audience that makes communication advantageous to the communicator. In conclusion the communicator develops the argumentative capacity to persuade, even if he does not always succeed; the listener develops coherence checking to assess the reliability of the communicator's arguments, even if he is often wrong. The communicator develops the capacity to be considered honest and reliable in testimony, even if he isn't; the listener develops fallible psychological instruments to identify whether the communicator is lying. According to Sperber in evolution, truth and rationality, falsehood and irrationality blend and the evolution of the social practice of communication are less univocally marked by the truthful ideal.

The presence or otherwise of cultural differences in the cognitive style of reasoning and decision-making is, according to Weinberg, Nichols, and Stich (2006), a fundamental epistemological fact when understanding which epistemological strategy to adopt in justifying knowledge. Why? One of the epistemological theories most in vogue over the past few years is the *internalist* theory. It affirms that the sole source of normative legitimation for our beliefs is internal, inside us. With a proper process of self-exploration we can discover the correct epistemic norms for belief formation and revision. By analogy with Romanticism in literature, Weinberg, Nichols, and Stich call this approach *Epistemic Romanticism* (2006). In fact, as in the case of Romanticism, only by exploring within ourselves can we make the real essence of our selves emerge, and also in Epistemic Romanticism we are the normative source of the epistemic principles. But in what way? One of the most debated solutions is that which identifies epistemic intuitions as the main cause, namely the spontaneous judgment about the epistemic properties of some cases. Now, the validity of IDR (Intuition Driven Romaticism), in its various versions, is based on a condition: that universal intuitions exist which can be used to determine universal norms for the formation and revision of beliefs. If, on the contrary, for the same type of events and cases the intuitions were different in relation to cultural, ethnic and social contexts, then it would not be possible not to admit some form of *epistemic relativism.* This would reveal the impossibility of IDR strategies to generate a normative theory of knowledge. The results from some intuition probes seem to prove that East Asians and Westerners are sensitive to different features of the situation, different epistemic vectors as Weinberg, Nichols, and Stich call them (2006). East Asians are very sensitive to communitarian, contextual factors, while Westerners respond to more individualistic, dispositional ones. The conclusion is that since IDR relies upon epistemic intuitions that are not universal but local to one's own cultural and socio-economic group, it is not able to lead to genuine normative conclusion.

In conclusion, the cultural variability of inferential styles and the errors and biases of human reasoning and decision-making appear to outline an epistemological picture characterised by relativism and irrationality. This picture is countered by a number of normative factors, following the internalist theory and linked to the "little scientist" hypothesis: the universal endowment of inferential principles that are both innate and adaptive in the sense of evolutionary psychology; the presence from birth of a method of theory and concept change based on empirical falsification, pragmatic consequences and problem-solving which also appears to be explained, in evolutionary terms, by its capacity to promote successful environmental adaptation. These innate principles of reasoning and the method of theory change are universal and characterize man's shared capacity, irrespective of any cultural context, to create hypotheses involving the physical, biological, psychological and social world, to learn from mistakes and to correct his theories in order to make them empirically and pragmatically successful.

The third chapter "*Cognitive Diversity in Western and Eastern Thinking*" introduces the research carried out in recent years into the diversity of thought in the Far East and in the West. One theory is that differences in the way language is organised in the two cultural areas seem to be at the origin of the different organisation of knowledge. Asians – particularly Chinese, Korean and Japanese – show less interest than Westerners – particularly Anglo-Americans – in creating abstract categories of objects, learning new categories by applying rules to properties and using categories in inductive activities (Nisbett 2003, p. 248). On the other hand, they are more interested in highlighting relations, relationships and interaction than Westerners are. How can these differences be explained on a linguistic basis? Categories are denoted by nouns (which refer to groups of objects that share the same properties) and relations by verbs (which usually denote an action that connects two objects). So we can presume that the languages that give more importance to nouns will be the ones in which the representation of knowledge is based more on conceptual categorisations of objects and phenomena. On the other hand, languages that attribute more importance to verbs reflect an organisation of knowledge that is based less on categorisation and an ontology of discreet, definite objects, and more on functional, relational and contextual aspects and a continuous relationship between objects. When we refer to the importance of nouns or verbs, it is not intended as a judgement based only on quantitative factors, for example the higher number of nouns present in a language, but also on qualitative factors, for example the position of nouns and verbs in a sentence. In Chinese, Japanese and Korean, verbs are placed primarily at the beginning and end of a sentence. These positions are more important and evident than others, because they stimulate attention mechanisms more. In European languages on the other hand, and English in particular, verbs are hidden in the middle of the sentence and this decreases their cognitive salience. As Nisbett observed (2003, pp. 157–158), Indo-European languages' preoccupation with and focus on nouns and categories is underlined by another typical feature of Anglo-Saxon languages and, to a lesser extent, even Latin languages: the prominence of the subject. A sentence in English is always polarised on a subject that represents an object or an event. The opposite is true of Far Eastern languages. Instead of being subject-prominent, they are oriented towards the issue and the context. For a Westerner, it is the Self that acts, whereas for the East Asian what acts is something that is undertaken in agreement with others or that is "the consequence of an individual action in a field of forces" (Nisbett 2003, p. 158). The grammar of Western languages is "agentive" in the sense that it highlights the role of the subject in determining the action. East Asian languages on the other hand focus on the context. Language seems to be a powerful component in determining the variety of the structure of thought, while on the other hand the structure of language tends to correspond to the representation of knowledge based on categories and objects. This different cognitive structure, which is present in the individual mind, conveys forms of knowledge that have different levels of understanding in people who belong to different linguistic communities. The greater the conceptual difference expressed by the language, the greater the diversity of the cognitive content and the smaller the capacity of the person receiving the message to understand the knowledge.

However, the difficulty of transmitting knowledge is not determined only by language. Together with language there are cultural factors that play an obvious role in generating knowledge and the standards for its justification and acceptability. Different styles of generating and justifying knowledge determine different propensities to acknowledge it, accept it and understand it. The Chinese seem more comfortable with contradictions than Westerners are. In tests that proposed conflicting assertions, East Asians tended to accept a much higher number of them than Westerners did. Unlike bivalent Western logic, East Asians seem to be guided by a "middle way logic". Between two contradictory values, they do not try to find the true one and exclude the false one, but to highlight intermediate values, or to value both horns of the dilemma. East Asians tend to classify objects and events on the basis of family relations and resemblances, while Americans tend to classify them on the basis of categories based on rules. Westerners have a tendency to give causal explanations of phenomena, based on the properties of the object and, in the case of human action, on internal dispositions. East Asians, on the other hand, are not obsessed with providing causal explanations and when they are, give greater significance to contextual factors and to the causal field between objects, and less to the properties of the individual object and, in the case of human action, to dispositional factors.

Choi and Nisbett (2000) analysed the differences between Westerners and Asians in committing "hindsight bias". Their hypothesis was that differences in causal reasoning between the two cultures would generate differences in that context. Westerners, who are more prone to explicitly abstracting causal links of ordinary historical events, should have been less prone to make facile forecasts. In fact, definite and limited causal antecedents can only generate a few final outcomes. East Asians, on the other hand, who use less explicit models of causal reasoning that consider a much larger number of factors as potential causes, are more likely to find some event that is responsible for the end result. This hypothesis was confirmed in the experiments carried out. The East Asians tended to be less surprised by events that they had previously considered improbable. They tended to rationalise them easily, unlike the American students.

The cognitive tendency of East Asians to attribute significance to the *causal field*, rather than the causal object, and of Westerners to attribute it to the object rather than the causal field, seems related to what happens in the perceptive sphere. In psychology of perception experiments we can see that East Asians tend to focus attention on a large number of context factors, while for Americans the focus is primarily on the objects in the foreground and not on those in the background.

It has been shown that the inferential component of tacit knowledge, defined as "Implicit Cognitive Rules", seems to depend directly on the principles contained in "Background Knowledge", which include moral values, and ontological, metaphysical and epistemological principles that are the background to our interpretation of reality. Even the cognitive and perceptive differences outlined earlier seem to be linked to a radical difference where "Background Knowledge" is concerned. First of all, Asian thought, and Chinese thought in particular, can be described as *dialectical*. It concentrates on the contradictions and on how to transcend them, or to find elements of truth in them. Peng (1997) outlined a number of principles that could underpin dialectical thought, set out in order of their general and implied importance. The world is not static but dynamic and constantly changing. Because the world is changing constantly, it is full of oppositions, contradictions, inconsistencies and anomalies. At the moment that a thing exists, it is already becoming something else. As a result of the principles of change and of contradiction, nothing can exist in isolation and independently. Every object and event is connected to numerous others inter-dependently. To understand something we have to understand all the relations that link that object to other objects and the various parts of the object with itself.

The thesis of the fourth chapter "*Adaptive Theory Change as an Epistemological Universal*" is that the norms of theory change – that we discover in the best examples of the growth of knowledge – can represent a naturalistic methodological criterion to assess the reasons for generating and changing a belief and consequently an epistemological universal.

The rationality emerging from some results in a study on a sample of applied scientists (Viale and Cerroni 2002) seems to have particular features: it is comparative, realist and procedural. Moreover the results of this test are coherent, to a great extent, with the results of the historical test contained in the volume of A. Donovan, L. Laudan and R. Laudan (1988), that represents the methodological behaviour of the upper level basic scientists of the past. The conclusion is that we can claim that in this sample of applied science, the methodological beliefs seem, to a great extent, similar to those of the best basic science of the past and to the normative criteria of rationalist philosophy of science. Contrary to the previous example there are other empirical data that support a disturbing image of the rational ability of scientists. One of my concerns stems from a study of the conjunction fallacy carried out with the same sample of scientists as the previous example (Viale and Osherson 2000) that showed 70% of the scientists fell in the probabilistic fallacy. Are the scientists guided by probabilistic principles when reasoning about technical matters related to their specialization? The answer seems negative. Many tests on probabilistic and deductive reasoning show an image of scientists that commit probabilistic and deductive fallacies.

Children resemble scientists in their method of theory change. One theory can substitute another when it fits the empirical evidence better and allows one to make better predictions. Counter-evidence to a theory is ignored unless it manifests itself persistently. These criteria remind me of those selected in the previous questionnaire submitted to adult scientists. The Methodological criteria of theory change in big and little scientists are not the guarantee of truth and representational success. Many false hypotheses are generated using these criteria. But nonetheless they seem to be a guarantee of conceptual learning from errors to generate theories that fit the world better. Norms and criteria of theory change and conceptual development in children give a positive representation of the rational attitude of humans. On the contrary, as in the case of big scientists, there is a dark side of the coin. Little scientists seem not to satisfy elementary canons of correct reasoning. For example, one candidate principle of inductive reasoning concerns the diversity of evidence in support of a general hypothesis. It is widely claimed that greater diversity entails greater support. American adults seem to support a general or a specific conclusion more when the premises are more different than when they are more similar. On the contrary, studies made by Lopez et al. (1997) and Gutheil & Gelman (1997) among 6 year olds and 9 year olds show an opposite attitude. In conclusion, little scientists seem to suffer from a schizophrenia similar to that of big scientists. They seem to follow sound criteria of conceptual and theory change, but at the same time, they lack important inferential principles of induction such as the diversity principle.

Adult man goes to the moon, that is, he is quite able to adapt to his social and natural environment. He is able to understand, predict and control many aspects of his life and his environment. He is able to plan his career, to make diagnoses from his symptoms, to discuss rationally many problems. In the same time he presents an irrational image because he commits a lot biases and errors in reasoning and decision making. There are two important aspects of human irrationality that can find a moderate interpretation. The first concerns sub-optimality in assessing co-variation among events, that is a crucial ability for generating hypotheses. Outside the laboratory, in real life, there are many circumstances that allow good performance in co-variation. The second and most important concern about human rationality is the "perseverance bias". People tend to persevere in their beliefs even when faced with data that falsify them. This behavior doesn't seem so irrational according to the following two considerations: (a)The maintenance of a theory in front of anomalies, until we are sure that it is systematic, seems a sound methodological rule also in the scientific community. (b) The adult seems more close to the model of the technologist rather than the scientist. He needs to apply theories in everyday problem solving. He has no time to worry about the truth of the theory. What is important is that it functions in solving practical problems. He fears more a casual error in applying the theory in a given pragmatic context than a systematic error that would need the generation of an alternative theory. Nevertheless, as in technology, the solution works if the embodied theory is valid. Therefore even the adult is obliged to change, sooner or later, ill-functioning theories.

When we analyse the cognitive rationality stemming from the cognitive tests on everyday reasoning, one important question concerns the cultural variability of the styles of reasoning. Are cognitive abilities universal or context-dependent? Can we discover common patterns of thinking among different cultures or does each socio-cultural environment shape its system of thought? An answer to this question comes from a recent article of Nisbett et al. (2001) on the differences between Asian and American thinking. They rely on an impressive amount of cognitive tests that try to compare the way of reasoning of North Americans, mainly university students and East Asians – Korean, Chinese and Japanese – mainly university students. As I show before East Asians and the Americans respond in qualitatively different ways to the same stimulus situation in many different tests.

It is likely that there are not fixed irreversible differences in cognition that stem from relative different and fixed metaphysical and epistemological theories about the world, as in Nisbett et al. thesis (2001). Many data show that the cognitive abilities are dependent on knowledge, expertise and on pragmatic needs. These factors are able to reduce and, in some cases, to neutralise the cultural diversity of the cognitive abilities. This conclusion is well known in cognitive anthropology. Education can quite easily shape cognitive attitudes making them, trans-culturally, similar. And the problem solving ability is much stronger in real world scenarios linked to particular pragmatic contexts and practical needs than it is in abstract tasks. The need for practical problem solving can trigger cognitive abilities that were hidden in abstract and uninteresting tasks (Boudon and Viale 2000).

What does this remark mean in my discourse? That the relative plasticity of cognitive abilities in different cultures reflects the dynamics of theory change of the little scientist hypothesis. Human cognitive abilities depend on his theories about the world. But these theories are not fixed, irreversibly, by his local socio-cultural condition. They can be changed in relation to pragmatic feed-backs, empirical evidence and the new information coming from the environment. The relative theory change is driven by methodological norms that are effective during childhood, and we meet it again, in a similar fashion, inside the scientific community. The methodological norms of theory change seem, to a great extent, universal.

Part I

Cognitive Rationality and Society

Psychologism and Antipsychologism

2

The social sciences focus on the effect of man's actions. Whether these regard immigration, employment, financial markets, technological innovation or political elections, any phenomenon that is the aggregate outcome of individual behaviour involving choice and human action is studied by a particular branch of the social sciences.

So far, in general, no objections can be raised to the definition of the aims of the social sciences. The situation becomes more intricate when we try to answer the following question: how can we explain the effect of human action? In the first place, some social scientists deny the relevance of this question. As they see it, the cognitive purpose of social sciences is the relationship between statistical aggregates of individual actions. Whether dealing with the relationship between internal demand and the rate of inflation or between the percentage of clandestine immigration and the level of assault, the ultimate goal is to identify statistical techniques and key quantitative figures that enable the researcher to signal the presence of a causal link between the aggregates. Seen from this point of view, to ensure that the question makes sense, we should decline it in the plural: how can we explain the aggregate effects of human actions? The answer is given in the aggregate terms of other human actions that play a causal role in determining the effect in question. Furthermore, they also identify the causal effects of the social phenomenon in the form of other aggregates of human actions. To sum up, the statistical explanation of a particular social phenomenon is sought by analysing the underlying causes and the consequent effects, always in the form of quantitative macrovariables of aggregates of human actions.

Those who would unhesitatingly answer the first question are the social scientists who, for a variety of reasons – metaphysical, epistemological and methodological – do not consider it possible to decline the question in the plural. If the goal of the study is to identify the laws and causal explanations, the line of inquiry must be directed at the real causal determinants of human action in the singular, whose aggregation is responsible for the social phenomenon. The relationship between statistical aggregates cannot a priori have any causal relevance because it represents mathematical invention, not real entities endowed with causal power.

R. Viale, *Methodological Cognitivism*,
DOI 10.1007/978-3-642-24743-9_2,

Anyone who does not hesitate to answer the question about explaining human action, should not have any doubt in identifying the causal factors responsible for action in the mind. What else except the mind, through its processes of reasoning, judgement and decision, could produce the outcome of action? The goal of the social scientist should therefore be to identify the psychological mechanisms that generate a particular action and can be generalised to the same type of action accomplished by others. The social phenomenon, translatable in the aggregate of several actions of the same type, can be explained by laws and by starting conditions that refer to the psychological mechanisms of reasoning, judgement and decision.

However, this solution is not accepted by a third group of social scientists who, on the contrary, share the answer to the first question. Human action cannot be explained causally, as with natural events, but must instead be interpreted rationally. It is not possible to reduce action to a natural event and try to derive it from causal laws. There are several reasons. On the whole, the most important seems to be the one that highlights the specificity of intentional human action, complete with meaning and a subjective content that cannot be deduced from general natural laws. Moreover, the action is chosen by the individual and interpreted by the researcher on the basis of a principle of rationality that is assumed to be general but which, being a priori, cannot be explained in naturalistic terms.

This chapter is dedicated to a short historical excursus on the fortunes and misfortunes of psychologism (a term coined by E. Husserl) in methodology of social science. A number of key positions will be illustrated, without any desire for historical completeness but with the aim of establishing the premises for the arguments developed later in the book.

2.1 The Psychologism of J.S. Mill

Although numerous important contributions to the methodology of the social sciences were made earlier, the work of John Stuart Mill represents a milestone for the psychologist position. In Book VI of *System of Logic Ratiocinative and Inductive* (1st edition 1843; 8th edition 1956; Italian translation 1968) the brilliant "official of the East India Company" provides a relatively complete and to a certain extent definitive exposé of the theoretical primacy of psychologism in the social sciences. Book VI, which is entitled *The Logic of Moral Sciences* and was published at the end of the other five books dedicated to "a comprehensive explanation of the principles of evidence and methods of scientific investigation," summarises the conceptual signposts of a position that would be neglected by later social science methodology. The book starts with a classic question "Are human actions subject to invariable laws like all other natural events? Are they really ruled by the constant of causality that underlies every scientific theory of successive phenomena?" (Mill, 1st edition 1843; 8th edition 1956; Italian translation 1968, VI, I, § 1, p. 827). Mill's answer is complex. The actions of individuals can never be predicted with certainty owing to the variety of circumstances and initial conditions that precede the action itself. On the other hand, "approximate generalisations" can be formulated that do not apply to all the actions of the members of a society, but only to the majority. In this case, it is possible to expect with certainty that a particular phenomenon will take place at a mass level, even if some individuals may act in a contrary manner. Seen from this point of view, the approximate generalisations that may assume universal validity for a given society from which they are derived and to which they apply, only reach the "base status of empirical laws." In order to ensure that the study of society meets the requisites of scientific study they must be connected in deductive terms to the causal laws on the nature of human action. In fact, an empirical law is a true uniformity in all cases of the predicative field of observation. However, this does not guarantee its validity for a wider sector of reality because its generalisation is based on contingent and external aspects of reality and not on the intimate causal mechanisms of human nature: "Empirical law derives its truth from causal laws, of which it is the consequence. If we are familiar with those laws, we know the limits of the derived law; instead, if we have not yet justified the empirical law – if it is based on observation alone – then there is no guarantee in applying it outwith the limits of time, place and circumstance in which the observations were made" (Mill, 1st edition 1843; 8th edition 1956; Italian translation 1968, VI, V, § 1, p. 853). The empirical laws of those phenomena that depend on known causes, according to the general theory, have no other function except to verify the conclusions of the theory.

Causal laws that can justify empirical generalisations must refer to the human mind. However, in Mill's opinion, there are two theoretical levels concerning the causal representation of the mind. At a lower, more general level are the principles of "ethology" or science of the character, and at a higher level the psychology or science of the elementary laws of the mind: "The principles of ethology are really average principles, the *axiomata media* (as Bacon would have said) of the science of the mind, because they can be distinguished, on the one hand, from the empirical laws based on simple observation, and on the other from higher generalisations" (Mill, 1st edition 1843; 8th edition 1956; Italian translation 1968, VI, V, § 5, p. 861).

Ethology is a deductive science, namely a system of corollaries of psychology which, on the contrary, is an experimental science. It is therefore necessary to generate the simplest laws of causality of psychology by induction, and then to derive the more complex laws of causality of ethology by deduction. In turn the science of character can be verified by empirical laws. How can ethology be represented? As the series of causal laws on the general character of the members of a given society in relation to the different cultural, material, political and other circumstances responsible for developing the character in one direction rather than another. In other words, the laws of ethology, derived deductively from the laws of psychology, should allow us to explain the different characters of social or national contexts in the presence of different starting conditions. Mill is concerned to underline that, in addition to this a priori activity of the deductive type, it is essential also to use an experimental kind of a posteriori activity: "The inference given by theory regarding the type of character formed by particular circumstances must be proved by the specific experience of those circumstances, if it can be obtained" (Mill, 1st edition 1843; 8th edition 1956; Italian translation 1968, VI, V, § 6, p. 865).

Mill's position was either neglected or criticised by later contributions to scientific methodology. These were marked by a generalised antipsychologism expressed by authors whose theses were radically divergent on other essential methodological questions. Marx, Weber, Menger, L. von Mises, Popper, von Hayek, Watkins, Boudon, Elster all share a stringent criticism of Mill's psychologism and, more in general, of the thesis concerning the reduction of social action to causal mechanisms of the human mind.

In order to illustrate the general tenets of antipsychologism, it seems appropriate to refer to the position of Karl Popper that is most clearly contrary to Mill.

It is significant that in *The Open Society and its Enemies* (5th edition 1966; Italian translation 1974) Popper takes Marx as one of the main objects of his critical analysis, but he finds himself in complete agreement with his antipsychologism. For Popper, the aim of the 14 chapter – *The Autonomy of Sociology* (*The Open Society and its Enemies*, 5th edition 1966; Italian translation 1974, vol. II, pp. 119–131) is to illustrate Marx's famous maxim: "It is not men's conscience that determines their being, but, on the contrary, their social being that determines their conscience" (Marx, Italian translation 1971, p. 5). According to Popper, the fact that Marx attacked psychologism and, consequently, contributed to reinstating the autonomy of sociology and social laws is his greatest achievement as a sociologist. In fact, "The error of psychologism consists in claiming that methodological individualism in the field of social sciences entails the need to reduce all social phenomena and all social regularities to psychological phenomena and psychological laws" (Popper, 5th edition 1966; Italian translation 1974, vol. II, p. 131).

2.2 The Historicist Accusation

According to Popper, the reasons why this reduction is unacceptable can be summed up as follows. In the first place, psychologism is "obliged to adopt historicist methods." According to Millian psychologism, all the regularities of society, its institutions, traditions, customs and culture must be explained and reduced, in the last resort, to the "actions and passions of human beings." This is not the same as the historicist claim that, starting from the laws of the mind and the initial circumstances of the human species, it is possible to "determine a priori the order in which human development must occur and as a result predict the general facts of history up to the present time" (Mill, 1st edition 1843; 8th edition 1956; Italian translation 1968, p. 906). Nonetheless, for Popper this admission is not enough to save Mill from the accusation of being a historicist. In fact, Mill appears to mean that, although it is not proposable to explain the complete development of human history, it is however possible to explain the "idea of the *first steps* of this development." But this implies that there must be a stage when the explanation of social regularities like institutions, culture and traditions is only based on pure, uncontaminated psychological factors, independent of social elements.

"Psychologism is therefore obliged, like it or not, to operate with the idea of a *start of society* and with the idea of a human nature and human psychology which exist prior to society" (Popper, 5th edition 1966; Italian translation 1974, vol. II, p.124). The theory of a pre-social human nature is, however, according to Popper, a historical and methodological myth. Because it is likely that man's forebears were "social before being human." This implies that the social dimension and the laws that explain it existed before the subjective human dimension and its relative psychological laws. "If a reduction is to be attempted at all costs, it would be more promising to attempt to reduce or interpret psychology in terms of sociology rather than the other way round" (Popper, 5th edition 1966; Italian translation 1974, vol. II, p.124). This criticism of Mill's supposed historicism is motivated by the equally debatable hypothesis (one need only consider the studies on sociobiology and cognitive primatology) regarding man's ancestors who were "social before being human." Popper's assertion appears to presuppose a genetic and hereditary basis of sociality that would account for its manifestation in species predating man's appearance. Sociality as instinctive behaviour would leave out the psychological component for explaining the action and could therefore not be reduced to it. This ingenuous vision of the relationship between mind and heredity overlooks a number of points. Firstly, the hereditary component is not presumed to be a prerogative of sociality, but of more fundamental cognitive activities like causal attribution, which is present in man and in primates right from the very earliest age (Viale 1999). On the other hand, sociality understood as instinctive behaviour without mental activity is present and is a feature of species that are very distant from humans, like ants. Thirdly, the combination of sociality with reflex and instinctive behaviour, like that in ants, is the basis for justifying the organicistic and teleological theses of society as a body whose individual parts act unconsciously solely for the purpose of ensuring the survival of the community. This outcome is in contrast with Popper's supposed methodological individualism. This apparent contradiction reveals, in my opinion, an anomaly that undermines all the individualistic theses contrary to psychologism. Even when they do not create such explicit contradictions as that proposed by Popper, they end up by legitimating a conceptual and ontological superiority and priority of the contextual and social dimension – for example, situational logic or the symbolic context – compared to the individual dimension. Consequently, they implicitly reduce individualism to a masqueraded form of contextualism, or in other words methodological holism.

In short, to return to Popper, if we are interested in referring to the sociality of man's forebears as the premise of our sociality, this should not be thought of as resembling the reflex behaviour of termites, but rather that tendency to interact, to organise ourselves collectively and to create a division of roles in order to solve problems which is guided by their (the forebears) and our own cognitive and perceptive activities, whose foundations are, above all in our earliest stages of life, mainly hereditary. Sociality without an underlying mental activity can only be of the reflex and instinctive type. In this case, the individual, like a cell in the body, acts according to positive or negative mechanisms of action and retroaction that have been selected through evolution depending on their effect in terms of the individual's better adaptation to the environment. However, in these cases, individual adaptability has been selected as being dependent on his role within a particular society of individuals of the same species, organised in a more or less hierarchical fashion. Sociality in this instance is obligatory, it presents constant organisational configurations and the individual, whether it is an ant or a cell, has no chance of autonomous survival outside these configurations. In conclusion, by taking this position Popper either supports strong theses of the innate type – which suggest that our sociality stems from and is founded on the conditional instinctual reflex of socialisation – which even the most radical modern sociobiology does not dare to affirm and which imply an organicist derivation, or he does not intend to support these theses, but could not avoid admitting that sociality – understood as an intentional or non-intentional artefact produced by human actions – although it may perhaps also be present in some superior primates – and therefore in pre-human species – can only be traced, even in these cases, to the psychological laws that explain human or pre-human actions in causal terms.

2.3 The Psychological Irreducibility of Unintentional Consequences

The second reason for opposing psychologism can be found in Popper's affirmation that while institutions, traditions and social groups are the result of human actions and decisions, this does not mean that they can be explained on this basis. "On the contrary, even those that occur as the outcome of conscious and intentional human actions are usually *the indirect, unintentional and often undesired by-products of these actions,*" (Popper, 5th edition 1966; Italian translation 1974, vol. II, p. 124). Any institution barring a few rare exceptions, is not the product of a conscious plan of construction, but instead is the unexpected result of human actions. And even when an institution is directly related to a conscious project, its final characteristics elude the original intentions of its creator. If this is true therefore, in Popper's opinion, society, in all its various forms, cannot be reduced to mental activity, given that it is not its direct expression. Popper's anti-psychologistic arguments, which are also shared by other authors like von Hayek, are based on a serious misunderstanding of the concept of mental. They are founded on the rationalist prejudice that mental equals rational. If mental is identified with rational, then any outcome of human actions that does not correspond to the original rational decision cannot be explained solely on this basis, but requires external explanations of a social and environmental nature. Millian pyschologism is not distorted by this "Cartesian bias." Instead, in his description of psychological and ethological laws Mill reveals an interest in the least rational and intentional aspects of the mind, for example character, personality, etc.

At all events, it is strange that Popper did not take into due consideration in the first place the difference between absolute rational action, relative rational action and intentional action. An intentional action is such if it is a means chosen consciously to reach an end based on given beliefs regarding the world (which may be true, false, complete or incomplete). A relative rational action is such if it is the best means consciously chosen to reach a goal in relation to given beliefs regarding the world (which may be true or false, complete or incomplete). An absolute rational action is such if it is the best means consciously chosen to reach a goal based on true and complete beliefs regarding the world. The term best means is conventionally understood to mean, in this case, that deriving from the theory of rational action, namely the maximisation of expected subjective utility.

The use of the terms information and beliefs does not only mean those immediately local and relative to the present, but also the expected future effects of our actions on surrounding phenomena. This is particularly important when the variables involved are not of the parametric type, but our action must strategically consider the interaction of other individual actions. The decision-making problem is further complicated when the goal of our actions is not immediate but protracted over time, thus opening up the possibility of the combinatorial explosion of the decision-making tree. It could be said that the complexity and consequent incompleteness or falsity of information is directly in proportion to the number of strategic players involved and the increased length of time required to achieve the goal. A last clarification concerns the resources we must use to reach our goal. In a world of infinite and unlimited resources, our information and our inferences aimed at attaining a goal, for example studying to achieve a good social position, might overlook complex analyses over time of the effects of the strategic interaction with other players pursuing the same purpose. On the contrary, in a world where resources are scarce, if we are pursuing the goal of social ascent, we are compelled to think strategically with medium and long-term plans. Otherwise, we will find ourselves making choices together with many other players, for example the mass pursuit of a particular profession, leading to the final perverse outcome that the supply well outstrips the demand leading to professional dequalification and failure to achieve our aim of social advancement.

In short, an intentional action may be irrational for two reasons: because it is based on incomplete or false information or because it uses inferential-deductive and inductive-fallacious procedures to choose the action. A relative rational action can only be irrational for one reason: because it is based on incomplete or false information. To these three categories we can also add that of unintentional actions, namely those carried out thoughtlessly, as in the case of reflex actions, or those deriving from violent emotions, or from lapsus and forgetfulness (that, according some authors, like Gigerenzer, that conceive intentionality and rationality as distinct concepts, can also be rational).[1]

All these categories of actions can be explained by psychological laws regarding the nature of the mind. Except for absolute rational actions, which are possible in

[1] In the second part of the volume I will introduce the current debate on duality of mind and ecological rationality. According to this debate most of mental activity is not intentional, but unaware and in the same time adaptive and rational as a good solution to the environmental decisional problem (Gigerenzer 2007).

principle but impossible in practice, apart in rare cases of transparent decision-making settings, with few parametric variables and with immediate outcomes and not medium-term deadlines and unintentional actions, the other two categories of action may produce unintentional consequences. How can we explain these undesired consequences? Through two elements. The first refers to informative limits or to the limits of the social player's inferential ability. Instead, the second refers to the resulting aggregate motive for the interaction of various individual actions generated on the basis of the informative and inferential limits. A simple classical example will suffice. How can we explain the overcrowded motorways and queues on the night before the start of the holidays? All other reasons being equal, like enjoying travelling by night or making use of every available minute of the holidays, the people who decide to start their journey during the night tend to base their choice on information that is incomplete, e.g. not taking account of the strategic dimension of similar actions taken by other individuals like them, or false, e.g. believing that the majority of holidaymakers leave the following morning, a statistic based on incorrect data published for the previous year. Based on these assumptions, they take the rational action of travelling by night with the aim of travelling comfortably on the motorway with no heavy traffic and queues. The aggregate result of all these similar relative rational actions aimed at achieving the purpose of travelling in comfort and the presence of a relative scarcity of the resource, namely road space, causes the unintentional phenomenon of queues and traffic jams which frustrates the hopes of the would-be crafty motorists. In this way, an unintentional social phenomenon can be explained in psychological terms, namely the cognitive mechanisms underlying the relative rational action of numerous motorists and the presence of an environmental constraint, like the relative scarcity of road space.

2.4 The Subalternity of Mental Causes to Situational Logic

The third reason why Popper affirms that psychologism is not acceptable is linked to the *logic of the situation* (Antiseri, 1996). The analysis of the situation plays an important role in all social sciences, starting with economics. Situational logic is dictated by the external circumstances in which the action occurs. It is the environmental constraints that shape the subject's rationality. "...when we talk of 'rational behaviour' or 'irrational behaviour', we mean a form of behaviour that is or is not in harmony with the logic of that situation" (Popper, 5th edition 1966; Italian translation 1974, vol. II, p. 129). The psychological motives are subordinate to the situational logic. In fact, "the psychological analysis of an action in terms of its motives (whether rational or irrational) presupposes (...) that the criteria for what should be considered rational in that situation have been defined beforehand" (Popper, 5th edition 1966; Italian translation 1974, vol. II, p.129). What Popper seems to be saying is that the situation, understood as the context in which the individual finds himself acting, dictates his explanatory priorities over the psychological mechanisms that are responsible for the action. It is as if the action is swallowed up by the contextual situation and without it has no possibility of being deciphered.

There are two ways of interpreting Popper's thesis. The first, which I would describe as weak, could be summed up as the need when explaining any social action to identify the context of the problem to which it is addressed. Every action could be defined as a solution to a problem, and in order to explain it we must therefore first clarify what it is addressing. This weak interpretation, which is easy to agree with, does not present the antipsychologist claims present in Popper's thesis. In fact, it could easily be compatible with the psychological tradition of decision analysis as a problem-solving activity which attributes the explanation of the action to the psychological mechanisms – heuristic, problem representation, empiric and deontic rules, etc. – responsible for the solving processes.[2]

The second interpretation, which could be called "strong," reverses the viewpoint of the relationship between situation and action. It is not the action which, as the response to a problem, allows the crucial characteristics of a situation to be defined, or in other words allows the formation of its semantic field, but rather the situation which contains all the possible explanatory meanings of the action. It is the situation that lays down the boundaries and determines the lines of strength if not the specific courses of human action. It is the situation that rationally structures the factual map so that the course of human action can be adequately explained through these facts. In short, Popper appears to suggest a reduction – in terms of rationality – of individual human action to the collective logic – namely the social context – of the situation in which the individual acts. By doing this, Popper appears to favour a form of holism that we might call *contextualism* or *methodological situationism*.

A number of critical considerations can be made regarding the position taken by Popper. First of all, it is not clear how a situational logic can exist with an independent foundation, external to individual logic. If by this, he means that the situation presents contextual constraints to the decision-making process – e.g. scarcity or otherwise of material resources, objectives and strategies of other players, time constraints, etc. – it is not clear what this has to do with logic. Even in the metaphorical sense, when we use the term logic we mean a set of a priori rules of an analytical type used to derive assertions from other assertions.

In the case of constraints on the situational context, if we want to unearth some sort of logic at all costs, it can be identified to a greater extent in the rules guiding the player's representative and decision-making processes which underlie the representation of the problematic situation, the search for a solution and the consequent action. In fact, the so-called environmental constraints characteristic

[2] As we will see in the second part of the volume, bounded rationality thesis represented by the metaphor of two blades of the scissors (Simon 1956; Gigerenzer and Selten 2001a) conceives rationality as the fitting of the environmental complexity represented by the structure of the problem and inferential ability of the problem solver. Therefore the rationality of a solution or of a decision is also assessed in relation to a problem that is contextually based.

of the situation have no logical form other than how they are represented by the player. The scarcity or otherwise of material resources present in a particular situational context is always relative to the objectives and the means chosen to achieve them, elaborated by a player using representative and inferential processes. If the material resources present in a given environment are equal, their relative scarcity or abundance is a function of how we represent them, the player's aims and the consequent actions taken to achieve them – e.g. the limited supplies of fossil fuels on earth makes this a resource that is scarce or abundant depending on the choice between combustion technologies and alternative energies and on consumption and energy saving policies.

The same argument could be applied to the constraint of time. Like material goods this, obviously, is a limited resource. However, its greater or lesser scarcity depends on the needs in terms of the player's aims and decisions, as well as on other variables regarding the situation. If other constraints are equal, the time variable either will or will not become a scarce resource depending on the aims and decisions of players requiring more "time consuming" actions – for example, in a chess match, the decision whether or not to adopt a decision-making strategy of the optimising type compared to a "satisficing" one. At any rate, it is the player who determines the value of the time variable, and not any form of external situational logic.

The third and most important aspect of a social situation is the interaction between players. In this case, situational logic can be compared to all the decision-making logics used by the players, each of whom attempts to pursue his own goal, trying to evaluate and foresee the moves made by the other individuals with whom he has to interact. Other people's decision-making logics represent important constraints on inferential processes and individual action. From this, can it be supposed that the logic of individual choice is annihilated by that of the situation? No. Let us take two extreme examples. In the first, the player interacts with other subjects who, for various reasons – lesser decision-making ability or rigid routine behaviour – present a less sophisticated rationality than his own, so that he can regard them as parameters within his decision-making processes – e.g. the manager of an organisation whose employees follow rigid routines. This is the case that comes closest to an example of situational logic. The decision-maker can formulate his choice on the basis of a rigidly structured environment. If he has a goal, he can only reach it by moulding the choice of the means to the rigid form of the parametric behaviour of other individuals. If we compare this situation with that represented by an interactive strategic-type environment made up of players who symmetrically possess sophisticated rationality – e.g. negotiations regarding an employment contract or the acquisition of a company, or talks on nuclear disarmament – the difference is clear. Because of the symmetric condition of the capacities of reasoning, decision and strategic interaction, the social player knows that the choices of other players in the situation cannot be foreseen using deterministic methods, nor is their behaviour rigidly conditioned by routines and decision-making models, but instead there is a potential symmetry in the opportunities for decision and action. The situation therefore becomes a continuous evolution in which the player's ability to calculate, interpret and anticipate the behaviour of others is at the basis of his strategic choices. Social action is closely dependent on the psychological ability to evaluate and foresee actions taken by other players in the social situation. Therefore, there is no logic outside the reasoning and decision-making capacity of the individual situational player. The only forms of logic are the representational, inferential and decision-making logics that oversee, as Mill would say, the mental activity of the individual in his attempt to interact strategically with other situational players. In a situation of this type, the barycentre is obviously at the level of the other individual social players involved. On the other hand, in the previous situation, it appears to be focused on the rigid constraints of the routine behaviour of the active members in this context. On the surface, this extreme case might be seen as situational logic capable of explaining individual action. This interpretation should be rejected on a number of grounds. In the first place, in the real world, no situations exist where routine behaviour is so rigid that it does not leave space for individual variability. Variability may derive from a variety of reasons: for example, it may be caused by the incorrect, but involuntary application of the assigned routine, or by the voluntary attempt to create decision-making spaces in the margin of one's own assigned role. In doing this, the individual assumes decision-making characteristics of a strategic type that present the aforesaid characteristics of non-predictability. The same could also be said of hypothetical social contexts peopled by parametric individuals whose rational abilities are less sophisticated than their own. Those who act in these contexts cannot assume with certainty the predictability of other people's actions. For the simple reason that there is no homogeneity in the expression of this rationality. Instead, subrational behaviour is often, owing to its instability and variability, less easy to interpret and foresee than rational behaviour.

Secondly, even in these parametric cases, the player who wants to formulate a decision does so on the basis of the constraints and characteristics deriving from his unique ability to represent reality. The elements making up the real situation with which he intends to interact have no life and meaning for the social player if they are not "reified" (*"mentalized")* as social entities by his mental processes of representation. Outside the cone of shade of attention and representation, they are simple entities without a role or social value. But mental social reification occurs both according to inclinations, distortions and "biases" that amplify or underestimate special aspects of the situation, and above all in different ways by different minds. The first order of effects has been studied and demonstrated by cognitive psychology. It leads to various phenomena – of a perceptive and inferential type – concerning the suboptimal representation of reality – e.g. perceptive distortions based on expectations or the mistaken estimate of the characteristics of an object based on overconfidence or "heuristics of representativeness." The second order of effects is based not only on the findings of psychological experiments which show a constant, albeit infinitesimal variability in the responses given by individuals. It is also justified by the variability between one individual and another in neuronal structure – in terms of the number of neurons and type of synaptic connections – and the unique personal experience that has resulted in the unique structure of his central nervous system and relative psychological abilities.

2.5 Mental Atomism and Psychologism

The reasons for the criticism of psychologism raised by Popper and many other authors can be traced back to methodological individualism. The structure and complexity of this school of social science methodology is often not taken sufficiently into account (Antiseri, 1996). The contraposition of methodological individualism (MI) to the various holistic theses often overshadows that the fact that it contains incompatible and contradictory positions. The first reason for this confusion is the lack of differentiation between the different philosophical dimensions present within this approach (Bhargava, 1992).

In the first place, a distinction should be drawn between at least three forms within MI: *explanatory individualism* (EI), *ontological individualism* (OI) and *semantic individualism* (SI). The first can be summed up in the thesis that all social phenomena can, in principle, be explained using methods that refer to individuals and their properties. The second aims to demonstrate that because only individuals and their properties exist, then social phenomena must be identified with them. *Semantic individualism* is based on a different thesis from the first two, although it can be derived from them. Every noun and attribute referring to social attributes can be reduced to nouns and attributes referring to individual entities.

The structure of psychologistic or antipsychologistic theses belongs, mainly to the dimension of OI, even if, according to the position expressed in EI, consequences can be derived in favour of one or other position.

In the first place (see Fig. 2.1 taken from Bhargava 1992, p. 33), there are two main variants of EI which correspond respectively with support or lack of support for the *nomological-deductive model*. As far as concerns the first family of EI, *support of the nomological-deductive model* is combined with the formal constraint that the explanation is an argument in which the matter to be explained, the explanandum, must be deduced from at least two premises, the explanans. The two principal members of the nomological-deductive family are the *reductionist* option which affirms the possibility of reducing social laws to laws on individual behaviour combined with either bridge laws or assertions of identity (microreductions), and the *non-reductionist* option which follows the standard nomologic-deductive model of deducting the particular social event from general laws on individual behaviour and the starting conditions for individuals and their properties.

At first sight, the *reductionist* version and above all the *microreductionist* version seem to be closer to psychologism. By asserting the identity of social phenomena, on the one hand, and individuals and their psychological properties on the other, the epistemological barycentre of social analysis shifts towards the reality of individual minds. To do this, however, we must assume the existence of social laws, the object of the reduction. If this type of assumption corresponds to an

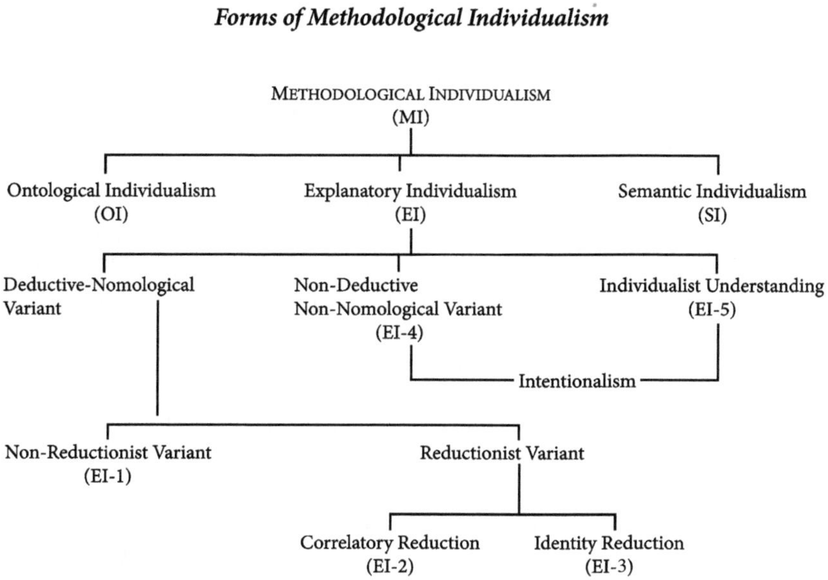

Fig 2.1 Forms of methodological individualism (Bhargava 1992)

affirmation of the epistemological reality of social laws, this would not be accepted by Millian psychologism because, according to it, only the laws of the human mind are real. The reason for this position is clearly ontological, because a scientific law aims to establish regular relations between real entities. According to the Millian position, a social law cannot exist because the social phenomena do not exist. In the words of scientific realism, it is impossible to accept as scientific a law describing the behaviour of entities that are not real.[3] Therefore, given that the reality of social entities is denied by psychologism at an ontological level, it is not possible to talk of social laws that describe constant relations between them. The only epistemological position that might support the role of the social laws at an explanatory level would be a radical conventionalistic position that affirms the conventional nature of both the entities and the scientific laws.

[3] This goal is not only pursued by the epistemological current known as scientific realism. Even the supporters of a conventionalist position on the reality of scientific laws, namely the lack of correspondence between the linguistic assertion called law and the world, might have a realistic position in terms of the entities to which the law applies (Hacking, 1983). For example, it is possible to support a Humean conception on the conventionality of causal laws and at the same time to support the epistemological reality of the entities to which the law applies. Even if it is asserted, for example, that the law of gases refers to the regularity of relations between real entities like the pressure and temperature of gas, it is still possible to deny its epistemological reality as a causal law.

On the contrary, according to the *non-reductionist* option, what can be explained is only the particular social event[4] and the explanation is based on laws and the starting conditions of individuals and their properties.[5] This variation of EI has no substantive ontological implications relating to what we propose as laws on individuals and their properties. The possibility of social laws is implicitly denied because the ontological existence of social phenomena is rejected. It is not assumed, however, which type of entity and individual properties are important for the explanation. The entities might be everything related to individual action. They might be psychological entities causally linked to action, like memory, reasoning, emotion, decision, and so on. Or they might be intentional entities linked to action through some principle of rationality. In fact, while psychologism may be favourable to *non-reductionist* option of EI, its greatest supporters also include convinced antipsychologists like Popper (1960) and Watkins (1973).

The *non nomological-deductive* version denies that social phenomena must be explained deductively with the aid of general laws. Social phenomena can only be explained or understood through particular facts on individuals. Singular facts like the dispositions and the intentions are the explanans that enable us to explain the social explanandum in a non-deductive manner. This allows us to establish causal relations of a particular type without the aid of deductions from general laws. Intentional and rational explanations are an example of this position (Elster 1983). Or, in the case of the "*understanding*" variant, through the description of beliefs, desires, individual intentions, an attempt is made to understand the social action, without trying to explain the meaning of social phenomena in causal terms. Hermeneutic understanding or empathic analysis are examples of this approach.

There are a number of well-known arguments (Hempel 1966; Rosenberg 1988) which demonstrate the implicit use of general laws also in this type of explanations. The hermeneutic model of beliefs-desires-intentions represents a general psychological theory known as "folk psychology." The implicit use of these theories or general laws is often done in a deductive manner, even if the resulting deduction is not usually complete. At all events, the methodological negation of the use of causal laws for social explanation obviously places this variation of EI in an antipsychologistic position. In fact, as Mill pointed out, the laws of the nature of the human mind represent the barycentre for the explanation of social phenomena.

Situational logic can be included in the category of *non-reductionist* EI, or if deprived of its nomological-deductive component also in the *non-nomological-deductive* variant of EI (Popper 1960, pp. 147–152).

In conclusion, the epistemological analysis does not, at first sight, appear to be resolutory for the acceptance or otherwise of the psychologist thesis (except for reinforcing and detailing the explanatory model with a series of epistemological

[4] Social event is considered as a linguistic fiction with pragmatic utility for the discussion but without any real content.

[5] Therefore this EI can be considered an explanatory reduction of a social event to the laws and facts of individuals.

constraints on the causal nature of laws and on scientific realism). Historically, the psychologistic and antipsychologistic theses of MI have found the strongest arguments in their favour only at an ontological level.

Ontological Individualism (OI) deals with the domain of the application of individualist theses. What characteristics and properties of the individual are crucial and determinant at an explanatory level? In the first place, the most likely attributes are those of a physical and psychic kind. An individual is made up of a physical and a psychic component. As will be seen later on, this simple and banal consideration presupposes some form of dualism, if not of the substance at least of the properties, which present several areas of weakness. For the time being, let us consider psychic as referring to the mind-brain concept, leaving a critical analysis of the dualism of these properties to the next chapter.

Psychologism assumes that the relevant properties for explaining social actions are mental and not physical. Clearly, individual behaviour – gestures, communications, etc. – produce reactions from other individuals. All social interactions are based on behaviour. From verbal and written language to non-verbal and body language man's social expressiveness is conveyed through his body. However in the individual, this is the effect of a cause that precedes the various types of behaviour. It is the mind that causes action and social communication is generated by the individual's mental and psychological activity. Even social interaction is first represented at a mental level and then made operative at a behavioural level. It is true that in some cases the action does not correspond to the original intention. In some instances intention is not translated perfectly into behaviour due to disturbance linked to the emotional and unconscious sphere. Or in other cases, corporeal expression appears to be entirely derived from the subconscious sphere or from reflex mechanism, and not from conscious knowledge. At all events, even in situations in which the action cannot be explained by a conscious mental mechanism, it can always be traced back to a psychological type genesis. Psychologism does not constrain the psychological entities and properties solely to the conscious dimension. Rather, it is the entire set of individual neurocognitive entities and properties that is causally responsible for the social action.

In any case, psychologism does not include *physical atomism* which seeks to explain social events on the basis of the physical and behavioural properties of single individuals. On the contrary, psychologism can be interpreted as a form of *psychological atomism* that intends to trace social events back to the individual's mental properties.

This is the aspect that most clearly distinguishes psychologism from antipsychologism. As pointed out by Bhargava (1992, pp. 42–45), psychological atomism can be regarded as the version of OI that supports the following theses:

1. The only acceptable explanations of mental states are those accomplished by empirical science, by knowledge on human psychology. Only causal laws of the mind rather than the conceptual analyses of philosophy can be used for the explanatory purposes of EI. The antipsychologism of Weber (1978, p. 19) and Dilthey is aimed precisely at challenging this position.

2. The only relevant facts for individualistic explanation are the mental ones. This form of psychologism is disputed by various authors like Popper (1966; Italian translation, 1974, pp. 75–76), Agassi (1973, pp. 187–188), von Hayek (1973, p. 40) and Elster (1983). In addition to those illustrated earlier when describing Popper's antipsychologism, the reasons for their opposition also include the refusal to exclude, as psychologism requests, the physical causes and the role of the action.

Von Hayek criticises both versions of psychologism. In his criticism of scientism, he takes on the opposition of the first version. According to von Hayek (1952a), scientism seeks to deny the subjective character of the social sciences and aims to construct a science founded on the objectivist methods used by the natural sciences. His polemical goal is clearly the scientist claim of some schools of methodological holism, like statistical structuralism. His criticism also touched on the scientific claim of psychologism which, in his opinion, tried to overturn the subjective and special character of human action, making it a natural and objective fact that could almost be described as a physical phenomenon. Moreover – and this is the criticism of the second version – von Hayek (1952a) thought that the social sciences fail to explain the action because this remained a task of psychology. The problems that social sciences tackle are those determined by the unforeseen effects of the interaction of a multiplicity of actions, in particular when these show a certain regularity or order. Unintentional orders are produced as the unplanned effect of individual actions which are the result of beliefs and individual ideas. However, as Watkins (1973) underlines, these beliefs should not be identified with psychological states. They are dispositions that do not refer to any one individual, but rather to a sort of "anonymous" individual, and therefore the explanations are of the "anonymous" type. "The reduced demand for consumer goods caused by an increase in prices" is just one example of anonymous type of explanation.

As I pointed out before, the psychologistic position does not claim to deny the presence of the physical and behavioural causes of social interaction. Instead, it acknowledges that all forms of social interaction are conveyed by individual actions and behaviour. The aim of psychologism is to explain these physical causes. The response is that they are a downstream effect of an upstream cause, the psychological cause. It is precisely these explanatory aims that make us search for regularity at a level that precedes the physical and behavioural one. This is justified above all by the complexity of social interaction. An individual's physical, linguistic or other behaviour may play a causal role in determining the physical and behavioural response in one or more individuals. This however takes place using a different mechanism from that in an amoeba, in which the physical stimulation by an individual on the body of another individual generates a peripheral reflex mechanism that causes a movement or an internal biochemical modification. In man, as in most of the animal kingdom, the generation of a behavioural response derives from a cortical type mental representation – or a subcortical reaction – by the "target" individual of the behaviour deriving from the "source" individual. Only after having represented the behaviour of the source individual and having made this representation the premise of a process of reasoning and decision is the target individual able to generate or otherwise the response action. The explanation of social interaction cannot therefore be satisfied by physical-behavioural atomism, as it was for the purposes of the behaviourist school. However, this does not rule out that different causal levels exist within the individual, ranging from the conscious cognitive level to reflex reactions of the peripheral type.

2.6 In Defence of Psychologism

While the main stream of MI was antipsychologist until the recent past, from the 70s onwards the Millian tradition started to put forward new interpreters. Goldstein (1958, 1974) criticises Watkins position on the anonymity of social explanations. For him methodological individualism only makes sense if it can demonstrate the relevance of psychological characteristics in explaining and describing social institutions. The reference to anonymous rules does not seem an appropriate way of complying with the requisites of methodological individualism which, according to Goldstein, presupposes the reference to special individuals with their psychological peculiarities. However, Goldstein seems to confuse the criticism of antipsychologistic dispositions and the need for generalisations, not only of Watkins thesis, but of any genuinely psychologist programme. If we take EI of the nomological-deductive type and psychic atomism as OI, then our aim is to construct generalisations of the psychological mechanisms underlying the actions that we use as the premises for our social explanations.

This goal is pursued to a certain extent by Homans (1967, 1970). He supports EI of the nomological-deductive type, and on this basis he denies legitimacy to the other types of explanation put forward by the social sciences: the structuralist explanation because it does not meet the nomological-deductive requirements; the functionalist explanation because of the empiric non-falsifiability of the general propositions on social balance and survival; the historical explanation because it is a disguised form of the psychological explanation.

Social explanation must use two kinds of proposition as general premises: that of *rationality* and that of *behavioural psychology*. The first takes the following form: "..every man, in choosing between alternative actions, is likely to take that one for which, as perceived by him at the time, the value *(v)* of the result, multiplied by the probability *(p)* of getting the result, is the greater; and the larger the excess of *pxv*, for the one action over the alternative, the more likely he is to take the former action" (Homans 1970, p. 318). According to Homans, this is a fundamental proposition for a widely varied range of explanations, in particular historical and above all economic. However, this proposition is sufficient for explanatory purposes when individual values and perceptions can be taken as data and are shared by a large number of persons. In the field of microeconomic explanations, the proposition of rationality has often proved sufficient. In other explanatory fields of the social sciences, it is important to add the second type of premises, those taken from behavioural psychology. There are the two main types of proposition. The first, which is also known as a "success proposition" would run as follows: "if a man takes an action that is followed by a reward, the probability that he will repeat the action increases" (Homans 1970, p. 321). The second referred to as a "stimulus-situation" is summed up as follows: "if in the past the occurrence of a particular stimulus-situation has been the occasion on which a person's action was rewarded, the recurrence of the stimuli in the present makes it more probable that the man will repeat the action" (Homans 1970, p. 322).

Homans' thesis is that the explanation of social events by psychological propositions cannot be proved philosophically. It is a matter of empirical investigation and analysis. "There is no philosophical argument that will resolve the issue. (....) there are no general sociological propositions at present that meet the two following conditions: they cannot be derived from psychological ones, and from them many features of social behaviour can themselves be derived. (...) But a sociological proposition with the right properties may be discovered tomorrow, and if it is, mere argument will be at an end in face of the fact" (Homans 1970, p. 325).

Homans seems to assume a sceptical aptitude towards methodological holism. He states that all social phenomena can be analysed without residue into the actions of individuals. And since methodological individualism entails psychologism, all sociological facts can be explained by the use of psychological propositions. However, he leaves the door open to emergent sociological propositions and properties. The psychologism of Homans has three weaknesses.

The first weakness is his lack of philosophical justification. If psychologism is only a matter of pragmatic choice when faced with the empirical data and if it is not the necessary consequence of explanatory or ontological individualism, it lacks any persuasive force in the methodology of social sciences.

The second weakness concerns the rationality proposition. Homans regards it as a psychological general proposition with respect to the behaviour of men, rather than with respect to societies or social groups as such. As will be shown in the following chapters, the rationality proposition is not so general. On the contrary, it applies only to a very limited set of decisions taken in ideal conditions for the rational computation of the choice.

The third weakness regards the proposal that behavioural psychology is the main psychological theory. Homans is a product of the time when the behavioural approach was dominant. The concept of stimulus and reward are an example. Nowadays cognitive science has completely changed the possibility of applying psychology to the social sciences.

Homans is an example of the handful of previous attempts that have been made to pursue the Millian approach. The following chapters will show how the Millian approach has found in cognitive science the proper foundation for a theory of social action that fulfils the desiderata of psychologism.

2.7 Beyond Methodological Individualism: The Methodological Cognitivism

This final paragraph will draft the outline of an hypothesis, which I dub *methodological cognitivism*. It can be regarded as an evolution of methodological individualism given that it appears to neutralise some of its epistemological and methodological difficulties and is more firmly rooted in the fabric of scientific knowledge, which is now more widely accredited in the study of human society.

It is an hypothesis whose arguments will be developed in the chapters of the two volumes. Therefore it should be considered the abstract of the entire work. For this reason it is elliptical and a little cryptic.

The first component concerns the *type of explanation* we prefer to use (see also Viale forthcoming, *Epistemology, Cognition, and Innovation*, part I, for a better analysis of this topic). In order to respond to the "social interrogatives", various models of explanation have been put forward over the past years. After the failures of the *nomological-deductive explanation* model due to the well-known paradoxes that it allowed and to the difficulties of generating nomological universals in the social world (Salmon 1984), the proposal of Hempel's *inductive statistical* model of explanation, or subsequently of Salmon's model of *statistical relevance*, and finally the more elaborate *screening-off* variant was thought to overcome some difficulties (Salmon 1984). Nevertheless their critical analysis produced a series of drawbacks: the high probability that is a requisite of the inductive statistical model does not allow relevant explanations to be drawn; and Salmon's elaboration of the statistical relevance model and the screening-off variant cannot avoid misleading explanations, the fallacy of substitutive causation and epiphenomenism. Finding high levels of correlation cannot avoid the trap of results lacking explanatory value. Moreover, the explanatory value appears to have coordinates that are not only epistemological but also pragmatic. In short, two key problems have emerged regarding explanation: one *pragmatic*, the other *causal*. The first was examined in an interesting article by van Fraassen (1980), above all concerning the logic of answers to the questions "why", using what he also called *erothetic logic*.[6] The pragmatic context K, which includes all contextual factors, ranging from knowledge of the phenomenon to our philosophical points of view and our interests, is what makes us select the reference class of the *explanans* when we try to provide an explanation. This factor is particularly valid when we are dealing with several causal chains, whose choice and selection cannot be justified solely on methodological grounds, or when we have to decide the level of aggregration at which to stop the explanation. However, factor K cannot rule out a spurious explanation or strong regularities without explanatory value. This difficulty leads us to the second problem, the *causal* one. What matters in an explanation is not the formal

[6] While the main task of logic is to define the consistency (or inconsistency) of ideas (sentences) and the definition of inference in the erothetic logic the definition of questions and rules have to ascertain whether a sentence can be conceived as an answer to a given question.

subsumption among assertions, as in the case of water and various combinations of H_2O, but the physical subsumption among facts. This is based on the nomological- or probabilistic-type causal relation that describes the physical connection – either *constitutive*(the micro intimate causes of the macro) or *non-constitutive*(the causal relation between phenomena at the same level of aggregation) – between facts. It can be identified for its *productive* or *propagative* typology, through the empirical control of conjunctive and counterfactual conditionals on the effects of the perturbation or modification of the causal chain. Therefore, only in causal mode is it possible to avoid the false steps of earlier models. Instead, in explanations for the social sciences social scientists are usually satisfied by the requirement for statistical relevance which, although generally meeting the criterion of predictive adequacy, does not, as was seen earlier, satisfy that of explanatory adequacy (see also Viale forthcoming, *Epistemology, Cognition, and Innovation*, part I) .

The causal problem, that is the explanatory need to identify the causal chain that "constitutes" the social phenomena, brings us to the heart of the debate on methodological individualism. Given that the epistemic purpose is causal explanation, in particular of the constitutive type when attempting more fundamental explanations, the study of social phenomena must use an individualistic type approach. But what kind of individualism is this? As we have seen above the candidates for this role include three versions of individualism.

The first, that of Watkins and the Popperians in general, can be ruled out because it uses the logical-argumentation model of explanation, which, as I mentioned earlier, cannot select and separate valid explanations from the spurious ones. The second is a form of reductionist individualism, which attempts to reduce social laws and theories to those of the actor through the use of "bridge" laws or correlation. This type of individualism, which has been adopted by authors like Nozick, Levine and Sober, appears to be quite vulnerable to the anti-reductionist arguments, in particular to that of *supervenience*.[7] According to some authors, society is supervenient on the individual because we are dealing with two different sets of properties, and while the individual's identity implicates that of society, the opposite is not true since various combinations of individuals can generate a given social property (*multiple realization*). If this argument is valid, the necessary nomological correlation between society and the individual cannot be present and therefore it is impossible to find "bridge" laws that allow the reduction of one property to another. In addition to this conceptual attack, there is also the clear absence, on the "market", of these connecting laws, even in the weakest disjunctive form. How can one respond to this attack? The lack of laws of correlation or the multiple realisation is not sufficient to demonstrate the impossibility of the reduction. Firstly, because multiple realisation, as Davidson affirms (Vermazen and Hintikka 1985, p. 252), is also present in the relationship between phenomena from the natural

[7] A set of properties *A* supervenes upon another set *B* just in case no two things can differ with respect to *A*-properties without also differing with respect to their *B*-properties. In slogan form, "there cannot be an *A*-difference without a *B*-difference".

world, as in the case of water and various combinations of H_2O, but, for example, this does not prevent us from reducing water to its molecular structure. Secondly, the impossibility of highlighting correlations may simply be due to the fact that one of the two terms to be correlated does not exist, given that the property of the society is identical to that of the individual. This consideration introduces the second type of reductionist individualism: the reduction must occur between laws and social theories and laws and individual theories with the help of assertions of identity. This microreduction allows the social macro properties to be identified with individual micro properties, which may have an unlimited number of specific combinations. Indeed, the identity is not token-token or type-token, but *type-type* (Bhargava 1992, pp. 68–78). Furthermore, this microreductionist individualism offers fundamental, rock-bottom explanations, whose essential nature is decided – by convention – according to the pragmatic Factor K mentioned earlier with reference to van Fraassen. This type of individualism therefore offers causal and constitutive type explanations that seem to satisfy our epistemic desiderata. As we have seen before at first sight, the *reductionist* version and above all the *microreductionist* version seem to be closer to psychologism. By asserting the identity of social phenomena, on the one hand, and individuals and their psychological properties on the other, the epistemological barycentre of social analysis shifts towards the reality of individual minds. To do this, however, as we saw above, we must assume the existence of social laws and social properties, the object of the reduction. If this type of assumption corresponds to an affirmation of the epistemological reality of social laws, this would not be accepted by psychologism because, according to it, only the laws of the human mind are real. On the contrary, according to the *non-reductionist* option, what can be explained is only the particular social event and the explanation is based on laws and the starting conditions of individuals and their properties. This variation of EI has no substantive ontological implications relating to what we propose as laws on individuals and their properties. But since our aim is to establish constitutive causal explanations the preferred laws are psychological. The possibility of social laws is implicitly denied because the ontological existence of social phenomena is rejected. The exclusion of social laws and properties makes the use of social terms only a conventional and pragmatic choice without any ontological engagement on their real existence. From this point of view this option can be dubbed *eliminative*.

Having outlined the epistemological framework of our individualist hypothesis, we must now clarify its scientific content. If the ultimate aim, the motive for our research, is to explain, if the best form of explanation is causal or constitutive, if the methodological individualism that meets this causal model is eliminative individualism, as defined earlier, then at what level of aggregation should we position our fundamental explanations? I define the proposed methodology as *methodological cognitivism* precisely because I feel that the conventional base level of our attempts of explanation must be the cognitive. I use the cognitive attribute in a narrow sense compared to most sociologists, but in a broader sense than cognitive scientists, to include all the psychological mechanisms responsible for the decision and therefore the action. Therefore, not only the superior psychological processes, like memory, learning, reasoning, but also emotion, instinct, perception.

Explanation based on cognitive mechanisms cannot always be accomplished. In some cases the state of our knowledge of the subject will make us raise the level of aggregation to the concepts of *folk psychology*, or commonsense psychology. But given that that this psychology is a theoretical fiction, with instrumental value, its use in social explanations can only be temporary. Instead, it is at the cognitive and, in prospect, at the neurocognitive level, as indicated by the programme of Patricia Churchland (1986) and Paul Churchland (1989), that these rock-bottom explanations must be sought, in macro-micro explanation.

In conclusion, we can sum up the epistemological reasons for choosing cognitive science as a source of models to give scientific content to our individualist hypothesis (Viale 1994a):

1. *Causality*: cognitive science, in all its variants, includes the search for compatibility of mental states and processes with their cerebral substratum. This physicality of mental activity meets the requisite for continuity and spatial and temporal contiguity that is typical of all causal relations. The type of explanation of action offered by cognitive science is of a constituent nature in that it aims to identify the intimate causal mechanisms responsible for behavioural output. These mechanisms, most of which are of a theoretical type, can be inferred both through experimental research using tests and through computer simulation using the principle of the common cause.
2. *Empirical nature*: cognitive science gives considerable importance to empirical research for the construction and checking of hypotheses. In experimental research, in the form of tests and in computer simulation, it is possible to make an independent determination of the starting conditions and the falsification of the hypothesis. Both when describing an event through the subsumptive model, and above all in causal explanation, the danger of the linguistic reformulation of the *explanandum*, albeit present, is not of a structural and constitutive type, as in \commonsense psychology.
3. *Irrationality*: cognitive science satisfies the principle of symmetry so dear to the Edinburgh School of cognitive sociology of science. Not only so-called rational behaviours but also irrational ones are explained by the same type of hypothesis (Simon et al. 1992; Gigerenzer 2007). One need only think of the studies on decision psychology by Kahneman, Tversky, Hogarth, etc. Given that the quantity of mental life deviating from rational schemes is not marginal, a psychology, like commonsense psychology, which does not guarantee explanatory cover of this part, is destined to become insignificant in social sciences.
4. *Theoretical support*: cognitive science is not alone, instead it has or tries to have the theoretical support of some of the most accredited hypotheses of the scientific community. The search for this link is shown by the current debate on whether an overly strong characterisation of cognitive activity in linguistic terms is compatible or not with evolutionary theory, in view to the evolutionary delay with which language appeared. There are also significant links with Shannon's

information theory, with Wiener's cybernetics, with Turing's and von Neumann's mathematical and computational models, and with the predominant theories of neurochemistry, neurobiology, neurophysiology and neuropathology. Support for cognitive science could also be found in the opposite direction. The importance of language and of inferential activity in moulding social relations is beyond doubt. The relationship is clearly biunique, but the constraints and limits with which the mind elaborates and filters return input from social relations are fundamental to explain the role of social factors in individual action. These constraints show a certain degree of regularity, which allows generalisations to be drawn that are useful, also at a predictive level, and which can provide support for compatible so-called *social theories*. One need only think of the potential importance of the decision-making heuristics in relation to economic theory, or of the theory of mental models in relation to the sociology of knowledge.

It is worth noting the epistemic advantage of this model compared to microreductionist attempts. Instead of proposing two types of explanation, causal for physical constraints and intentional for action, there is only one type for both. Instead of being a timid and incoherent microreductionist hypothesis, ready to surrender before a mentalistic, dualistic-type language, lacking empirical content to explain the action, it arrives at the point where empirical hypotheses, accepted in the scientific community, are available to explain the real mechanisms of the action. Instead of proposing a priori assumptions of rationality that are systematically falsified by human behaviour, rationality is built a posteriori, along the lines of the *fil rouge* leading from Quine, to Goldman and Stich, as an empirical generalisation or cognitive theory of probabilistic and deductive reasoning (Viale 1997a).

Moreover, in conclusion, this approach offers a number of advantages. I refer only to two. Unlike the rationalist models that find it difficult to explain the various forms of social change, *methodological cognitivism* emphasises the creative and innovative aspects of thought, above all in problem-solving, inductive reasoning and conceptual learning, which manage to explain the introduction of novelties and new models of social interaction. Moreover, the difficulty of explaining the social structural stability of many social theories is solved at a more fundamental level than that of social language or rules. Indeed, it seems that cognitive procedures, underlying much of the fallacious reasoning, are responsible for the commensurability of communications between individuals, for the possibility of building common meanings, and in short, for synergy and inferential coordination (Viale 1991, pp. 288–298).

The Mind-Society Problem

3

In most methodologies of social sciences one of the crucial problems is the relationship between mental and social phenomena. Often the problem is mediated by concepts like individual action or decision. In other cases the problem is implicit or even hidden. Nevertheless, every methodology of social sciences must, sooner or later, "cross the street" that connects mind and society. In the same way as the parallel mind–body problem, the mind-society problem concerns a number of variegated fundamental philosophical questions. These are metaphysical when they deal with the existence of one or more ontological levels of reality between mind and society; with the efficacy of social causation as distinct from individual mental causation; with the feature of social properties as second order properties compared to the first order mental properties; with *supervenience*, epiphenomenalism or realizationism between the mental and social dimensions; and so on. They are epistemological when they privilege the problem of explanation and representation. Can we explain social phenomena by connection with other social events or only by reduction to individual mental phenomena? Can we establish genuinely autonomous scientific laws at the social level or should they only be derived from the laws that represent the psychological dimension?

There are many answers to these questions. In analogy with the *mind–body problem* in the philosophy of mind we can describe different theories of the *mind-society problem*. The first distinction is between substance dualism that claims that society and mind are two different and separate kinds of phenomena, each with their own special laws and concepts, and *property dualism* that would argue that both are made of the same substance, namely human beings, but the properties of society are different from those of mind. In the category of property dualism we have the main popular positions. *Emergentism* views the social phenomena as something inexplicable born out of the individual mental dimension; *epiphenomenalism* invokes the causal relation that connects mental to social dimensions and explains it; for *mental realizationism* social properties are second order properties defined over first order

The present chapter is a modified version of Viale, R. (2000). *The mind-society problem*, published in Mind & Society, 1, vol. 1.

R. Viale, *Methodological Cognitivism*,
DOI 10.1007/978-3-642-24743-9_3,

mental properties. Lastly, there is *monism* that excludes any autonomous ontological or epistemological reality for the social dimension: *mental reductionism* supports the reduction of social phenomena to the mental ones and *radical eliminativism* would eliminate any language of society in favour of the mental one.

No attempt can be made here to make a full analysis of the previous philosophical positions. Rather the aim is to give an overview of this problem. Since the mind-society problem is often implicit in social theories, I would like to introduce it by discussing some well known methodologies of social sciences that, for different reasons, rule out the possibility of explaining society using mental concepts. Therefore, the arguments will be mainly epistemological. Nevertheless, metaphysics remains in the background of the discussion. In particular, in my opinion, three metaphysical problems are crucial to every epistemological discussion of the mind-society problem: the concept of causality (that will be analyzed in the first part of the second volume), the mind–body problem and realism in science.

Lastly, the arguments in favour of the mental explanation of social phenomena will mainly rely on cognitive psychology. Therefore the original problem will shift towards the cognition-society relationship. This move is made with the awareness that overall mental life, causally responsible for social action, cannot be reduced merely to cognitive processes described by cognitive psychology. Nevertheless, cognitive psychology now seems to be the only scientific psychology that is able to create a causal link between mental processes and social action.

3.1 Applied Cognition to Social Events

Let us start with a brief example of the cognitive explanation of social phenomena. There are two important cases in international politics that have been studied for a long time by political scientists. Superficially they have much in common, but a completely different outcome.

The cases are the Korean War and the Cuban missiles crisis. Both developed during the period of the Cold War with the Soviet Union. Both were originated by an hostile initiative of a pro-Soviet country. Both were perceived as a dangerous threat to American interests and its international role. Moreover, in the Cuban missiles crisis there were many initial conditions that prompted military intervention: stronger anti-Communist public opinion; missiles close to the coast of America; the direct involvement of the Soviet Union; Monroe's doctrine against Soviet presence in the Western hemisphere. Instead in the Korea affair the initial conditions were not so strongly predisposed to war: the beginning of the Cold War; Korea's weak strategic importance and weak economic role; many military risks in being involved in the war.

As everyone knows the outcomes of these initial conditions were very different: military American escalation in Korea; naval blockade and quick solution in the Cuban crisis. How did two such different results occur?

Traditional political theories cannot give a persuasive answer.

A realist approach, based on structuralist and functionalist methodology, sees international relations as based on power relations alone. The only player is the state and the only actions are finalized to improve its power. Every phenomenon is explained in a teleological way: it must be suitable to fulfil some internal function of a given nation or to maintain equilibrium in the international community.

It is hard to apply this kind of explanation to the previous two cases: initial conditions seem to support completely opposite outcomes compared to what really happened.

Another fashionable approach to international politics is the theory of rational choice. Using this theory, social scientists explain the outcome of international relations as a result of rational individual decision making. The main players are the government leaders and they act to maximize some function of expected subjective utility.

Even by this approach it seems quite mysterious why, starting from the previous premises, one more inclined to war and the other more inclined to peace, the outcomes resulted so different. A defensive answer might be that we do not know precisely the subjective utility of leaders involved in the events. But this ad hoc move makes the appeal of rational choice theory very weak for social scientists.

Some social scientists have tried to use the tools of cognitive science to explain the different outcomes of the two cases. For example, if we represent the decision-making process as a problem-solving activity and we apply the concept of "group-think" elaborated by Janis (1982) we begin to understand that the initial different representations of problems – in the case of the Korean War as an aggression to American interests organized by Soviet Union; in the case of the Cuban Crisis as a move to defend the Castro regime – and the way in which meetings were managed in the White House – in the case of the Korean War with Truman's authoritarian agenda power and little chance to express alternative views; in case of the Cuban Crisis with Kennedy's tolerant approach and a pluralistic discussion – were quite relevant causal factors to produce different decision-making processes and outcomes.

If we apply to this representation another cognitive tool, the "Prospect Theory"[1] elaborated by Kanheman and Tversky (Tversky and Kanheman 1986; Quattrone and Tversky 1988; Jervis 1992; Tetlock 2005) we can gain a better understanding of the events. In case of the Korean War the initial representation made by Acheson, the Secretary of State, of a probable increasing loss in terms of the status quo caused the elaboration of risky options as the initial soft military intervention. This initial investment was ineffective, but it was not treated as a "sunk cost." On the contrary, it led to more risky options to recover the loss and, consequently, to the classical process of cognitive irrational escalation, that in this case meant military escalation.

In the case of the Cuban Crisis, the initial representation made by McNamara, the Minister of Defence, emphasised the limited loss of status quo and did not

[1] Prospect theory is an empirical theory of choice, which claims that people in a loss condition have a greater risk propensity than those in a gain condition (see Chap. 2, Part II of this volume).

provoke the elaboration of a too-risky option. Moreover, the blockade was completely successful in stopping the Soviet Union. In fact, the Soviet Union had not finished the installation of missiles and there was no official announcement of the new status quo. Therefore Soviet Union leaders did not perceive the naval blockade as a loss compared to a new status quo and consequently they did not elaborate risky military options to retort to USA's move.

3.2 Apparent Hermeneutic Surrender

I began with this example of cognitive explanation of two social events to emphasize how the cognitive theory of social action, de facto, is already an approach that is gaining ground in social sciences. Often science is ahead and does not take note of philosophical and methodological conundrums. Unfortunately, the fortune of cognitive explanation in social sciences or, in other words, the reduction of social phenomena to mental ones, is not so straightforward among social scientists.

If we think of the previous example, we could say that social scientists tried to suggest an explanation for a social event by reducing it to individual cognitive causal mechanisms, mainly decision-making processes described by scientific cognitive psychology. This strategy is rejected for numerous different reasons by most methodologies of social sciences. A description of some of these critiques will enable us to gain a better understanding of the mind-society problem.

There are two strong critiques to the tentative reduction[2] of social phenomena to cognitive mechanisms. The first and most powerful critique is what we might call the "hermeneutic surrender." The second can be termed the "holistic illusion."

In its most radical version the first critique claims that every individual action is so full of subjective social meaning that it can never be explained objectively, but only interpreted as we do for paintings and poems. The champion of this approach is Charles Taylor (1985) and the methodological model is Max Weber's concept of *verstehen* (1949). This affirms that there are no generalizations that allow us to predict or explain the social action, nor we can hope to discover them.

We can divide this position in two claims: (a) the interpretation of social action is not made according to generalizations; (b) the meaning of social action is not reducible to general natural facts of the human mind.

If we fully accept the first claim – that there are no explanatory generalizations in social sciences – the most coherent conclusion is that it would be impossible even to describe the external behaviour of the social actors. In fact every description implies a certain amount of general categorization expressed by concepts being used in the description – e.g. laughing, crying, winking, etc. Moreover, many of the behavioural concepts imply some kind of general psychological hypothesis. How do we attribute the word "laugh" to the peculiar movement of lips and mouth

[2] I'm using the term reduction in a broad meaning inclusive of reductionist and non-reductionist approaches introduced in the previous chapter.

if we do have not some general inductive psychological hypothesis to understand the meaning of this behaviour and to distinguish laughing from other similar behavioural gestures, such as neurotic tics?

Moreover, the use of general psychological hypotheses is unavoidable if, as prescribed in the *verstehen* methodology, we want to understand the mental states of the agent. How can the hermeneutic social scientist infer the agent's mental state from a knowledge of his behaviour and of the social and cultural context? By applying some general hypothesis regarding the relationships between his beliefs, desires and actions. Namely, by applying a general theory that we usually call *common sense* or *folk psychology*.

If we analyse the work of some distinguished interpretative anthropologists, like Clifford Geertz, we will discover a massive use of general psychological hypotheses. In his interpretation of the cultural significance of cockfighting in Bali (1973) he fills the concepts of folk psychology with all the symbols, meanings, practices and traditions of Balinese culture. Interpretation is often based on a general psychological theory that links beliefs, desires and actions and the link is based on some kind of instrumental or problem-solving rationality that is not so remote from that used in our everyday life. In fact, according to Geertz, the Balinese agent "uses emotions for cognitive ends," has religious beliefs that drive his actions of grooming, training, feeding, watching and betting on the birds.

The denial, in principle, of the use of general hypotheses is linked to the second claim of hermeneutics: the mental states of people advocated by hermeneutics cannot be described by science. This claim has two different parts.

(a) According to the first part, the meaning of a social action relies on how the agent represents it using symbols, values, models, traditions and so on that form part of his culture and that he applies in the given social context.

In Balinese funerals the procession makes very unpredictable turns and zigzags. Moreover, it is sometimes washed by sudden sprinklings of water that a foreigner, like me, interprets as a way to mitigate the burning heat. Faced with events of this kind, hermeneutics claims that there is no scientific way to understand the meaning of this social action, that, in this case, is represented as a means of confusing the dead person's soul, thus not allowing him to find the way back home.

The only way to cope with the problem of meaning is, according to hermeneutics, when someone's peculiar subjectivity tries to interpret someone else's peculiar subjectivity by penetrating the network of his particular values, practices, models and so on, linking them to the contingent social context. It is like the interpretation of a painting or a poem: every interpretation is unique in a double sense. Because who is interpreting is unique and what it is interpreted is also unique.

In my view, this claim is too radical for two symmetrical reasons that are particularly relevant in the interpretation of paintings. Whoever is interpreting a painting is not unique because they use concepts and general hypotheses common to other investigators, as most of history of art teaches us (e.g., the work of Ernst Gombrich). What is interpreted is not unique because painters in every period share common values and criteria of beauty and aesthetic progress with other painters, as Vasari has emphasized in his history of Renaissance art (Viale 1995, pp. 4–6).

In reality the hermeneutic's tenets are more a declaration of principles than a new style of investigation. Even authors like Geertz or Wolf who are against every kind of causal explanation, nonetheless try to establish general hypotheses that are valid for a given cultural context and not only for a single individual. Geertz established some generalizations that were valid for the Balinese microuniverse. And Wolf (1978) pursues the same goal for a bigger microuniverse: China. It is well known that in order to be universal, a statement does not need to refer to the globality of space and time, but may be valid for a local part of them. In fact, many scientific laws are, in this sense, local, such as Kepler's laws or the biological laws.

(b) The main reason for this impossibility to generalize the meaning of social action relies on another powerful assumption that corresponds to the second part of the second hermeneutic claim. This affirms that mental activity, which is responsible for the meaning of action, is not part of nature and therefore cannot be explained using the laws of nature. It is not clear what kind of dualism is implicitly involved by this claim. It might be a *substance dualism* that holds that there are two kinds of substances in the world, mental and physical. Or it might be a weaker form of dualism, the *property dualism* that states that all particular objects or events are physical, but also says that mental properties are not identical to physical properties. For the sake of discussion, the relevant differences between the two dualisms are not important. What is important is that, according to hermeneutics, mental properties are not reducible to physical properties. Therefore they cannot be explained by laws referring directly to the properties of aggregate physical entities or to properties that are reduced, in the last instance and in principle, to properties of physical entities, like the elementary particles described by physics (as in the hypothesis of the completeness of physics supported by physicalists like Lewis or Amstrong).

If hermeneutics implicitly supports the previous concept of mind, it therefore entails the impossibility to make an appeal to any form of causal explanation of social action. In fact, causality is a property of matter and can refer only to relations between events in the physical world. Moreover, if the thesis of completeness of physics is correct, any causal relation at any level of aggregation of reality should be reducible to an explanation at an inferior level. Lastly, I would add, any claim of causal relation at a given level can be accepted if a causal explanation is available based on the properties of entities at the underlying level of aggregation of nature. It seems that property dualism cannot allow this kind of causal explanation.

Hermeneutics proposes the method of empathy to interpret the meaning of a social action. One has to interpret how the network of beliefs and goals composed by values, practices, knowledge and so on gives meaning to a given action in a given social environment. In concise terms, one has to try to re-experience the psychological situation that has driven the person to act in a given way. No single belief appears to have meaning if it is not interpreted in relation with other beliefs. The perception of the empirical world produces a belief through its connection with values, cultural models and other beliefs. If a Balinese looks at a Benjamin fig-tree, he sees a god because of his other beliefs, whilst if I look at it only I see a tree, owing to my different beliefs. If someone wants to interpret what the Balinese or I am seeing, he has to understand the network of other beliefs that is responsible for the meaning given to the particular perception.

This picture resembles the *network theory* or *holistic theory of meaning* (Churchland 1979; Field 1977). This affirms that the meaning of every statement is a function of the role that it plays in the internal economy of an agent's representations, namely how it is linked to his sensorial inputs and his behavioural outputs and how it plays a role inside inferential and reasoning dynamics. As it is well known, this theory is an important support to the functionalist theory of mind (Fodor 1975; Dennett 1978). According to the latter, the nature of our psychological states is a function of causal roles played in the internal system of other states, that are situated between sensorial inputs and behavioural outputs.

The general methodological model for understanding the meaning of an action appears to be similar in hermeneutics and functionalist theory. Both emphasize the functional interpretation of a belief in relation to the network of other beliefs linked to it. What seems to differentiate the two approaches is the causal picture of mind that is clearly refuted by hermeneutics.

The claim that mind is not part of nature and therefore it cannot be analysed using general laws and causal explanation is, typically, a metaphysical position. The opposite claim of the functionalist theory is symmetrically also metaphysic. But apart from the metaphysical claims, how do the two theories treat the problem of causality?

We have already seen that hermeneutics uses implicit general hypotheses to interpret mental states – e.g., folk psychology and network theory at least – and formulates universal hypotheses on the meaning of social action. On the other hand, the functionalist theory of mind explicitly appeals to the same kind of theories, but it emphasizes that its theory of mind is causal. What kind of causality is involved in functionalism?

The most common and naive version of the functionalist theory of mind represents mental activity as described by the concepts of folk psychology. It is the causal relation between sensory inputs, beliefs, desires and action that constitutes mental activity. The mental states are functional states of the brain in the same way that software states of the computer are functional states of its hardware. Its philosophy of mind is called "*token identity theory*," namely a kind of *property dualism*, since it supports the view that mental properties, those described by folk psychology, are different from the properties of any kind of hardware that implement them. If this is a reliable description of functionalism, the consequence, in my view, is that the claim that there are causal relations among mental states is quite problematic. Why? The reason stems from our concept of causation.

If we assume an Hempelian nomological account of causation supplemented by an account, given by the Mill-Ramsey-Lewis tradition, of how to define the laws of nature,[3] no claim can be put forward by folk psychology regarding a causal relation

[3] According to this tradition, a law of nature should be part of a deductive system of laws, each of which is linked logically to the others.

between mental states. This is because folk psychology cannot be considered a law of nature and therefore cannot nomologically deduce the causal relation between events. Moreover, it is manifestly empirically unfalsifiable by independent empirical control of its main concepts and therefore it cannot function as an empirical general premise in our argument (Viale 1994a, pp. 303–308).

In fact, if we agree on an account of causation conceived as a nomological explanation derived from one of the laws belonging to an ideal Hume corpus, namely the unified deductive theoretical system of the world, we cannot say that *c* causes *e* unless we derive a description P of *e* from a description F of *c*, that is unless we prove that "there is a derivation of P that belongs to the best unifying systematisation of an ideal Hume corpus such that there is a premise of the derivation in which reference to F is made" (Kitcher 1989, p. 495).

In my opinion, this account implies (1) that the theory of mind must belong to this ideal Hume corpus, where it can be derived from a more general theory (for example the theory of brain) and where a less general theory is derivable from it (for example the so called *theory of society*); (2) that the relation between phenomena at the level described by the theory of mind should be derived from relations between phenomena that compose the mental phenomena, described by a different reducing theory, for example the theory of brain; (3) that the reducing theory is member of the ideal Hume corpus.

In short, we cannot claim that there is causal relation between two mental events unless we produce an explanatory account at an inferior level of aggregation, for example at the level of the neural network.

These conditions are not met by folk psychology and therefore the claim made by the functionalist theory of mind to give a causal account of mind seems to me weak. If this is correct and, therefore, the functionalist theory of mind is empty of any true causal content, there is an argument to support a greater proximity between hermeneutics and naive functionalism.

Apart from declarations of principles, an analysis of the use of general hypotheses and the generation of general descriptions of social action, and the non-causal account of the human mind indicate that the two theories may seem quite similar.

3.3 The Mind–Body Problem

If the previous remarks are correct, the critique of functionalism might introduce a possible answer to the mind-society problem. The answer, called *methodological cognitivism*, aims to provide a causal theory of mind that explains action. How can this goal be achieved without making an appeal to folk psychology and, at the same time, answering the challenge of hermeneutics regarding the meaningful aspect of social action? In short how can we provide a cognitive theory of action that is causal, in the strong sense previously described, and semantically adequate?

I will limit myself to making a few remarks.

Any answer to the mind-society problem should start from an analysis of the mind–body problem, as we have seen before in analysing the hermeneutic thesis. In fact it is clear from the previous discussion about hermeneutics and naive functionalism that one of the central pillars of the entire theory is their concept of mind and its relation with the physical world. This is why it is useful at this point to introduce a brief note on the concepts of mind. In the philosophy of mind there are two main sets of solutions to the nature of mind, *psychophysical dualism* and *psychophysical monism*. According to the former, mind and brain are separate entities, whereas according to monism, they are one and the same in some way. However there are considerable differences between the components of each of the two sets of solutions to the nature of mind.[4] Psychophysical dualism has been the official view of the West for a couple of millennia. It was supported by some well-known arguments.[5] In any case it comes up against many well-known difficulties. The main difficulty is that dualism detaches properties and events from things. To describe mental activities, such as perceiving and deciding, as parallel to or interacting with, but radically different from brain events is like talking about chemical combinations that are parallel to the combining atoms or molecules, or of social events parallel to the actions of their actors. Modern science started by rejecting the Platonic idea of autonomous form (properties) and events as being the relicts of animism. Science construes properties as properties possessed by something or other. This construal is reflected in the formalization of the concept of a property as a function whose domain includes the set of things possessing the

---

[4] Psychophysical dualism is composed of the following main alternative doctrines:
(a) *Autonomism:* it conceives body and mind as mutually independent.
(b) *Parallelism:* for Leibniz, body and mind are parallel or synchronous to one another.
(c) *Epiphenomenalism:* for Broad and Ayer, body affects or causes mind.
(d) *Animism:* for Plato and Augustine, mind affects, causes, animates, or controls the body.
(e) *Interactionism:* for Descartes and Popper-Eccles, body and mind interact.

Psychophysical monism is composed of the following main alternative doctrines:
(a) *Panpsychism:* Whitehead and Theillard de Chardin think that everything is mental.
(b) *Neutral Monism:* for Russell and Schlick, the physical and the mental are so many aspects or manifestations of a single entity.
(c) *Eliminative Materialism:* for Behaviourism, nothing is mental.
(d) *Reductive Materialism:* for Lashley and Smart, mind is physical.
(e) *Emergentist Materialism:* for Darwin, Hebb, and Bunge, the mind is a set of emergent brain functions and activities.

[5] (a) Mind must be immaterial because we know it differently from the way we know matter: the former knowledge is private, the latter is public.
(b) Phenomenal predicates cannot be reduced to physical predicates, so the mind must be substantially different from the brain.
(c) There must be a mind animating the brain machinery, for machines are mindless (Popper and Eccles 1977).
(d) Dualism squares with emergentism and the hypothesis of the level structure of reality.
(e) Whereas neurons fire digitally, we can have continuous experiences (Sellars 1963).

properties concerned. If we remove the things occurring as members of the domain of the function, the function itself will disappear. The dualistic theory of mind demands that an exception be made for mental properties and events. Whereas every scientific theory needs a single state space to represent the states of its referents, the dualist would need two disjointed state spaces. Indeed it would need one state space to locate brain states and another to locate mental states. Moreover, if the mental properties are detached from the brain how can it acknowledge evidence of the molecular and cellular roots of mental abilities and disorders (e.g. brain injury and drug action)?

According to Fodor (1975), every acceptable concept of mind must solve two sets of problems: one related to *mind–body interaction* and the other to *knowledge of other minds*. One popular solution to these problems was afforded by *behaviourism* (Skinner 1953; Hull 1943). Its radical claim was that it is possible to describe the mind with terms that only express behavioural properties. There are many objections to this claim. One is linguistic and logical, and regards the *intensionality* of mental terms. The behavioural and physical propositions are *extensional*, i.e. they have the property to be transparent. Transparency means following Leibniz's law that affirms that "*if a and b are equal, then their properties are also equal.*"[6] On the other hand, mental terms like believing, willing, and hoping are irreducibly *intensional*, i.e. they are not transparent and they fail to follow Leibniz's law. It is not possible to exchange their terms without twisting the truth.[7] This implies that it is not generally possible to *extensionalize* transparent propositions (for example behavioural ones) that are logically equivalent to propositions including non-transparent *intensional* expressions (for example the mental ones). Hence the behaviourist pretension to translate the mental into behaviour is impossible.

Another difficulty of behaviourism is the possibility to *know other minds*. If mental attributions are literally assigned on the basis of facts relative to manifest behaviour, then behavioural propositions should always refer to the same mental proposition. But we know that often the same behavioural propositions refer to different mental ones and the same mental propositions refer to different

[6] For example if *a is equal to b,* i.e. if Mary is equal to my sister, then we can say that *Fa,* i.e. Mary has stomach ache, *is equal to Fb,* my sister has stomach ache. We may exchange Mary with my sister without twisting the truth.

[7] A classical example comes from Frege (1982). In astronomy, the entity denoted by the expression "the morning star" is identical to the one denoted by the expression "the evening star", so it should be logical to expect that, on the basis of the Leibniz law, these expressions could be interchangeable in every linguistic context. On the contrary, these substitutions are false in propositions including predicates that express mental states like "believing that". For example, *if a is equal to b,* i.e. the "morning star" is identical to the "evening star", *Fa,* i.e. "the ancients believed the morning star was identical to the morning star" is not the same as *Fb,* i.e. "the ancients believed that the morning star was identical to the evening star".

behavioural ones.[8] Radical behaviourism is not able to solve these difficulties. And its incapacity derives from its theory of *mind as a black box* and the fact that it denies any mental causation. Nor is the alternative of *dispositional behaviourism* convincing (Ryle 1949). It does not deny mental causation but reduces it to the display of a *behaviour disposition.* More precisely mental causation is what happens when an organism has a behaviour disposition and the antecedent of the behaviour condition which expresses this disposition is true.[9] Indeed the antecedent of the hypothetical phrase only refers to stimuli and the consequent only refers to behaviour responses. The dispositions are only a weak kind of physical causality. Paradigmatic examples of dispositions are the magnet or fragility. But while the behaviourist acknowledges the display of the disposition as the only type of mental causation, physical sciences acknowledge other types of causation. For example, one type of causation, which also includes the dispositional type, is *event-event causation.* According to this, a physical event causes another physical event. The dispositional theory is also not capable of translating the propositions about mental causation of behaviour dispositions because it is an example of event-event causation.[10] Indeed it is only in the face of these propositions that the dispositional behaviourist proves to be able to acknowledge only facts regarding relations between stimuli and responses. Therefore it is reduced to *pickwickian* radical behaviourism.

The radical solution to overcome the anomalies of behaviourism is the *Central State Identity Theory* (Armstrong 1968).[11] According to this, mental states are neurophysiological states, and the property of being in a certain mental state is

---

[8] For example, if we establish that "Mary has stomach ache" means "Mary touches her stomach, takes the pills, complains, etc.", then every time that "Mary touches her stomach, takes the pills, complains, etc." it means that "Mary has stomach ache". But what if Mary simulates a pain that she does not feel, or she truly has stomach ache but does not display "stomach ache behavior"? Then the proposition "Mary touches her stomach, takes the pills, complains, etc." may also be synonymous with propositions like "Mary simulates stomach ache", and vice versa "Mary simulates stomach ache" may be expressed by "Mary touches her stomach, takes the pills, complains, etc.. . .".

[9] For example, the causal proposition "Mary took the medicine because she had stomach ache means that "if there had been medicine, Mary would have taken it and the medicine really was there".

[10] For example it is impossible that the dispositional analysis of "If Mary has a stomach-ache" can mean "Mary is disposed to exhibit stomach ache behaviour." It is impossible because it is a typical example of event-event causation: the stomach ache mental event causes the disposition mental event to exhibit stomach ache behaviour. The fact that she may or may not exhibit it depends on the other events interacting at a mental level, such as the desire to get rid of the stomach ache, a belief in the existence and efficacy of the stomach ache treatment, etc.

[11] The CSIT is divided in two main alternatives:

(a) *Reductive Materialism:* the CNS is a physical identity that only differs from the other physical system in complexity. Hence an explanation of the mental should require only physical concepts and theories in the narrow or technical sense of physical. Reductive materialism involves both ontological reduction (i.e. levelling) and epistemological reduction (i.e. transformation of psychology into a branch of physics).

identified with the property of being in a certain neurophysiological state. The mental causation of behaviour is a particular case of physical causality. The mind–body problem seems to find a solution in the knowledge of other minds.[12]

The defect of this kind of materialism, also called *type materialism,* is that it confines mental properties only to CNS properties. No other material instantiation of mental properties is allowed. Intelligent computers or humans like martians are forbidden. *Token Materialism* tries to overcome this exclusion. According to it, only mental contingent particulars and not properties are neurophysiological. Every pain, whim or thought identifies itself with a certain state of a particular neuronal system.

3.4 Strong Identity Theory and Mental Causation

If our goal is to provide a causal account of mind that suits the desiderata of nomological derivation, the first question to be answered is what kind of identity theory gives a suitable philosophical account of the mind–body problem.

As we see above according to the *token identity theory* (or *token materialism*) mental properties are not identical to physical properties. The relations between body and mind can be different – for example, law-like causal relations according to Searle or, on the contrary, relations without any kind of law-like regularities according to Davidson. What it is constant among many interpretations of the property dualism is the impossibility of a complete reduction of the mental level to the physical, in primis to the neural level. If the mind cannot be reduced to the body, an important question is how we can conceive a causal role for mental phenomena. If mind and brain are identical from a substantial point of view, but different with regard to their properties, how can we represent a separate causal dimension for mental life? How can mental events cause other mental events or can they have any causal role towards the physical world? If mental and physical are the same thing and if we attribute a causal dimension to the physical base, it is very difficult to justify a parallel separate causal role to mental events. In other words, if

(b) *Emergentist Materialism:* the CNS, far from being a physical entity, is a biosystem, i.e. a complex thing endowed with properties and laws peculiar to living things and moreover very peculiar in itself, i.e. not shared by all biosystems. Mental functions would be CNS functions, and far from being purely physical processes, they would emerge in relation to the physical level (Bunge 1980).

[12] According to this theory, typical mental state attributions are deductions by *inference of the best explanation*, which move from the behaviour effect to the supposed mental causes. Mary takes the medicine because she has stomach ache. This movement is possible because we acknowledge the existence of the mental causes that are identified with the neurophysiological causes. This logical inference is never demonstrative, but may supply some explanation that reflects the evidence better than other alternative hypotheses. On the other hand, with regard to causal relations, it is clear that if there are two states S1 and S2, and S2 is the effect of S1, it might be possible that the same situation may occur not as an effect of S1. A causal relation from the effect to the cause is always contingent. Every effect might have had a cause that is different from what really happened.

the neural event *N1*, that corresponds to the mental event *M1*, for example a memory of a pleasant fact, causes the neural event *N2*, that corresponds to the mental event *M2*, for example a strong emotion, there is little space to think of other alternative causal relations that can explain the final result *M2*. In fact, either we rely on an unacceptable causal overdetermination that states the parallel separate causal role of *N1* and *M1* to produce *M2* or we must abandon the ontological identity between mind and brain and accept an autonomous and separate causal dimension for mental activity. But the problem of mental causation becomes even more complicated if we try to represent the interaction between mind and the physical world, namely the autonomous causal role of mind in generating effects outside mental life – e.g. deciding to lift up a glass of wine. If the neural event *N1*, corresponding to the mental event *M1*, deciding to drink a glass of wine, causes the physical effect *P1*, lifting up the glass of wine, and we want to avoid unacceptable causal overdetermination, we must conclude that the causal relation occurs between an event that has no physical properties – the mental event *M1* – and a physical event *P1*. But a relation of this kind violates the principle of causal closure of the physical world according to which a physical effect can only be caused by an event that has physical properties; this is not the case of the mental event, according to the property dualism of the token identity theory. The conclusion of this argument is that mind and mental states may only be, from a causal point of view, mere epiphenomena of the real causal agent, namely the brain and the relative neural states. They cannot be taken as real causal events, but they may be used as conventional metaphors referring to the hidden causal agents.

Therefore if we want to establish a causal picture of the relations between mind and action we must avoid having to rely on any kind of property dualism. Only a strong identity theory between mental and neural properties can let us work out causal models that try to explain the mechanisms of individual action. It is obvious that some methodologies of social sciences like hermeneutics do not share either the premises and the conclusion of this argument. They do not try to justify mental causation because, from their point of view, the relation between mind and action is not causal. On the contrary, the justification of mental causation continues to be a serious problem for functionalism and its token identity theory.

The natural consequence of the foregoing remarks is that *type identity theory* (or *type materialism*) seems the most suitable candidate to meet the desiderata of our concept of causality. In relation to examples taken from nature, type identity theory seems the only one that can cope with the causal problem. Let us think of the example of water. If water is analysed from a phenomenological point of view it seems to present superior and emergent properties compared to its molecular structure H_2O. It is transparent, dense, clear and so on. But if we analyse the causal properties of water, for example its ability to extinguish fire, we cannot avoid making its molecular structure responsible for the chemical reaction that puts out the fire. We cannot claim that water causes the extinction unless we explain it using the causal relation between their molecular structures. And also the same phenomenological properties can only be explained by appealing to the causal effects of the peculiar molecular structure of H_2O in relation to our perceptual apparatus. Nor is it valid to make the critique that possible worlds may exist where there is a substance that has many of water's causal properties but a different molecular structure, and that therefore its causal properties are contingent and cannot be identified with its molecular properties. This is not a valid argument because when we speak of causal properties we mean the entire repertoire, not only some of them. And if a molecular structure has the entire repertoire of water's causal properties, then it cannot be anything other than H_2O. According to Kripke (1980), the identity between H_2O and water is a metaphysical necessity not only a nomic necessity. In other words, its necessity is not only a matter of contingent relations valid in worlds where there are the same scientific laws.

A traditional critique to this kind of example comes from the *multirealizability argument*. We cannot establish strong identities between mind and brain because for any mental property there are many possible physical realizations. The same mental property, for example pain, is realized by many different material hardware, e.g. the human nervous system or that of other animals that experience pain. Moreover, even among humans the same property is implemented by different physical hardware. The difference might lie in the number of neurons, the types of neural connections or the number of neuromediators. This multirealizability appears to justify abandoning any attempt to reduce mind to brain using biconditional assertions – mind $\leftrightarrow$ brain (as in the Nagel model of reduction). Moreover, it is well known that the traditional solution put forward for the problem of multirealizability, namely the *supervenience thesis,*[13] cannot avoid some of the anomalies about causality, introduced before, in particular the epiphenomenal character of mental causation (Kim 1998).

What is the possible solution to the problem of multirealizabilty? There is an option that can be called *default identity theory* (Viale 1999, p. 159). It applies to

[13] "A set of properties *A* supervenes upon another set *B* just in case no two things can differ with respect to *A*-properties without also differing with respect to their *B*-properties. In slogan form, "there cannot be an *A*-difference without a *B*-difference." This slogan can be cashed out in many different ways. But to illustrate the basic idea, imagine that there is a perfect forger. Her copies of paintings not only fool the art dealers, but are in fact exact duplicates of the originals down to the precise placement of every molecule of pigment – indeed, down to every microphysical detail. Suppose that she produces such a copy of El Greco's *A View of Toledo*. It is of course different from the original in various respects – it is a forgery, it was not painted by El Greco, it is worth quite a bit less at Sotheby's, and so forth. But the forgery is also *exactly like* the original in other respects. It is the same shape, size, and weight. The surface of the canvas contains the same arrangements of colors and shapes – a blue rectangle here, a green swirl there. Indeed, it *looks* just the same, at least to a single viewer under identical lighting conditions and so forth. Perhaps it is even just as beautiful as the original, though that is more controversial. The properties that the forgery is guaranteed to share with the original are those that supervene upon its microphysical properties. Two paintings that are microphysically just alike are guaranteed to be just alike in the arrangement of colors and shapes on their canvases. That is, you cannot change the arrangement of colors and shapes on a painting's canvas without changing its microphysical properties. This is just to say that the arrangement of colors and shapes supervenes on its microphysical properties" (Stanford Dictionary of Philosophy).

the mind-brain identity the same argument that is valid in any natural identity. When we say that water is equal to H_2O we take for granted that the many samples of H_2O molecular structures are variable with regard to their position in space and time and other microphysical features. Likewise even the phenomenological properties of water – from colour to taste and transparency – are not constant among the various samples. You cannot think of two real samples of water that are perfectly identical. Nonetheless, the identity *water* $= H_20$, like other conceptual identities in nature, does work quite well. The reason is that natural identities always lie within a core of phenomenological and microphysical properties, and in addition there is a default rule that allows the inclusion of every new case that satisfies the core identity, but presents variations compared to the previous examples. This is also true of the mind-brain identity: we know that even in the same person a given mental property is realized by different neural configurations at different times. The neural networks are not stable and the neurons die. Nevertheless, in principle we can establish a default identity between mind and brain that refers to a core of mental and neural properties plus a default rule. At the neural level the core will be based on prototypes of the structural configurations of the central nervous system that realize given mental properties in a given species. Every particular instance of a mental state will be equal, in principle, to the given neural prototype plus a set of contingent and variable particular conditions of the nervous system allowed by the default rule.

As affirmed by Kim (1998), the identity between mental properties and neural properties does not imply the elimination of the mental dimension. Even if the claim of identity is that the causal role is played exclusively by the neural realizers of the mind and there is no autonomous and separate mental causation, it is possible to preserve the property dimension of the mind for practical reasons. The mental property will be considered second order property of the neural first order property, that is a property of having a property in the neural base with given causal potentials. To achieve this kind of reduction we need to functionalize (Kim 1998, pp. 98–103) the mental property by constructing its relational causal role with other properties and phenomena. And the first order neural property exactly should fit the causal specification of this functionalization.

As we will see below, this kind of functional reduction is what is claimed by the sophisticated functionalist theory and is pursued, in principle, by cognitive psychology.

If we identify mind with brain because of our goal to represent the causal properties of mind, how we can link the representational features of mind to the causal structure of the brain? There appear to be two main options.

One solution is given by a sophisticated functionalist theory: the idea is of a mental syntax that is realized in the causal structure of the brain. As Fodor pointed out: "you connect the causal properties of a symbol with its semantic properties via its syntax" (Fodor 1990, p. 22). Using the comparison with the computer, the causal properties of its processors (for example, outputting current when and only when it receives electric currents from both inputs) realizes the syntactic properties of the symbol (in this case the formal properties of the logical conjunction) that realizes the semantic properties of the symbol (in this case truth preserving, using the rule of conduction). According to this analogy, the AND-GATE processor (that of conjunction) can correspond to a given neural connection in the brain. Therefore the goal of cognitive science is to find the formal syntactic rules that process the representations and are realized by given neural connections, analogs of computer processors.

Using this programme it would be possible to connect mental states with the causal properties of the neural connections of the brain via the mental syntax.

The second possible solution starts from a critique of the unbiological features of the previous functionalist description. The computer model of mind aims at a level of description of the mind that abstracts away from the biological realizations of the cognitive structures. As far as the computer model goes, it does not matter whether our gates are realized in grey matter, switches or other substances. But if mind is identified with the causal structure of the brain, an answer to our questions therefore lies in how the neural structure works. The analogy of the mind as the software of the brain is misleading. It seems to imply two ontological or explanatory levels. But in the same way that we cannot say that water and H_2O are different ontological and explanatory levels, the same applies to mind and brain. This follows the analogy that the external and phenomenological properties of water and the language that we use to represent them correspond to the psychological properties of mind and to the language that we use in describing them. That is, they are elliptical and metaphorical concepts and terms that do not refer to a new level of reality, but have the utility of summarizing a complex description of our inner reality and adapting it pragmatically to our need to communicate. Therefore they can be eliminated from scientific language.

Computational neuroscience (Anderson and Rosenfeld 1988; Churchland and Sejnowski 1992) and its artificial counterpart, connectionism, are the programmes that pursue this eliminative goal. According to computational neuroscience, the basic unit of occurrent cognition is apparently not the sentence-like state, but rather the high dimensional neuronal activation vector (that is a pattern of excitation levels across a large population of neurons). And the basic unit of cognitive processing is apparently not inference from sentence to sentence, but rather a synapse-induced transformation of large activation vectors into other such vectors. In this way, speaking of representations of the reality means speaking of prototype vectors in the higher populations of cortical neurons.

Strong identity theory and our causal desiderata seem to incline towards the second eliminative option, computational neuroscience. But the sophisticated functionalist solution also meets the desiderata of identity and causality, according to the version of functionalist reduction (Kim 1998). The first programme tries to derive psychological concepts starting from neural phenomena, while the second starts from the mental level of rules and representations and tries to find the neural counterparts. In other words, one is bottom-up and the other is top-down. Only scientific research will prove if our mental activity is merely a distributed pattern of neural activation or if it has to be modelled as the neural embodiment of syntactic rules processing representations.

But for the purpose of explaining social action according to causal cognitive mechanisms, it seems that until now computational neuroscience has not provided useful concepts and hypotheses to achieve this goal. Even Churchland in his recent analysis of the neural representation of society and morality (1995) has little to say about it.

Instead current cognitive psychology, which attempts to discover the syntactic rules or procedures that process representations without overly resorting to folk psychology, has provided the best generalizations to explain social action to date. What it is lacking is a clear connection between these concepts and neural realizers and therefore its claim of causality is *sub judice*.[14]

3.5 Cognitive Therapy to Avoid Holistic Illusion

Let us discuss briefly the second critique. The critique is towards the *holistic illusion*. As we saw in the previous example of international politics, theories are still present in the methodologies of social sciences that support an autonomous and separate level of social phenomena. Structuralism and social functionalism are two examples. What I want to emphasize in the present paper is not that social phenomena should be reduced to individual action, as in the traditional thesis of methodological individualism, but that social phenomena should be reduced to the causal mechanisms of the human mind, which is the central tenet of methodological cognitivism. One of the main reasons for this kind of reduction was outlined before in the analysis of the mind–body problem and mental causation. If we want to establish causal models of action we should refer to the cognitive or, in the future, neurocomputational models of action. Therefore it is not satisfactory to explain social phenomena by reducing them to the belief-desire-intention triad generating the individual action.

The first consideration is that if we want to reduce something, the reducible phenomenon must be real. And the separate ontology of social phenomena is, in my opinion, more dubious than that of water compared to its molecular structure. If this is true, concepts and language about social phenomena are only, and not always, useful elliptical metaphora referring to group of individuals and the explanations of social phenomena are the explanations of the behaviour of these groups of individuals. As in the previous eliminative programme about mind-brain identity, there is no reduction but only the elimination of one non-existent level by the other.

The social dimension is quite dubious even from a conceptual point of view. Often the social concepts only have an *intensional* life, in other words they only live in the heads of social scientists and they lack any *extensional* reference. In other

[14] As I will show in the following chapters of this volume, nowadays there are many data coming from brain research, realized mainly with FMRi and other techniques, that seem to be quite successful in discovering a correspondence between particular neural structures and mental events (Gazzaniga et al. 2002; Smith and Kosslyn 2007).

cases their extension is definable only with reference to individuals and their behaviour. Concepts like state, class, government, race and so on are statistical or elliptical terms used to summarize given real groups of individuals, their concrete actions plus a set of entities, such as laws, rules, symbols, principles, culture and so on.

A holistic critic would immediately point out that the presence in the definition of this set of extraindividual entities proves the irreducibility of social concepts to individual concepts. In my own opinion, this critique does not hit the mark because the mere existence of these normative or cultural entities, created by individuals, are, if taken separately from individuals, devoid of meaning for the social phenomenon. They are inert and inanimate things, like the chairs or carpets in some ministerial office. They only begin to live when they become part of individuals' mental representations and therefore drive their reasoning and decision-making processes. Moreover, the fact that these rules and symbols are common to many individuals, in other words they are social, does not eliminate another fact: namely, that it is the individual mind that filters and implements them in a way that often differs from that of the other individuals.

The ontologial and conceptual dimensions of social phenomena are not the scope of the present paper. Let us assume as if social phenomena are real and that the semantic properties of social concepts refer to existing phenomena. The striking weakness of the holistic approach is at the level of explanation. Holism supports the view that it is possible to explain a social phenomenon using another social phenomenon. The explanation may have many forms depending on the various methodologies: causal, teleological, structuralist, and so on.

Let us set aside those explanations that do not follow the criteria of empirical controllability and intersubjectivity such as the Levi Strauss structuralist approach.

If we analyse the other two models of explanation we will see that it will always be possible to establish a better explanation, that is an explanation that has more generality, scope and controllability, by making reference to individual decision-making and action.

Teleological social *functionalist* explanations, as Elster and Boudon have shown, can always be interpreted causally as individual actions reinforced by positive feedback from the environment to the mental representations and decision-making processes of the agent. The Vietnamese rational peasant described by Samuel Popkin (1979) is a brilliant example of how it is possible in anthropology to avoid teleological explanations in favour of individualistic ones.

The systematic empirical insufficiency of causal *structuralist* explanations, and their subset of sociometric causal explanations, has been revealed in the past few years. They systematically fall into the countless traps of spurious causal explanations, like post hoc fallacy, epiphenomenalism and substitutive causation. The reason, as I previously emphasized, is that they follow an inadequate model of causal explanation. In fact, we cannot claim to have discovered a causal relation between two social events if we cannot offer an explanation based on the description of the causal relation between the components of the two social phenomena, namely a description of the causal relations between the individuals that are the components of the social phenomena.

At this point, I would like to add my own thesis that these components must be represented as the cognitive mechanisms of actions and not only as individual actions, as some structuralists would concede.

Let us come back to the initial examples of international politics. An important theory of international politics is the *Deterrence Theory*. It tries to overcome some inadequacies of the realist theory in explaining the behaviour of nations when faced with the hostile behaviour of other nations. It tries to establish some regularities in the causal relation between the hostile behaviour of one nation and the reaction of another. It is clear that there are many difficulties, stemming from the clause *ceteris paribus* to the individuation of "where," "when" and "who" in the real processes of decision making. Political scientists have even tried to apply the game theory to extrapolate some regularities in the empirical international arena. All these regularities were not without exceptions and made no reference to the cognitive mechanisms of reasoning and decision making. One regularity, established by Schelling (1966), claimed that coercion more readily maintains rather than alters the status quo. This regularity was corroborated but it was not offered a deeper explanation of the reasons of this phenomenon.

The picture was changed by the *prospect theory* (see Chap. 2, Part II of this volume). It seems that the fact that actors react very differently to the prospect of losses compared to the chance of making gains has important explanatory implications for international bargaining and conflicts. If loss aversion is present, state leaders defending the status quo should have a big bargaining advantage. They will be willing to pay a higher price and run higher risks if they are facing losses compared to a situation in which they are seeking to make gains.

The first implication is that conflicts and wars are most likely when each side believes it will suffer significant losses if it does not fight. Moreover, deterrence will be effective when the hostile leader fears losses and tries to coerce the other country that is seeking gains. According to this, it is possible to explain many conflicts or successful bargaining in causal terms. For example, the lack of a spiral of greater hostility in the Cuban crisis between Usa and Soviet Union. The Soviet perception of non losses with regard to the status quo by the naval blockade did not stimulate a more hostile reaction to Usa. It would have been a completely different outcome if there had been a military intervention in Cuba, leading to a consequent change in the status quo.

The example just given uses prospect theory, an hypothesis that appears to be behavioural, but is explained by cognitive mechanisms, like the heuristics of probabilistic judgement introduced by Kanheman and Tversky.

Faced with this kind of cognitive explanation a likely criticism from the structuralist side (but hermeneutics would also agree) would be that cognitive explanations leave out a large number of social actions that are not based on conscious representation. Social rules, cultural symbols, moral values, social practices drive an individual's actions without his awareness of their causal roles. They form the social structure that crosses the individual mind of many social actors and causes their common but unaware social behaviour. Instead cognitive explanation presupposes a conscious and aware representation of the rules and prescriptions, allowing them to govern the decision-making processes.

I think this critique is weak because it relies on a rationalist picture of the cognitive theory of action. It has the Cartesian bias of assimilating cognition to intentional rational choice and thinks that the concept of mind present in cognitive science is what is described by folk psychology. Instead cognitive psychology, that supplies the conceptual tools for the cognitive theory of action, is trained to cope with unintentional and unconscious behaviour.

Individuals are often not aware of how they reason (Gigerenzer 2007). They are aware of the results, not the mechanisms. What they say about their reasoning does not tally with its real nature. One of the main goals of heuristics of reasoning, framing effect, mental models theory and inferential rules theory is to explain the role of contextual variables in changing the results of reasoning and decision-making processes, unaware to the agent. Why do we have a greater propensity to risk faced with loss compared to a situation of gain? Why does the individual change the answer if you change the format and the frame of the problem of choice? And so on.

Moreover, cognitive psychology is aware that the majority of our thought and knowledge is tacit. And considerable space in cognitive science is dedicated to the top-down effects of unconscious thought and memory on perception and reasoning processes. The work of Nisbett and Ross (1980) on social biases and stereotypes are an important example.

Another holistic remark tries to show that social phenomena are emergent and are not reducible to individual cognition. For example, unintended consequences of action or social learning cannot be explained in terms of cognitive mechanisms of action. At first glance these phenomena seem to have something that goes beyond individual cognition. Let us briefly analyse using the language of folk psychology how these phenomena are structured. We can divide the behaviour of individuals producing the so-called social phenomena into three main idealized categories.

(a) Individuals who reach the same belief without any form of group interaction. It might be a political conviction or a particular taste or a sense of frustration regarding the government. The social phenomena in this case merely amount to a statistical aggregate of all individuals sharing the same belief. The explanation will try to identify the mental mechanism that is responsible for the given belief starting from contextual inputs.
(b) Individuals who want to reach the same goal without any group interaction, but in trying to do so they produce unintended consequences. For example, the parametric behaviour of those who leave to go on holiday during the night in the hope of finding themselves alone on the motorway and instead find a queue stretching for miles. In this case the social phenomena does not amount to a statistical aggregate of cognitive events, but to an aggregate of actions depending on given environmental constraints.

A queue on a motorway, the perverse effect of intellectual unemployment, the bankruptcy of a solid bank are unintended social phenomena that cannot be reduced to individual cognition because the consequences are not present in the agent's mental representations. But is this a sufficient reason to claim that they are emergent social phenomena? On the contrary, in my opinion, they can be satisfactorily analysed as the results of cognitive mechanisms of action limited by environmental constraints, for example scarcity of space on the motorway, or the scarce supply of intellectual employment in the labour market, or the scarcity of financial deposits in the bank compared with the sudden global demand of clients.

Moreover, these phenomena will usually produce a kind of social learning because it will be less likely that the unintended consequences will manifest themselves in the same way after the first instance. In other words, it is unlikely that the supposedly smart drivers will repeat the same unsuccessful action after the first trial. Also in this case I do not see any clues for emergent social phenomena. The first unintended consequence changes the knowledge of the possible means of achieving the goal of a comfortable drive and therefore drivers will try to find a new solution the next time. Even in this case there may be a cognitive explanation of action depending on the new knowledge gained from the first trial. This kind of explanation can be called, using another language, negative feedback from the environment. In all cases of social feedback the correct explanation should always be seen in terms of changing the mental representation of the problem.

(c) Individuals that interact in a co-operative way to reach a common goal. In the case of co-operation the individual must share the mental representation of the common goal and the knowledge of the means to achieve it. But individuals should also have representation of the representations adopted by other co-operative agents in order to share the same goal and means.

The social learning resulting from this co-operation might be unintended, even in this case. The positive or negative feedback from the co-operation will change the mental representation of the knowledge of the means (reinforcing or decreasing belief in them) or will change the common goal of the group. Therefore social learning can be easily explained, as in the previous case, as individual cognitive adaptation of the behaviour of the members of the group towards a common goal.

How can the social learning be represented? For example, let us take the example of an idealized group of scientists who share a common goal to discover the treatment for a disease. Let us assume that they start with no organizational culture but with strong constraints of money and time. Let us assume that they have the same expertise at the beginning. After the first trial in which everybody did the same things, in other words tried to reach the same goal using the same means, they discover that, given the complex structure of the problem composed of various parallel different sub problems, it would be better, and more likely to increase the speed of the discovery, if everybody begins to tackle one or few of the different sub problems. The general goal remains the same, but they change the individual sub goals and the means of reaching them. This is a typical case of division of labour in science. Even this example of social learning, which is often presented as a case of emergent social phenomenon, can be given a cognitive explanation.

The same analysis applies when the interaction is not co-operative, namely individuals try to pursue separate goals, which may even be the same. The social learning in these cases can be explained mainly by two classical mechanisms: imitation, as in the case of the diffusion of a technological innovation inside a group of enterprises, and adaptation, as in the case of product differentiation among the members of a group of enterprises in the competitive market. In the first case imitation of a technological innovation corresponds to a change in the knowledge of the means to solve a given technological problem; in the second case, the entrepreneur changes the production means and goals until he finds a solution, namely a product niche, that allows his economic survival and development.

3.6 Conclusion: Far From a Unified Cognitive Theory of Social Action

A few last words on the candidate psychological models for the theory of social action.

Until recently first place was occupied by the strongest model that social sciences have ever had: the *theory of rational choice as subjective expected utility maximization*. It has been pervasive in economic theory. It is now of growing importance in political science and a little less in sociology.

One of the critiques that comes from this theory to the cognitive approach is the scant theoretical unity and lack of generality characterizing cognitive models of action compared to the decision rules of rational choice theory. This is a true remark. In fact, rational choice theory is conceptually very compact and it applies to many different and varied fields, as is shown by authors like Gary Becker. Unfortunately for this theory, there is a clear trade-off between compactness and truth and between the generality and empirical reliability (Viale 1992; 1997b). The rational choice theory does not suit any of the philosophical desiderata listed earlier for a psychological theory of social action. It relies heavily on the concepts of folk psychology. Therefore it is far from the desiderata of causality and mind–body identity. Moreover, its principle of action is not based on an a posteriori empirical description of reasoning and decision-making processes but it is a priori and normative. Therefore a social theory that relies on it may, with much difficulty, be described as empirical and even scientific. The theory of rational choice has done much in the past to change the perspective of social investigation from aggregate social phenomena and from the empire of super individual forces to the central role of the individual actors and his rationality. But nowadays, as is affirmed by supporters of methodological individualism like Boudon (1994), the same methodological programme can be pursued with better chance and stronger conceptual tools using the empirical knowledge coming from the cognitive psychology of reasoning and decision making.

The psychology of reasoning and decision making has given birth in the past few years to many different research programmes. Therefore today we cannot speak of a cognitive theory of social action but of many alternative theories.

Turning to the *neurocomputational* approach, it augurs well for the future, but nowadays it does not seem to offer convincing conceptual tools for explaining the individual cognitive mechanisms of action. In particular, a lot of work still needs to be done to understand "how the entire spectrum of sensory inputs processed in the rear half of the brain finally gets transformed into some appropriate motor outputs formulated in the front half of the brain" (Churchland 1998, p. 243). Nevertheless, there is an important hypothesis that stems from the present neurocomputational research. It is very likely that both moral and social thinking and behaviour are embodied not in a rule and verbal language-based architecture, but in a hierarchy of learned prototypes, in a well-tuned configuration of a neural network's synaptic weights. This thesis is well suited to the prototypical theory of categorization and it represents an important and outstanding example of convergence between neurocomputational and cognitive research.

In conclusion, it may be useful to enumerate the present main candidates for methodological cognitivism (without any pretence of completeness).

- *Mental Model Theory* by Johnson Laird (1983; with Byrne 1990) and others. It deals mainly with deductive reasoning, but tries to develop some explanations, also of inductive and causal reasoning. It is one of the few cognitive theories that attempts to offer a picture of the mind-brain connections. According to Johnson Laird (1988; it. transl. 1990, p. 207) there are two levels of mental activity, that of conscious processes analysed as explicit processing of separate symbols and the level of subconscious processes analysed as parallel processing of implicit distributed representations. The high level symbolic processing, analysed by cognitive psychology, is translated into low level sub symbolic distributed processing, analysed using a neurocomputational approach. It seems to pay little attention to decision making and to contextual environmental variables, crucial for any application to the social context. It is a semantic theory and therefore rejects the idea that reasoning depends on formal rules of inference, which, on the contrary, is one of the main research goals of cognitive psychology according to the functionalist theory.
- *Theory of Inferential Rules* (and the relative T*heory of Pragmatic Schemes*) by Cheng and Holyoak (1985, 1989) and others. It claims that inductive and deductive reasoning depends on formal rules of inference. These are not equivalent to rules of formal logic or probability calculus and they are represented in the long-term memory as production rules. The strength of this theory is its ability to explain the function of moral prescriptions, social rules and laws. Moreover it pays considerable attention to contextual variables. It is more suited than the others to a functionalist architecture of the mind.
- *Heuristics of judgement and decision making* by Kanheman, Slovic and Tversky (1982) and others and the relative *Prospect Theory* (Kahneman & Tversky 1979b). These have been developed to represent probabilistic judgement and decision making. They have been generated mainly to correct the anomalies of the expected utility model and to propose alternative hypotheses to the current theory of economic rationality. They are the most suitable to analyse context of choice where the crucial variables are risk and uncertainty.

- *Smart and Frugal Heuristics* by Gigerenzer et al. (Gigerenzer et al. 1999; Gigerenzer and Selten 2001b; Gigerenzer 2007). They are the most suitable to cope with the duality of mind, the growing role of intuition, emotion and affect. They represent the most coherent development of bounded rationality theory and of its thesis of the ecological and environmental dimension of choice. They are justified by some of the main results of evolutionary psychology.
- *Problem Solving* models by Newell (1990; with Simon 1972) and others. Now less fashionable than they were in the past, they developed quite apart from research on reasoning and decision making. In my opinion, the reason is more contingent than epistemological. In fact, as Newell (1990) has claimed, the problem-solving frame can capture all aspects of reasoning, judgement and decision making. Every decision is taken as a result of a problem-solving activity and every problem-solving activity needs a complex set of reasoning and decision-making processes. It might be the right way to achieve the aim of a unified theory of cognition.

Until now there have been no cognitive theories of action that were able to fulfil properly the desiderata of causality and the mind-brain identity of methodological cognitivism. Moreover, cognitive psychology is widespread in many theories or empirical generalizations that apply to single aspects of the action process. What can a social scientist do? He or she should help to develop a unified theory of cognition and ought to apply, using a pluralistic and pragmatic approach, the latest cognitive tools that he or she deems most suitable to explain a given social phenomenon.

Cognition and Rationality of Beliefs in the Social Sciences

4

4.1 Introduction

Rationality comes into play every time we have to make a choice or decide what to do.

According to Kant, philosophical tradition identifies three chief contexts for choice: that of belief, that of action, and that of evaluation. They correspond well to our modern-day trio in the social sciences of belief, action and purpose (or preference or desire, etc.), which make up the theory of rationality. A rational agent is one who chooses the action that he believes to be the most appropriate (best or satisfying) means of achieving the end. Belief in the appropriate means will, in turn, have a series of connections with other beliefs in the world, in the causal relationship between means and end, etc.

The wealth of studies on rationality has resulted, as often happens in these cases, in some confusion about the meaning of the term. Used as an adjective, rational comes close to a series of other terms, like intention, plan, order, etc. Even if some of these terms seem to have acquired an independent meaning, in practice they are derivative terms. A rational plan, for example, describes a future action that the agent believes is the most appropriate means of achieving an end. A rational order is the one based on a series of rational plans, etc. I had originally planned to draw a tree diagram to show the various categories to which the term "rational" can be applied as an adjective, but I had to give up the attempt because of the rapid spread of the branches. Instead, I have preferred to show only individual rationality, without citing the various theories that have led to the development of different areas of the tree, and without showing the branches in too much detail (Fig. 4.1).

As it can be seen, an initial and important division must be made between *behavioural rationality* and *mental rationality*. Clearly, behavioural rationality can be described as a form of behaviour derived from rational preferences and beliefs. However, some authors prefer to describe rational behaviour only at a behavioural level, as an optimal adjustment to the environment. In this context,

R. Viale, *Methodological Cognitivism*,
DOI 10.1007/978-3-642-24743-9_4,

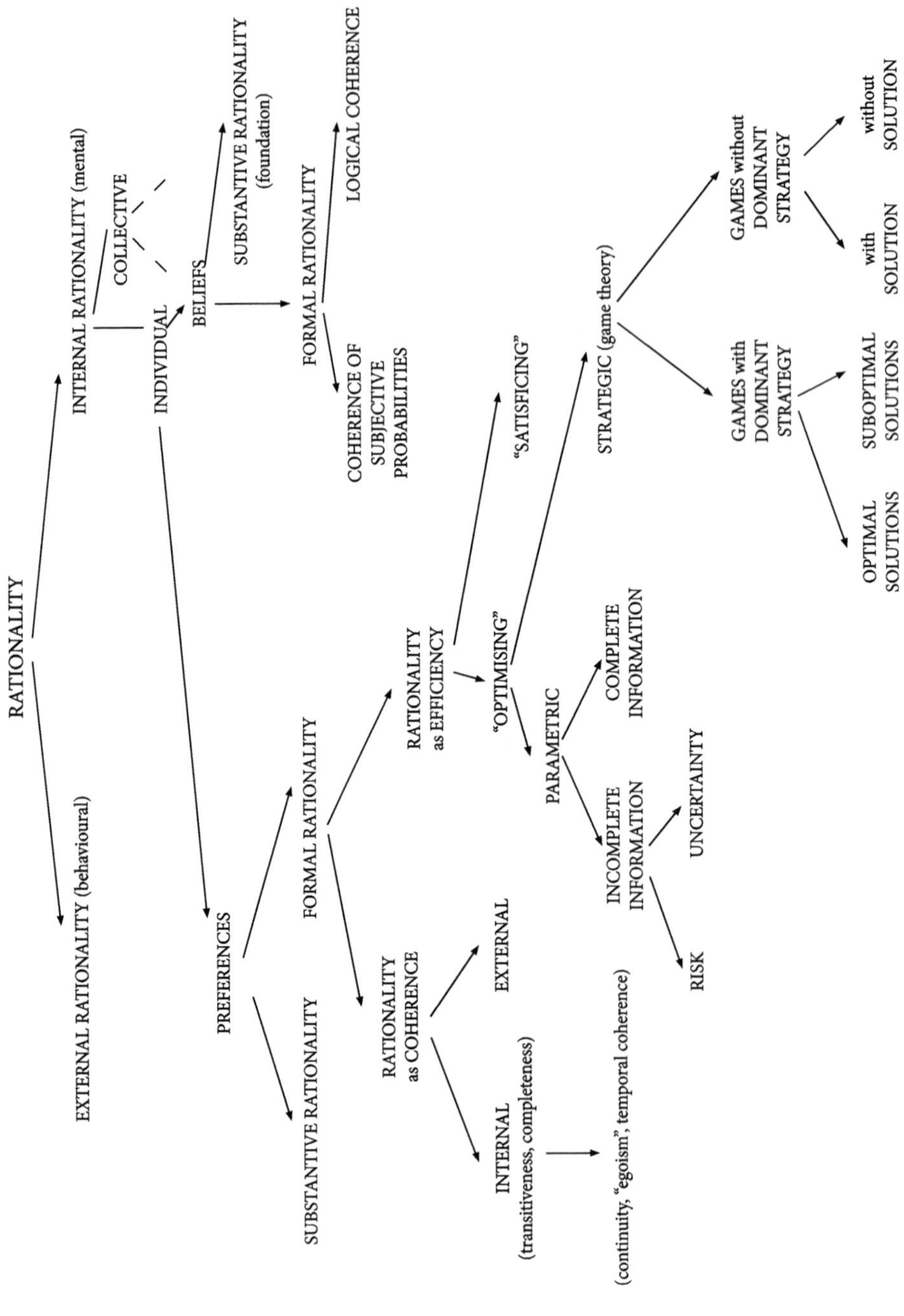

Fig. 4.1 Forms of rationality

reference can be made to Nelson and Winter's evolutionary theory of enterprise or to Popper's situational rationality.

Turning to focus on rationality at a mental level, namely rationality in terms of the agent's internal preferences or beliefs, an initial separation can be made between *individual rationality* and *collective rationality*. I will leave the latter aside because it would take us too far from the theme of this chapter. Clearly, this separation between collective and individual is often motivated more by academic rather than theoretical reasons, given that collective rationality can refer both to collective decisional processes (as in the theories of social choice) and to the overall outcome of individual decisions. In both cases, individual preferences are deemed to have been given and rationality is defined mainly as the relationship between preferences and the social outcome (as in the case of Arrow's theorem of the impossibility of a function of social wellbeing).

The diagram clearly shows the dense theoretical branching at the level of the *formal rationality of preferences*. It comprises *rationality as efficiency*, which is relative to instrumental rationality, namely to the problem of how, given a particular end, it is possible to find the best or most satisfactory means of achieving it. In the *optimising variant*, the end will generally be specified through some objective function of utility to be maximised. In turn, the optimising variant has given rise to the interesting division between *parametric rationality*, namely rational behaviour in an environment that the agent assumes to be made up of natural objects governed by causal laws or of other agents, whose behaviour is irrelevant to the agent (the agent thinks of himself as a variable and of others as constants, or he thinks that if the others adapt to the environment, he is only one to adapt himself to other agents' adaptation) and of *strategic rationality* defined using an axiom of symmetry: the agent acts in other actors' environments, but none can be deemed less rational or sophisticated than him (each actor must anticipate others' decisions before his own, knowing full well that the others will try to do the same to him) (Elster 1983). Both parametric and strategic rationality, with game theory, have led to a massive output of mathematical studies, and to what is defined, rather presumptuously, as the mathematics of rationality.

Bringing this rapid *excursus* to an end, we find that the important chapter of rationality is an *internal coherence of preferences*. It provides the minimal notion of the coherence of preferences underlying the notion of a rational human being, namely the condition of the transitiveness and completeness of the preferences and the three auxiliary conditions that, together with the first two, characterise the dynamic notion of economic man in the rational consumer theory, namely continuity, "egoism", and the coherence of the temporal succession of preferences.

Why did I start with this schematic illustration of the subdivisions of the rationality theory?

As is clear from the diagram, my aim was to show – also in visual terms, along the lines of what is done using some bibliometric methods of scientific research – where the theoretical focus has mainly been concentrated over the past few years when analysing the concept of rationality. That it has focused, above all, on the side of the *formal rationality of preferences* is a reliable indicator of how scientific interests have become polarised in social sciences, as in ethics and in political philosophy. This would have been even clearer if I had added the major theories and hypotheses produced in the past few years.

One question comes naturally to mind: why have researchers concentrated mainly on the formal aspects of rationality, and on preferences in particular, neglecting to analyse the *substantial aspects of rationality*, in particular the extremely important question of beliefs? The most probable response might arise from the fact that the theoretical elaboration of the concept of rationality has above all been provided by economists, who are clearly interested mainly in the formal relationship between preferences and consumer choice, and only secondarily in the question of contents and the foundation of beliefs and expectations.

4.2 The Role of Procedural Rationality in Economics

Economists have introduced two key meanings for rationality. There is a *broader definition of rationality*, which more closely resembles a paradigm rather than a specific theory. It is felt that an actor acts rationally, for example, when he has a utility function whose arguments are defined as alternative uses of the resources with which he is endowed. The quantity of these resources are seen as constraints to the possible choices available to the decision-maker, so that rational behaviour consists, in terms of solving a problem of bounded maximisation, in determining the whole panoply of resources to dedicate to each of the possible uses. This concept offers a principle that establishes a relationship between changes in one or more constraints on the available resources and changes in the quantity of phenomena to describe, which can be the supply of a product or other phenomena, like changes in crime figures, birth rates or the number of marriages. There is no need to make psychological-type assumptions in order to apply the paradigm of rational choice.

The second definition of rationality is a *narrow* one, which has replaced the broader definition in many descriptive contexts. Rationality is seen as the maximisation of expected utility, which is instead based on strong a priori psychological assumptions. It assumes preferences as being given and coherent, a corpus of beliefs corresponding to a true description of the world, and an unlimited decisional power for the decision-maker. Therefore, there is no need to draw a distinction between the real world and the decision-maker's perception of it, given that he has a true representation of the world. We can therefore predict the choices that the rational decision-maker will make from our knowledge of the world, together with the knowledge of its function of utility, without having to know the specific characteristics through which the decision-maker has perceived, elaborated and memorised his beliefs in the world.

Contrary to these assumptions, if instead we accept the empirically confirmed finding on the limited capacity of knowledge and the computational power of the human decision-maker, then we must distinguish between the real world and the representations of it formed by the decision-maker. In other words, we must elaborate an empirical theory of the cognitive processes that lead to the decision. This will therefore include the perception, representation and memorisation of beliefs in the world and the deductive and probabilistic reasoning on the factual base it produces. This is what Simon defines as *procedural rationality*.

As Simon has underlined, neoclassical economy differs from other sciences in the way it confronts the problem of rationality. Economics is characterised by its silence on the kind of preferences and beliefs, its assumption of a broadly coherent behaviour and rationality towards the total environment, both now and in the future. On the contrary, other human sciences pay more attention when confronting the problem of rationality to (1) determining the processes, both individual and social, used to perceive, elaborate and memorise selected aspects of reality which make up the corpus of beliefs on which the decisional rationale is based; (2) defining empirically the nature and origin of values and their changes; (3) understanding the computational strategies used in reasoning which allow a very limited level of information processing to tackle a very complex reality; (4) describing and explaining how emotional, motivational and sensorial-type causes can influence and disturb attention mechanisms and the definition of the real situation which forms the factual base for rationality (Simon 1986, p. 26).

The neoclassical economics approach to rationality has instead hampered the development of effective methods to investigate the processes through which selected aspects of reality are perceived, or how a representation is formed of the situation of choice, or how inferential processes are responsible for particular conclusions based on the previous representation. When faced with descriptive and predictive difficulties, neoclassical economists are generally willing to add any auxiliary theoretical assumption about the form of the functions of utility or about the way in which actors create expectations about the future or about their focus or lack of focus on particular environmental variables. Everything seems to be allowed in order to maintain the postulate of maximising utility, even preserving unconfirmed empirical assumptions. As has been demonstrated by authors like Simon, the tautological and non-falsifiable nature of the postulate upheld by the neoclassical economy prompts its supporters not to realise that the strength of its predictions rests mainly on the often uncontrolled and ad hoc auxiliary descriptive assumptions of the decisional environment. It is clear from various examples given by Simon (1986, pp. 29–38) that many explanations of neoclassical economics taken with the ad hoc addition of auxiliary assumptions could have been reached using the postulate of limited procedural rationality without the assumption of the utility maximisation. For example, the neoclassical theory cannot explain the phenomenon of the economic cycle without resorting to auxiliary irrational assumptions, like that of *monetary illusion*, which clearly correspond to a deviation from objective rationality. If we refer to Keynes's *General Theory* (1936), which coincides on several points with the model of neoclassical rationality, it is trade unions that suffer from monetary illusion because they cannot distinguish between monetary changes and changes in the purchasing power of wages. However, if instead we refer to Lucas (1981), the economic cycle is derived from the auxiliary assumption about monetary illusion by entrepreneurs who are incapable of distinguishing between general prices rises and changes in their own business sector. In both cases, the economic cycle can be said to derive from auxiliary assumptions and not from assumptions of rationality. Instead, the phenomenon of monetary illusion is connected to the processes used by people to create expectations about future events, a field of enquiry in empirical research according to the postulate of procedural rationality.

The limited theoretical and cognitive utility of a formal and a priori rational concept seems quite clear. The judgement that a certain kind of behaviour is rational can only be made within a context of empirically formulated premises. These include the situation in which the behaviour takes place, the preferences and ends that it is trying to achieve, and the cognitive means available in order to determine how the ends can be achieved. It is precisely this third aspect that makes Simon's *procedural rationality* so different from neoclassical examples. Procedural rationality becomes the causal premise of the rationality of action.

At this point we could characterise the rationality model in three successive stages, each featuring a specific type of rationality. The informative process gives the agent a range of more or less accurate evidential data (*perceptive rationality*), which are represented and memorised (*rationality of beliefs*); using logical and probabilistic forms of reasoning, the decisional process infers the possible action from the information (*decisional rationality*); and the implementation processes transform, with more or less accurate results, the potential action into real action (*rationality of action*). Decisional rationality can, in turn, be broken down into two main forms of rationality: *cognitive rationality*, linked to processing the available data in order to define the agent's expectations about himself and the surrounding environment, and *instrumental rationality*, which, based on these expectations, tries to select the most appropriate action. Perceptive and decisional rationality correspond to Simon's procedural rationality.

4.3 Perceptive Rationality and Rationality of Beliefs

But what does procedural rationality mean? It is well known that Simon has no qualms about committing the offence of naturalistic fallacy and he would not hesitate to respond that procedural rationality is identical to the empirical theory of cognitive decisional processes. However, there is a normative side to Simon's argument that tends to detach itself from the purely descriptive aspect of cognitive processes, and which biases procedural rationality towards the instrumental side. As Simon writes (1986, p. 25): "People have motives and they use reasons (both good and bad) to respond to these motives and attain their ends". In this case, the "good and bad" means whether or not they use the best means at their disposal, for example the best heuristics, to achieve a given end. Therefore, it is possible to judge the rationality of a decision-maker against a set of criteria to assess the efficacy and efficiency of the processes he uses to achieve a given aim. This set of criteria is derived, in the first place, from the empirical study of the various general heuristics, both weak and strong, involved in problem solving and from identifying the specific techniques and methodologies that have been successfully applied in this particular problem space of a problematic area. In this sense, the procedural rationality of a decision-maker is a general concept that can be used not only in economics but also in scientific decisions, and in all kinds of general problem-solving activities.

This Simonian solution seems to have given a definitive response to the problem of defining the concept of rationality. The magical phrase '*problem-solving heuristics*' appears to offer the normative key to describe the instrumental efficacy of certain cognitive processes reaching the goals pre-established by the problem space. It therefore seems possible to avoid the epistemological traps set by the normative characterisation of the term 'rationality'.

My thesis is slightly more problematic. As we have seen, any decisional rationality theory needs a theory of 'rationality of beliefs' to define the accuracy of information and the representation of beliefs. It is not possible to characterise rationality of beliefs without referring to acceptability criteria, namely how to form the corpus of beliefs about the world, which represents the information base from which choice is inferred. These acceptability criteria necessarily refer to epistemological values, like truth, coherency, accuracy, etc.

To my way of thinking, Simon's normative solution is too biased towards instrumental rationality and fails to focus sufficiently on the problem of rationality of beliefs, the accuracy of representing the world (and also of representing the problem of choice) which forms the information base for heuristic inference. This inference will be more or less effective depending on whether the representation of reality is more or less correct, more or less significant and not banal. How can the accuracy of the representation, and of the factual base be assessed, except by making reference to epistemological values like those mentioned above? Perceptive rationality is a necessary condition of rationality of beliefs that is the necessary condition of cognitive rationality, which in turn is the necessary condition for instrumental rationality. But while decisional rationality can be characterised by satisfying the conditions of instrumental rationality, namely the efficiency and efficacy of the cognitive processes in problem solving and the identification of appropriate means to achieve a given end, rationality of beliefs should be characterised with reference to epistemological type analysis.

While the rationality of real decision-making processes can be assessed, if scientifically possible, by gauging the correspondence of these processes to given decisional heuristics capable of achieving given aims, with greater or lesser efficacy (as described by Langley, Simon, Bradshaw and Zytkow in their 1987 book on scientific discovery and by Gigerenzer, Todd and the ABC Group, in their 1999 book on smart and frugal heuristics), the rationality of representing informative inputs presents problems of an epistemological nature which are still far from being resolved using a cognitive and simulative approach.

An epistemological solution to these problems might be the radical one that sustains that the rationality and reliability of our belief formation processes is guaranteed a priori "by ourselves" and that no empirical and experimental study would be able to question the rationality of these processes. If anything, they could only describe them. Quine's naturalisation programme of epistemology (1985) moves in this direction. Instead of asking how we ought to go about forming our beliefs, we should ask how do we actually go about it. For Quine, this position is caused by the failure of the fundamentalist programme that tried to demonstrate the existence of a class of beliefs – those based on our sensorial experiences – which were sufficient to justify the rest of our beliefs. Therefore, it is best to discover how knowledge of the world develops in reality. Epistemology becomes a chapter of psychology and natural sciences, and its focus of study is the natural phenomenon, human beings.

This *a priori* position is strongly supported, in a different way, also by Davidson: "...if we are intelligibly to attribute attitudes and beliefs, or usefully to describe motions as behaviour, then we are committed to find in behaviour, belief, and desire, a large degree of rationality and consistency" (1980, p. 237). A theory of interpretation cannot be correct that makes a man assent to very many false sentences: it must generally be the case that a sentence is true when a speaker holds it to be" (1984, pp. 168–169).

A similar position is also supported by Dennett (1981) whereby (1) the beliefs of a system are those which it must have in view of its perceptive capacities, its epistemic requirements, and its biography; (2) the desires of a system are those it must have in view of its biological requirements and the most practical means of satisfying them; (3) the behaviour of a system must consist of those acts which an agent with these beliefs and desires would find it rational to carry out.

4.4 Limits of Perception and Memory in Humans

The best way of starting to respond to this thesis is to illustrate what happens in the practical formation of beliefs in humans. I will limit myself to highlighting some characteristics of the belief perception and memorisation processes.

Perception is a central theme in both psychology and epistemology. One of the standard approaches in the psychology of perception is based on pattern recognition. People recognise the presentation of a particular object as an example of a certain pattern. Perception output implies a classification of the stimulus. The perceived stimulus is not a mere *qualia*, but a classification of a certain segment of the environment. The perceptive stimulus is developed into a perceptive belief. Both Marr (1982) and Rock (1983) emphasise different stages in perception. There is, in brief, a lower stage of 'perception of forms' in which the stimulus is not recognised and is characterised as round, elongated, etc. Then, there are higher stages in which access to long-term memory leads to the categorical recognition of the stimulus. All stages, however, require descriptions of the stimulus.

Perception is ultimately made up of two kinds of elaboration: bottom-up elaboration, in which information flows from small perceptive inputs to larger units made up of those inputs, and top-down elaboration, in which background beliefs influence the interpretation of the most elementary perceptive units. In language perception empirical evidence of the importance of context in the perception of words is available. For example, the 'reintegration of the phoneme' effect when the missing phonemes in a word are automatically and unconsciously restored by the listener in experiments, so that they conform to the context. (Sternberg 2009; Smith and Kosslyn 2007). Recent work suggests that, whereas the very first stage of the visual pathway represent only what is in the retinal image of an object, later-stage representations emphasize the viewer's current interest or attention. Moreover vision for different things can take different forms. Visual control of action is mediated by cortical pathways that are different from those involved in visual control of the perception. In other words, when we merely see an object, such as chair, we process differently that if we intend also to pick up the object. Usually we perceive the object holistically. But if we intend to act on them, we perceive them more analytically so that we can act in an effective way (Ganel and Goodale 2003).

The influence of memory on perception, on the other hand, has been shown by a number of experiments such as those on the visual perception of fragmented and incoherent images which, after having been identified with a given object, are then easily recognised using the previously memorised pattern.

As these examples clearly show, top-down elaboration of perceptive stimuli often tends to add something which was not present in the stimulus itself: some internal constructive process mediates between the entry stimulus and the perceptive result. This can lead to an improvement or to a decline in the reliability and truth of the perception, depending on the kind of perception and on individual mnemonic patterns.

Moreover, a trade-off phenomenon between rapidity and reliability of perception is evident. Strong emotions, such as desires and fears, generally related to primary needs, lead to an improvement in perception rapidity to the detriment of reliability. Partial correspondence of some portion of the perceptive stimulus with a memorised pattern having a high affective value is enough to produce a strong activation of the pattern itself and thus the recognition of the perception. For example, the child with an intense desire to see his mother will recognise her face in other women's features. At a pragmatic level such a phenomenon can have a positive value, but this is not always the case as far as the reliability and accuracy of our perception of reality are concerned and it is responsible for the production of false beliefs. Here too, the presence of such a phenomenon will be related to the particular emotional and affective constitution of the individual.

Another fundamental component of the correctness of informational inputs of perceptive rationality is related to the mechanisms of memory. The fact that an individual holds a belief now does not imply that he will in the future. This depends on mnemonic power. In the same way, if a man has a belief today, because he thinks he has had it some time ago, it is not certain that his belief is the same. That will depend on the accuracy and reliability of memorisation mechanisms. The corpus of beliefs, the factual foundation of rationality, depends therefore on memory. As we know, memory can be subdivided into three sections: besides the memory of sensory information which does not concern us here, there is short-term memory, where a small part of rapidly disappearing information can be stored and where the operational centre of the information processing is located, and long-term memory, which is the filing cabinet of information, with virtually unlimited capacity. I do not address myself here to the question whether short-term memory exists separately from long-term memory or corresponds to states activated by it. The first consideration to make concerns which database is used in the inference. Various experiments, as well as everyday observation, clearly show that the factual database used often corresponds only to a part of the beliefs available in long-term memory and useful for inferences (Sternberg 2009). People cannot gain access to a significant part of their knowledge and consequently the resulting inferences are generally wrong. Sometimes the individual cannot connect all elements, useful for inference, existing in his memory. The holistic theses of some authors, like Quine and Harman, are therefore problematic, since according to them inductive inference must have all the corpus of earlier beliefs as a premise. If inference is a causal process in which the premises must be causally operative in producing a new belief then, at a psychological level, only activated beliefs and not residual ones will be causally operative. At the root of the problem of belief activation is apparently the codification process which determines the communications through which activation spreads through the mnemonic network. Man codifies information in a semantic structure which goes beyond individual information. This can happen both at the time when the informative input presents itself and when the information is retrieved through memory. This often leads to a diminished reliability of memory. For example, people tend to use information after an event to construct the memory of the event itself. Moreover, one is not always able to make out the original sources of information.

Associated to memory we find the irrational phenomenon of perseverance in the belief, carefully studied by Nisbett and Ross (1980). People are inclined to preserve a belief even after it has been proved false by new evidential data.

The reason for this perseverance can be found in the emotional refusal of new beliefs, deemed unsatisfactory, and in the search for factual validation of old beliefs through the retrieval of supporting information from memory. This phenomenon seems to be, among other things, at the root of the confirmation bias, a phenomenon studied by the cognitive psychology of science, which points in the opposite direction to Popper's falsification rule (Johnson Laird 1983).

There is also another characteristic of memory which goes against the rational principle of revision of beliefs in the face of new informational data. According to psychologists, long-term memory is not a blackboard from which propositions can be wiped out on the basis of new evidence. On the contrary, there seems to be no real loss of informational material from memory unless as a result of physical damage. Every piece of information memorised, and every belief acquired, is stored in memory and cannot be erased even after it has been proved false. If information cannot be erased from memory, it will contain contradictions and time structures. The wrong steps worked out while solving a problem will be memorised together with the correct ones and may be recalled when the solution of the problem is repeated. Residual beliefs can, like the phoenix, always revive from long-term memory through a semantic interference with other beliefs causing an incorrect and incoherent response. It is clear that also in the case of memory the tendency to incoherence or to accuracy of beliefs will show individual degrees of variation.

4.5 Minimal Model of the Social Actor and Rationality of Beliefs

In view of this overview of cognitive deficits relating to the logical coherence, factual reliability and deductive completeness of perception and memory, is it still possible to sustain the thesis of a priori rationality? What general model of rationality emerges from such a variegated picture? Some a priorist might respond that the aim is not to put forward a general model of rationality, but that each individual, whatever his particular level of incoherence, factual unreliability and deductive incompleteness, is a rational being given that he is an intentional and talking agent.

If we can agree that, ultimately, every criterion for rationality and truth, including the truth of logic, stems from human intuition, this does not detract from the fact that a rationality theory of this kind is of no use whatsoever for the social sciences.

It is well known that every scientist needs to construct concepts in which the predicative field is greater than the field of empirical proof. The idealisation of a concept serves to allow descriptions and predictions about singular facts to be derived, using the appropriate initial conditions.

Now, to sustain that the field of proof for rationality is represented by the cognitive features of all thinking and talking humans means removing, de facto, all heuristic and explicative function from rationality, and even to deny that the term has a theoretical role.

So what are the theoretical characteristics of the concept of rationality of beliefs that allow it to fulfil the heuristic, descriptive and predictive functions? This can be solved by specifying two elements: (1) the general conditions of rationality of beliefs; (2) the actor model for rationality of beliefs.

1. The principal condition of rationality of beliefs is that the factual base, the corpus of beliefs, is founded, and corresponds, as reliably as possible, to the real world. Clearly, the danger of this assertion is that it involves us in epistemological problems of a theory of truth or likelihood. Undoubtedly, however, the act of referring to epistemic terms, like degree of confirmation, burden of proof, the accuracy and reliability of the factual base, and correspondence to the real world, inevitably recalls the notion of truth. The assumption underlying the concept proposed here is that the truth being studied is distinct from the processes of empirical control. This position refers to a theory of truth known as metaphysical realism. For Dummett (1982, p. 55) realism implies that a given class of assertions are related to a reality that exists independently of our knowledge of it, so that reality makes each assertion of the class true or false, even though we are not in a position to know or discover its truth value. Dummett's position is characterised by the principle of "verification-transcendent truth"; an assertion is true or false irrespective of our knowledge and verification of it. Verification is not an epistemic matter. Indeed, in order to verify a proposition our senses must receive information about the object to which the proposition refers. However, there may be distorting effects in the environment in which the information is conveyed or the brain may not be

constructed to register the information completely or correctly. So, it might happen that a proposition is true although we are not in a position to verify it. The function of verification is therefore the one proposed by Wimsatt (1981), Campbell and Cook (1979) and Levins (1968). Our conception of reality is the conception of something robust, an object or property that is invariant under multiple modes of detection. The use of multiple procedures, methods or assumptions to get at the same putative object, trait, or regularity is commonplace in individual cognitive experience and in science. For example, we use different perceptual modalities to observe the same object, or the same sense to observe the object from different perspectives and under different observational circumstances; we use different experimental procedures to verify the same empirical relations, that is alternative procedures are used to 'valididate' one another; different assumptions, models or axiomatisations are normally used to derive the same result; we use agreement of different tests, scales or indices as a sign of validity of a trait-construct; lastly, we seek matches and convergence of theoretical description of a given system at different levels of organisation and aggregation. This need for *triangulation* is based on the assumption that the truths about the object under study are distinct from the processes of verification or control.

Any particular method yields putative information because of its own peculiarities, its biases and distortions. Triangulation serves to correct such biases in order to know the real properties of the phenomenon being studied. Truth as correspondence to reality can be well expressed by the following metaphor used by Alvin Goldman (1986): unlike the metaphor of truth as a mirror of precategorised nature, truth can be seen as a garment that is tailor-made to fit reality using a variety of instruments. The styles, and also the categories, produced by man, may vary and differ, what is important is that they achieve the result of "clothing" reality.

What implications does this concept have for rationality of beliefs? In perception, man sometimes tends to have a distorted view of the perceptive input and genuine belief can often not emerge in the memory. What hope can we have if the most direct interface between the mind and the world, the guarantee of correspondence between the world and belief, contains errors and distortions? The answer is that if it is true that the path to achieve fittingness with reality is triangulation, then an operating condition for rationality of beliefs is not to raise the question of the epistemic justification of the factual base, but rather the "trial" approach aimed at justifying the formation process of the factual base. In this case, triangulation would entail using all the decision-maker's cognitive, heuristic and methodological resources, critically and cross-referenced, in line with the techniques identified by cognitive science. They would be used to construct a corpus of beliefs, a factual base that has a reliability and likelihood that has been produced and verified independently by different cognitive processes. For example, if we are aware of dealing with contextual situations (as in the case of patterns with high affective value), with a distorting effect of the top-down processes on perceptive input, then, according to the laws of triangulation, it would be best to identify the object of the input using different "perceptive angles" and at different moments of time.

If the corpus of beliefs available to inference has to be complete a triangulation technique adopted to achieve greater completeness is the *depth of processing*. When a person memorises a word, he may link it to other things he knows, forming a denser network of associative connections. The closer integration between the informative input and part of the beliefs already memorised will improve the ability to recovery memory of the input. Moreover, if at the time of memorising an informative input, all the implications of this input are developed towards the other beliefs already memorised, then, when the majority of the information available on a given problem are retrieved from the memory, the completeness of the factual base will become more probable.

Reliability of the factual base can also be achieved by comparing the beliefs, intersubjectively and critically, and refining them by using various measuring instruments or tests and resorting to diversified sources of information. Incoherence and contradiction will certainly be indicators of inaccurate beliefs and must be corrected.

2. Having briefly identified the main condition of perceptive rationality, the question to be asked is how all this can be used by the social sciences? Any predictive theory of the social sciences must appeal to the notion of actor. Clearly, an economic and social actor is an abstract and general concept that, as such, has no predictive and descriptive capacity without the aid of appropriate initial conditions, and in some cases auxiliary assumptions. As we saw earlier in economics, the concept of economic actor was constructed through a strong idealisation of his capacity for memory, coherence, knowledge and calculation. This strong idealisation of the maximiser actor concept has forced neoclassical economists often to introduce auxiliary assumptions to correct the predictions of the theory.

What value can a theory then have that does not allow predictions to be made about the real economic behaviour of man without making *a posteriori* use of suitable conventional stratagems? For example, how could a maximising theory, without empirical assumptions of procedural rationality, explain the commonplace diversionary behaviour used in our everyday games where, in order to improve one's own position, one leads one's rival to believe that one is incapable of assessing the cost of a move so as to persuade him to opt for different and more vulnerable strategies?

As we have seen in the case of rationality of beliefs, and much clearer empirical data are available in the case of cognitive and instrumental rationality, man is a limited being with a limited capacity for active memorisation, reliable beliefs, logical coherence, evidential revision, etc. It is therefore necessary to construct a minimal concept of rationality of beliefs for the human sciences actor who has both a descriptive and prescriptive component. The descriptive component will be used to highlight the lower and upper limits of cognitive performance compared to the epistemic criterion of correspondence between beliefs and reality, as an effect of the cognitive and methodological triangulation process. This will be done by describing the contexts and the optimality and suboptimality conditions of the performances.

The *theory of the minimal actor* in terms of rationality of beliefs would stem from a generalisation of the perceptive and memory performances that reach high limits of reliability and accuracy. The assertions describing the cognitive and environmental conditions in which these performances fall short of optimal will be included, when they occur, as the initial conditions in the explanation. Along with the initial conditions, appropriate additional assumptions will be introduced to describe the causal relations between specific cognitive and environmental conditions and specific reductions in the performances. For example, where the perceptive input is related to patterns with a high affective or emotional value, then it can be supposed that there is a strong possibility that the top-down process is distorting the perceptive input and provoking suboptimal performances. Therefore, in addition to the initial conditions describing the perceptive input in question, additional assumptions will also be introduced which describe the perceptive distortion in the presence of patterns with a high emotional value.

Clearly, as in every scientific theory involving man, there will always be individual variability. However, this variability will not prevent relatively accurate predictions and descriptions being made about the factual base of the human decision-maker. Furthermore, in conclusion, the generalisation of the cognitive processes that allows the factual base to be used in highly accurate and reliable performances also has the prescriptive significance of promoting the maintenance of high levels of reliability and accuracy of the factual base by utilising subjective and intersubjective triangulation procedures in order to construct and verify beliefs.

Brain, Mind and Social Action

5

5.1 Introduction

The aim of social sciences is to understand[1] human behavior (Taylor 1985). Whether setting out to explain an institution like marriage, an organization like a political party or a practice such as cheerleading in sport, the starting point is always the same: to understand the significance of such phenomena for the individual and how, beginning from a single action, they have been generated or could be generated through the aggregation or interaction of multiple actions.

Consequently, one of the most important concerns of contemporary philosophy of social sciences is the relationship between the researcher and human behavior, specifically the modality employed by the social researcher to understand or predict the actions of a social agent through the identification of her mental states.

This is not a new theme. Max Weber (1949) had already been influential in describing the main problems in the relationship between the researcher and social action. The researcher attempts to identify empathetically with the agent's mental life, pinpointing the reasons and motivations that caused him to act in a certain manner. In so doing, he also requires essential information about the setting in which the agent acted. Contextual information, together with specific psychological information about the agent, permits a more precise, more realistic process of

[1] This paper uses the term understanding (*Verstehen*) as a synonym for explanation (*Erklären*) without claiming the necessity and universality typical of the analytical and neopositivist tradition (Von Wright 1971).

This chapter is a new version of: Viale, R. (2009). Neurosociology, mindreading, and mindfeeling: how the social scientist explains social action. In M. Cherkaoui & P. Hamilton (Eds.), *Raymond boudon: A life in sociology*. Oxford: Bardwell Press. With kind permission from the Publishers; Viale, R. (2011). Brain reading social action. *International Journal of Economics*, Springer-Verlag. DOI: 10.1007/s12232-011-0130-0; Viale, R. Cognizione sociale e neuroni specchio. *Sistemi Intelligenti*, n. 2, (in corso di pubblicazione).

R. Viale, *Methodological Cognitivism*,
DOI 10.1007/978-3-642-24743-9_5, © Springer-Verlag Berlin Heidelberg 2012

verstehen,[2] or understanding of the action. This investigative approach is adopted for both predictive analysis and retrodictive analysis. In predictive analysis, of particular interest to economists, the researcher attempts to predict the agent's behavior by identifying with the agent's mental life, determining his beliefs and goals and inferring his choice of action from them. In retrodictive analysis, favored in particular by sociologists or anthropologists, the researcher uses the action as a basis to reconstruct the possible underlying beliefs and desires, in other words, the meaning of the action. What principle guides the researcher in inferring a choice of action from particular beliefs and desires of the agent or in reconstructing the beliefs and desires that caused an action? Through the identification process, the researcher should be able to intercept the inferential principles guiding the agent, even when those principles differ from his own. As when dealing with members of other cultures or other psychic groups, like the immature or deviants, the researcher should quarantine his own principles of inferential rationality and identify those of the agent. Cognitive identification and simulation is the necessary premise to understand an action and generalize it into an ideal-type representing aggregate social behavior or a social phenomenon.

5.2 Problems in Mindreading

Weber's analysis introduces, albeit with a different terminology, the main topics of interest to contemporary philosophy of social sciences in the debate on the relationship between researcher and social behavior. These are the problems that characteristically arise in mindreading, to use another terminology, as the social researcher attempts to identify the causes of an action or to predict it. The objectives of the researcher's mindreading are largely theoretical, unlike those of mindreading in everyday life, which are essentially practical.[3] In theory, moreover, mindreading by the social researcher should be conscious and intentional, whereas mindreading by the layman should often be an automatic, unconscious process. In practice, as we shall see, the neuropsychological mechanisms and modalities active in mindreading are so powerful and pervasive that they are probably common to both the researcher

[2] The paper distinguishes between empathy (E*infühlung*), a psychological process of identification with the subject's mental states, and understanding (V*erstehen*), the ability to determine, through analysis of the context and empathy, the reasons that led the subject to act in a certain manner. Another German term exists, E*rlebnis* (sympathetic repetition of the experience); this refers more specifically to the simulation of propositional attitudes, while empathy is a more appropriate term for simulation of emotions and feelings. Another way to separate the emotional from the cognitive identification is to characterize cognitive empathy and emotional empathy. In the first the identification and simulation is about propositional attitudes whereas in the second the identification and simulation is about emotions and feelings.

[3] This distinction is not acceptable to advocates of Theory Theory (Gopnik and Meltzoff 1997) and others who maintain that the layman and the scientist employ the same type of deductive hypothetical activity to build theories about the world.

and the layman. On this point, studies of mindreading cover a variety of questions. Of these, four interrelated topics are of particular interest for our analysis:

1. *Theory Mindreading Versus Simulation Mindreading*. In studying social action, the researcher tries to reconstruct the mental process that led or could lead the agent to act in a certain way. There are various candidates for her mindreading, which may be conducted with one of three main methods: through simulation by the researcher of the target's mental states; through theoretical inference of the target's mental states based on a folk psychology theory; through inference of the target's mental states based on a scientific theory. There are two theories about the first method, simulation mindreading: according to the first theory (Goldman 2006), the researcher sets out to identify and then assume the target's mental states, processing them mentally to derive an output in the form of action or another mental state and then project the result on to the target; according to the second theory (Gordon 1995), the researcher-mindreader makes a re-centering of the egocentric map or "egocentric shift". He transforms himself into the target and experiences his mental states. With the second method, the researcher identifies the target's mental states and applies folk psychology theory to them to derive an output in the form of action or another mental state of the target. With the third method, he uses the models of a theory (e.g., neoclassical economics or discourse theory or social identity theory) to identify the target's mental states, processes these mental states on the basis of the theory's concepts and assumptions, and derives an output in the form of action or another mental state.
2. *Mindreading Versus Mindfeeling*. Through mindreading, the researcher aims to identify the mental states directly responsible for an action. So his attention will focus largely on propositional attitudes like beliefs, desires, decisions, plans, hopes. Mindreading of these mental states typically takes place at conscious level with a certain degree of willpower (Goldman 2006, p. 147). The reader may interrupt, slow down or speed up the reading. He can decide which mental states to include in or exclude from the reading process. He has a partially clear conscious idea of the various steps in the reading process. In the relationship between mindreader and target, however, the target's mental states are also read at another level. This level corresponds to emotional empathy (or with a new term *mindfeeling)* reading of sensations like feelings and pain and of emotions like disgust and anger. The characteristics of this low-level mindreading (Goldman 2006) differ from those of the first type of mindreading. It is an automatic reading, independent of the will. The reading is often not conscious, although subsequently it may become so when we become aware of its effect. We cannot govern the process. In part, we can reproduce it mentally through a re-enactment of the image that caused the sensation or emotion.
3. *Normative A Priori Attribution Versus Empirical A Posteriori Attribution*. What principle does the researcher adopt when mindreading and processing the target's choice of action? In trying to make sense of his target, the attributor "will try for a theory that finds him consistent, a believer of truths, and a lover of the good" (Davidson 1980, p. 253). Dennett advances a similar thesis (1987). In attributing propositional attitudes to a target, the attributor's reading will be

based on precepts of rationality and normativity, in other words, he will adopt an "*intentional stance*":

> First you decide to treat the object whose behavior is to be predicted as a rational agent; then you figure out what beliefs that agent ought to have, given its place in the world and its purpose. Then you figure out what desires it ought to have, on the same considerations, and finally you predict that this rational agent will act to further its goals in the light of its beliefs. (Dennett 1987, p. 17).

According to Davidson and Dennett, mindreading is possible if the mental states are identified on the basis of a priori normative principles. Without such principles, reconstruction of the reasons for the target's action is impossible. Likewise, some contributions from social psychology (Hamilton and Sherman 1996) and pragmatics of language (Grice 1989) highlight attributors' tendency to adopt principles of consistency, wholeness of information and truth in understanding or predicting others' actions. In interpreting the meaning of a discourse, the listener often produces a particular mindreading whereby, according to the *principle of cooperation* and one of the consequent conversational theoretical maxims such as quality and quantity, hidden linguistic content is attributed to the speaker through what Grice calls "*conversational implicatures*". But what happens when we deal with people from other cultures, with liars, with mental deviants, with Dadaist and surrealist artists, with creative imaginative people who do not apply our normative principles? And can we exclude variability in principles of rationality, truth and consistency? The plurality of rationality principles is a theme familiar to social and cognitive scientists, from Simon's bounded rationality (1982, 2000) to the adaptive rationality of Gigerenzer et al. (1999). In the same way, truth does not have a single interpretation, but depends on context variables and on cognitive and perceptual feasibility (Goldman 1986; Viale 2001a). Finally, consistency of beliefs presupposes deductive closure and the inconsistency avoidance of beliefs, an objective beyond the cognitive reach of the individual. Thus, in contrast to normative a priori attribution we have empirical a posteriori attribution, which aims during the mindreading process to identify the principles governing mental state attribution and action prediction, whilst avoiding Quine's inscrutability-of-reference problem (1960). Quine despaired of the possibility that we can infer the specific content of the mental states of a target. The only way is to bootstrap from our mental states and to proceed by empathetic imaginative projection (McGee 2005). To do this, the social attributor must avoid projecting his own normative principles and concentrate on the target's life, history, reference context and empirical data, using this inductive knowledge and active imagination to attribute a posteriori the principles used by the target (in a similar fashion to Quine in his attempt to understanding the meaning of Gavagoi, a word uttered by a member of some strange tribe on seeing a rabbit, when we are not familiar with the tribe's language or the principles that establish the meaning of the words it uses).

4. *Predictive Versus Retrodictive Mindreading*. Studies of social action fall into two main epistemic categories. In the first category, the social mindreader's goal is to predict the agent's action by identifying the mental states responsible for it.

In the second category, given a specific action, the mindreader sets out to understand the mental states that caused it. All the social sciences are interested in both types of epistemic goal, but whereas economics focuses predominantly on predictive objectives, sociology, anthropology and, obviously, history are more concerned with retrodictive objectives. The two types of mindreading involve different kinds of difficulty. The predictive approach often has no certain information from which to begin, and must pay greater attention to situational and contextual information in order to imagine the mental states – beliefs and desires in particular – from which to derive the prediction. The retrodictive approach has a clear starting point, the action. In theory, therefore, the mindreading process should be easier since the action, according to some economists like Samuelson, is a revealed preference. This makes it easier to infer the other propositional attitudes responsible for the action. However, this simplification by neoclassical economics fails to take account of the fact that behavior often deviates, to a greater or lesser extent, from the agent's preferences. Moreover, backward mindreading is psychologically a different process from forward mindreading. In this sense, the epistemic objectives of predictive mindreading and retrodictive mindreading are not symmetrical.[4]

5.3 Philosophies of Social Sciences and Mindreading

Three philosophical approaches to these fundamental problems in mindreading can be identified in the social sciences:

1. *Normative Intentional Approach.* This is the mainstream approach in analysis of social action. Commonly used in economics and its applications (Downs 1957; Olson 1965; Coleman 1990), the normative intentional approach holds that mindreading should focus on the propositional attitudes responsible for an action in order to predict or explain it. To do this, it has to begin from an explicative theory about social action (e.g., Downs' economic theory of democracy, Samuelson's consumer theory or Olson's theory of collective action) or at the very least from a folk psychology theory. In reconstructing the relationship between beliefs, desires and action, a rationality principle must always be assumed a priori (Elster 1983), as well as, depending on the author, a truth and consistency principle. The normative principle together with knowledge about the decisional context will enable the action to be explained or predicted. Some authors including Popper (1972) believe the rationality principle postulated a priori should be attributed automatically to every action once the situation that

[4] This epistemic and cognitive asymmetry has nothing to do with Hempel and Popper's philosophy of science thesis on the symmetry between explanation and prediction in both natural and social science (Hempel 1965). Epistemic asymmetry relates to context of discovery, while the asymmetry between prediction and explanation postulated by philosophy of science relates to context of justification, according to Popper and neopositivist stance.

generated it is known (situational logic). Conversely, Pareto (1944) and the neoclassical economists adopt a narrow version of rationality, excluding all choices that fail to match its a priori principles (e.g., maximization of expected subjective utility). The epistemological objective is symmetrical with the prediction and explanation of social action, beginning from the symmetry of predictive and retrodictive mindreading and from the possibility that the prediction and explanation can be generalized to multiple individuals, based on the normative approach and knowledge of the situational context.

2. *Cognitive Approach.* The cognitive approach presents a series of important subtle differences with respect to the normative intentional approach. It is common to several authors, notably Weber (1949), Simon (1982, 2000) and Boudon (1984, 1993a, 1993b). It too focuses on mindreading of high-level propositional attitudes (with the exception of *methodological cognitivism* that has a broad interpretation of cognition including also emotion and sensation). The area of interest to this approach is the level of representation of the problem, of definition of goals, of the choice of the means to achieve the goals or solve the problem. Attribution of mental states always begins from a general theory such as Information Processing Psychology for Simon or Folk Psychology for Boudon. However, no normative rationality principle is applied a priori to predict or explain the action (apart from the very general pragmatic type of principle whereby to achieve/resolve an objective/problem, a method/solution appropriate to the purpose/problem is sought[5]). The objective is to define a posteriori, using an empirical approach that analyzes the agent's history, context and cultural characteristics, the particular *good reasons* (Boudon 1984, 1993a; Boudon & Viale 2000) that led the agent to act in a certain way. Or, to use Simon's terminology, to identify the subjective level of psychological satisfaction that led the agent to choose an action because he considered it "*satisficing*" for attainment of his goal (to use Gigerenzer's terminology, the most adaptive solution for the problematic context). Levels of satisfaction, like types of reason, may vary slightly from one individual to another in the same culture, but they will vary radically from one culture to another. It therefore seems possible, although greater caution is required, that retrodictive mindreading can be adopted in order to develop general explanations for social action. Whereas, given the greater difficulties of predictive mindreading, the possibility of making a general prediction about action is more remote.
3. *Hermeneutic Approach.* This approach draws on a part of the Hermeneutics school (Schleiermacher 1998; Dilthey 2002; Gadamer 1960, It. Transl. 1972) and on Interpretation Theory (Geertz 1973; Taylor 1985), and differs

[5] As Elisabeth Anscombe maintains (Anscombe 1957), this minimal pragmatic rationality principle could take us back to Aristotle's *practical syllogism*, described in the *Nicomachean Ethics*: the starting point, or major premise, of the syllogism refers to a goal, or the purpose of an action; the minor premise links an action with this goal, more or less with a means-end relationship; the conclusion is the use of the means to achieve the end.

significantly from the two mindreading approaches described above. First of all, the *verstehen* objective of the hermeneutic approach leads it to attempt empathy through 360°. The social scientist's mindreading considers not only the target's propositional attitudes but also his emotions and sensations. For Dilthey (2002), understanding occurs when the interpreter is able to recognize the inner state of another by means of that other person's empirical expressions. For example, on seeing a facial expression the interpreter understands the emotional state of the other. The only way to do this is through simulation. Of the two simulation models, the method centered on the mindreader is generally preferred. In some cases, some authors also favor the second method, centered on the target. For example, Schleiermacher writes that "The *divinatory* method is the one in which one, so to speak, transforms oneself into the other person and tries to understand the individual element directly" (1998, p. 92). But he adds immediately that although one cannot actually place oneself in the thinking of the other, one can guess or intuit how the other thought by comparison to how one thinks oneself, since every person "has a receptivity for all other people" (Schleiermacher 1998, p. 93). This receptivity is based "on the fact that everyone carries a minimum of everyone else within themselves, and divination is consequently excited by comparison with oneself" (Schleiermacher 1998, p. 93). In trying to place oneself in the position of the other whose thoughts are freely flowing, one tries oneself to freely associate from one idea to another, and this could lead to the other idea that the author had. The interpreter then can project by analogy the associations that the other person might have had. In simulating mental states and choices, the interpreter does not assume a priori normative principles, but attempts to understand the principles that guided or might guide action by identifying with the life of the subject and through active imagination. According to Dilthey, there are two modes of "active re-creating or re-experiencing" (2002, p. 235) the states of the other person. One mode is that the presentation of the milieu and external situation aids in re-experiencing. The second mode is that "imagination can increase or diminish the intensity of attitudes, powers, feelings, strivings, and thought tendencies that characterize our own life-nexus in order to recreate the psychic life of any other person" (Dilthey 2002, p. 236). By virtue of both its genesis from interpretation of literary and historical texts and its epistemological objectives, the hermeneutic approach favors retrodictive rather than predictive mindreading. As Geertz points out (Geertz 1973), the objective of human sciences is to interpret the meaning of an action as represented mentally by the agent. Since every action is a culturally unique action, a predictive approach is not possible.[6]

[6] This claim differentiates the hermeneutic approach from the mindreading of everyday life. Contrary to Geertz claim in everyday life people tend to predict often the third person behaviours. The theory of mind is used for mindreading in order, mainly, to make predictions more than retrodictions of third person action.

5.4 Brain-Driven Social Scientist Mindreading and Neurosociology

Mindreading has an important role in social research. It is the necessary premise for an understanding of the meaning of social action and, according to some authors, for construction of a general ideal-type for the action and related explicative theory. The main social science methodologies envisage a stage of field research for mindreading purposes. Even when this is not possible, for example in historical research, or not explicitly contemplated, as in statistical sociology, a form of indirect, implicit mindreading always takes place. Consider for instance the reconstruction of the reasons for the action of historical figures through study of historical documents, or the simulation by the researcher drawing up a sociological questionnaire of the possible options that can be chosen by the social agent.[7]

The previous section outlined the main philosophical positions of the social sciences with regard to mindreading. This section attempts to analyze those positions in light of the constraints and restrictions on mindreading highlighted by neurocognitive research, above all by mirror neuron theory. Neurocognitive research has not yet examined social scientist mindreading at experimental level, so its indications are obviously based on analogy. In short, we have no data comparing attribution of mental content in mindreading by a social scientist studying social behavior with mindreading in everyday social interaction. I shall analyze the various points with reference to the previous paragraphs:

1. *The Predominance of Simulation*. In conducting empirical research, the social scientist, like every other scientist, is generally conditioned by the theories of his field and his background knowledge. Observations are "theory laden" said Karl Popper and, later, Feyerabend and the philosophers, sociologists and psychologists of science have done nothing but confirm this. If that is the case, then identification of the mental states that caused an individual to act in a certain way should be based on theoretical inferences. Knowledge of the decisional context and the agent's behavioral patterns together with the theoretical models of the researcher's discipline should permit inference to the best explanation of the mental states responsible for the action. From a normative viewpoint, however, interpretation of mental states on the basis of the models of the theory under control is not ideal. A reconstruction of the causes of an action using the theoretical assumptions of the theory under control would not provide any genuine information to confirm or disprove the theory. It would probably end up as simply another case of "confirmation bias". To avoid this epistemological illusion, the social scientist ought to quarantine his theory and develop

[7] The application of neuroscience of mindreading might be both in analyzing the social behavior (neurosociology) and in analyzing the behavior of the social scientist studying the social behavior (neuromethodology of social sciences). Data and reflections of this chapter have been applied both to neurosociology and to neuromethodology of social sciences.

his mindreading with the least possible conditioning from theoretical models and preconceptions. It would be best if mental state attribution and the processing of a course of action realistically corresponded, as far as possible, to what happened or will happen in the target's head, without any idiosyncratic or theoretical distortions on the part of the mindreader. Is this possible? And if so, how?

According to Theory Theory (TT) (Premack and Woodruff 1978), attribution of other people's mental states is possible only through construction and development of a theory.[8] Our mental states and others' mental states are unobservables empirically linked, in the first case, with sensorial input and, in the second, with external behavior and action, and consequently any attribution is of a theoretical nature. On the basis of these theoretical entities, beginning in infancy we build our theoretical assumptions on third person's mental activity and first person's mental activity. Thus, every time we mindread a target, we apply a Hempel model where our theory, generally a more or less complex version of folk psychology, represents the major premise of the explanans. By analogy this deductive hypothetical activity also takes place in social research. In order to identify the causes of a social agent's action, the mindreading on the various individuals will be guided deductively by the folk theory and its concepts. The mindreading will lead to the development of the scientific hypothesis under investigation. At the same time, the folk theory that guided the mindreading will be enhanced with new conceptual details relating to the mental states the scientist has just analyzed. So on one hand every theory the researcher builds about the social action from his mindreading is a technical development of the folk theory. On the other, the folk theory itself changes as a result of the mindreading, developing conceptually. Ultimately, a biunivocal causal interaction is created between the two theories. It will be difficult to work without the social theory the next time we check it in order to disprove it, confirm it or develop it further. Even if we could activate some form of inhibitory quarantine enabling us to do without the social theory, we would still have to use the extended folk theory now incorporating part of the social theory. If Theory Theory is right, theory-free control of social action theories is not possible. But is Theory Theory right?

As Goldman has convincingly shown (2006), various experimental cognitive and neuroscientific findings appear to diminish the theoretical importance of TT in mental attribution.

(a) First of all, experimental findings on false-belief task performance, appearance-reality, deception in children indicate the weakness of TT as a mental attribution theory in developmental psychology. Successful performance in false-belief tasks, i.e., attribution to another person of a belief that is false

[8] Unlike the empirical law that refers to terms and concepts denoting empirically observable or measurable entities, the theory refers to theoretical entities that may be empirically controlled not directly, but indirectly through experimental bridge laws.

with respect to what we see, requires an ability to inhibit reference to reality and to identify instead with the other's thought processes. Studies have found that inhibitory control is an executive ability that enables someone to override dominant tendencies. Birch and Bloom (2003) recently showed a correlation between childhood improvement in false-belief task performance between 3 and 5 years and relevance of inhibitory control. Based on a wide-range study on false-belief tasks and inhibitory control and other studies on the role of the frontal lobes in development of both mindreading activity and executive control functioning activity, Carlson and Moses (2001) suggest that inhibitory control and mindreading attainments share a common developmental timetable and a common brain region and their joint absence appears to yield autism (Goldman 2006, p. 198).

(b) One of the cornerstones of TT, the theoretical aspect of mental states, has been questioned by a series of studies on first person attribution. There is asymmetry between the access to third person and first person mental states. The access to first person mental states resembles the visual perception. The representation of mental types is direct 'perception-like recognition process in which a given occurrent token is mapped into mental category selected from a relatively smallish number of types' (Goldman 2006, p. 253). The representation of mental content instead utilizes the redeployment (and in the case of visual format the translation from visual code to belief code) of the content already present in mind to produce the content assignment contained in the metarepresentation. (Goldman 2006, p. 254). This model of introspective self-attribution supporting a strong asymmetry between first person and third person attribution seems to be supported by neuroscientific data. Craig (2002) proposal of *interoception* that is the perception of the physiological condition of the entire body seem to rely on the "interoceptive cortex" a dedicated thalamocortical relay nucleus, the posterior part of ventromedial nucleus or VMpo. Embedded in VMpo there are the representations of several distinct sensations, like pain, temperature, muscular and visceral sensations, and so on, that are mediated by different classes of neurons. The introspection, according Goldman (2006, p. 252), is the meta-representation and classification of those perceptions. This neural mechanism is dedicated to sensations-type and not for propositional attitudes. In any case it proves the introspection as perception-like recognition process and opposes the theoretical feature of first person attribution maintained by TT.

Therefore if first person attribution is perception-like, through empirical recognition and "observation" of one's own mental states, the individual is able to mindread the mental states of a third person by reproducing them in his own mind, in other words by simulating them. Direct reading of one's own mental states, therefore, is a prerequisite for simulative reading of others' mental states. Furthermore, social researchers know that self-reflection is the source of the main intuitions regarding an hypothesis as well as its first test-bed. If the researcher is free to simulate the relationship between mental states and action directly in his own mind without reference to a folk theory, he will have a better chance to catch genuine features of the causes of the social action.

(c) A reliable mindreading of the target's mental states requires the researcher to put aside his theoretical models and idiosyncratic positions and simulate those of the target without distortions. The greater the match between the two states, the greater the cognitive value of mindreading. As we have seen, TT rejects the possibility of theory-free reading. Simulation theory, on the other hand, regards it as one of its distinguishing characteristics. This is not to say there are no egocentric tendencies nor that the mental state content is that of the target. Specifically, there appears to be evidence that:
   - Mindreading in everyday life has a tendency to make egocentric attributions with regard to knowledge (Camerer et al. 1989), preferences (van Boven et al. 2000), feelings (Van Boven and Loewenstein 2003). Behavioral economics offers extensive literature on this point.
   - In attributing propositional content, the attributor necessarily takes his personal conceptual and ontological constructs as a basis. Even if the way he builds the representation and derives the inference tends to correspond with that of the target, the building blocks are those of the mindreader. Generally speaking, in a given culture the same building blocks are used. For example, the Western world shares a common ontology of objects (Soya et al. 1991). Difficulties arise when, as in the case of anthropologists, contact is made with other cultures where, for example, color ontology envisages only two colors, black and white (Berlin and Kay 1969); or when, as Nisbett and his team have shown for Chinese culture (2003), society favors a holistic metaphysic rather than the individual-oriented view prevalent in the West. In cases like these, where the building blocks differ so greatly, mindreading is impossible until the nature of the differences has been clarified. Once generalizations about the target's conceptual exoticity have been processed, then mindreading guided by those generalizations is possible.

   Nevertheless, neurophysiological tests have found mechanisms in the brain that inhibit egocentric tendencies during mindreading (Goldman 2006, pp. 170–172). Samson et al. (2005) describe the case of a patient, WBA, who presented a lesion in the right inferior and middle frontal gyri extending into the right superior temporal gyrus. This area seems to be involved in the ability to inhibit one's own perspective (Vogeley et al. 2001). During the tests Samson et al. performed on WBA, the patient showed continual problems in executive control and self-perspective inhibition, and consequently made egocentric errors in many mindreading tasks. He failed false-belief tasks requiring high inhibition of personal knowledge in attribution of the false belief. The findings seem to indicate that a specific area of the brain is responsible for self-perspective inhibition, a vital function if the mindreader is to quarantine his egocentric projective tendencies. When the mindreader is a social scientist, a double effort is required: to quarantine egocentrism and to inhibit the interpretative role of the scientist's professional knowledge, in particular of the social theory for which he is performing the mindreading. The scientist may be unable to achieve this dual inhibition by himself and may require external aids to conduct a critique of his personal viewpoint in order to quarantine it. This could take the form of intersubjective comparisons with other researchers or, better still, with non-experts using the three-step mindreading procedure proposed by Goldman (2006, p. 170) on the basis of Gilbert et al. (2002).

> They first imagine events without temporal information ("atemporal representation"). Next, they use their hedonic reactions to these mental images ("proxy reactions") as the basis for a preliminary prediction. Third, they correct or adjust their preliminary forecast by explicitly considering the target event's temporal location ("temporal correction").

In other words, predictive mindreading would use the result that maximizes intersubjective convergence on the result of the three-step procedure (a similar method could be proposed for retrodictive mindreading, too). To sum up the Simulation Theory seems to be superior compared to TT in explaining the mindreading. There is the possibility for a social scientist to quarantine her egocentric bias and theoretical schemes in order to simulate and mindread the social actor (also with the support of the three step procedure). The possibility of a partial theory-free mindreading seems to support the hermeneutic approach and to condemn the normative intentional one.

2. *The Mindreading Iceberg*. The main approaches in social sciences favor mindreading at the level of propositional attitudes. Understanding or predicting an action requires mindreading of the mental states – beliefs, desires and intentions – responsible for the action. This is achieved through conscious, intentional metarepresentation of the target's mental states by the attributor, using folk psychology theory. Forms of automatic, unconscious reading of intentional mental states are not contemplated nor does reading of emotions and sensation play an important part. This is the thesis shared by the normative and cognitive approaches in social sciences and advocated by TT. Recent neuroscientific research, however, appears to show otherwise. Recent studies on a human cortical network composed of the rostral part of the inferior parietal lobule and the caudal sector of the inferior frontal gyrus plus the adjacent part of the premotor cortex (Rizzolatti et al. 2001) found a type of neuron, the *mirror neuron*, that seems to intermediate automatic unconscious attribution of intentional content to a third person observed in action. When we see *transitive* hand/arm gestures (involving an object, such as picking up a cup) or *intransitive* hand/arm gestures (not involving an object, such as a dance step), there is an activation of part of the same motor circuits that are recruited when we ourselves perform that action. The mirror neuron system encodes not only the gesture under observation, but also the intention with which it is performed, as demonstrated by recent research by Iacoboni et al. (2005). Additionally, other studies with fMRI found a functional connection between the areas in the mirror

neurons, the insula and the emotional areas of the limbic system, in particular the amygdala (Carr et al. 2003). The mirror neurons are activated when we see other people expressing emotions as if we ourselves were making those facial expressions. The activated neurons also transmit signals, via the insula, to the emotional cerebral centers of the limbic system, so that we ourselves experience what the person we are watching is experiencing (Iacoboni 2008). Both types of attribution are simulative processes, albeit a type of automatic and unconscious embodied simulation. While cognitive simulation of the intentions behind an action is generally a conscious, voluntary activity (Goldman 2006), like the metarepresentative, disembodied mindreading postulated by TT, the motor-mediated type of action understanding of mirror neuron theory is automatic and unconscious. As is the emotion understanding of others' emotions through the mirror neurons-insula-amygdala viscero-motor mechanism. "*It is likely that other's emotions can also be understood on the basis of the cognitive elaboration of the visual aspects of their expression. (….) It is likely that the direct viscero-motor mechanism scaffolds the cognitive description, and, when the former mechanism is not present or malfunctioning, the latter provides only a pale, detached account of the emotions of the others*"(Gallese et al. 2004, p.). The hypothesis being developed by these studies is that the conscious, voluntary, cognitive component of simulative mindreading of others' actions and emotions is just the tip of the iceberg, whereas most mindreading activity in everyday life is automatic and unconscious, through embodied simulation generated by mirror neurons (for a full description of all the discoveries and implications of mirror neurons, see Rizzolatti and Sinigaglia 2006; Iacoboni 2008). Should this hypothesis be confirmed by future research, it will have a considerable impact on understanding of social action. Embodied simulation of mirror neuron theory is creating difficulties not only for the normative approach, already undermined by the weakening of TT and the other approaches positing theoretical mindreading, but also for the cognitive approach. Cognitive simulative action mindreading often seems to be overridden by automatic, unconscious attribution of intentional content. And this is not just a question of attribution of "a motoric plan" (Gallese and Goldman 1998, p. 498) because the "real attributor does not go back to a distal goal or set of beliefs" (Gallese and Goldman 1998, p. 498), as mirror neuron researchers themselves believed a few years ago. On the contrary, as recent research by Iacoboni et al. (2005) has found, the real attributor does indeed go back to a distal goal or set of beliefs! Moreover, the emphatic resonance might penetrate action understanding in a forceful manner. It might add emotional overtones to the context in which intentional content is automatically attributed to the observed action. The viscero-motor simulation of the emotional expression of the observed subject might enhance the somato-motor simulation of the observed action, providing a better focus on the internal reasons for the action. The hermeneutic approach seems to be the only approach to anticipate and be consistent with the results of research on mirror neuron theory embodied simulation, in particular because of the importance it attaches to emotional and affective simulation and to the corporeality of the simulation.

3. *Bootstrapping from our Reasons.* The fact that a considerable portion of mental state attribution takes place at an automatic, unconscious level does not lighten the mindreading workload for the social scientist. His mindreading activities are often related to field research examining problems of social interaction in everyday life and his own culture, where automatic attribution through embodied simulation could have a significant weight. In these cases, problems of high-level simulation of the inferential principles that generated or could generate an action would not arise. The simulation would be automatic without awareness of the particular inferential principle used. In other cases, however, simulation must necessarily be conscious and voluntary, and at times require metarepresentation of the normative principles enabling attribution. There are two such cases, complete opposites:
   (a) When the target presents predominantly conscious and voluntary rational reasoning.
   (b) "Gavagoi" situations (Quine 1960), where cultural and anthropological differences prevent activation of conscious simulation of the target's mental states.

An example of the first case is the study of a person engaged in a business deal, union negotiations or a political conflict. Before drawing up questionnaires or creating experimental settings, the cognitive economists and social psychologists studying these instances of decision-making should observe real cases or try to mindread players in historical cases. This permits identification of the propositional attitudes and reasoning principles leading to specific decisions and actions. Consider, for example, Allison's reconstruction of the Cuban missile crisis (1971). The researcher can use Allison's reconstruction to attempt a retrodictive simulation of the mental states of the players involved, in this case Kennedy, McNamara and Khrushchev, based on theoretical and general reasoning principles, such as prospect theory (Kahneman and Tversky 1979b). In this way, he can explain the absence of an irrational escalation leading to armed conflict in the Cuban crisis, as opposed to what happened in the Korean war or other episodes in contemporary international politics. The greater the a priori normativity of the reasoning principle applied, as in the case of maximization of subjective expected utility, the lower the reliability of the researcher's understanding of the action. Conversely, the greater the empirical and descriptive range of the principle, as with prospect theory, the greater the likelihood of a correct mindreading of the causes of the action. So in this type of decisional setting, if the researcher has no appropriate empirical hypotheses about reasoning models for the setting under analysis, the most reliable approach is to simulate the target's mental states by applying his own inferential principles and quarantining the a priori rationality models described in the textbooks.

In "Gavagoi" situations, on the other hand, cultural and anthropological differences mean simulation with internal principles of reasoning or with other, external theories of our culture is not possible. In these cases, the embodied simulation of mirror neurons could also prove unreliable. As an automatic, unconscious simulation, it would lead us, on the basis of our previous experience, to attribute intentional content to actions whose reasons have a different cultural and contextual root. In "Gavagoi" situations, the reasons for an action can only be determined through a lengthy, repeated process on multiple subjects, based on simulation and theoretical adjustment of the three-step procedure type (Goldman 2006, p. 170), with E-imagination (enactment imagination) playing a vital role. To conclude, in situations of intense competitive pressure, when the stakes are clear and we have no inferential theories that can be applied to the decisional context, and in situations where there is no cultural overlap, the cognitive approach appears to be the only convincing choice. Bootstrapping from our reasoning principles seems to be the only option in the first case when we have no valid theoretical hypotheses to apply to reasoning in the decisional setting, and in the second case, when the target's principles are inscrutable due to cultural differences. On the contrary an empathetic and corporeal simulation of the type proposed by the hermeneutic approach could take us off track. The relevance of emotional overtones and shades of actions and expressions differs in different cultures. Consequently, the automatic result of embodied simulation mindreading and mindfeeling should be filtered in light of the results of repeated cognitive simulation.

4. *Automatic Retrodictive Mindreading*. According to Goldman (2006), Simulation Theory alone cannot explain retrodictive mindreading. Unless a mental process can run backward, simulation does not seem applicable. Mental processes are by-and-large unidirectional. Therefore a hybrid method that employs generate-and-test strategy can explain retrodictive mindreading. Moreover there is the problem of complex intentional content, where identification of propositional attitudes depends on knowledge of multiple factors such as the subject's behavioral history, the situation in which he acted, the cultural context, and so on. Take reconstruction of the reasons that led an historical figure or politician to act in a certain way, for example Colin Powell's declarations to the United Nations Security Council on the nuclear threat posed by Iraq, or understanding of Alan Greenspan's reasons for introducing a sharp reduction in interest rates despite the risk of a speculative bubble on the real estate markets. From the point of view of the mindreader's attributive possibilities, these actions, and other less widely reported actions characterized by the peculiarity and inferential complexity of the situation, can only be explained with a hybrid simulative-theoretical model. This is the experience of social scientists endeavoring to understand actions in economic, strategic, military, administrative and other spheres.[9] But we also have to consider the broad area of field research into everyday behavior in the scientist's own cultural environment. The suspicion here is that mirror neuron embodied simulation plays a very substantial part. Not only of course in low-level mindreading as Goldman would say (2006), in other words in empathetic

[9] Despite the prevalence of the hybrid model in these situations, a sizeable degree of attribution ability continues to be associated with automatic empathetic simulation. Take, for example the importance of emotional factors in business negotiations (Neale and Bazerman 1991). Researchers studying these phenomena will be dealing not only with intentional non-automatic mindreading, but also with emotional and intentional automatic mindreading, or mirroring.

simulation of emotions and feelings, or emotional mirroring, but also in automatic attribution of intentional content to many actions that are part of everyday behavioral models and important elements in the development of explicative social hypotheses. Consider the majority of situations in our social lives: interaction with family and friends, workplace relations, the family budget, parties, celebrations, deaths, etc.. In all these situations, there is often a script consisting of a variable number of repeated actions, each with a "local" significance stemming from a wider contextual and social significance expressing the actions as a whole. The scripts are common to a specific social community whose members share and learn their meanings. The social sciences have developed various concepts to represent this phenomenonology. Clifford Geertz (1973) introduced the concept of *ritual* – a rule-guided sequence of behavior consecrated by religious meaning (to understand social phenomena such as cock-fighting in Bali or funerals in Java); Victor Turner (1974) proposed the theory of *drama* – an extended interaction between a number of characters over time – which emerges in situations of conflict; Pierre Bourdieau (1977) developed the concept of *practice* – practical, deliberate human action within the context of social, cultural, material constraints – as a framework for interpreting repetitive behavior. Leaving aside their differences, what these concepts have in common is that they all group multiple individual actions within a general frame as an expression of their social meaning. A social researcher who shares these meanings, since he belongs to the same frame community, will observe individual actions and automatically attribute intentional content to them. At this point, the question that corresponds to a possible working hypothesis is this: is it likely that the ability to attribute social significance to an individual action as part of a general frame depends on a superior neuronal interaction within mirror neuron theory, or can it only be explained in a traditional manner, through non-automatic mindreading that voluntarily simulates the meaning of the action? If the answer to the first question is yes, it should be possible to find a superior order of mirror neurons whose function is to control and integrate the other mirror neurons. The experiment by Iacoboni et al. (2005) found that context-dependent action seems to be interpreted automatically through mirror neuron mediation. Another series of tests currently being conducted (Mukamel et al. 2007) seems to confirm the presence of so-called *super* mirror neurons in the orbitofrontal cortex, the anterior cortex of the cingulum and the presupplementary motor area, whose function is inhibitory control of the other mirror neurons. The presupplementary motor area also appears to house mirror neurons capable of organizing simple imitative actions into more complex forms of imitation (Iacoboni 2008, p. 173). If the hypothesis about a superior order of mirror neurons is correct, we would have a neurocognitive basis to justify the possibility of automatic mindreading of the social significance of an action. The countless repeated gestures and acts of a social script would be automatically interpreted with respect to their general higher-order significance, since they would correspond to action models already executed or culturally learned by the observer. This automatic attribution mechanism would be effective only when the social researcher belongs to the same frame community. In this case, the hermeneutic approach, which could now also be called *neural hermeneutics* (Frith 2003), seems to be the philosophical position closest to the mechanism in question. The story changes when different cultural contexts are involved and the frame community is not that of the researcher. Then, automatic mindreading can prove treacherous, leading the researcher into erroneous intentional and emotional content attribution on the basis of inappropriate cultural frames. The social researcher must be able to inhibit, to quarantine these false attributions, and perform predictive and retrodictive mindreading with the cognitive approach, employing intensive use of E-imagination and the three-step simulation procedure.

5.5 Mirror Neurons and Social–Social Cognition

One of the most frequent criticisms leveled at social psychology, first in the behavioral tradition, subsequently in the cognitive tradition, is that it forgets society and looks only at the individual. The paradigmatic position quoted as evidence is Gordon Allport's definition of social psychology:

> The attempt to understand how the thought, feeling, and behavior of individuals are influenced by the actual, imagined, or implied presence of others. (Allport 1985, p. 3)

It is evident from the definition that the "others" tend to be seen as separate, distant entities, mild irritants. The definition mentions the influence of others, but makes no reference to the individual and others as entities that develop mutually. A similar criticism is made of social cognition, that is, current social psychology drawn to the information-processing metaphor.

A recent new edition of a Social Cognition manual makes the following criticism of the individualistic aspect of contemporary social cognition research and concepts:

> Unfortunately the information processing models central to social cognition focus on cognitive processes at the expense of content and context. As such, societal, collective, shared, interactive, and symbolic features of human thought, experience, and interaction are often ignored and forgotten. Contemporary social cognition research is individualistic because it searches within the cognitive and perceptual domain of the person to understand social phenomena such as attitudes, attributions and identity. Social cognition will never explain adequately the totality of human experience so long as it remains at the individual level of analysis alone. (Augoustinos et al. 2006)

This is the position of the main alternative social theories to what we could call Individualistic Social Cognition (ISC): social identity theory (e.g., Tajfel and Turner 1986), social representation theory (e.g., Moscovici 1984; Doise 1986) and discursive psychology (e.g., Edwards and Potter 1992), which could be grouped under the heading of Social Social Cognition (SSC). Could mirror neuron theory be a response to these criticisms?

In 1998 Gallese and Goldman ruled out a role for mirror neurons in understanding action when they stated that:

> One difference is that the real attributor does not go back to a distal goal or set of beliefs. He only goes back to a motoric plan. (Gallese and Goldman 1998, p. 498)

Similarly, Gallese et al. (2004) assign a fairly unambitious role to mirror neurons, for the moment at least. In their view:

> It is important to stress here that in the present review, we discuss only how the meaning of action is understood and not how the intention of the action's agent is captured. (Gallese et al. 2004)

So it is not clear why Jacob and Jeannerod (2007), as a critique to Rizzolatti et al. work, maintain that motor theory of social cognition has the ambitious goal to derive human social cognition from human motor cognition.

In my view, the explanation offered by mirror neuron theory for imitation, empathy, and mindreading mechanisms addresses successfully some of the fundamental problems raised by social social cognition.[10] Specifically, the dimension of "we", of sociality, seems to be a distinguishing characteristic of the discovery of mirror neurons with respect to other contributions from the neurosciences. An interaction mechanism assisting understanding of others' gestures or emotions through a viscero-motor and somato-motor embodied simulation is an important concept for an explanation of human sociality. We could venture the idea that mirror neuron activity is a sort of sociality neuroindicator. This seems to be borne out by a recent study by Pfeiffer et al. (2008), which found, in children, a correlation between emotive empathy, measured with the Interpersonal Reactivity Index, and mirror neuron activity during observation of facial emotional expressions. Moreover, during imitation of facial emotional expressions, interpersonal attitudes were also strongly correlated with mirror neuron activity. The more socially outgoing children, with more relationships, friends, and interactions, with a greater popularity index on the Interpersonal Relations Scale, showed greater mirror neuron activity (Iacoboni 2008, p. 145).

The discovery of mirror neurons therefore appears to be of importance to the self-others relationship. In this light, I would disagree with the criticism made by Singer et al. (2003, p. XVII) that social cognitive neuroscience has mostly ignored the study of self-concept and of interpersonal relationships. That is true if we exclude mirror neurons.[11] Even though at basic level mirror neurons are fundamental for both phenomena. It is true that social cognitive neuroscience is in its infancy and is as yet unable to answer many questions raised by SSC, above all SSC's

[10] Some, but not all: as Sperber points out (2005), there are many forms of social cognition that do not involve mindreading.

[11] There is evidence that also cerebellum is involved in inferring other's people intentions from their actions. It monitors the correspondence between intended and achieved states (Blakemore and Decety 2001).

criticisms of the ISC approach to areas like social perception, social attitudes, prejudice, ideology, etc. Nevertheless, I believe that mirror neuron theory offers some answers to SSC criticisms with regard to two areas of social cognition.

1. *Attributions.* SSC criticizes ISC theories on attributions for their inability to explain the automatic aspects of attribution and their neglect of contextual, situational, cultural and social aspects. The theories advanced by Kelley (1967) and by Heider (1958) and his followers vest the attributor with a scientist's processing and causal hypothesis development ability. This processing is decided and performed at conscious level. With the Fundamental Error of Attribution (Ross 1977), attributions of dispositional causes of action are considered to predominate. Individual dispositional elements are considered responsible for the action and the influence of the agent's social environment is neglected. As we saw earlier, mirror neuron theory responds to the criticism of the lack of attribution automaticity. Unlike high-level simulation (Goldman 2006), which is conscious and guided by will, attribution of intentions through observational or auditory perception of the action seems, like empathy, to occur automatically through mirror neuron embodied simulation. This automaticity in social perception also seems to have been recognized recently by a number of social psychologists of the ISC school (Gilbert et al. 1998; Uleman 1999). While mirror neuron theory offers a convincing response to the criticism over the automaticity of intention attribution, its contribution in responding to the second criticism, underestimation of social causes in attribution, is not so simple, in the current state of the art. It is true that the experiment by Iacoboni et al. (2005) shows that the attributor differentiates action intentions in relation to context. So far, however, we have no data showing that this differentiation takes place with a complex social context. In my opinion, the experimental data on the relationship between mirror neurons and empathy offers promising indications on this point (Carr et al. 2003; Gallese et al. 2004). Social identity, membership of a group, seems to be channeled mostly not by cognitive factors, but by emotional and affective factors (e.g., emotional identification with a leader, a group, with cultural symbols and social practices; or affective involvement with family, friends, teachers, etc.). A neural mechanism like mirror neurons that explains mindreading of actions and mindfeeling of emotions stands a good chance of explaining the social reasons for an action.
2. *Self-Others.* ISC models of the self (Higgins and Bargh 1987; Higgins 1997; Markus and Kunda 1986; Carver and Scheier 1981) are concerned with the ways in which knowledge that people have about themselves becomes relevant in particular circumstances, and how this self-knowledge guides behavior and affect. SSC questions its assumption that the 'self' is located within the individual and transported by him into various social situations in which various parts of the internal cognitive 'self structure' become activated. Selves do not go out into the world to display their pre-existing attributes and to impose their pre-existing agendas, but selves emerge from the social structures, relationships and contexts in which people find themselves. In particular, according to Tajfel (1981), an

important part of every self is membership of some social group. This social identity is "... that part of the individual's self-concept which derives from his knowledge of his membership of a social group (or groups) together with the value and emotional significance attached to that membership" (p. 251). At the same time, the ISC decontextualized interpretation of the self appears to be a cultural product of a particular historic time or geographical area rather than a universal aspect of human nature. Western conceptions of an autonomous demarcated self contrast markedly with those found in other cultures (Geertz 1973; Markus and Kitayama 1991). For example, the Chinese dimension of self is relational, shaped to integrate with the community, to foster social harmony, to blend into the continuous flow of human interaction (Nisbett 2003; Nisbett and Masuda 2006; Viale 2006). It is social representation (Moscovici 1984) or, in other words, social discourse (Foucalt 1972) that determines construction of the decontextualized, desocialized self prevalent in the West, which ISC holds to be universal. On the contrary, according to the symbolic interactionism of Goffman (1963), when an individual interacts with a third person she does not interact with that person but with her symbolic representation of her. And these representations, including those we develop of ourselves, develop through social interaction, reflecting those aspects which the particular social context makes meaningful. We develop symbolic representations of ourselves as a result of our interactions with others. Cooley (1902) adopted the metaphor of the *looking-glass self*. We develop a sense of ourselves and of the attributes and qualities that we possess through the reflected appraisal of others. We form a sense of our psychological selves through seeing ourselves reflected in the *social mirrors* of the people around us (Gergen 1994). How can mirror neuron theory contribute to other attempts by ISC to respond to these criticisms? For example, one of the most social theories advanced by ISC in response to SSC criticisms, the *working self-concept theory* (Markus and Kunda 1986), postulates a change in possible selves depending on social context. The self is conceived as a multifaceted dynamic structure which can appear very different in different social contexts and in relation to different situational necessities. The theory, however, preserves an essential distinction between the individual interior cognitive self and the external social context which the self encounters. Conversely, mirror neuron theory identifies development of the self and self-recognition with imitation of others. Personal identity is formed through mirroring in others, as the mirror neuron theorists often observe by quoting phenomenonologists like Merleau-Ponty and Dan Zahavi: the self and the other "illuminate one another and can only be understood through their interconnection" (Zahavi 2001). First of all, the hypothesis, not yet directly confirmed by experimental findings, is that the newborn baby develops mirror neurons through the repeated imitation of its expressions by the adults around it. The child's brain is therefore able to associate the sight of a smiling face or other actions with the motoric plan required to replicate the actions. The mirror neurons that develop in infancy are the result of the reflection of our behavior in others. With mirror neurons, we see ourselves in others. Self and others, therefore, are intrinsically bound together. Indirect confirmation that self-recognition and imitation develop in parallel comes from studies by Asendorpf and Baudonniere (1993) demonstrating that children who recognized themselves in a mirror were better at imitating themselves than children who had not attained that ability. The phenomena of external imitation and, above all, internal imitation or automatic simulation in adults have been demonstrated experimentally by mirror neuron theory. The embodied simulation at the basis of mirroring recalls the thesis of symbolic interactionism on the looking-glass self and social mirrors. Mirror neuron theory also seems to offer an explanation for the postulates of social identity theory (Tajfel 1981). Although data is still limited, it shows that mirror neurons are activated every time a process of social identification occurs. Such activation was found in response to an advertising message (Iacoboni 2008) and in identification with political leaders (Schreiber and Iacoboni 2005). A recent study by Iacoboni with anthropologist Alan Fiske (Iacoboni et al. 2004) attempted to control mirror neuron activation with respect to two forms of social relationship, sharing of common property and authority hierarchies. Using fMRI on subjects watching videoclips representing the two types of social relationship in different ways, greater mirror neuron activity was found during the relational sections of the videos, i.e., when the social relationships were stronger and more intense. The study also found activity by the *default state network* (present in the precuneus and the dorsomedial prefrontal cortex), which is activated when the brain is in a state of repose, i.e., not engaged in cognitive tasks (which in this case would mean considering thinking of social relations as the default condition, normal routine for the psychic life of the brain). All the data on human mirror neurons seems to confirm that the social dimension of human cognition is a constituent element of the self rather than a culturally acquired element. Thus social representation theory appears to be correct in warning against considering the individualist conception of self expressed by ISC which operates in Western culture but not in Eastern culture to be universal. Our fundamental errors of attribution and our self-perception of separateness and distance from others is not a constituent fact but probably a metarepresentation of the way we relate to others.

5.6 Conclusion: What Does Neurosociology Tell to Philosophy of Social Sciences?

Neurosocial data offer material for a series of reflections on the methodology and philosophy of social sciences. The considerations set out below refer mainly to the cognitive approach, specifically the approach endorsed by Boudon, and should also be taken in consideration also by *methodological cognitivism.*

The superiority of Simulation Theory in explaining mindreading implies that the possibility exists for the social scientist to quarantine her egocentric bias and theoretical schemes in order to mindread the social agent and explain social action. The only philosophical approach that seems fully to match this condition is the hermeneutic approach. When Schleiermacher writes that "the *divinatory* method is the one in which one, so to speak, transforms oneself into the other person and tries to understand the individual element directly" (1998, p. 92), he proposes a simulation through empathy without any preconceptions, theories and subjective models. Nevertheless, Schleiermacher himself says that absolute empathy is extremely difficult to achieve, because the individual can only simulate the reasons for the other person's action through a comparison with herself. Within the cognitive approach, Boudon's position is very close to the simulative requirements presented earlier. The researcher who tries to understand the reasons for action tries to reconstruct the situation that, *a parte subjecti,* led the subject to embrace certain beliefs. As Weber noted (1949), the social researcher will not be able to provide an explanation for social action unless she uses her imagination to reconstruct internally, i.e., simulate, the reasons (Boudon 1990). The main point on which Boudon diverges from the hermeneutic approach is the role of simulation. For hermeneutics, simulation is essential to understand the reasons for action, whereas Boudon sees it more as the final step in the understanding process, to be used to check the result of the situational analysis (Di Nuoscio 1996). In any case, hermeneutics too places importance on the presentation of the milieu and external situation that aids the subject in re-experiencing the reasoning processes of the other person (Dilthey 2002).

The cognitive approach regards simulation as a voluntary, conscious activity whose goal is to recreate the experiential conditions that led the subject to behave in a certain manner. The emphasis on conscious identification of the reasons that led the subject to consider certain beliefs as true and justified and to act accordingly is very evident in Boudon (1990, 1993a, 1993b). In short, the simulation effected by the understanding scientist is what Goldman (2006) defines as high-level mindreading, that is, simulation of propositional attitudes like intentions, beliefs and desires. The hermeneutic approach, on the other hand, sees the ability to understand human action as centered not just in cognitive empathy, or high-level mindreading, but also in emotional empathy, or mindfeeling of the other person (although it is not clear how much of this mindfeeling is regarded by hermeneutics as automatic and how much as voluntary, through active re-experiencing and re-enacting of the other person's mental processes).

What neurosocial data suggest (see the section above on the *Mindreading iceberg*) is that a large proportion of attribution activity occurs automatically and is an emotional rather than cognitive process. The individual tends to simulate automatically, in other words to re-experience internally the other person's feelings and emotions – sadness, anger, disgust – through automatic mirroring, triggered by the visual stimuli of facial behavior recognition (FaBeR) or by other visual or auditory clues to verbal or non-verbal behavior. Moreover, there is growing evidence of automatic simulation of propositional attitudes, in the form of intentions (Iacoboni et al. 2005), which would reduce the role of voluntary high-level mindreading proposed by Goldman (2006) and Boudon (1990, 1993a, 1993b). Attribution of intentions through observational or auditory perception of the actions seems, like empathy, to occur, often, automatically through mirror neurons embodied simulation. This automaticity in social perception has been recognized by a growing number of social psychologists (Gilbert et al. 1998; Uleman 1999). The presence of automatic attribution of intentions and the importance of emotional empathy in attribution mechanisms can both be seen as new data to help to change the cognitive approach of Boudon and Simon and to perfect the *methodological cognitivism*. The reasons are as follows:

(a) The cognitive approach (Simon 1982, 2000; Goldman 1986) including Boudon (1990, 1993a, 1993b) concurs with the anti-Humean thesis that normative objectives cannot be proposed for human knowledge unless they are feasible for the neurocognitive system. Boudon, for example, introducing the concept of cognitive rationality and the theory of good reasons, calls into play the computational constraints of the human mind, in other words, Simon's *subjective bounded rationality* (1982). If information processing is subject to the inferential limitations of the human mind, then there is no place for Olympian theories of rationality like Pareto's *narrow theory* (1944). The generation of beliefs and the processing of knowledge about the world, including knowledge about other people's social action, are conditioned by the *feasibility* of the mind-world interaction (Viale 2001a). When new contributions from the neurocognitive sciences challenge his methodological theories, if Boudon wishes to be consistent with his concept of cognitive rationality he should either acknowledge the new data and modify his theory, or modify the *feasibility* constraint.

(b) Boudon (1993a, 1993b), for example, adopts Simmel's Kantian-based theory of knowledge, whereby we acquire knowledge because we have cognitive a priori that simplify, structure and order the variety and heterogeneity of our experience. For Boudon these a priori are of acquired origin, non universal and temporal, and they change in response to reality. They are largely logical, epistemological and linguistic structures, frames and principles forming part of what Searle calls our background knowledge, and play a heuristic role in information processing and individual production of knowledge. Neurocognitive studies of children and of adults (Viale 2006) have found that the a priori we use to process knowledge include variable structures of acquired origin, but also universal, atemporal structures (of hereditary origin). Even the moral values of right and wrong seem to be governed by an innate grammar of moral a priori similar to the universal grammar proposed by linguist Noam Chomsky (Hauser 2006).

To stay with the theme of this chapter, neurocognitive research into mindreading appears to indicate that mirror neurons are in part innate. In any case, the mirror neurons formed from birth to the present that channel emotional and cognitive mirroring functions tend to be constant, even if the milieu changes. For example, if a person tends to simulate an emotion like sorrow through the facial behavior recognition of the other person, she will continue to do so even if, in a different milieu, those facial expressions are associated with other emotions (such as deference or submission).

(c) Boudon (1993a, 1993b) tends to identify rationality as the voluntary processing of beliefs in relation to the contextual situation. Even if the beliefs are false, they should be considered rational if the underlying reasons are held to be true and sufficient by the subject, in relation to the context and background knowledge. According to this interpretation, all cognitive activity that takes place automatically, without voluntary control of reason, is to be excluded from rationality. Consider for example, one of the central phenomena of social cognition and neurosociology, imitation. Imitation distinguishes man from the other species. Looking at knowledge-transfer mechanisms, the mechanisms used to transfer technological or business know-how are based largely on imitation, which involves voluntary elements, but above all automatic elements. These automatic elements can be explained by the mirroring processes generated by mirror neurons. Boudon, however, places imitation among the irrational forces that determine beliefs. Describing *Tocqueville's model* (1993a, p. 15), he praises the French scholar's cognitive approach which, in examining the development of American democracy and the end of the Ancien Régime in France, avoids explaining the spread of certain beliefs as the effect of imitative phenomena. Boudon's "aversion" to imitation stems from the fact that he equates the automaticity of psychological phenomena with irrationality. Anything that is not controlled by the conscious will is irrational. In many cases, this is not true. Automatic behavior is often an adaptive solution, learned over time, to problems encountered in daily life or in the workplace. Organizational routines are an example. People in an organization learn tasks and duties and subsequently replicate them in an automatic fashion. This is a great advantage in terms of organizational rationality and efficient decision-making, compared with situations where automatisms of this type are not present and each member of the organization is obliged to process *ex novo*, in a conscious voluntary manner, the behavior appropriate to their role (for example, in a hypothetical company where everyone constantly changes job).

Going back to our theme, we can conclude, from what has been said, that understanding the mental life of another person is a question of understanding her propositional attitudes through voluntary, conscious mindreading. According to Boudon's thesis, knowledge acquired automatically through emotional empathy or mindfeeling or mirroring of intentions is not rationally acceptable. Neurocognitive data, however, seem to indicate that most attributor activity is a mixture of voluntary and automatic activity. So, if we apply Boudon's cognitive approach rigidly to the letter, it would be very difficult to accept any form of understanding of other people's actions since mindreading would inevitably be polluted by automatic elements, especially emotional elements.

(d) Unlike the hermeneutic approach, the cognitive approach takes a negative view of emotional elements in explaining social action. Researchers attempting to attribute the mental states of a social agent should be guided exclusively by cognitive simulation based on conscious, voluntary processes of reasoning and inference. Boudon writes that <<*understanding* does not mean trying to experience the same feelings as the agent, an enterprise certainly doomed in advance to failure and one that in any case is uncontrollable.>> (Boudon 1984, It. Transl. 1985, p. 73). As we saw earlier, this *desideratum* is not feasible, given the pervasiveness of emotional automatic processes in social action mindreading. Moreover, as noted in recent literature in cognitive sciences (Damasio 1994; Kahneman 2003; Slovic et al. 2001; Viale 2005b), individual decisions and judgments are often anticipated and guided by emotion, to the point that we now talk about *mind dualism* in decision making. Next to the rational, conscious, serial mind is a parallel emotional, automatic mind, which has acquired growing importance in neurocognitive studies in the last 10 years. Emotional processing, often in the form of somatic markers (Damasio 1994), improves the ability to put problems into focus and take decisions rapidly. We now also have an extensive body of literature demonstrating that fast, simple, smart and frugal heuristics (Gigerenzer et al. 1999; Gigerenzer 2007), such as *ignorance heuristics,* which process judgments in a fast, almost automatic manner on the basis of limited information, often produce decisions that are better, normatively speaking, than those based on the algorithms of standard rationality. So this preconception regarding the automaticity of mindreading mechanisms, and emotional empathy in particular, appears to be misplaced. At intuitive level, too, it is evident that simulation of the emotional nuances of the mental activity of another person helps the mindreader attribute meaning to certain action that neither the manifest behavior nor knowledge of the situational context and past action can shed light on. For example, in negotiation phenomena (and various types of strategic interaction, from chess-playing to international political conflicts) predictive mindreading of the opponent's behavior is based largely on emotional clues (Neale and Bazerman 1991). Consequently, anyone attempting to reconstruct the meaning of subjective action or predict the decisions of the subject must necessarily take into account the information deriving from the emotional sphere of the subject.

Emotional empathy clearly plays a heuristic role in the process of understanding the reasons for action. Nevertheless, its importance is largely confined to cultural milieus sharing a common view of the causal relationship between emotion and behavioral/verbal expression. When the social scientist moves out of her native cultural environment into a milieu with different emotion-expression relationships, the automaticity of emotional mirroring may produce misleading attributions. Certain facial expressions, for example, might lead her automatically to attribute emotions like sadness, whereas in fact, in that particular culture, they simply denote deference toward the speaker.

Exotic emotional expressions exacerbate the well-known "Gavagai" problem, i.e., the inscrutability-of-reference introduced by Quine (1960). In these cases, the social scientist has to quarantine egocentric perspective, formulate hypotheses about the reasons for behavior and simulate the relationship between reason and action. This is a hybrid approach combining ST and TT, which also aims to neutralize the automatisms of emotional mirroring. In these instances, the cognitive approach, seems to be the best path toward understanding the meaning of individual action and from there formulating explanations for social action. Here, the search for the good reasons for behavior should begin from a situational analysis and past experience with similar decisional situations. Simulation should not take place until all the other possible reasons have been identified. In searching for the reasons for action, the social scientist must quarantine the traditional models of rationality, as well as her subjective principles of rationality. In these contexts, the attributions produced by a hermeneutic approach centered on emotional empathy will inevitably prove deceptive.

Part II

Cognitive Economics

Developing Simon's Bounded Rationality 6

Herbert Simon is the father of the empirically based microeconomics. His economic theory is founded on a new concept of economic rationality. Herbert Simon's contribution to the theory of economic rationality can be characterized by one *pars destruens* and one *part costruens*. The first part is the attack to the neoclassical Olympic rationality. The second is the proposal of an empirically based bounded rationality theory. In this chapter I will develop and assess the first and second contribution of Simon showing that while the first is justified theoretically and empirically the second shows some serious flaws.

Neoclassical economics is based on a theoretical hypothesis of the rational actor with the two following characteristics:

1. He knows all physically or even logically possible options, and all physically and logically possible states of the world which could be relevant to his decision.
2. As Bayesian agent, he has a coherent preference structure. Therefore, he is able to estimate his expected utility for each option and then choose the option with the highest expected utility.

In neoclassical economics, the rational agent is a maximizer.

In science there are two basic ways to control a theoretical hypothesis (a) indirectly, by upholding the general propositions to which the hypothesis is deductively connected; (b) directly, through the control of factual, singular propositions that can be derived from the hypothesis, in the form of initial conditions.

In posing the problem of controlling the theoretical hypothesis of the rational maximizing actor in neoclassical economics we can refer to either way.

This is a revised version of Viale, R. (1992 [2008]). Cognitive constraints of economic rationality. In H. A. Simon, M. Egidi, R. Marris & R. Viale (eds.), *Economics, bounded rationality and the cognitive revolution* (pp. 174–193). Cheltenham, UK and Northampton, MA: Edward Elgar Publishing Ltd. With kind permission from the Publishers.

DOI 10.1007/978-3-642-24743-9_6,

6.1 Control of Theoretical Support of the Rational Actor Hypothesis

To which general propositions is the economic actor hypothesis connected in neoclassical economics?

According to Simon (1987, p. 26) this model of rational actor is mainly connected to the following hypotheses:

1. His beliefs about aims and values are given and not liable to change in time and through experience.
2. His beliefs are internally coherent.
3. The agent is capable of an objective description of the world.
4. His abilities to elaborate data to define his expectations, that is, respectively, his probabilistic and deductive reasoning, are not limited.

We could express these properties otherwise by saying that, in the neoclassical economic actor, perceptive rationality and rationality of beliefs (see Part I Chap. 3 of this volume) – the rationality which is assumed in the representations of informational data – and decisional rationality – the rationality which is assumed in inferential activities which lead from data to decisions – are non-limited (from the point of view of some prescriptive canons) (Viale 1993).

These propositions of deductive support for the neoclassical rationality hypothesis may be, in principle, empirically controlled. Cognitive science has been engaged in testing them for some years, through experiments and observation.

Neoclassical *perceptive rationality* and *rationality of beliefs* presupposes an objective representation of the world, in the form of coherently organized true beliefs.

Empirical control of this hypothesis has been effected mainly through cognitive study of perception and memory mechanisms and of the codes of representation of informational data (Viale 1991). Up to now these controls have shown that the representation of informational data is often unreliable[1] and incoherent.[2]

---

[1] The reliability of a mental activity like perception or memory may be evaluated by the rate of true beliefs it is able to generate. In this case truth may be defined as some kind of correspondence belief-real world ("realist" position) or as some kind of internal coherence between prediction and predicted fact ("instrumentalist" position). A belief is a mental state whose content may be not only a proposition but also an image or a mixture of the two, like in the mental models (Johnson-Laird 1983).

While it is likely to find some ways to prove the correspondence or quasi isomorphism between a mental image and a real fact this seems much more difficult for the correspondence between proposition and fact. In this case the instrumentalist position seems more acceptable even if non unproblematic.

[2] A logical incoherence is usually considered a flaw which must be promptly eliminated. There are two reasons for this: because any proposition can be derived from a contradiction; and because at least one of the two propositions must be false. The rule prescribes therefore the prompt identification and elimination of the incoherence. This is not so desirable, however, from a pragmatic and epistemic point of view. First, a coherent belief system is not necessarily better than an incoherent one, from the point of view of its truth. It could be a coherent system of false beliefs. In addition,

Perception is a central theme in cognitive research (see Chap. 3 of Part I of this volume). One of the standard approaches in the psychology of perception is based on so-called pattern recognition. People recognize the presentation of an object as an example of a certain pattern. Perception output implies a classification of the stimulus. The perceived stimulus is not a mere *qualia*, but a classification of a certain section of the environment. The perceptive stimulus is developed into a perceptive belief. Both Marr (1982) and Rock (1983) highlight different stages in perception. There is, in brief, a lower stage of "perception of forms" in which the stimulus is not recognized and there are higher stages in which access to long-term memory leads to the categorical recognition of the stimulus. Perception is ultimately made up of two kinds of elaboration: bottom-up elaboration, in which information flows from small perceptive inputs to larger units made up of those inputs, and top-down elaboration, in which background beliefs influence the interpretation of the most elementary perceptive units. Top-down elaboration of perceptive stimuli often tends to add something which was not present in the stimulus itself: some internal constructive process mediates between the entry stimulus and the perceptive result. This can lead to an improvement or to a decline in the reliability and truth of the perception, depending on the kind of perception and on individual mnemonic patterns. Moreover a trade-off phenomenon between rapidity and reliability of perception is evident. Strong emotions such as wishes and fears, generally related to primary needs, lead to an improvement in perception rapidity to the detriment of reliability. Partial correspondence of some portion of the perceptive stimulus with a memorized pattern having a high affective value is enough to produce a strong activation of the pattern itself and thus the recognition of the perception. At a pragmatic level such a phenomenon can have a positive value, but, as far as the reliability and accuracy of our perception of reality are concerned, it is clearly not always so, and it is responsible for the production of false belief.

Another fundamental component of the correctness of informational inputs of perceptive rationality is related to the mechanisms of *memory*. The fact that an individual holds a belief now doesn't imply that he will hold it in the future. This depends on mnemonic power. In the same way, if a man has a belief today, because he thinks he had it some time ago, it is not certain that his belief is the same. That will depend on the accuracy and reliability of memorization mechanisms. The corpus of beliefs, the factual foundation of rationality, depends therefore on memory. As we know, memory can be subdivided into three sections: besides the memory of sensory information which does not concern us here, there is short term memory (STM), where a small part of rapidly disappearing information can be stored and where the operational centre of the information processing is located, and long term memory (LTM), which is the filing cabinet of information, with virtually unlimited capacity.

when faced with an incoherent belief system, it is sometimes better to wait for further data before proceeding to eliminate the incoherence, so as to be sure that a true belief is not being sacrificed in favour of a false one. Sometimes, therefore, pragmatic and epistemic reasons prevail over the reasons of logic.

The first consideration one has to make concerns which data base is used in the inference. Various experiments, as well as everyday observation, clearly show that the factual data base used often corresponds only to a part of the beliefs available in long term memory and useful for inferences. People can't gain access to a significant part of their knowledge and consequently the resulting inferences are generally wrong. Sometimes the individual cannot connect all elements, useful for inference, existing in his memory. At the roots of the problem of belief activation is apparently the codification process which determines the communications through which activation is propagated in the mnemonic system. Man codifies information in a semantic structure which goes beyond individual information. This can happen both at the time when the informative input presents itself and when the information is retrieved through memory. This often leads to a diminished reliability of memory. For instance people tend to develop the recollection of an event using information subsequent to the event itself. Moreover, one is not always able to make out the original sources of information.

Associated to memory we find the irrational phenomenon of perseverance in the belief, carefully studied by Nisbett and Ross (1980). People are inclined to preserve a belief even after it has been proved false by new evidence. The reason of this perseverance can be found in the emotional refusal of new beliefs, deemed unsatisfactory, and in the search for factual validation of old beliefs through the retrieval of supporting information from memory.

There is also another characteristic of memory which goes against the rational principle of revision of beliefs in the face of new informational data. According to psychologists, long term memory is not a blackboard from which propositions can be wiped out on the basis of new evidence. On the contrary, there seems to be no real loss of informational material from memory unless as a result of physical damage. Every piece of information memorized, and every belief acquired, is stored in memory and cannot be erased even after it has been proved false. If information material cannot be erased from memory, it will contain contradictions and time structures. The wrong steps worked out while solving a problem will be memorized together with the correct ones and may be recalled when the solution of the problem is undertaken again. Residual beliefs can always revive from long term memory through a semantic interference with other beliefs causing an incorrect and incoherent answer.

At the root of the availability of information inputs are the cognitive modalities through which information is represented. They are another powerful cognitive constraint against the hypothesis of objective representation of the world in neoclassical rationality. One first general fact emerging from cognitive research is the pervasiveness of hierarchical organization in mental representations (Goldman 1986, pp. 228–237). Hierarchically structured representations can be identified in the structure of linguistic propositions, in semantic memory, in visual representations, in time sequences as well as in other domains, such as behaviour planning and problem solving. There is, moreover, a pervasive tendency to favour certain hierarchical organizations and certain compositions of the represented phenomena: in vision, only certain parts are recognized as such, memorized and exploited to recall the whole picture (Bower and Glass 1976); a musical sequence is hierarchically memorized – according to the laws of pictorial completeness, similar to those of the *gestalt* – and is retrieved through a top-down mechanism (Deutsch and Feroe 1981); representation of movement, too, takes place according to cognitive constraints which tend to favour the interpretation of movement of solid bodies, along straight lines and towards objects which are nearer than others (Ullman 1979).

"Hierarchization" can often result in errors and distortions which make of mental representations an unfaithful image of reality. On the other hand, "hierarchization" contributes to the power and flexibility of the cognitive activity. Since it makes it possible to move from one level to another, varying the resolution level of the analysis according to the problem and the decision maker's "interests", it allows one to highlight only details which are significant from the contextual point of view, disregarding all others. Besides, "hierarchization" considerably increases the power of mnemonic retrieval. When a plan of action has to be decided upon, for instance, one should be able to represent in STM the various stages of the plan and its consequences. Because of space limitations in STM this is not possible. The bottleneck can be bypassed by subdividing the plan in various related parts and focusing on them one at a time. This is possible because in LTM the "plan" macro-unit is hierarchically organized in "stage" micro-units of the plan itself.

Substantially, many authors seem to agree on the characteristics of hierarchical organization in mental representations; opinion is more divided about the forms of the representations. A common feature shared by a number of cognitive scientists is the unvarying tripartition of representations: according to Langley et al. (1987) the three possible forms are list structures, propositional representations and images; according to Johnson-Laird (1983) mental models, propositional representations and images; according to Anderson (1983) time sequences, abstract propositions and space images; etc.

The form of representation which seems to play a central role in the peculiar human way of representing informational data is the image. As explained by Kosslyn (1981) the mental image is an instrument of representation much more powerful than the proposition. It allows the simultaneous and interdependent representation of information such as shape, size, orientation and position of an object. The mental image is however susceptible to various forms of interference. Since representations having higher emotional content, concreteness, simplicity and ability to evoke other images will be preferred, distorting effects on the accuracy of the representation of reality may often ensue.

Serious cognitive constraints to the "Olympian" pretences of neoclassical rationality have also been empirically brought to attention in regard to *decisional rationality*. In elaborating the available data to define expectations about environment and agent and to select, on the basis of these expectations, the most appropriate action, people seem to deviate from the rules underlying the neoclassical rational agent.

This is evident in many studies of *probabilistic reasoning*, which have shown that man forms estimates about the likelihood of future events, assigns numbers and percentages, combines probabilities and values in a way which does not conform to the theory of probability.[3] Only a brief reference to these empirical results will be mentioned here.

The selection of information deemed relevant for decisional purposes is not carried out through an exhaustive examination at mnemonic level of all relevant information (Tversky and Kahneman 1973). Man tends to select examples of large classes rather than of small ones, even if they are just as relevant in the decisional context (heuristic of availability).

Another tendency discovered by Tversky and Kahneman is the propensity to give counter-normative judgements according to the degree to which the salient characteristics of an object or person are representative of or similar to characteristics conceived as peculiar to some category. This is known as the heuristic of representativeness. Representativeness is formally described by a relation between a model M and some event X associated with that model. A sample X is more or less

[3] There are arguments against the pretension of adopting some theory of probability as a canon for the rationality of probabilistic inferences (Cohen 1981, pp. 319–320). The concept of probability has not yet found a universally accepted interpretation. If we take as syntactic reference point Kolmogorov's (1950) axiomatization – where probability is axiomatically defined in terms of sets and theory of measure – various definitions can be considered coherent in relation to the constraints set up by axiomatization: the frequentist definition (Reichenbach 1949; von Mises 1957) according to which the probability of an event is the limit towards which the relative frequency of the event tends when the number of occurrences tends to infinity; the subjectivistic definition (Ramsey 1931; de Finetti 1931) according to which the probability of an event is the degree of confidence that an individual, on the basis of the knowledge he possesses at a given moment, has that the event will occur; Carnap's (1950) conception of probability as logical connection between propositions; Popper's (1959) and Mellor's (1971) conception of probability as causal propensity; etc. All these interpretations seem to conform to the constraints of Kolmogorov's axiomatization. The choice of any one interpretation as a rational canon is not indifferent, however. First, probability is treated as a function of propositions if it is measured as a degree of subjective confidence or established as a logical relationship; as a function of sets if it refers to relative frequencies; as a function of properties if it refers to causal propensities. These different functions are not equally appropriate to the evaluation of the probability of events. Second, while different degrees of subjective probability of an event are not considered mutually incoherent, the assertion of different relative frequencies, of different logical relationships or of different causal propensities about the same event are logically incoherent.

In the face of these differences it is difficult to decide which interpretation is viable as a theory of human probabilistic inferences without relying on an empirical evaluation, based on people's intuitive judgements of appropriateness.

Furthermore, if the syntactic characterization of Kolmogorov is apt for the previous semantic interpretations, its appropriateness is dubious when other, non classical interpretations are concerned.

Finally, one can apply to these axiomatizations, as in the case for the truths of logic, the consideration that their ultimate foundation can only be of an intuitive sort. It does not seem possible to do without intuition, both when evaluating which semantic interpretation is viable as a theory of human probabilistic inferences, and where the ultimate foundations of syntactic axiomatization in the theory of probability are concerned.

representative of a model *M*. Four kinds of cases can be identified in which the heuristic of representativeness may be present:

1. *M* is a class and *X* is one value of a determined variable in that class: the average income of the teachers in a school may be thought as representative of that class.
2. *M* is a class and *X* is an example of that class: Rita Levi Montalcini may be considered as being representative of Italian scientists.
3. *M* is a class and *X* is a sub-set of *M*: Post Office workers may be considered more representative of the category of Italian civil servants than the employees of the Ministry of Culture.
4. *M* is a causal system and *X* one possible consequence: Keynesian economic policy (*M*) can be considered a cause of Italian national debt (*X*).

In these cases *X* may cause a counter-normative judgement of the characteristics of *M* since the judgement of *M* is completely oriented (biased) by the sample *X*, and it disregards the general characteristics of *M*.

Various studies have compared probability estimates made by people with the estimates that should be derived from Bayesian theorem. Some experiments have shown that subjects underestimate the effects of new evidence and that this underestimate is reflected in their evaluation of the subsequent probability, evaluated as lower than predicted by Bayesian theorem. This behaviour has been called conservative by Edwards (1968).

On the other hand, subjects have more often been found to ignore completely, in certain situations, previous probability. Tversky and Kahneman (1980) conducted some well-known experiments on this using the "taxi-cab problem". Previous probability seems to combine correctly with new evidence only when the former is interpreted in a causal way and when the nature of the other evidence is not more specific than the data of the previous probability.

The importance of causal patterns in everyday reasoning has been pointed out in many experiments. Several of them refer not to statistical reasoning but to the more general phenomenon of causal attribution (Nisbett and Ross 1980). Standard interpretation of this kind of experiments differentiates between causal reasoning (from cause to effect) and diagnostic reasoning (from effect to cause). People feel more at ease with causal reasoning. Even when the information content is the same in both directions, people favour the causal pattern over the diagnostic one.

Bayesian information model, on the other hand, considers only the information content and ignores the difference between causal and diagnostic reasoning. This is another instance in which the normative model obviously breaks away from the actual decisional behaviour of people.

A decision is generally elaborated by combining probabilistic and *deductive reasoning*.[4] One implicit logical form which can often be identified in the argument

[4] Various arguments can be opposed to the pretension of assuming classical logic as the canon of deductive rationality (Cohen 1981, pp. 318–319; Johnson-Laird 1983, pp. 26–28, pp. 34–39; Viale 1989, pp. 111–115): if classical logic were accepted as the canon of deductive inferential rationality one would reach the absurdity of having to accept the countless conclusions, trivial

at the basis of inferences is the syllogism. In it premises and conclusion can have various forms, among them universal, particular, probabilistic or hypothetical propositions, so that we can speak of categorical syllogisms, statistical syllogisms and quasi-syllogisms.

Empirical results of experiments on syllogistic reasoning have shown very low levels of performance. One of the first theories on performance in syllogistic reasoning was suggested by Woodworth and Sells (1935). With their "atmosphere effect" theory they maintained that people cannot reason logically because of the nature of the premises which creates an atmosphere leading the subject to derive certain conclusions. More specifically, they suggest that positive premises lead the subject to accept positive conclusions while negative premises lead him to negative conclusions. If one of the premises is positive and the other negative, then the subject inclines towards a negative conclusion. They also took into consideration universal propositions (such as, "all As are B") and particular propositions (such as "some As are B"). According to the atmosphere effect, universal premises predispose people to accept a universal conclusion while a particular conclusion is accepted after particular premises. The subject also prefers a particular conclusion when one premise is universal and the other particular.

The atmosphere effect theory has been questioned by Johnson-Laird and Steedman (1978). According to the atmosphere effect subjects should have been equally ready to accept each of the wrong conclusions in the following syllogisms:

1. Some As are B
   Some Bs are C
   Then some As are C

but correct, which are implied by a set of valid premises. This would have fatal consequences for man's ability to adapt to his environment. Other inferential rules are therefore needed to select and skim significant deductions from trivial ones. This seems to be the function of the heuristics which select relevant conclusions, according to feedback of a contextual and pragmatic kind, and are usually, but not always, able to preserve the semantic informational content of the premises. Secondly, it is not clear why one should favour classical logic over any of the several types of logic which have been developed in our century: modal types of logic, which offer the advantage of formalizing the concepts of possibility and necessity, or non-monotonic types of logic and "fuzzy" logic, which can emulate the ambiguity, poor resolution and contradictoriness of human reasoning. Third, justifying the validity of a logical theory is one thing; ascertaining the possibility of its application to cognitive reality is a different matter. In the case of propositional calculus, for example, its application has to do with the meaning assigned to the logical particles "if", "and", "or", based on the intuitively perceived legitimacy of deductive relations between the propositions where these particles appear. Fourth, there is one final consideration underlying this whole line of reasoning: outside intuition, there is no logical theory through the application of which one can justify the validity of human inferences, since logic itself finds its ultimate justification in human intuition. The main strategy aimed at avoiding the recourse to intuition in founding the truth of logic is obviously ineffective: the empirical-inductive strategy sets logic as an adjunct to science and grounds logical truth on the truth of the holistic system which forms scientific knowledge. This strategy is not effective both because of the classical arguments against neopositivism and for the impossibility of establishing important methodological principles in the methodology of science, such as simplicity, coherence and generality, without resort to intuition.

2. Some Bs are A
   Some Cs are B
   Then some As are C

The subjects in the experiment were more inclined to accept the wrong conclusion in syllogism 1 than in 2. This has been explained with the presence of another particularly strong and resilient phenomenon: the "figural effect". People tend to accept a conclusion having A as subject and C as conclusion if there is a chain leading from A to B in one premise and from B to C in the other.

A further difficulty in the atmosphere effect theory comes from alternative interpretations of the same experimental results. According to some, a wrong conclusion may be accepted because of a bad interpretation of the premises. According to Chapman and Chapman (1959) and their "conversion hypothesis", subjects commonly interpret in an inverted way both universal affirmative propositions ("all As are B" is understood as "all Bs are A"), and negative particular propositions ("some As are not B" is understood as "some Bs are not A").

In deductive inference do not follow some law of formal logic but appear to be developing a mental model, using whatever means at their disposal, with the aim of representing significant information in an easily accessible and manageable way. In syllogistic inference, according to Johnson-Laird (1983), first a representation of the inference symbol is developed, and then a mental model of the first premise is formed. The information of the second premise is then added to the mental model of the first premise. The conclusion finally reached expresses the relation between the symbols existing in all the models of the premises. A control of the resulting model is then enacted through the search for an interpretation of the premises which is incoherent with the model. If that is not achieved then the inference is valid.

One of the most important inference rules that has been studied till now is the *modus ponens* of material implication. It rules that given the proposition "if A then B", and given also A, then one can validly infer B.

Most people find little difficulty in accepting arguments based on the *modus ponens*, but often have problems with another inference rule known as *modus tollens*. This rule dictates that, given the proposition "if A then B", and given also the fact that B is false, we can infer that A is false.

Both these inference rules seem quite obvious, but people find some difficulty in applying them. The difficulty arises from the inability to behave in a way which fits with the correct interpretation of the rules, and from the inclination to draw conclusions which are not justified.

1. As far as the rule of the *modus ponens* is concerned, it is not justified to conclude that B is false on the basis of the premises "if A then B" and "non-A".
2. As far as the rule of the *modus tollens* is concerned it is not justified to conclude that A is true on the basis of the premises "if A then B" and "B".

In human reasoning the drawing of false conclusions based on (1) and (2) has often been observed.

Rips and Marcus have worked experimentally using hypothetical examples (1977). They submitted all possible combinations of premises and conclusions. In the case of the *modus ponens* all subjects selected the correct conclusions.

With propositions of other kinds, however, a large proportion of subjects made logical errors from the point of view of the logic of material implication.

In case (1), for instance, one cannot say that B is "never" true since that cannot be ascertained. Yet 16% of the subjects gave "never" as an answer. This particular error is called "fallacy in the denial of the antecedent".

Another example has to do with case (2) which, as the former, is not a valid inference. A cannot be said to be "always" true, even if it can be true sometimes. Yet, 23% of answers maintained that it was "always" true. This error is known as "fallacy in the affirmation of the consequent".

Many errors were found also in the application of the *modus tollens* rule. The correct conclusion in the *modus tollens* is that A is "always" false, but only 57% of the answers were of this kind. Thirty-nine per cent answered "sometimes".

The conclusions of these studies seem to point to two important principles (Viale 1989, p. 123):

1. Individuals do not behave in accordance with the logical principle of trying to falsify a rule, except in particular circumstances.
2. These circumstances are those in which the interpretation of the problem is achieved through its mapping out in a description of the situation existing in memory, which successfully incorporates a suitable testing procedure. Just as problem-solving procedures are determined by the initial representation of the problem itself, the same is true of this particular test of logical reasoning.

Not only does the precise form of the problem determine the strategies used by the subject; it has also been found that, even if a correct answer has been given to a specific concrete problem, the subject rarely behaves correctly when faced with a subsequent abstract version of the problem itself. In brief, he doesn't even appear to have learned to transfer his knowledge from the concrete situation to a structurally identical abstract one.

Logical properties of conditionals are determined by the interrelated propositions and by the kind of relation they represent. Every proposition generally defines its own context and in the case of the conditional this is achieved in three ways: once for the antecedent, once for the consequent and once for the relation between the two. According to the seemingly more plausible theory, the subject uses his beliefs and knowledge stemming from the interpretation of the conditional to develop a mental model of a scenario in which the antecedent will come true. At this point the consequent is interpreted in the light of that model and scenario (Johnson-Laird 1983, pp. 54–62).

To conclude, empirical control of the propositions at the basis of the model of rational actors in neoclassical economics appears to falsify them.

Common man's inferential and decisional performances diverge from the prescriptions of the hypotheses underlying maximizing rationality. This reason alone would be enough to reject the hypothesis itself.

Advocates of the neoclassical model could object that these conclusions apply only to the common man, while economic theory is interested in an economic actor capable of surviving in the market by learning. This, however, is merely a peripheral objection, since the results of cognitive research have established systematic limitations to the expression of maximizing rationality which are built into the psycho-physiological structure of the decision maker. These constraints are therefore present and active in various contextual and learning situations, among which are market situations (which have been the object, among other things, of experimental research in cognitive science).

For the sake of methodological completeness one could also control the factual predictions inferred from the model of neoclassical rationality. If the predictions too were falsified by empirical data of an economic kind, one would have another strong argument against preserving the hypothesis of maximizing rationality.

6.2 Control of the Factual Consequences of the Rational Actor Hypothesis

There are two main ways of controlling the factual consequences of an economic theory: through observation in artificial experiments or through historical recording in the so-called natural experiments.

From a methodological point of view economists are rather doubtful about whether *artificial experiments* can be considered as a reliable testing ground for the rational actor theory. There are three specific constraints for an experiment to be acceptable by economists (Hogarth and Reder 1987, pp. 11–13):

1. Subjects in the experiment must have experience as maximizing actors in the specific market sector.
2. Subjects must be appropriately motivated so that rewards are a progressive function of the correctness of their answers.
3. Experimental settings must correspond with a context in which competition market forces are active.

These constraints stem from one of the fundamental conditions of the rational actor theory: only through competition do individual actions become liable to that learning feedback which forces them either to become competitive, hence maximizing, or retire.

Kahneman and Tversky (1987, pp. 90–91) have questioned the actual possibility of learning of this kind in actual market conditions: feed-back is often inadequate because there is no clear connection with the results; variability of environment diminishes feedback reliability; there is often no clear information on the consequences of alternative decisions; many decisions do not occur a second time and therefore are not useful for learning purposes.

This strict methodological requirement does not therefore seem to have much foundation. However, some experiments have been carried out in recent years to reproduce the conditions of choice outlined by economists. Results are contradictory. In some experiments which aimed at reproducing motivational patterns in relation to the correctness of answers, results have been counter-normative. Thaler (1987) and Kahneman and Tversky (1987) have quoted studies in which an inverse relation between incentives and rational behaviour has emerged. Other studies, conducted on experts in experimental realistic settings, have highlighted a proportion of errors analogous to the one of non-expert groups (Eddy 1982).

Kahneman and Tversky (1987) have put forward a possible interpretation of these results, assuming the importance of the framing effect in making the problem of choice plain or opaque. When in the problem context the presence of disturbing elements does not allow the creation of a well structured problem space, then the problem becomes opaque and even the expert is inclined to behave in an irrational way.

In artificial experiments the possibility of selecting and isolating the most relevant decisional variables allows, in principle, direct control of the maximizing rationality hypothesis. Verifying the rational choice hypothesis in the so-called *natural experiments* is a different matter.

Economic science has a pre-eminently deductive nature. Given the general framework of the rational choice hypothesis – in its enlarged version of constrained maximization of the utility function or in the restricted version of maximization of expected utility – economists are interested in extending the applicable domain of the hypothesis. This is achieved through various conventional stratagems, but chiefly through an abundant use of suitable, and often ad hoc, auxiliary assumptions, which protect the rational choice hypothesis from falsifications, without increasing the empirical content of the theory.

This protection is often achieved also in a more "metaphysical" way through the extension of the explicative domain to areas where significant empirical control data are not available.

The confirmation of deductive consequences in neoclassical economics is therefore often reached by adding auxiliary hypothesis of a factual kind, with the function of defining the situation. As Simon (1987, p. 28) maintains, without these factual assumptions on the forms of the utility function, on the way in which agents form expectations about the future or on their attention to specific environmental variables, the maximization of utility hypothesis offers no predictive or explicative value. The limited usefulness of the maximizing hypothesis is proved by the fact that, in many cases, it can be replaced by much weaker hypotheses of "satisficing" behaviour without any loss of explicative power. Some examples made by Simon (1987, pp. 29–38) are enlightening in this respect.

One example comes from Becker's numerous efforts at extending the rational choice hypothesis to domains outside the traditional boundaries of economic science. Becker's theory (1981) on education and intergenerational mobility, or his other theory (1981) on the dynamics in the American family after the Second World War II are an example. In the former he aims at proving that remedial educational programmes cannot reach their purpose because parents of attending children reallocate elsewhere the resources they would have invested in their children. This is based on the assumption that the parents' utility grows in positive terms with their consumption and their children's income and that the children's income is an additive function of the parents' investment and their children's fortune. The conclusion thus does not depend on the maximization hypothesis, but on the auxiliary assumption – empirically unchecked – that the interaction between fortune and income is of an additive rather than a multiplicative kind. Maximization of utility in this case is a condition neither necessary nor sufficient for the compensatory behaviour of parents.

As far as the second example is concerned, according to Becker (1981), the steadily growing proportion of married women in the workforce has been a consequence of the growth in women's wage power as the American economy has developed. This has led to an increase of the housewife's cost of choice and has raised the relative cost of children, with a subsequent reduction in their demand.

According to Simon (1987, p. 31) the whole of Becker's explanation is based on an unexplained change in the demand curve of women's labour. In this case, too, action depends not on the hypothesis of maximization of utility but from factual assumptions about change or stability of demand and offer curves.

Among the examples offered by Simon (1987, pp. 33–34) to illustrate the fundamental – rather than merely auxiliary – role played by auxiliary assumptions, one of the clearest is the explanation of the economic cycle. Both in Keynes' (1936) interpretation and in the opposite one by Lucas (1981), the economic cycle is explained not in reference to maximization hypotheses but to the "money illusion" which workers, according to Keynes, and businessmen, for Lucas, undergo. The former cannot differentiate between changes in real and in nominal wages, while the latter cannot differentiate between general changes in prices and changes in their own industry. Both supplementary assumptions refer to processes leading agents to form certain expectations about future events. Only by studying empirically these processes would it therefore be possible to formulate an empirical theory, capable of genuinely explicating and predicting the economic cycle.

To conclude, both the control of the general propositions at the basis of the model of rational actor and the control of the factual consequences of this theory seem negative.

The successful explanation of the economic behaviour doesn't rely only on the neoclassical theory of rational actor plus the initial conditions but needs the post hoc addition of new assumptions. These assumptions, in many cases, have the form of empirical psychological laws about economic decision making. These laws often add empirical content to the theory, therefore their introduction may be considered non ad hoc and then accepted.[5] But in many cases they rob the neoclassical theory

[5] The principle of the acceptability of a theoretical adjustment on the basis of the increase of the empirical content may be found in many authors, for example in Popper (1959) and Lakatos (1970). This normative principle has found a descriptive support from some methodological and hystorical studies (Donovan et al. 1988).

The possibility of new theoretical adjustments through the introduction of auxiliary hypothesis is allowed when the *ceteris paribus* clause is not put in the unproblematic background knowledge. In general it is always preferable a conventional decision, among the scientists, on when to put this clause on the unproblematic background knowledge and consequently on when stopping the *post hoc* introduction of new assumptions and initial conditions that may save the theory under control. Usually this decision should be taken when, after a certain number of theoretical adjustments the new empirical content has not found any kind of empirical confirmation.

of rational actor of its predictive primacy. The "maximizing" theory itself becomes an auxiliary assumption that may be substituted by the "satisficing" one without any loss of explicative power.

In other cases the post hoc assumption, doesn't add any empirical content nor function as a semantic device to define the situation.

These are typical ad hoc adjustments that show the inadequacy of the theory.

6.3 Unsatisfactory Realism in Simon's Bounded Rationality

In his historical analysis of the economic rationality concept, Simon (1997) rightly espouses what he calls the moderate approach: which means not viewing posterity from the heights of contemporary science's success, but identifying with posterity's cultural and social outlook to understand the reasons for *its* success. The reasons why Simon makes this choice are, first and foremost, because the concept of scientific progress as an accumulation leading to truth is relatively untenable, and, above all, because it enables him to use the theoretical lens of bounded rationality to stress how, in some cases, the trend has been one of descent from, rather than ascension to, economic classics.

If we analyse theses connecting motions in greater detail, we may be able to understand how Simon's concept of bounded rationality is positioned, and what implications it has for economic actor theory.

The first differentiation is to be found in the ontology of the economic actor concept. Does it refer to the general characteristics of the agent, or does it simply single out the functions of the actor who is present in economic contexts? Or, to put it another way, does it describe the real man or only a part of him specialising in economic interaction? If we think back to two of the founding fathers of economic theory, Adam Smith and John Stuart Mill, the difference is clear. In Smith's view (1776), man's self interest conduct, the object of economic study, was not aimed solely at increasing his pecuniary wealth, but rather at sentiments such as honour, ambition, social esteem, love of dominion and so on – themes of psychological study; Mill (1848), instead, saw it as a hypothetical exemplification isolating a select set of the functions, such as the maximisation of wellbeing and the desire for leisure time, which underpin economic behaviour. *Homo oeconomicus* is thus an abstraction of only a part of human conduct, not of the whole. This "fictional man" differs from the real man proposed by other authors, such as Neville Keynes (1917), according to whom the economic actor is not an abstraction of a specific part of behaviour, since self-interest and the pursuit of subjective utility are pervasive and predominant over other forms thereof, such as altruism and solidarity.

In this conflict, the realistic position would appear to enjoy clear predominance in most of modern and contemporary economics. But the question is: what kind of realism are we referring to? How can the economic actor theory be generated from the characteristics of the real man? One way would be to construct generalised psychological functions that are significant for economic action: this is the way suggested by Hutchinson (1938) and by bounded rationality theory. The other is to use intuition or introspection to separate a limited number of principles which govern the behaviour of the real man, and which characterise him as *homo oeconomicus*. This is the way followed by virtually all economic theory from Senior (1836; 1965) onwards, and the one which characterises the neoclassical global rationality concept. Its aim is to describe the economic agent in terms of a general behavioural principle, that of maximisation of individual utility functions.

These characteristics are introduced by a somewhat "unrealistic", superficial analysis of an extremely limited psychological nature, that of the aims-desires-action triad. Moreover, the psychology adopted is not scientific at all but, rather, of the common-sense, folk variety. The outcome of this supposedly "realist" formulation is thus not all that different from Mill's antirealist or "fictional" version.

Corresponding to this antithetical construction of *homo oeconomicus* is the bifurcation of global and bounded rationality, which is accentuated in the second differentiation, that of the epistemological and methodological basis for actor theory. Once they have been introduced, are the principles which characterise the economic agent aprioristic and unfalsifiable, hence empirically uncontrollable, or are they, instead, falsifiable, controllable and, in the final analysis, corrigible? The first is, of course, the epistemological option which prevails in economics. It does not matter how assumptions are introduced – whether by observation, introspection or intuition or completely hypothetically – but once they have been, they are turned into aprioristically unfalsifiable truths. This type of apriorism is to be found in many authors, such as Robbins, von Mises and even Friedman (1953), according to whom, indirectly and paradoxically, it becomes important for a hypothesis to be descriptively false in its fundamental assumptions. What counts most is its predictive capacity.

This takes us to the methodological differentiation of empiric scope and control capacity of hypotheses in economics, which gets to the heart of the realism–antirealism diatribe in economic actor theory. Leaving aside the extreme apriorism of classical economics, which is concerned not so much with controlling theory's predictions as with its ad hoc application to reality, we can single out two forms of relationship with empiric data. The instrumentalist form considers economic actor theory as a "black box", introduced hypothetically and judged acceptable as long as it produces correct predictions. Whenever anomalies occur, the outer belt of auxiliary hypotheses might protect the hardcore of fundamental assumptions, unless this leads – to use Lakatos's term (1970) – to "degenerating problem-shifts"; that is, to a decrease in empirical content. In this case, it is necessary to replace the theoretical core with other hypothetical assumptions. This formulation, which we might link to Friedman's, differs from the empiricist position of Hutchinson and Simon, who also consider empirical research as a way of helping to perfect and improve fundamental assumptions – the theoretical core – insofar as it makes the latter correspond increasingly to reality.

These methodological desiderata are very different from the reality of contemporary economics. Whereas, in principle, the leading neoclassical economists declare their willingness to sacrifice basic assumptions when faced with falsified predictions and degenerating problem-shifts, in practice, contemporary economics is very close to the "classical" approach, well represented by John Stuart Mill, which is, instead, prepared to use the *ceteris paribus* condition to the bitter end specifically to neutralise every anomaly. Simon's procedural and bounded rationality theory thus differs sharply – empirically and realistically – from the apriorism and ad hoc conventionalism of much of past and contemporary economics.

What are the implications for Simon's bounded rationality of this sharp realist and empiricist characterisation? Let us analyse the concept of rationality in greater depth. As we have seen in the first part of the book it may be broken down into three parts, each corresponding to a stage in the decision-making process. The informative process provides the agent with more or less accurate evidential data, which are then represented and memorised *("perceptive rationality and rationality of beliefs")*; through forms of logical and probabilistic reasoning, the decision-making process infers the possible action from the information *(decision-making rationality)*; and implementation processes transform the potential action, more or less accurately, into the real action (*rationality of the action*). Decision-making rationality may, in turn, be broken down into two forms of rationality: *cognitive rationality*, which concerns the processing of available data to define the agent's expectations of himself and the surrounding environment, and *instrumental rationality* which, on the basis of these expectations, seeks to select the most appropriate action. Perceptive rationality, rationality of beliefs and decision-making rationality correspond to Simon's *procedural and bounded rationality*.

The first problem arises when we address the at once descriptive and normative character of Simon's rationality concept. The old dilemma of positive or normative economics has "jumped with its feet together" insofar as he commits the naturalist fallacy of asserting that bounded rationality corresponds to the empirical theory of cognitive decision processes.

Simon (1997) writes that "People have motivations and use reasons (well or badly) to respond to these motivations, and to reach their goals". In this context, "well or badly" signifies the use or otherwise of the best means available – the best heuristics, for instance – instrumental to reaching a given goal. It is thus possible to judge a decision-maker rationality normatively through a set of criteria for assessing the effectiveness or efficiency of processes used to achieve a given objective. This set of criteria derives, first of all, from the empirical study of the various general weak and strong problem-solving heuristics, and from the identification of specific techniques and methodologies successfully applicable in the particular type of problem space in a problematic area.

Plainly, the identification of normative with descriptive is unsatisfactory, but a key role is played by the epistemological concept of rationality's instrumental value, which is tacitly added as a key to assessment of the actor's decision. Hence, Simon's naturalist theory whereby procedural rationality corresponds to the empirical theory of cognitive decision-making does not hold. It is necessary to add the prescriptive attribute of "instrumental".[6]

The problem becomes even thornier if we consider perceptive rationality and rationality of beliefs. In this case too, it is very problematic to assert that it corresponds to the cognitive theory of perception and memory. Perceptive rationality and rationality of beliefs is concerned with how we build the database on which we make our inferences, hence our decisions, and thus refers prevalently to perceptive and mnemonic inputs. If by cognitive theory we were to understand the general psychological modalities whereby man remembers, hears and sees, it would comprise all the errors, contradictions and illusions which systematically cram our daily perceptive and mnemonic activity, and which have been highlighted in recent years by cognitive science. But we would be hardly likely to construct a concept of rationality on errors, illusions and contradictions. If, instead, by

[6] In contemporary epistemology, the other two most important attempts to justify rationality empirically – the evolutionary and "reflective equilibrium" attempts – entail a number of drawbacks.

The first sets out from the premise that, in evolution, natural selection is discriminatory, favouring the emergence of organisms that tend towards optimality of the phenotype. Hence man's present cognitive apparatus, the fruit of a million years' evolution, is very close to optimality in its reasoning and inferential capacities. This thesis is based on a simplistic interpretation of evolutionary mechanisms: the latter are represented not only by natural selection, but also by genetic drift, migration and differential mutation rates, which may also lead to the stabilisation of negative characteristics of the phenotype. Moreover, in natural selection there are phenomena, such as pleiotropy, heterozigotic superiority and meiotic drive, which select less adaptive phenotypes than those potentially available. Besides, even if evolution always tended towards optimality, for it to justify rationality empirically we would have to demonstrate that inferential capacities are necessarily determined by the genome, and that inferential rationality increases individual fitness on a biological and social level. Neither claim appears plausible.

The second epistemological thesis is that of reflective equilibrium, introduced by Nelson Goodman (1965). How can we justify an inferential principle? Through its adequacy to what common sense intuitively regards as legitimate inferences. How can we justify inferences? Through their subsumption by inferential principles that are considered legitimate. It is from this reciprocal interaction that the test to justify inferential rationality principles may empirically derive. Despite its undoubted appeal, this principle, applied empirically by Stich and Nisbett (1980), has led to somewhat unsatisfactory results, such as the acceptance of inferential principles like those on which the "gambler's fallacy" is based, and conservative basic frequency estimates. Nor does it seem possible to apply defensive strategies, such as "wide reflective equilibrium" (inferential principles plus all the philosophical and social principles which govern individual judgement) or "expert reflective equilibrium" (thus restricting the sample of who is called to judge to experts in formal reasoning). Perhaps the most tenable position is the so-called neo-Goodman one, which constructs a cognitive theory of the natural processes at the basis of the intuitive justification of inferential principles. This theory might become the test of the latter's acceptability, and the foundation of inferential rationality itself.

This option differs from Simon's inasmuch as the descriptive level is not that of cognitive decision processes, but the metalevel of the cognitive processes underlying the intuitive justification of the principles which govern cognitive decision processes. Besides, the object is not the cognitive capacity instrumentally effective to problem-solving, but the intuitive capacity to justify inferential rules and principles (Goldman 1993; Viale 2001a).

perceptive rationality and rationality of beliefs we mean the perceptive and mnemonic modalities of correct and coherent representation of the real world, then we can perform this screening by tacitly introducing two important epistemological and prescriptive principles; that of coherence[7] and that of truth.[8] In my view, it is,

[7] Traditionally, one of the first prerequisites of rationality has been that of logical coherence not only in terms of beliefs, but also of the logical implications of such beliefs. The prerequisite of the closure and coherence of the logical implications of a system of beliefs contrasts with a series of reflections on the computational limits and cognitive performance of the human mind. The point of departure is what Cherniak (1986) calls the "finitary predicament", which characterises the life of man: it refers to the finite nature of biological time and resources of calculus, which make knowledge of all the logical consequences of our system of beliefs impossible. There is also a series of demonstrations by the theory of complexity. In assessment of the computational feasibility of some classes of algorithms, it has been shown that many familiar algorithms require a computational power so great as to be inexpressible by the human brain. For example, as far as coherence is concerned, it has been demonstrated that a system of beliefs containing the conjunction of 138 independent logical propositions, assessed using the simple truth table method, requires an absolutely fantastic power of calculus and amount of time. Since the human memory contains a much higher number of beliefs than 138, it is evidently impossible, in principle, to achieve every prerequisite of logical closure and coherence.

These considerations are accompanied by the many results of empirical research, which demonstrate how man maintains sets of defective, contradictory beliefs. Suffice it to cite Nisbett and Ross's phenomenon of "belief perseverance" (1980), according to which a belief, even if falsified by empirical evidence, is often maintained in the long-term memory alongside the new, true belief.

In view of these reflections, the prerequisite of coherence as a characterisation of rationality seems irrelevant. This does not exempt us, however, from seeking to identify criteria of assessment and acceptability of the formal characteristics of our database, and thence to draw inferences. According to our new criterion, it will be possible, with the inevitable variability given by underdetermination, to judge the rationality or otherwise of our inferences and decisions. For example, if we proposed ourselves a pragmatic-epistemic aim such as the utility of truth, the prerequisite of swift, prompt elimination of all inconsistencies would no longer seem so desirable. A coherent set of beliefs is not necessarily better from the point of view of truth than an incoherent set. It might be a coherent set of false beliefs. Moreover, faced by an incoherent set of beliefs, before eliminating the incoherence, sometimes it is better to have more data to be certain that we are not sacrificing a true belief for a false one, Viale (1992).

[8] The problem of the reliability of beliefs has various complications. The first is to understand what is meant by true belief – whether there is correspondence to facts of the real world through some belief-mapping function, or coherence between belief and its implications through feedback with the environment. The first interpretation is a realist one and forms the basis for causal-functional theories of the semantics of mental states (such as those developed by Hilary Putnam, Saul Kripke, Hartry Field, Ned Block, Michael Devitt, William Lycan, Colin McGinn and Kim Sterelny). The second is pragmatist and is well represented by the theory behind the programme of Holland, Holyoak, Nisbett and Thagard (1986), which uses concepts such as "default hierarchy" to construct beliefs and hypotheses about the world on the basis of environmental feedbacks.

The second complication is to decide on what bases it is possible to justify truth as an ultimate criterion for assessment of our database. The most convincing response is the instrumental one: if we have true beliefs this improves our chances of achieving other aims, such as happiness and survival. As Stich (1990) has rightly highlighted, this is likely if we compare true beliefs and false beliefs. The problem is that, at the mental level, there seems to be a vast computational space occupied by states that have no conditions of truth, that are neither true nor false. Albeit

above all, the principle of truth or likelihood, in its various forms of correspondence to reality – a veritable labour of Sisyphus in contemporary epistemology – which acts as a conceptual stumbling-block in the way of Simon's programme to reduce the normative theory of procedural rationality to the descriptive theory of perception and decision. To reach his objective, therefore, Simon first has to solve the normative problem of how and why a perceptive, mnemonic data-base is correct, and hence acceptable as a point of departure for our inferences and decisions.

The second problem we encounter is that of the scope of the realism of the rational actor hypothesis. Insofar as Simon's bounded and procedural rationality seeks to be a realistic representation of human cognitive activity, it finds its *raison d'étre* in the hypotheses and knowledge of psychology. The first question we have to ask is: "what type of psychology?". There are almost as many types of psychology as there are psychologists! Although he sometimes seems to leave leeway to common-sense psychology – which seems to me devoid of empirical content and explicative capacity,[9] – Simon (1987) naturally enough, favours cognitive

non-semantic, these mental states, such as emotions or the subconscious sphere, may contribute to the attainment of other aims such as survival and happiness to an extent comparable to true beliefs. It is also necessary to explore the thesis that to have true beliefs is a sure way of achieving our most important ends, such as survival and happiness. At a social and biological evolutionary level, it is possible to demonstrate instead that truth has costs both in terms of internal resources such as time, waste of energy and the limitedness of physical hardware and of adaptation to the external environment.

In the first case, it is possible to demonstrate that a natural selection process may tend to select a less truthful inferential system as opposed to a more truthful one, insofar as cost-benefit analysis may reveal the first to be more economical in terms of hardware and that the marginal utility of the second decreases as the capability of processing true information increases.

As for adaptation to the environment, it is easy to imagine how very prudent organisms which tend to increase beliefs about dangers erroneously – that is to generate many positive falsehoods – may have more chances of avoiding dangers, and hence to survive, than organisms which process a greater number of true beliefs, but also the odd fatal negative falsehood.

It is better to be a relatively unreliable organism, risk-adverse and generating positive falsehoods – as in the belief that a mushroom is poisonous when it actually isn't than to be relatively reliable, prone to risk but occasionally processing negative falsehoods – for example, that a mushroom isn't poisonous when it is.

[9] Common-sense psychology is based on the ascribing of semantic content to mental states such as believing, desiring, wishing and so on. One of the main objection to this type of psychology is that it is chauvinistic; that is, it is incapable of representing the mental activity of persons culturally and cognitively different from ourselves, such as children, members of other cultures, the mentally disabled and so on. When we ascribe content to a mental state, we must compare the latter to our own. We assert that a person is in a mental state – believing p, for instance – if in the same conditions we would have asserted the same belief p. Plainly, this attribution process cannot happen in the company of individuals with a different cultural and cognitive background from our own. This is a conspicuous and serious limitation for a psychology which claims to be scientific. It also has another limit insofar as it is uncontrollable and unfalsifiable as an action theory. It is never possible to check its predictions independently without presupposing the theory itself in the check. Finally, in asserting the irreducibility of the semantic dimension of mental states, this theory is based on a dualist conception of the mind, which seems today to be unlikely by the latest developments in cognitive science.

psychology, of which he was one of the main founding fathers. Yet, especially over the last few years, the sea of cognitive psychology too has grown increasingly stormy.

As a model of mental activity, Simon uses production systems composed of the condition-action rules which are stored in the long-term memory, and are governed by the programmes which operate in the working memory. This model presupposes a unitary architecture of the mind, a simple structure of the memory[10] and of the control processes which govern the execution of mental tasks and, finally, the assumption that the processes which govern learning and memory depend upon explicit symbolic rules.

Our first critical consideration concerns methodology: since production systems have the unlimited power of Turing's universal machine, their claim to be a general model of mental activity is unfalsifiable by any empirical psychological evidence. Although we may reject a particular production system which simulates a given cognitive function, if we find it explicatively inadequate, it will always be possible to elaborate another particular production system capable of incorporating any coherent configuration of empirical results. Therefore, since the system cannot be confuted as a general model of mental architecture in any empirical research activity, it becomes difficult to accept the hypothesis of their correspondence with mental reality. This is a body blow for the theory's realist and empiricist claims.

The second consideration is a scientific one. The best way to check whether a hypothesis is realist is of course to see at close quarters how reality – in this case, the mind and the brain – is made up. Lately, cognitive science has cast doubts on the scientific validity of the mental activity of Simon's model, which ought to represent the content of bounded and procedural rationality.[11]

One initial doubt concerns the code of mental representations, which Simon considers entirely reducible to list structures. Are we really sure that propositions and, above all, representations in image-form are built into the long-term memory as list structures? Simon himself has recognised that they cannot represent the images' metrical and spatial continuity properties. As recent neurophysiological

[10] The memory structure contained in production systems (even the most complex ones such as Anderson's ACT (1983), is too simplified with respect to the latest hypotheses drawn from psychology and neuropsychology, which identify at least five basic types of memory (1) the central executive system; (2) the sensory store; (3) the working memory; (4) the permanent memory for fundamental skills; (5) the long-term memory for experience and knowledge.

[11] It is undoubtedly true that any theory on a natural phenomenon is always an abstraction and an idealisation of the phenomenon, hence even a mental theory is different from the mind itself. Moreover, no one questions the methodological utility of computational models of the mind and related programmes for avoiding incoherencies, incompletenesses or lack of understanding at an intersubjective level. However, the use of such models – production systems, for example – sets out from the uncorroborated premise that the mind is a computational phenomenon like one of Turing's machines. If, in a near future, it was demonstrated that the effective procedures of the mind cannot be simulated by any computer, the principal reasons for the importance attributed to these models would no longer hold.

research would appear to suggest, the mental image is irreducible and it is produced by the activity of the same structure of the central nervous system as visual perception.

A second, and much more important, doubt regards the type of mental processing. Research in the fields of neuropsychology and artificial intelligence is increasingly reinforcing the thesis that memory, learning and mental activity in general happen not through the manipulation of separate symbols according to explicit rules as in Simon's production systems, but through the parallel processing of distributed representations created by the fusion of many separate experiences. It is the thesis underlying connectionism and neural networks that represents a raw nerve for Simon. I wonder, along with many other cognitive scientists such as Johnson Laird (1988) whether it is not possible to identify a compromise between the two approaches envisaging different levels of representation – a high level with explicit, separate symbols and a low level with distributed configurations – and making conscious processes depend on the manipulation of separate, explicit symbols and unconscious parallel processing of distributed representations.[12]

This proposition is of founding value to the very concept of bounded rationality for a very precise reason. We know that the greater part of mental activity is related to, or controlled by, the emotional sphere and needs. We perceive the form of a well known face in an unknown person because it is connected, for instance, to our expectation and desire to meet that person. We memorise sometimes complex recollections at a computational level when they have emotional value, and we persevere in our beliefs, even if they are false, if they are connected with the affective sphere. We learn only a limited series of skills or knowledge in a limited time because the emotional and motivational sphere allows us to focus our attention on the most significant aspects, and to reinforce our memory of the various procedural stages that are successful. We produce a limited number of inferences and "reasonings" with respect to the huge quantity that is possible in principle, because it is our needs, motivations, emotions, as well as our pragmatic interests, which direct and select our inferential processes. Finally, even the result of these processes often seems determined by causes in our unconscious emotional life, as studies from Kahneman and Tversky onwards on decision psychology have demonstrated. The fact is that, whereas all this limits and constrains our rationality

[12] Although a structural correspondence between connectionist architectures and the mind-brain unit does not as yet appear relevant, some experimental results seem to go in this direction. In a recent experiment, Geoff Hinton (cited by Johnson Laird 1988) established distributed associations between words and characteristics of their meaning, and then nullified some of the hidden units used to establish the associations. The result was an increase in errors of interpretation of the various words, rather than a complete loss of meaning of a specific word. Many of the errors consisted of elements of meaning appropriate for a word different from the one previously presented. This phenomenon is reminiscent of the profound dyslexia which is verified in certain forms of cerebral lesion, in which the request to read a word is met with a semantically correlated word. It is hard to imagine how this effect might arise in damage to a system based on structural rules.

and, more specifically, the rationality of the economic actor, as Mill and Keynes marginally observed, this important dimension of mental activity does not seem to be given the place it deserves in the psychology underlying Simon's bounded rationality concept. This happens precisely because production systems based on rules and explicit symbols seem inadequate as models of unconscious mental life and mental events such as emotion, which seemingly display characteristics of impenetrability and cognitive holism. It is these considerations which give rise to my doubt about the realism of the human cognition theory at the base of the bounded rationality concept, and the need to improve it and supplement it in the future with cognitive models based on the cerebral nervous structure and activity.

I do not believe, in fact, that Simon wishes to shun the epistemological aim of constructing theories to represent reality that are more than mere simplifications, useful only for drawing inferences, as some cognitive scientists and many economists seem to suggest. A non-conventionalist approach, therefore, ought to prompt a greater willingness to accept hypotheses, such as that of neuro-computational programme, which seek to construct a closer correspondence between mind and brain, without detracting from the historical merit of the production systems hypothesis as a useful fiction for studying one part of mental activity.[13]

6.4 Conclusion: A *Big Bang* of Rationality?

In conclusion, I wish to ask a question which may sound a little provocative. Faced by what Quine (1969), in philosophy, has defined as the programme of naturalised epistemology, which for Simon means founding a concept that has always been sharply normative such as rationality in an empirical theory such as human cognition, are we so sure that the moment has not come to question the term "rationality" itself?

It is possible to extract two epistemological criteria from Simon's bounded rationality theory to assess the rationality of our inferences: one is antiutopian, the other consequentialist.

According to the first principle (the term of which ís borrowed by Larry Laudan (1984) who applies it to scientific rationality), the question we have to answer is: can a given inference, computation and reasoning be processed in the human mind? If a given inferential and computational model presupposes Olympian skills of reasoning beyond the scope of human cognitive possibility, it may be interesting theoretically, but inapplicable as a criterion for judging man's inferential rationality.

[13] One of the most sophisticated models based on production systems is John Anderson's ACT (1983). It seeks to embrace both memory and learning by combining a bottom–up approach with a top–down one, but it is unconvincing in its explanation of how learning right take place in a production system.

The second assessment principle is the consequentialist one. What type of consequence does this modality of reasoning entail in relation to the aims we have proposed ourselves, and to environmental and contextual constraints? Plainly, in this case the judgement on inferential rationality is comparative: that is, an attempt is made to compare different inferential procedures and to analyse the one which – aims and environmental and contextual constraints being equal – is most effective in achieving the objective. If these are the two criteria for assessing rationality, one inevitably wonders whether the moment has not arrived to abandon the very term "rationality", and break it down into the attributes which characterise an inferential-type human activity effective in achieving the objectives of a problematic context. In drawing inferences, why not break the term down into its attributes of power, accuracy and velocity? This might have a number of advantages: it would adapt better to the consequentialist and instrumental character of reasoning activity; it would be more suited to the characterisation typical of the analytical concepts which describe an inferential activity as procedure and heuristics; finally, it would be more effective in expressing the limitedness of time, power of calculus, memory and perceptive reliability, which characterise the activity of the mind-brain unit.

Feasibility and Realism in Cognitive Economics

7

7.1 A Growing Dissatisfaction with Economics

Economics is not in good shape. Over the past 20 years even *The Economist* has debated the case for abandoning the traditional neoclassical economic tools, since they seem unable to explain, let alone predict, most economic phenomena. In an article published on 23 April 1994, *The Economist* affirmed that, according to financial economists, only the study of decision-making psychology could shed any light on what is apparently irrational and inexplicable financial market behaviour. The neoclassical economists believed that markets are efficient, in other words prices reflect fundamental information and they change only if that information changes, rather than in response to the whims of fickle investors. Quoting George Soros (Wall Street guru as well as Popper's student) and the Stanford economist Bill Sharpe, who won the Nobel Prize for his part in developing efficient-market theory, *The Economist* maintained that prospect theory and framing effects offer better explanations than neoclassical economics for both short- and long-term oddities in financial markets.

The Economist's thesis is only one of the many complaints concerning the empirical inadequacy of economics put forward by different corners of the academic and economic world. The key question they all address is how to deal with the empirical anomalies and inadequacies of economics? In summarizing the various methodological solutions, I have attempted to extrapolate three positions.

The first is the Popperian position or non-sophisticated falsificationism expressed by authors like Mark Blaug (1980, pp. 160–161). In Blaug's opinion neoclassical economics does not fit the methodological desiderata of an empirical theory. For example, consumer theory is full of economic laws that are only ad hoc and ex post facto rationalizations of all final demand outcomes. Samuelson himself writes

---

The present chapter is a modified version of Viale, R. (1997). From neoclassical to cognitive economics: The epistemological constraints of feasibility and realism. In R. Viale (ed.), *Cognitive economics*. Fondazione Rosselli, Quaderni Lascomes, Lascomes Series, I.

DOI 10.1007/978-3-642-24743-9_7,

that, considering all economic laws from “Bowley’s Law” of constant relative wage share to “Everybody’s Law” of a constant capital–output ratio, the conclusion is that “*If these be Laws, Mother Nature is a criminal by nature*” (Samuelson 1966, p. 1539). If this criticism is taken seriously, all taxpayers and economic bodies should ask the neoclassical economists for a refund of all the moneys paid for market analyses and forecasts because neoclassical economists have told fibs by declaring the scientificity and reliability of their economic advice. However, fortunately for them, for the past 20 years puritanical Popperian methodology has been undermined by methodologies with looser morals and more easy-going virtues.

The second is represented by McCloskey’s *The Rhetoric of Economics* (1986, reprinted in Hausman ed. 1994), which is an example of the new libertarian, “anything goes” approach. He argues that the methodology of economics should limit itself to studying the linguistic style and the shape of the arguments, namely the rhetoric, that economists use in their reasoning and theorizing.

One may be also attracted by pluralism in the philosophy of science, but what about the criteria for theory choice and theory generation? If “anything goes”, there is no chance of a reasonable discussion (I do not ask for a rational one) inside the scientific community. In science this discussion might be a conventional game, as some might think, but, as in every game, it must be played by the rules. Therefore we must establish the criteria of demarcation between what we consider to be an acceptable economic theory (game) and what is not acceptable.

The third and final position is Friedman’s anti-realist “as if” proposal (1953), which, in my opinion, is a methodological game played with exact rules. We may know that our economic theory is false or we do not care about its truth. What is important is that it saves the phenomena, that it makes good predictions.

This position reminds me of one of Duhem’s heroes, the medieval Piccolomini who described the Ptolemaic astronomers in these terms:

> for these astronomers it was amply sufficient that their constructs save the appearances, that they allow for the reckoning of the movements of the heavenly bodies, their arrangements, and their place. Whether or not things really are as they envisage them – that question they leave to the philosophers of nature (Duhem 1969, p. 82).

This instrumentalist and anti-realist position might be also acceptable, from a pragmatic point of view (which I do not share), provided the theory produces good predictions and successful technological applications and no better theory exists with regard to empirical accuracy and computational simplicity. But, faced with the empirical failures of neoclassical economics, even Friedman’s “as if” fiction no longer works and therefore we must confront the problem of building a different representation of the economic phenomena which we want to explain and predict. To achieve this goal we must solve the following dilemma: can the descriptive and predictive power of economics be increased by developing and improving the neoclassical theory or, as Blaug maintains, must we abandon the neoclassical postulates and look for an alternative theory?

There are three main philosophical flaws that, in my opinion, condemn neoclassical economics to a barren desert of research with no prospect of development and improvement.

The first is related to the *model of mind* used in economics. This model, which is based on the belief-preference-action triad, seems empirically empty and unfalsifiable. Even if this model of mind were valid there is a second flaw that impedes the improvement of neoclassical economics: this is a *theory of rationality* built in an a priori way and justified by an old-fashioned rationalistic epistemology.

Lastly, even if the first two flaws could be overcome, neoclassical economics subscribes to a *philosophy of science* that is too similar to that of physical science in the past. Nowadays the primacy of theoretical explanations and of goals like coherence and deductive elegance are questionable in physical sciences, but they continue to be popular in economics. This methodological attitude constrains and impedes genuine and bold empirical research.

The weaknesses of neoclassical economics and the possible solutions to them point us towards the development of what we can call a cognitive approach to economics. The need for this new approach in economics is an indicator, even from the permissive point of view of economic rhetoric, that the neoclassical arguments have become increasingly less satisfactory and unappealing to the community of economists.

It is worth examining each of the three flaws mentioned above in greater detail.

7.2 The Empirical Vacuum of Folk Psychology Used by Economics

Economic theory assumes that economic causes should be systematically categorized into classes of preference and belief in order to explain actions like buying and selling, and the movements of markets, industries and economies to which these actions are aggregated. Late nineteenth-century marginalists like Wicksteed saw clearly that microeconomics is but formalization of this commonsense notion, and the history of consumer behaviour is the search for laws that can express the relations between preference, belief, and action, first in terms of cardinal utility and certainty, later in terms of ordinal utility, revealed preference, and expected utility under varying conditions of uncertainty and risk. The failure to find such laws seems to rely, among other things, on the empirical and conceptual anomalies of a model of action based on such variables as belief and preference.

According to the first consideration, since the triad belief-desire-action stems from the common sense of everyday life – and in fact the relative psychology is called "commonsense or folk psychology" – the interchangeable and confused use that is made in economics of concepts related to belief and desire is incorrect and goes against the commonsense meaning of the words. For example, the economics uses synonyms for preference words like desire – while it is possible to prefer something that is not desirable – goal – while I might be constrained to follow a certain goal without having preferred it, let alone desired it – want, and so on.

Also belief is sometimes exchanged with opportunity and expectation, although there is a clear difference between them: expecting that something might happen, or having an opportunity to do something does not imply believing in either.

In addition, according to commonsense psychology, the mental machine responsible for economic action is impressive for its poverty. How can we limit the causal variables of action only to belief and preference? We know from personal experience how many other factors are involved in decision and action. These include emotions towards external or internal experiences, and particular motives that strengthen our decision to behave in a certain way. Then, there is the sensibility that influences our perceptual ability; and lastly, the numerous other cognitive and emotional factors, such as regret, confidence and creativity.

The theoretical poverty of the mental machinery of the economic actor may be also explained by the goals that this model of action should pursue. The central aim of neoclassical economics was to explain the general economic equilibrium. In the Walrasian auctioneer model the economic actors do not need a variegated and powerful mental life to choose the equilibrium price. Their rationality does not need to be strategic but only parametric (Egidi 1992, p. 470). Their simplified mind does not need tools and operators to solve poorly structured problems, or to innovate or produce new knowledge. The consequence of this simplified model of action is that the Walrasian theory of a perfectly competitive market fails completely when dealing with goods like knowledge, information and innovation. But this failure does not stem only from the public-good nature of information, innovation and knowledge, as Arrow (1971) pointed out. It stems also from the poor cognitive endowment of the neoclassical economic actor: this simple-minded actor is not able to behave as an innovative and adaptive agent, or to invent the future; he is not able to devise new solutions, for example new economic institutions, useful for the complexity of the market and for the need for more and better information; finally he is not able to change by learning fixed routines and deterministic behaviour.

Second, during the past 20 years there has been a great debate among those specializing in philosophy of the mind and psychology about the empirical adequacy of commonsense psychology. This is not the time or place to analyse the debate in depth, but it is worthwhile highlighting some critical remarks.

The claims of folk psychology might be represented by this general statement or law:

> *L: if a person x desires d, and x has belief c that a is the best action to attain goal d, then, ceteris paribus, x will do a.*

How is it possible to control L? We must be able to control its predictions. Let us try to check if we are able to do this.

Imagine a nomological deductive explanation that is covered by L:

1. L
2. Soros desires d, to earn money
3. Soros believes c, that a, the action of buying shares on the Italian Stock Exchange is the best way to attain d, to earn money
4. Soros does a, buys shares on the Italian Stock Exchange.

The main problem is how to successfully control the correctness of the initial conditions 2 and 3. One way is to observe the behaviour and to draw inferences from the action in relation to the beliefs and desires. As every inference to the best explanation the conclusion might be very risky: the desires might be many and incoherent with each other or they might be different from what we think is more likely. For example, Soros might wish to lose money in order to alter expectations concerning his rational infallibility (in fact, the history of the Italian Stock Exchange should warn any rational investor from investing in it to earn money). Or the belief itself might be different, for example, investing in State Bonds to earn money, but the action did not correspond to the belief because of irrational perturbations between the intention and the action.

But even if it were possible, and reliable, to draw inferences from the action with regard to the beliefs and desires, it can only be done by presupposing L, that is the real focus of our enquiry. The same problem arises if we refer to analogous actions that happened in the past or if we try to reproduce them experimentally. In principle we cannot overcome the vicious circle even by asking Soros what his beliefs and desires are, since his answer will be a verbal action that we will always evaluate by presupposing L on the basis of hypothetical beliefs and desires. In conclusion, L cannot be controlled empirically because every control presupposes the truth of L.

This result conceals another serious drawback: the tautological dimension of L. Every description of human action according to L is equivalent to a repetition of the event to be described. We cannot describe an action without reference to the beliefs and desires that contain the action and we cannot describe the belief without reference to the desires and actions. Therefore L, which is folk psychology, contains the features of the definition (Rosenberg 1988, pp. 26–38; Viale 1994a, p. 304).

Third, another strong criticism of the model of action based on belief and preference is that it is a theoretical fiction that does not correspond to any natural kind, and it cannot be reduced or supported by any other accepted scientific theory.

According to Rosenberg (1983, reprinted in Hausman ed., 1994, p. 384), belief and preference do not seem to correspond to natural kinds because we are not able to identify any empirical method that can answer questions like what do they refer to? How can we identify them? How are they generated? How can they be altered and modified? What is their physical substratum and so on? And while common-sense psychology has tried to deepen and develop, at least conceptually, the meaning of belief and preference, neoclassical economics has remained constrained by these concepts which have gradually lost every shred of original, intuitive, semantic meaning, leaving just syntactic variables.

In addition, a well-known and shared criteria of science is to accept a law or a theory when it forms part of a theoretical network, when there is a deductive bridge that connects it to other accepted scientific laws or theories. There are some exceptions like the Mendel unit of inheritance which cannot be reduced to a molecular gene, but this exception has proved successful in terms of improving technological and predictive success. Instead the intentional concepts of economics cannot be reduced to any other theory in cognitive science and neuroscience nor can they be shown to meet the standards of predictive and technological success in their application to economics (Rosenberg 1983, reprinted in Hausman ed., 1994, pp. 384–387).

The predictive weakness of economics hinges on the intentional typology of the phenomena it explains and the causes it identifies. Its failure to uncover laws of human behaviour is due to its wrongly assuming that these laws will trade in preferences, beliefs, or their cognates. And the system of propositions about markets and economies that economists have constructed on the basis of its assumptions about human behaviour is deprived of improving explanatory and predictive power. Its assumptions cannot be improved in a way that transmits improved precision to their consequences.

Therefore, the mental machinery responsible for economic action must be enriched far beyond the folk concepts of belief and preference. Cognitive science and, in particular, cognitive psychology have developed many different empirical generalizations and laws that can give a richer and more accurate representation of the reality of the mental life, and in particular its reasoning and decision-making.

7.3 A Priori Rationality is Unfeasible

Economics involves searching for the law that describes the relationship between preference, belief and action. This search characterizes the aim of positive economics which, by trying to generalize the law of human action, might be seen as corresponding, in principle, to the naturalistic side of commonsense psychology. I write "in principle" because, as a matter of fact, positive neoclassical economics seems to have abdicated its empirical function and has, more or less implicitly, identified the law of economic action with the last version of the theory of Olympic rationality, now characterized as the principle of maximizing the function of subjective expected utility. As pointed out by Hausman and McPherson (1993, reprinted in Hausman ed., 1994, pp. 256–259), the normativity of the theory of rationality has created a powerful rhetorical argument for neoclassical economists which can be summarized as follows: since the positive theory of actual choice is also a normative theory of rational choice, it gives us one strong reason to accept and save the positive theory. In fact empirical anomalies, such as preference reversal, are not only in conflict with the positive theory of choice but also with the normative theory of choice. For that reason, according to defenders of neoclassical economics, irrational behaviour, like preference reversal, should be treated as unstable and occasional because it creates opportunities to be exploited by other normal rational agents and therefore quickly disappears from the market. In other words, either irrational people will learn not to be exploited and become rational or they will quit the market. In this way positive economics is saved – both rhetorically and ad hoc – by the non-falsifiable a priori theory of rationality.

I do not want to highlight the empirical refutations of this claim: the markets are full of systematic failures and of pervasive, crystallized, irrational behaviour. We may say that the market floats on irrationalities. What I want to point out is that this argument relies on old-fashioned epistemology which justifies rationality in an a priori way. Until recently, building a priori moral and rational justifications had been the prevailing philosophical tradition for many centuries. The neo-positivist programme used the same approach and tried to justify rationally inductive generalizations from empirical facts using propositional calculus and set theory. The failures of the neo-positivist programme, and also other a priori attempts, were mainly the result of two reasons, one linked to conceptual difficulties and inadequacies and the other to the unfeasibility of these prescriptions when applied to the reality, in the case of both scientific decision-making and moral behaviour. This second reason has given rise to an important new epistemological tradition named after Quine, Goodman, Simon, and more recently Stich and Goldman, or in ethics known as the Rawls approach. The common ground of this approach is a recognition of the philosophical consequences of what is ultimately the mental origin of our postulates and principles. Both in the case of formal principles as those of logic and probability calculus and in the case of moral principles as those of social justice and individual freedom, the ultimate justification stems from human intuition and reasoning. Moreover it is pointless to propose elaborate principles of rationality or justice for individual and collective action if they are unfeasible and inapplicable to human beings. Therefore we cannot avoid starting from human beings and, in particular from the mind, in order to build and justify our normative principles of rationality and ethics (other chapters in volumes I and II will explore this argument further). What matters here is to sketch the consequences for the theory of rationality. A theory of rationality relies on a common criterion of theory choice and on three alternative methods of theory generation.

The *criterion of theory choice* is called the "*feasibility criterion*" (Goldman 1993) and states that every standard of rationality can be accepted if it fits the feasibility of this standard by the cognitive constraints of the human mind. For example, with regard to perceptive rationality – namely, the data base for reasoning – standards like the logical consistency of our set of beliefs – in other words, rational beliefs which do not entail any contradiction – are clearly unfeasible for the cognitive limitations of the structure of long-term memory. Similarly, the limited possibility of computation of the human mind does not match the normative principles of reasoning for rational decision-making. In the theory of complexity it is well known that the evaluation of the coherence, for example, of 138 independent logical propositions requires a computational power greater than that of the biggest computer in the world. And most real problems processed using the formal criteria as "maxi-min" or consistency causes the same combinatorial explosion.

As regards the alternative *criteria of theory generation,* they all are a posteriori, but in different ways: the first supports a cognitive theory of rationality, that is a generalization of the cognitive mechanisms of how we judge and choose or, at a meta-level, of how we justify our judgements and choices (Stich 1990); the second is based on Goodman's (1965) concepts of reflective equilibrium, that is on generalizations of the pre-analytical intuitions of people or experts about what might be justified as a rational judgement and choice; the third, which includes generation and evaluation, is based on the pragmatic adequacy and feedback of rational choice concerning the results that the choice has produced in solving a problem or attaining a particular goal (Stich 1990; Holland et al. 1986; Langley et al. 1987; Gigerenzer, Todd, and the ABC Research Group 1999).

This chapter does not pretend to argue in favour of one or other of these criteria. What I want to stress is that nowadays the programme of "naturalizing epistemology" (Quine 1969) seems to overrule the dependency between positive economics and the theory of rationality. It is the a posteriori theory of rationality that may now depend on how, empirically and realistically, the economic actor judges and chooses, whether in the market or in economic institutions, and not the opposite, as in the a priori epistemology of neoclassical economics. This change of epistemological prospect justifies the increasing role of cognitive science in studying the constraints and limitations of the economic actor's reasoning and decision-making in comparison with expectations based on the principles of a priori rationality. This definitively justifies the ambition of cognitive science in trying to build new models of economic action.

7.4 Back to Galileo

The need for a new economic rationality representing the reasoning and decision-making of the economic actor is refused by many economists who regard it as a task for psychology and social science. Economics does not need to represent the processes of reasoning, learning and decision-making because the disciplinary fence of economics separates action from the mechanics of choice (reasoning, learning and decision-making). This position is well illustrated by the following citations from Montesano (1998):

> Economics takes into consideration agents who are assumed to choose according to a criterion. The existence of such a criterion makes the actions intentional (or rational) and the agents rational. The criterion of choice is usually represented by a regular (i.e. complete and transitive) binary preference system on the set of alternatives among which the agent can choose ... economic theory assumes that every agent chooses the action which he or she prefers ... The principle that agents are rational leads to the rule of internal consistency which is represented by the so-called axiom of revealed preference. (Montesano 1998)

> While rationality of agents is necessary to determine the actions that agents choose in a given economic environment (represented by the price of commodities, endowments, technology, etc.) rationality of preferences is not necessary .... (Montesano 1998)

According to this picture the economic actor is a black box with an input (the data represented by the environment) and an output, the chosen action, selected through the regular binary preference system on the set of alternatives. In fact "*since economics is a deductive science, economists make sometimes complicated calculations which are not necessarily assumed to be performed by economic agents (more or less like in mechanics, where the motion of a material body is represented by the solution of a differential equation)*" (Montesano 1998).

This picture of economics presents, in my opinion, a number of epistemological problems.

If we regard it as a programme to establish good correlations between input data and output action it might be a useful descriptive enterprise with no ambitions to elaborate genuine causal explanations. This programme would be acceptable until it produces good predictions and simple laws. This, for example, is the position of Lionel Robbins (1935/1983).

We cannot regard Montesano's previous description as completely descriptive because it introduces some a priori principles. The existence of the criterion of choice – a regular binary preference system based on the set of alternatives of choice and the rule of internal consistency – "makes the actions intentional (or rational) and the agents rational". If these a priori principles – which seem very weak, but in the case of the internal consistency are very demanding on the cognitive ability of the economic actor – have a normative meaning they change the epistemological dimension of the theory.

On the contrary, if these a priori principles are only psychological fictions, introduced in an intuitive way, to allow deductions and predictions, they may be accepted, from an instrumentalist point of view (which is not mine), until the hypothesis is empirically adequate and simple. But since this is not the case a serious methodology of science should oblige us to try, at least, to make some changes in the previous conceptual "repertoire".

For example, equating rationality and intentionality may be right to deprive rationality of any normative meaning. In fact the meanings of intentionality and rationality – as in the case of Simon's subjective rationality – are usually separate (in the common sense, in the philosophy of mind and in psychology): intentionality is present when one decides to act according to given beliefs and preferences (using the language of commonsense psychology); rationality is present when one tries to choose the optimal or *satisficing* action. We can have intentionality without rationality – as in the case where I choose an action that is harmful to me because I have been superficial and hurried. We can have rationality without intentionality, since the optimal but unintentional action generated randomly by chance may be rational even if it is not the product of our conscious reasoning processes.[1] This use of rationality is always normative: the only rational actions are those that overcome given thresholds either established, strongly, in an a priori way – e.g. maximizing expected subjective utility – or, weakly, in an a posteriori way – e.g. reaching subjective, psychological thresholds of *satisficing*. Instead, in principle, if economics aims to be an empirical science focused on "establishing a correspondence between 'data' (i.e. the environment or the conditions of the choice, i.e., technology, endowments, preferences, market regimes, policies, etc.) and the chosen actions or 'variables'" (Montesano 1998), it should refer only to the actual and real behaviours of choice, avoiding any normative concept of optimality or *satisficing*. From this point of view, it is fully justifiable to equate rationality to intentionality. In principle even intentionality is too narrow a concept to include

[1] Many authors, like Jon Elster, support a different thesis so rationality implies intentionality.

all the actual and real choices. Even unintentional or semi-intentional choices (e.g. many consumer choices correspond to an automatic and reflex behaviour based on subliminal conditioning) should be included into a descriptive economic theory (according to the previous definition taken from Robbins). Therefore it is unacceptable (as is made clear in Montesano) to both hold the previous descriptive goals and, at the same time, to introduce concepts like the rule of internal consistency of preferences of actions. Because either the rule of consistency is a normative concept, and is therefore incompatible with the previous descriptive aims of the theory, or it is an empirical abstraction, but in this case it has been falsified by an enormous amount of cognitive research. Moreover, by introducing this rule we do not satisfy the goal of the black-box model of economics expressed in Robbins's previous definition. In fact, in this way, instead of looking for good empirical generalizations between input data and output choices, the theory introduces concepts that try to describe internal features of the black box. But, in this way, we betray Robbins's original programme and the logical consequence is to open the door and make room for a different approach to the economic theory aimed at discovering what is inside the black box, for example by using an empirical representation of the reasoning and decision-making processes responsible for the actual economic choice.

We may ask ourselves the reasons for the previous shift from Robbins's original descriptive programme. This weak shift and the stronger one of introducing the rationality of preferences respond to an unavoidable epistemological need to improve the explanatory and predictive abilities. It is difficult to establish meaningful empirical generalizations only on the basis of statistical correlations among given external variables (as in the case of Robbins's programme) without any reduction to a deeper level of causal explanation. But even if we were able to find good empirical generalizations (empirically adequate with no anomalies) we would always need a causal representation at a minor level of aggregation of the phenomena in order to obtain some probabilities that we are in the presence of genuine empirical causal relations and not of epiphenomena or substitutive causations. There are a lot of epistemological arguments that justify this norm (see, for example, von Wright 1971; Salmon 1984; Mackie 1974, Viale 1994a). The history of science is also full of cases of earlier discoveries of empirical generalizations that were followed by research to discover the causal mechanism of the phenomenon. We need only think of the Mendelian laws of inheritance followed by the discovery of DNA. The Mendelian laws did not allow any causal explanation of the phenomena of inheritance and therefore the scientific community was not satisfied by the inferences allowed by the laws until Watson and Crick's discovery shed light on the causal mechanisms of inheritance.

To sum up, if we agree that we want the best empirical theory that links input data to output choices; that to reach this goal we need a causal explanation of the mechanisms that link input and output; that we must avoid any normative concept that is incompatible with our empirical aim; and that the use of abstract and non-realist concepts are allowed until the theory works and provided there are not better realist concepts, then the logical consequence is to enrich the economic theory by representing the reasoning and decision-making processes present inside the black box. According to these premises we cannot accept the axiom of revealed preference and we must build the rationality of the preference system on the basis of cognitive processing.

To give one example for all. The rationality of preferences is based on the determination of the preference system over actions. According to traditional models the function that represents the preference system "is rational if determined by a model the axioms of which embody the required rationality" (Montesano 1998). What are these models? They are the many a priori versions of the utility theory (von Neumann-Morgenstern, Savage, Cloquet, and so on). The new axiomatic models differ from each other in requiring a weaker rationality than the Von Neumann-Morgenstern model. A weaker rationality that includes, for example, the Allais and Ellsberg paradoxes.[2] But the new axiomatic versions introduced to cope with the empirical anomalies are only formal ad hoc adjustments. They want to cope with the reality of the preference system over actions, but do not represent the real mechanisms that affect the preference over action. In my opinion they represent a clear example of a Lakatosian "degenerating programme". A completely different approach is represented by the "*prospect theory*" of Kahneman and Tversky (1979b). This theory, based on cognitive research on probabilistic judgements, tries to describe the mental representation of the preference system over actions. It substitutes utility (the net welfare that one may reach) with value (gains or losses respect a neutral point of reference) to allow two different functions, instead of one as in utility theory, one for gains and another for losses (Fig. 7.1).

Moreover, prospect theory regards preferences as a function of "decisional weights" and postulates that these weights are inclined to overestimate the small probabilities and underestimate the medium and high probabilities (Fig. 7.2).

Lastly, it predicts that the preferences depend on the type of mental representation of the decision problem. If an outcome is judged as a gain then the resulting value function will be concave and the decision-maker will be inclined to take non-risky decisions. On the contrary, if an outcome is judged as a loss then the resulting value function will be convex and the decision-maker will be inclined to take risky decisions. Prospect theory differs radically from the traditional versions of utility theory and has been, many times, controlled and found quite empirically adequate. But apart the substantive value of this theory it represents the right way to study the behaviour of choice of the economic agent: finding the empirical causal representation of the mechanisms of the black box.

To conclude, there is a passage from Montesano that summarizes the anti-realist bias of the approach that he refers to: *since economics is a deductive science, economists make sometimes complicated calculations which are not necessarily assumed to be performed by economic agents (more or less like in mechanics,*

[2] The paradoxes of Allais and Ellsberg showed that human choices do not conform to subjective expected utility theory.

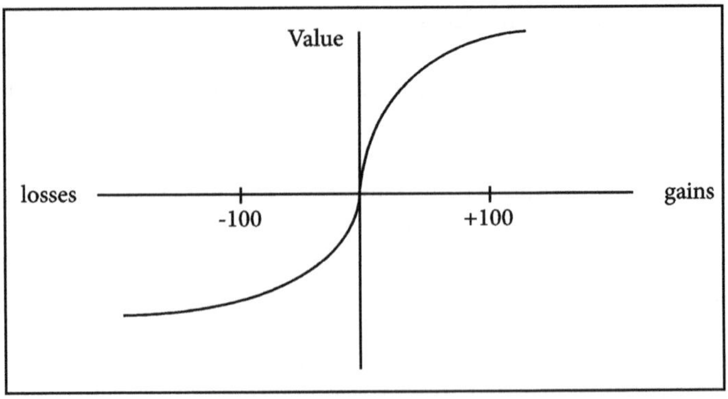

Fig. 7.1 Value functions of gains and losses according to prospect theory

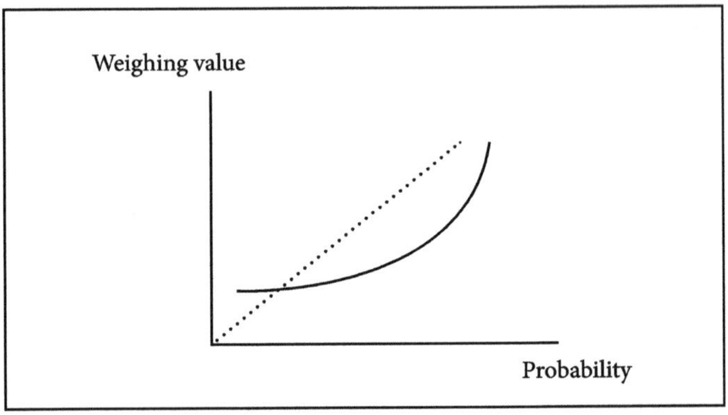

Fig. 7.2 Weighing curve according to prospect theory

where the motion of a material body is represented by the solution of a differential equation) (Montesano 1998).

It is a mistake to think that the formal modelling of the phenomena excludes a realist representation of them. Galileo can teach us something on this subject. He always looked for a realistic representation of physical phenomena and tried to represent them beyond the external appearances. He tried to go to the heart of reality and used mathematical language because he thought that nature was formulated by mathematics. He followed the platonic distinction between "real" and "phenomenic". To grasp the "real" the scientist should use abstract and ideal concepts, such as "free fall in empty space" or the "ideal pendulum", which are useful to eliminate the variegated features of the "phenomenic". Moreover, deductive systematization is the best tool to represent the "real".

Therefore it is possible to be realistic and, at the same time, to use mathematical modelling. The mistake is to become prisoners of our formal models and to separate them from reality. The mathematics is only a language to represent what exists in the external world. Therefore, as in the case of prospect theory, the study of economic decision-making must subdue formal modelling to the needs of genuine empirical causal investigation, not the contrary. The consideration that complicated calculations of economics cannot be performed by economic agents does not imply that formal modelling cannot be generated by the study of human decision-making in economic contexts. The notion that there is asymmetry between the real performances of economic agents and their formal models stems from a strong anti-realist bias.

7.5 Let's Not Ape Physics!

The final point I want to analyse is related to the philosophy of science followed by neoclassical economics. The model is clearly based on Newtonian mechanics but it carries two serious drawbacks.

As Rosenberg pointed out (1983, reprinted in Hausman ed., 1994, pp. 378–380), since the nineteenth century economists have been elaborating a theory whose form is identical to the great theoretical breakthroughs made in science from the sixteenth century onwards. The strategy is to view the behaviour economists seek to explain as reflecting forces that always move towards a stable equilibrium, which maximizes or minimizes some theoretically crucial variable. In the case of microeconomics, this crucial variable is utility (or its latter-day surrogates) and the equilibrium is provided by a level of price across all markets that maximizes this variable. This strategy is most impressively exemplified in Newtonian mechanics and in Darwinian theory of natural selection. In Newtonian mechanics the system's behaviour always minimizes or maximizes variables that reflect the state of the system which is mechanically possible, while in Darwinian theory it is the environment that maximizes the fitness of individuals of a species. This strategy is crucial to the success of these theories because of the way it directs and shapes the research. If we believe that a system always act to maximize the value of a mechanical variable – for example, total energy – and our measurement of the observable values of that variable diverges from the predictions of the theory and the initial conditions, we do not infer that the system described is failing to maximize the value of the variable in question. We do not falsify the theory, but we assume that we have incompletely described the constraints under which the system is actually operating. The axioms of these theories do not embody even implicit *ceteris paribus* clauses. With these theories the choice is always between rejecting the auxiliary hypotheses and test conditions or rejecting the theory altogether. Hence the only change that can be made to the theory is to deny that its subjects invariably maximize or minimize its chosen variable.

In Newtonian mechanics attempts to describe the systems under study more completely resulted in the discovery of new planets and new laws, like those of thermodynamics. In biology, the assumption that fitness is maximized led to the discovery of forces not previously recognized to effect genetic variation within a population and led to the discovery of genetic laws that explain the persistence in a population of apparently non-adaptive traits, like sickle-cell anaemia. But what about microeconomics? The success of this strategy in other disciplines may justify the attempts made by economists to make recalcitrant facts about human behaviour and the economic systems humans have constructed fit the economic theory. Moreover, this strategy allows the use of many powerful formal tools, such as differential calculus, topology and differential geometry. But many years of work in the same direction have produced nothing comparable to the physicists' discovery of new planets or new technologies, or the biological understanding of the mechanism of adaptation and heredity. Therefore it is time to question the merit of applying this approach to economics, since it carries all the disadvantages of empirical non-falsifiability without the advantages of the discovery of novel facts and applications.

There is also another general reason "not to ape physics" that stems from a recent philosophical debate in physics compared with the other sciences. Let us consider the methodological status of decision-making psychology proposed by Kahneman, Slovic and Tversky (1982) compared to the theory of mental models advanced by Johnson Laird (1983). My earlier critical evaluation of the first was that it had no theoretical depth, no general scope, and that it looked more like a set of empirical generalizations while, on the contrary, the theory of mental models tried to represent the underlying mechanisms of human reasoning responsible for a great variety of psychological phenomena. Thus, *ceteris paribus* with regards to empirical adequacy, the second ought to be preferred according to the established and shared methodological standards of theory choice used by the scientific community. I must confess now that I am not so sure of the validity of my position and I am inclined to think that my reasoning was biased by the models derived from the philosophy of physics. In contemporary physics there is a trade-off between explanatory power and factual content. As pointed out by Cartwright (1983, pp. 135–139), fundamental laws like Maxwell's equations or Schroedinger's equations have great explanatory power but do not describe the true facts about reality. The aim of these equations is to cover a wide variety of different phenomena with a small number of principles. If the fundamental laws set out to fit reality into the highly constrained structures of their mathematical formulae they will have to distort the true picture of what happens. Quantum mechanics is a good example. The central principle is Schroedinger's equation. This equation describes how systems subject to various forces evolve in time, but in order to know the evolution of a real system we also need to know the mathematical representation of the kinetic and potential energies of that real system. This is called Hamiltonian representation. In principle, if we wanted to have a realistic picture of the various systems, we ought to calculate a Hamiltonian representation of each real system we wish to study. Instead if we look at physics text-books we discover that they contain only a limited number of Hamiltonians, which do not fit real objects, like the hydrogen atom, but only highly fictionalized objects, like free particle motion, the linear harmonic oscillator, piecewise constant potentials, diatomic molecules, central potential scattering and so on. In fact the explanatory power of quantum theory comes from its ability to deploy a small number of well-understood Hamiltonians to cover a wide range of cases. But this explanatory power has its price. By limiting the number of Hamiltonians we set constraints on our ability to represent situations realistically and we lose the true representation of the system. In physics if we want to have a realistic representation of the phenomena we must abandon the fundamental laws and look at the phenomenological laws like those of Galileo, Ohm or Kepler. Fundamental laws usually explain phenomenological laws not in a deductive ways, as was asserted until recently – think of the Hempel-Popperian deductive-nomological model – but using a model which fits the phenomenon into the theory (Cartwright 1983, pp. 131–134). This picture of science fits Friedman's "as-if" instrumentalist methodology well: the theory is only a fictitious deductive machine to produce explanations and predictions.

This model of science seems to work only for the fundamental laws of physics. If we climb up the levels of aggregation of reality we find that already at the level of biology we are not able to find explanatory structures based on the three components – theory, model, facts – that are present in physics. Instead we find phenomenological laws with many exceptions that aim to describe complex phenomena. The same consideration applies a fortiori to the explanation of human behaviour. The great complexity and variability of behavioural phenomena precludes the discovery of genuine general phenomenological laws relating to particular domains of psychological reality. This absence does not allow any serious unifying mathematical abstraction, comparable to that of the fundamental laws in physics, which has the power to explain reality at the phenomenological level. The moral is that instead of "putting the cart before the horse", or in other words playing the game of the theoretical physicists and trying to elaborate fictitious, but useless, theoretical formal models of human decision-making, it would be wiser to study, patiently, the empirical phenomenology of human decision-making and to try to elaborate some useful, and genuine, empirical laws that are valid, locally and contextually, for a small fragment of human reality. From this point of view, the theoretical ambitions of Johnson Laird's mental model theory seem to be scarcely justified by the empirical adequacy and precision of its descriptions and predictions, while some achievements of the psychology of decision-making – like prospect theory, regret theory or the framing effect – are positive steps in the right direction. They provide phenomenological laws and generalizations, wrongly called theories, with the modest ambition of describing very small aspects of the human decision-making process. This is the only methodological approach possible if we want to endow economics with useful empirical knowledge about human economic behaviour in the present, and, perhaps, with some theoretical unifying abstractions in the future.

7.6 Conclusion: Why Cognitive Economics?

To conclude, I would like to offer some justifications for the choice of the attribute "cognitive" used to identify the new research programme in economics. These justifications are derived, clearly deductively, from my previous points.

If, for the reasons described earlier, we do not believe in the possibility of any a priori formulation of the theory of rationality; if we think that the concepts of folk psychology are empirically empty and too simplified to represent the richness of the mental life responsible for economic action; if we do not make unrealistic claims to build theoretical abstractions of the mental machinery of human decision-making, but instead our goal is to build genuine empirical laws and generalizations in response to the empirical and conceptual inadequacies of the neoclassical theory of economic action, we must conclude that only the piecemeal empirical work of cognitive psychology can offer correct and realistic answers to the question of how the economic actor judges and chooses in various empirical contexts.

The *experimental economics* of economists like Binmore et al. (1985, 1991) or Hey (1991) is, in my opinion, too closely linked to the concepts of folk psychology and to an ad hoc defence of an a priori model of rationality.

Instead the *computational economics* of researchers like Holland et al. (1986) is too prone towards an instrumentalist and not realist philosophy of science, and in particular to the theoretical physicists' game of building abstract theoretical explanations. The result is that their work falls into the trap of "*computational circularity*", namely when computational programs provide effective models of human cognition only because cognition must be described in computational language.

Both new branches of economics, particularly the computational one, have many merits in producing new empirical knowledge about economic action and institutions, but it is the interpretation of this knowledge that I often find biased by dangerous methodological vices. On the contrary, *cognitive economics* has no great short-term ambitions to substitute the neoclassical models, but in the long run it may represent a strong, solid alternative to the present standard models of economic action.

But in order to achieve this goal cognitive economics must follow the precious advice of scientific rhetoric (advice that I did not follow in this chapter). It must convince the economic community not to be too abstruse, not to debate problems that are of scarce relevance to economists, and, above all, to highlight concrete results that have overwhelmingly practical value!

8 Economic and Cognitive Rationality in Political Behaviour

8.1 Introduction

This chapter aims to analyse the weaknesses of the economic theory of politics and the potential advantages of an alternative, cognitive-type approach which can offer a better explanation of political action.

I would like to start with a brief introduction to what is meant by an economic approach to politics, and in particular to democratic politics.

We can start by referring to the research tradition led, among others, by Downs (1957). The voter is treated in the same way as an economic actor in a market. In the same way as an economic actor maximises profits by exploiting the available economic resources, so the voter tries to maximise his or her utility or benefits using the resources available to him, above all the right to vote. He is therefore likely to vote for the party that guarantees to form a government whose programme will bring the greatest benefits, or so he believes. On the other hand, parties, too, are maximisers and their benefit is, in this case, the votes. Each party tries to adopt a mode of behaviour that allows it to attract the greatest number of voters to the detriment of its rivals.

This model of political democracy has both a normative significance, given that it aims to justify democracy in rational terms, and an empirical significance because it aspires to take account of how modern democratic systems work. This model has ambitions that are respectively *normative* (the rational political actor is one who maximises his benefit) and *explicative* (the political actor is rational because he maximises his benefit).

This approach is open to two forms of criticism. The first highlights the formal inconsistency, the paradoxes or the impossibility of justifying the political choices based on individual rationality. The second emphasises the empirical falsifications

The present chapter is a modified version of Viale, R. (1996). Razionalità economica e razionalità cognitiva nella spiegazione del comportamento politico. In P. Legrenzi & V. Girotto (a cura di) (Eds.), *Psicologia e Politica*, Raffaello Cortina Editore, With kind permission from the Publishers.

DOI 10.1007/978-3-642-24743-9_8, © Springer-Verlag Berlin Heidelberg 2012

of the various consequences derived from the model (for a general overview of these criticisms, see Panebianco 1989, in particular the chapters by Petroni, Martelli and Pappalardo).

8.2 Formal Inconsistencies of the Economic Theory of Democracy

In formal criticism the approach based on individual rationality is compared to that of collective rationality leading to the discovery that there are systematic incongruences between the two forms of rationality.

In election theory one of the most interesting results is the so-called *voting paradox* noted by the Marquis de Condorcet in 1785. Suppose that three individuals have to choose between A, B and C, and they will express very different opinions: the first declares an order of ABC; the second prefers BCA, and the third CAB. On this basis it is not possible to form any majority. Let us suppose that, to get out of this impasse, the individuals are asked to vote on pairs (choose between A and B, between A and C, and between B and C). The outcome will depend arbitrarily on which pair is voted first. This collective decision satisfies the rational requirement of the transitivity of each individual preference ordering – namely, if A is preferred to B, and B to C, then A is preferred to C. In spite of this, it is impossible to arrive at equally rational majority decisions.

What does this outcome indicate for a political system? That it is logically impossible, based on individual preferences, to claim to represent the "general will" or, to put it differently, to identify the function of social well-being; that democracy consists of situations of unstable equilibrium in which alternating majorities on individual themes are formed and then collapse; that the importance of controlling the areas of interest on the political agenda stimulates the activation of strategies to manipulate the order of priorities and the tactical inclusion of new themes.

Kenneth Arrow (1951) clearly identifies a series of conditions that allow a collective decision to be rationally constructed on the basis of individual preferences. The first is that the decision-making procedure applies to all circumstances (provided that individuals are consistent and show transitive preferences); the second is that individual preference must be followed if it does not go against the preference of another individual (*Pareto's principle*); the third is that if the decision-making procedure results in preferring A to B, this result will not change if any individual changes his preferences in cases where other alternatives occur, but does not change his choice between A and B (*principle of independence from irrelevant alternatives*); lastly, the fourth consideration states that no one shall acquire dictatorial power if they find themselves in a position to impose vetoes or to determine alone the result of the decision-making process.

By deduction, Arrow demonstrates the impossibility of building a collective decision that can satisfy all four conditions simultaneously. His *impossibility theorem* asserts that, if an aggregation method allows voters to have any preference order, if it meets given conditions and excludes any form of imposition, then it will inevitably result in a non-transitive and inconsistent aggregate of preferences compared to those expressed by individual participants in the process of choice.

Another important aspect of political behaviour which cannot be justified by the rational action model is that of participation to the vote. The most significant inconsistence is *Downs' Dilemma* (Downs 1957), which is essentially the same as the Prisoner's dilemma multiplied to x-number of people. What prompts an elector to vote? Evidently individuals vote when the benefits of doing so exceed the costs. In this case the benefits are represented by the probability P that an individual's vote might affect the implementation of the government's manifesto, which has a higher benefit differential D compared to other rival manifestos. The product DP must, therefore, be greater than the costs C of voting:

$$\mathrm{DP} > \mathrm{C}$$

The value D is generally very low, because the expected benefit compared to the various rival manifestos does not vary much between one party's manifesto and another, above all in a bipartite system and, moreover, the probability that an individual's vote, among the millions of other votes cast in an election, might be relevant to the results is practically zero. This gives rise to the following paradox: when the probability of obtaining a benefit is little above zero it becomes irrational to vote, and therefore the only rational conduct is to abstain from voting. Hence, democracy cannot be rationally explained using an economic approach to democracy.

Condorcet's voting paradox, Arrow's general impossibility theorem, and Downs' dilemma of voting behaviour are three classic difficulties facing the rational model of democracy which are so strong that they suggest the need to relinquish the assumptions of rationality on which this model is based. Also because all the attempts made to date, aimed at overcoming these inconsistencies, have not produced any acceptable final result, except by distorting the assumptions underlying the model of *homo economicus*.

8.3 Empirical Falsifications of the Economic Theory of Democracy

The fate reserved for the explanatory and predictive power of these economic models of democracy seems no less harsh. In this case the principle of maximising rationality is assumed as the abstraction of *homo politicus*'s real behaviour. While recognising that man is not merely a machine for calculating benefits, all aspects of irrationality are regarded as secondary, and an idealised representation is used of *homo politicus* as being capable of tackling "every situation with one eye on the gains to be had, the other eye on costs, a delicate ability to balance them, and a strong desire to follow wherever rationality leads" (Downs 1957, p. 38).

The core of the rational theory of political competition from Downs (1957) to Enelow and Hinich (1984) borrows the spatial approach from economic models of competitive equilibrium among enterprises. It is expected that electors will vote for the closest party, namely the one that corresponds to their preferences; that competition will allow a single equilibrium represented by the position of the voter in the middle or at the centre of the field, and that parties can only get as close as possible to this if they want to maximise their probability of winning. This presents serious drawbacks: (1) the predicted direction of competition should always tend to converge towards the centre, although it is empirically proven that there are numerous exceptions (niche political parties, for example, like those on the far left or far right, or niche theme parties, like the greens); (2) if electors vote for the closest party and all parties converge towards the centre of the distribution chart, only two parties can be in equilibrium (because a third would fall between the two rivals, on the left and right, and would not win votes), and therefore, this makes multi-party systems inexplicable!

These anomalies in the model have been corrected in various ways, but the results continue to be inadequate. There is a temptation to weaken the maximisation principle in order to explain multi-party systems, for example, by introducing Simon's *satisficing* principle (1985), according to which an individual does not try to maximise but instead is content with decisions that exceed a level of personal psychological satisfaction. This principle allows parties to exist that are content with satisfactory election results and do not try to maximise votes, and this in turn produces a multi-party system.

Another sign of the limited explicative ability of rational models of democracy is the scant presence of one of the deductively predictable phenomena of the theory: electoral *volatility*. A floating voter is one whose choice is based solely on the calculation of how a party's manifesto corresponds to his or her own expected benefit. Therefore, these voters can easily swing from one party to another based on marginal changes to the manifesto statements made by individual parties. Instead, empirical observation tells us that the voter is weakly bound by manifesto contents, whereas those voters who often change voting preference are generally not well informed about manifestos and instead their decision is based on factors, that might at first seem marginal, like belonging to a particular faith or a political leader's rhetorical skills.

In conclusion, such a simplistic model of maximising economic rationality shows scant success in representing or explaining the complexity of political phenomena. It can claim some empirical success in explaining the decision-making processes of restricted groups, but not in macroprocesses, such as participation, competition between parties and coalition processes (Sartori 1987, pp. 214–253).

8.4 Conventionalist Stratagems in the Economic Theory of Democracy

Faced with empirical falsifications and logical inconsistencies in a theory, it may be methodologically correct to make changes to the "belt" of auxiliary hypotheses in order to neutralise the empirical problems and internal theoretical drawbacks.

Retaining the nucleus of key assumptions is allowed, unless this means that the same assumptions become increasingly less important and more marginal. By changing the "belt" of auxiliary hypotheses, it is necessary to ensure that the increased empirical content or *problem-solving* capacity is not only theoretical, but that it is also confirmed by observation or experiment. Where there are logical inconsistencies and empirical falsifications in the economic theory of democracy, these precautions do not seem to have been taken.

Nor, in view of Condorcet's voting paradox, can these problems be resolved by using the various alternative voting systems (single, double, elimination) proposed by Black (1958). The majority rule remains inefficient and ineffective unless other rules are used to regulate the presentation of motions, the number of amendments possible, the information available to users, the type of agreements that may be reached, etc. As well as being difficult to formalise, these new assumptions lead to other problems, such as the paradox of the "power of agenda setting" exercised by the presidency, namely the ability of the chairman of a committee to decide which items to include on the agenda. Indeed, if majority rule is not coupled with some agenda setting power, it turns into anarchy, while if it is coupled with absolute agenda setting power, it becomes dictatorship (Shepsle and Weingast 1982).

As for the paradox of social decision derived from Arrow's general impossibility theorem, one solution was to change some of the fundamental assumptions, such as the condition for transitivity (Sen 1970), or that of independence from irrelevant alternatives (Barry 1970). Another solution was to propose other assumptions, such as the condition of liberalism (Sen 1970) which states that society must respect individual decision concerning the private sphere. However, the latter transformation leads to new paradoxes between individual choice and social choice, as is shown by the *impossibility theorem of a Paretian liberal*, which highlights the fact that a liberal-democratic constitution must limit individual rights on the basis of any belief shared at a collective level so as not to counter collective decisions with individual ones (Sen 1970).

In the case of Downs' dilemma of voting behaviour, the conventionalist strategem is to introduce ad hoc extra-economic type hypotheses, such as, for example, affirming the "value of voting per se" and that citizens:

1. "Are moved by a sense of social responsibility that is relatively independent of their short-term gains and losses" (Downs 1957, pp. 266–267); and/or
2. Derive "satisfaction from behaviour that complies with voting ethics, from affirming their loyalty to the political system or their own party preferences"; and/or
3. Are interested in specific actions, such as how to keep themselves politically informed, take part in elections, choose a party, etc.

As for the empirical falsifications of some explanations of the economic theory of democracy, like convergence to the centre, the two-party system and electoral volatility, we have already seen how theoretical corrections, through the introduction of more realistic hypotheses and extra-economic variables, only demonstrate the empirical weakness of their fundamental assumptions. This confirms the inadequacy of the rational actor theory of neoclassical economics, also highlighted in the field of economics, in both the results of artificial experiments and in the observation of natural experiments (Viale 1992/2008). Indeed, as affirmed by Simon (1987, p.26), this theory presupposes an actor whose rationality is such that: (1) his beliefs are consistent internally; (2) he is capable of describing the world objectively; (3) his capacities for processing data to define his expectations, namely his probabilistic and deductive reasoning, are not limited; (4) his beliefs regarding purposes and values are given and not subject to changes over time and through experience. All these hypotheses are proved false by the empirical discoveries of cognitive science.

8.5 An Example of the Economic Theorist of Politics: Mancur Olson

What are the implications of all that has been said above for the theory of politics? In order to answer this question we will outline some of the characteristics that single out a cognitive theory of the political actor as opposed to an economically-motivated one.[1]

The *homo politicus* proposed here does not follow abstract and unrealistic calculations of benefit, but instead elaborates his own decisions in line with the subjective constraints of his cognitive ability, and with the objective constraints of the time available to choose and the complexity of the problem. This has both explicative and normative consequences. It serves to create a research programme that appears to be very promising and fertile at an empirical level. In order to control this hypothesis we can consider a classic example of an economic approach to politics: the model offered by Mancur Olson.

To illustrate this I will draw on Viale (1994b), starting with an historical reconstruction taken from Olson (1994). In 1920s China, Feng Yu-Hsiang, a general famous for his military prowess, was able, in spite of having fewer men, to defeat the army of a dangerous bandit leader called White Wolf. The general was loved by the population, whatever their background, and was also renowned as a careful administrator of his territorial possessions. This was the era of the warlords in China, namely settled bandits who could not claim any form of legitimation and who grew rich not from occasional pillage but through regular taxes levied from the populations they controlled. Why were these warlords preferable to the roaming bandits? Because if an itinerant bandit settled in a territory and decided to establish a regular monopoly on theft within his domains, he did so in a way that would not destroy the source of his revenue. Moreover, he protected his subjects from ransacking and violence at the hands of other bandits; he encouraged the productive output of his subjects; he did not extort any sums that would deter his subjects from creating wealth, but instead he tried to tax them to a

[1] For an analysis of the cognitive foundations of the theory of social action, see the part I of this volume.

threshold that would prompt them to produce more and grow rich. He was encouraged to improve infrastructure and to provide public services. He created irrigation canals, built better roads and improved medical services and public health. As if guided by an invisible hand, other itinerant bandits also settled down and found an outlet for the entrepreneurial skills, increasing their power and ruling over neighbouring lands.

In this way two forms of rationality appear to overlap: that of the bandit chief and that of the subject. People prefer the autocrat (a ruler who exploits and defends them) to open anarchy and the risk of pillage and violence at the hands of passing bandits. But what are the characteristics of the rationality of the autocrat? How greedily will he grasp his subjects' wealth? What level of taxation will satisfy him and what proportion of those taxes will he allocate to the production of public assets? In theory, a rational autocrat should choose a tax rate that provides him with the maximum quantity of resources for his own use (palaces, military power, personal consumption, etc.). Because he has a monopoly over violence in the area, he will tend to extract the greatest possible surplus for himself, increasing the rate to the point at which any further increase would reduce the overall tax yield. He will only spend taxes on public assets if such expenditure increases overall social wealth to a level that will allow him to recoup in the form of tax revenues exactly what he has spent. In general the autocrat will determine the level of expenditure on public services that will maximise his benefit. In this way, however, the high rates required to meet his autocratic interests will gradually tend to reduce overall wealth. His subjects will be obliged to support taxes that are much higher than they would be if their interests were taken into account and this will gradually undermine the structure of individual incentives. Income distribution in an autocracy therefore introduces massive inefficiencies in society by giving the dictator too large a share of the total taxable output.

On the contrary, at least in theory, democratic systems with strongly representative interests function better in terms of redistributive efficiency. On the one hand, even a political party that represents only a small percentage of the electorate is interested in redistributing a share of tax revenues to the sector of society that supported it and, on the other, no party is willing to raise taxes excessively with the risk of losing support of the electorate. Therefore, democratic governments are encouraged to provide public services, while also not overburdening their electors with tax. This situation is much more virtuous than that of autocracy in terms of economic and social efficiency and it guarantees a greater increase in net social income (that of well-being).

Olson elaborates the argument of the superiority of democracy compared to autocracy and to anarchy using his theory of collective action, presented in *The Logic of Collective Action* (1965) and applied in *The Rise and Decline of Nations* (1982).

What is collective action? It occurs when organised groups, whether large or small, act in collusion and apply pressure to improve the well-being of their members. Olsonian collective action highlights two main aspects: the "micro" aspect, namely how collective action is formed, and the "macro" aspect, namely the pressure group's impact on the efficiency of the system.

On the first aspect, Olson states that only organisations made up of a small number of members do not need added incentives to motivate their members to take action. Each person knows that, in combination with others, the result of his or her action will result in economic improvements shared by a small number of people. Therefore, the cost of individual action is generally not greater than the economic return.

Instead, in large organisations this does not happen since increased well-being has to be divided by a considerable number of beneficiaries and, generally speaking, the gain is far less than the cost of action. This is the reason why large organisations (trade unions, for example) have to introduce selective incentives, whether formal or informal, negative or positive, in order to encourage individual participation in collective action, which would otherwise be very weak. These incentives vary widely, ranging from conditions like the *closed shop* clause used by some British companies (no one may be hired in a factory unless he or she is a union member) to censure and social disapproval (one need only think of the subculture of the unionised miners' urban settlements in Britain in the early twentieth century).

The "macro" analysis of the social and economic impact created by the various kinds of collective action is equally interesting. Here, too, size is important. All pressure groups try to grab a larger slice of the cake, namely national wealth. Increased wealth, in the form of monopolistic advantages, revenues of offices, etc., will inevitably lead to a diminished efficiency of the system, and therefore also to reduced national wealth, and consequently a lower individual income for the organisation's members. For a small-sized group (a group that, say, represents one thousandth part of national revenues), the repercussions of a reduction in national wealth are often paltry compared to the gain resulting from collective action. Instead, according to Olson, a large organisation (a group that, say, represents one third of national revenues) faces many more general problems when it takes action to press for a claim. One third of any loss in the efficiency of the system would therefore affect the members of the organisation. Therefore, while small groups do not realise that their claims could weaken the country's economic efficiency, large social organisations are generally a driving factor that strengthens the country's economic growth.

Using this individualistic and economic model of collective action, Olson offers the key to interpret many social and institutional phenomena which have been traditionally examined using sociological and holistic type methodological instruments (for example, Parsons' formal theory of 1954 which calls upon the functional evolution of groups, starting from primary and primitive groups up to today's large-sized groups). Olson takes a view that is not telescopic, but microscopic. It is individuals, seen as economic rational actors, who represent the bricks that make up the institutional and social building. As Boudon would say (1984), social action can only be explained by disclosing the actor's reasons, and Olson offers a superb interpretation of this rule of methodological individualism.

8.6 Olson Revisited

Faced with a study like Olson's that is so methodologically transparent, it is easy to criticise and add clarification. I will limit myself to some fundamental remarks. In the "micro" part of his study, Olson proposes a social actor model that seems rather unsatisfactory. His social actor is without question an ingenuous caricature of a real social actor. Like a mechanical Pythagorean table, he calculates the individual benefit of the action, dividing global benefit by the number of persons who benefit and subtracting the cost of the action. If the result is positive he acts, otherwise he does not take part.

In the social sciences, as is well known, one must be tolerant with serious simplifications, both because there are few of them and they are difficult to elaborate, and also because they are essential as a tool for inference and research. However, they must be simplifications of the real characteristics of the social phenomenon. When evaluating the decision to act, it is important to take account, as comprehensively as possible, of all the "micro" factors that might or might not trigger the action based on the decision-making context. The following are just a selection.

The cost of participation in a collective action (industrial action, for example) can be calculated differently depending on the type of involvement. As cognitive scientists and economists who study the psychological phenomena of negotiation processes now know full well, we all have both a certain initial resistance to increasing an "investment" we have mentally set aside for a particular expenditure, and a certain propensity to spend even more just to make the most of an investment, once it has been made. There is an inferential propensity known as *mental budget allocation* that makes us reluctant to spend a certain sum for the first time, but, once it has been allocated, we tend to set aside even more than we might have agreed in the first place. Therefore, the perception of the cost of participating in a social action – for example, supporting industrial action – changes over time, depending on whether the person has been involved for some time or whether he or she has recently decided to join. Once a supporter has joined, he will not renege on the action even if it has proved costly and seems likely to fail (one need only think of the irrational obstinacy of the English miners in their strike against the Thatcher government) because of another psychological mechanism studied by cognitive science, namely the *regret* or sorrow that would result from abandoning investments or initiatives already loaded with history, projections and scenarios of success, attempted recovery, etc.

Faced with the dilemma of whether or not to act there is also another phenomenon that theoreticians of social action, like Olson, should examine carefully: the cost of acting. If there is an equal chance of losing, irrespective of whether or not the individual chooses to act, he or she will feel greater regret if action is taken, since this requires greater justification than not acting and leaving matters as they are. This phenomenon, together with the *mental budget allocation*, allows us, in part, to explain the tendency towards the conservative and non-participatory behaviour of many social categories, such as the newly employed and *newcomers* in general.

The actor's evaluation of the benefit and his or her consequent response change significantly depending on how the social context of action is presented. For example, a company that wishes to restrict the burden of negotiations should create a "front" of success and gain for the workers' organisation, while the trade union should underline the negative aspects of negotiations in order to motivate its supporters to fight back. Indeed, it is well known that there is a *bias* that makes the decision-maker more conservative in a context of certainty and victory, but emphasises the propensity for risk in situations of uncertainty and loss.

More generally, and as demonstrated by the *framing effect* (see Kahneman and Tversky 1979b), we reach decisions differently depending on how the choices are presented. Our decisions may therefore clash with the forecasts or prescriptions of the expected utility theory, a key component of the Olsonian model. Let us suppose, for example, that a worker has to choose between the following options:

(a) Going on strike with the certainty of a pay rise worth 200,000 lire;
(b) Not striking with a 1/3 probability of a pay rise worth 700,000 lire and a 2/3 probability of no pay rise;
Workers would probably opt for (a), to go on strike, although, in rational terms, this is clearly the suboptimal choice (also because the cost of strike action needs to be deducted from (a)).
Instead, let us suppose that they are faced with a choice between:
(c) Not going on strike and having the certainty of a pay rise of 200,000;
(d) Striking with a 1/3 probability of a pay rise worth 700,000 lire and a 2/3 probability of no pay rise.

They would very probably opt for (c), not going on strike, thereby reversing their preferences compared to the earlier choice. In terms of the expected benefit, (c) is inferior to (d) and is therefore irrational, providing that the cost of the action is less than $(700{,}000 \times 1/3) - 200{,}000 = 33{,}000$.

The framing effect is based on two mental mechanisms: acquiescence whereby, when formulating a problem, we accept it as it is explained, without spontaneously generating alternative versions; and segregation, whereby we isolate the problem from its overall context and do not evaluate the more general significance of our choice. In other words, we are hemmed in by the frame and, in a short-sighted way, we only take into account the actions that have an immediate effect on the situation. Clearly, this is a potential weapon that can be used by union officials to influence the choices of their members, and depending on the format of the communication, individual cost-benefit analysis will lead to action or inaction, with the results of Olson's rational calculation being equal.[2]

The above illustration serves to highlight the cognitive poverty of the Olsonian actor model. Greater sensitivity to these aspects of the decision-maker would have

[2] For an analysis of the cognitive foundations of the theory of social action see Part I of this volume.

allowed Olson to interpret the dynamics of the various forms of collective action differently. For example, when a worker chooses to take action in order to gain an economic advantage, he does not do so for the overall amount granted to the entire category to which he belongs, but for the local increase in his wage packet. The striking worker focuses on the extra tens of thousand Euros that he will bring home rather than on the hundreds of millions gained by the category, which then have to be divided with a huge number of colleagues in order to obtain his benefit, from which he will subtract the cost of action. This increase will be more or less valuable, namely its marginal benefit will vary depending on the worker's particular starting conditions. For example, it will be very beneficial if he or she has a large family, high expectations of quality of life, previously well-off living standards, good education, etc.; or it will be less beneficial if he or she comes from an underdeveloped background, has been unemployed for years, is unmarried, has no educational qualifications, no ambitions and no expectations. The pressure to take collective action depends on these motivations, and also on the clarity and transparency of the result to be achieved.

If consumers cannot put together an effective claim action, this is not necessarily because of the fragmentary nature of their social role in relation to the variety of goods, as Olson affirms, but rather because of the cognitive opacity of the result to be achieved. While a worker fights for a clear result tailored to his needs, such as a pay rise, and consequently manages to engage the motivational and decision-making machine, the consumer is faced with much vaguer and ambiguous objectives. This is also the case for an unemployed person faced with a complex situation (who can change his social condition and by means of what hiring methods?) that is difficult to attain on the basis of "previous probabilities". On the other hand, even if the supposed Olsonian calculation were to exist, it would not provide a convincing explanation for the differences in the propensity to take collective action based on the larger or smaller number of participants. Why would a worker from a company with a small number of employees have more reasons to go on strike for a pay rise than a worker employed by a large company? Indeed, based merely on a rational calculation, the individual benefit (the overall benefit divided by the number of beneficiaries) and the cost of action (strike, picketing, assemblies, etc.) do not vary much in relation to the number of those involved. Instead, the fact that workers belonging to smaller groups appear more motivated to take part is based on other factors, namely on the greater proximity and transparency of the objectives, on greater accessibility to decision-making processes, and on a stronger identification with local trade union leadership, namely on factors that are marginal in Olson's analysis.

In conclusion, many auxiliary hypotheses of an empirical nature seem to be required in order to apply Olson's social actor model efficiently to social reality. This might even be acceptable from a methodological point of view. Generally speaking, we should not be shocked when an abstract concept proves inapplicable in research without the help of hypotheses and bridging principles that adapt it to the specific context of empirical reality. However, doubts arise when these auxiliary hypotheses take on a leading role in deducing explanations and forecasts. In Olson's case, however, it cannot be denied that at a historical time when holistic theories, like those of Parsons, were predominant, his individualistic approach cast new light on the study of institutions and social phenomena. This can also be said of his work on the greater responsibility for national interests shown by social organisations representing a considerable part of the national revenue. In Italy, for example, one might cite the greater sense of responsibility (matured after a long period of ideological clashes) now shown by the three large trade union organisations in relation to problems of public finance and industrial competition, compared to the total lack of interest shown by smaller trade organisations like Cobas for the engine-drivers or the air traffic controllers, which, owing to the pivotal role played by their members, can hold the entire country to ransom. Likewise, one could cite considerations on the greater economic compatibility of redistributive policies that aim to boost the purchasing power of the less well-off compared to the supposed pro-market formulas of the economic right that often disguise the protection of cartels and industrial lobbies and, instead, tend to reduce the efficiency of the economic system. Or, lastly, one could refer to the explanation of the reasons for the superiority of democracy compared to autocracy set out at the beginning of the chapter.

Yet, many exceptions can be found to all these examples. In the latter case one could object that democracy is not always superior to autocracy in terms of efficiency. For example, in coalition governments, characterised by a high level of instability (as was the case for many years in Italy), those in power often do not behave like owners who care about the maintenance and decoration of their own properties, but rather like a group of tenants with an eviction order who no longer have any interest in improving the common property. It does not matter if there is a drop in national wealth or if tax revenues plummet; what matters is for politicians to line their own pockets, by ransacking public assets, given the probability that they will shortly be replaced by others.

Paradoxically, in these situations, democracy seems to be inferior to autocracy (of the oligarchic type): there is a perverse mix of progressively higher marginal rates (although the autocrat has an interest in not raising rates too high in order to avoid depressing and removing the incentive for manufacturers and savers), inefficiency in the infrastructure and public service system (the autocrat has an interest in making the system function in order to boost revenues and he is not conditioned by political considerations which produce artificial jobs while not imposing penalties for failures of efficiency) and the absence of constitutional or parliamentary budget constraints (instead, the autocrat is under pressure not to leave crippling finances for those family members who will succeed him to government).

8.7 Conclusion: The Fertility of the Cognitive Approach to Politics

These comments regarding the criticisms of the Olsonian social actor model enable us to understand the explicative potential of a cognitive analysis of political action. If we regard the voter not as merely a maximiser of benefit, but rather as a bound processor of information, we can attempt to explain a number of phenomena that are otherwise inexplicable.

Decision-making psychology has identified a series of a decisional shortcuts used by the individual to tackle many problems occurring in everyday and professional life. These shortcuts can be defined as *heuristics* because they accelerate the inferential process to the detriment of completeness and the formal rigour of reasoning. These inferential tendencies have been found and used to explain decision-making behaviour in various fields, ranging from economics to professional and legal use, but they have been less frequently applied to political conduct. As was seen in the section on the Olsonian model, an analysis of the decision-making heuristics responsible for the said effects appears to offer an interesting tool for interpreting political behaviour.

Tversky and Kahneman (1973) showed how individuals use the so-called *availability* heuristic to evaluate the occurrence of events or to assess the probability that they will occur. Based on these heuristics, the frequency of an event varies depending on the availability of that event in the memory, namely the greater or lesser ease with which it is evoked. For example, a voter will tend to assess the probability that a candidate presents defects or merits based on the number of times he has heard or read that a fellow party member presents the same defects or merits.

Some political events, like certain decisions on energy or military policy, are seen as one-off cases, generally making it impossible to assess the probabilities for that event to occur. A scenario is therefore created that leads to the event under evaluation. The plausibility of the scenarios which are presented or the difficulties of producing them are used as clues to evaluate the probability that the event will occur. It follows that if an individual cannot produce any scenario, he will consider the event impossible, but, on the contrary, he will view it as being highly probable if he is able to evoke a large number of scenarios or even one particularly consistent and convincing scenario. For example, take some errors of evaluation made by Western governments, like the energy policy before the oil shock, or environmental policy before Chernobyl. This suggests that it is advisable for the various levels of government to use computerised decision-making support tools, like DSS (*Decision Support System*), which are able to simulate and construct the missing scenarios in order to compensate for the limiting effects of availability heuristics.

These cases, as Simon (1987) would say, show how a theory of politics calls for a theory of attention to explain how some themes, among the countless ones available, are selected and placed at the top of the political agenda. While in the past information was a scarce resource for the politician, now it is time that is short supply: only a small proportion of information can be selected and taken into consideration by the ruling government, while the rest is ignored. The fact that governments limit and selectively focus attention on some topics to the exclusion of others is a result of the limited capacity of their members to process the information within the available time. The resulting effect is the creation of a parallel working structure, made up of committees, commissions, groups of advisors, etc. whose task is to process any information that has been marginalized. However, this solution is not sufficient to return topics that would deserve this type of attention to the political agenda. Indeed, this bottleneck often means that matters which are essential to economic well-being and to national security are relegated until such time that they are dramatically catapulted to attention after the explosion of some crisis or following a newspaper or television campaign.

Another heuristic, the *representativeness* heuristic identified by Kahneman and Tversky (1972), explains how we often make inferences that an object A belongs to class B, or the probability that event A is caused by B, based on the degree to which A is representative of B. An individual using this heuristic evaluates the probability of an uncertain event or a sample based on how similar it is in essential characteristics to its parent population, or how it reflects the salient features of the process by which it is generated. For example, an elector might think it very probable that a candidate A for party B which has had numerous brushes with the law is not honest, based on the degree to which this candidate is representative of this party. An elector might think that a particular policy A produced by coalition B is ineffective based on the degree to which the coalition which produced it is ineffective. This may lead to a number of prescriptive type suggestions to neutralise these effects. In elections the reduced number of candidates on each party list and the reduced size of the constituency can reinforce an evaluation made of the candidate's real capacities and skills rather than his or her representativeness of that party's characteristics.

Then there is the so-called *illusion of control* phenomenon, a systematic tendency based on which individuals create an expectancy of personal success probability in a task higher than the objective probability would warrant (Langer 1975). This expectancy of control is more likely to be manifest when factors, linked to situations in which success depends on an individual's skill, are introduced in situations governed by chance. This illusion, which is always impending, may have perverse effects in political decision-making when, for example, the evaluation of the probability of some interventions is overestimated due to the politician, minister or assessor overstepping the mark and intervening directly in areas that are outside his scope, therefore ignoring the prerogatives of the bureaucrat. From this point of view, a formal separation of the areas of responsibility between the politician and the bureaucrat is to be encouraged, in prescriptive terms, leaving the latter to manage *policy* and the politician to evaluate and control its efficacy. A further two forms of illusion concerning methods of controlling the outcome of an event are *wishful thinking*, which sees certain events are more probable than others, simply because they are seen as more desirable (Halpern 1985), and the "Pollyanna" effect in which, on the contrary, some outcomes are regarded as more desirable because they are more probable (Matlin and Strang 1978). Clearly, *wishful thinking* is responsible for the various irrational outcomes, with regard to both electoral choices and the government's decisions.

Lastly, there is the phenomenon of *hindsight* (Fischhoff 1975). Individuals very often judge events that have already happened as being highly likely based on known facts, while the probability attributed to their occurring, based on the same facts, would have been much lower before they happened. It is not difficult to realize that certain well-known events in the past are often seen in this way. People not only tend to regard what has happened as being inevitable, but also to consider it relatively inevitable even before it had happened (therefore, not only is there a tendency to say that something had to happen, but also to add that "I would have seen it coming if you had asked me"). Clearly, this phenomenon can alter a voter's judgment of the burden of responsibility of a particular political actor in relation to a past event. This can happen in two ways. Either by making a casual and contingent link between the actor and the event more deterministic; or by making the actor less responsible and less guilty since the event is, in part, seen as being inevitable. This highlights the ambivalent role of political information. While it does not harm the image and responsibility of a "seasoned" politician, given that the circumstances in which he has been involved have become part and parcel of normal historical and political life (this is the case of *Teflon men* like Reagan or Andreotti, for example, whose reputations are almost never sullied by the mud flung at them by their political opponents), information can undermine the position of a new politician who happens to find himself in a politically negative situation.

An important chapter in cognitive studies of political action concerns the ways of presenting political programmes and results. For example, as we saw earlier when illustrating the framing effect, preference reversal can be achieved or avoided depending how a particular problem is presented; or depending on which value a particular fact is linked to, there will be an anchoring effect to that value (Tversky and Kahneman 1974) which will distort the final judgment of the fact. For example, when a premier has to announce the economic results of his government's policies, it is preferable to announce the good results first, in order to anchor public opinion to a favourable view of the government's actions. Indeed, to a certain degree, there is an involuntary tendency to avoid applying the principle of *regression towards the mean* when announcing results (Kahneman and Tversky 1973). To give an example, if we are told that unemployment has risen by 1% compared to the previous month, we rarely evaluate this difference as a simple statistical fluctuation. On the contrary, we tend to regard it as the sign of a deteriorating economic situation, compared to the previous month, even if there have been many occasions in the past when similar fluctuations have occurred. In other words, normal statistical fluctuations, both up and down, which occur over long periods of observation and which do not alter the mean value of the phenomenon, are seen as events with a specific cause.

In conclusion, the points covered here reveal the empirical fertility of taking an approach to the problems of politics and democracy founded on the cognitive theory of the political actor. This theory does not rule out, indeed in some ways it includes, the logic of the economic approach. Its instrumental rationality is highlighted by concepts like the "means-ends analysis" heuristic in problem solving (Simon 1985), or the principle of cost-benefit analysis present in Beach and Mitchell's model (1978). The fundamental difference between these two approaches lies not in the type of purpose, whether benefit or utility function, to be achieved, but rather in the type of calculation underlying the decision, which only rarely can be maximization.

Lastly, it should be pointed out that a cognitive theory of the political actor is not neutral towards democracy. If, on the one hand, systematic errors of judgment by voters undermine the justification, in the traditional sense, of their rational role in forming the collective choice (thereby backing a possible supporter of technocratic solutions or enlightened despotism), on the other, similar shortcomings appear to characterize the central decision makers. Seen in this light, an interaction between the electorate and those elected, which is as free as possible from the elements seen earlier that disturb judgment, might create the conditions for a virtuous circle instead of introducing the risk of a dangerous, perverse spiral.

Which Mind for Cognitive Economics? 9

At the basis of economics, like other social sciences, there is always an agency theory. This identifies the key characteristics of the subjects who, through their actions, give rise to collective social and economic phenomena. Among these, the most important characteristics are those that explain the origin of the agent's behaviour: why (s)he acts in a particular way; how his or her choice is affected by context; what principles guide or characterise his or her decisions? In short, whether explicitly or implicitly, every action refers to a theory of mind. It is this that, with varying degrees of detail and direct involvement, represents the causal variables responsible for generating the action. However, in general, a theory of mind is neither explicitly nor fully described in economics. Above all, what is referred to are summary psychological indications or implicit assumptions inferred from the principles of choice attributed to the agent by the postulates of economic theory.

9.1 Theories of Mind in the Economic Tradition

There is no question that neoclassical economics is the most important economic theory of the last century. In its first phase – from Irving Fisher and Vilfredo Pareto to the late 1930s and the introduction of Paul Samuelson's weak axiom of revealed preferences – it inherited from the marginalist school a psychological representation of the economic agent as the intentional maximiser of his self-interest based on available beliefs. The theory of mind is based on the triad of belief–desire–action which corresponds to common sense psychology or folk psychology. Being very limited in conceptual terms, this psychology has not been backed by scientific psychology in recent years, nor does it present the characteristics of empirical science (Stich 1983; Viale 1997b, pp. 5–9). It does not seem credible to limit the determinants of action merely to beliefs and desires. One need only refer to everyday personal experience to understand how many other factors are involved in

The present chapter is a modified version of Viale, R. (2005). Quale mente per l'economia cognitiva. In R. Viale (a cura di), *Le nuove economie*. Milano, Editrice Il Sole 24 Ore, 2005.

DOI 10.1007/978-3-642-24743-9_9,

decision-making and action. There are the emotions regarding one's own experiences; the reasons that weaken or strengthen our resolve to act in a particular way; regret, confidence, sensitivity, etc. Not to mention the mechanisms that underlie memory, learning, reasoning and perception. As Egidi (1992) notes, this simplified psychology of the economic agent reflects the cognitive minimalism requested by the aims of neoclassical economics: namely to explain general economic equilibrium. In order to choose the equilibrium price one does not have to pretend that the economic agent has complex gifts of strategic analysis. A parametric capacity is sufficient, in other words an ability to represent the situation as if it were governed by simple, easily foreseeable phenomena. With his or her simplified mind, this economic agent is unaware of most of the complex events of economic reality. In particular, (s)he is completely unprepared when facing phenomena such as innovation, knowledge, institutional change and information, which can be seen as public assets and eludes the parameters of economic equilibrium in general.

Even the simplified theory of mind of the first phase of neoclassical economics was eliminated in contemporary neoclassical economics (from Samuelson onwards). Instead, we witness the progressive replacement of the traditional maximisation view in favour of the consistency view (Giocoli 2003, p. 7). In place of the mind the new economic agent has the equations of Bayesian decision theory. No psychology is needed to describe it. What matters is the a priori and "conventionalist" ascription of the computational capacities able to allow the agent to resolve the equations, in a formally correct manner, which guide his or her decisions. In this way, the theory of economic action leaves the enclosure of empirical science and becomes a branch of mathematics.

However, this terminal outcome of the theory of mind in contemporary neoclassical economics must not make us forget other contributions which, well before the orientations of the new science of economics, have made it a priority directly to tackle the psychology of the economic agent.

As was shown recently (Egidi and Rizzello 2003, pp. 221–245), this focus is certainly present in the work of Marshall, Veblen, Menger and von Hayek.

Over many years Marshall (1867–68) developed a considerable interest in the study of the mind. His research focused on representing neurobiological-type mental phenomena. He anticipated some of Simon and March's later positions in organisation theory. In order to explain the dynamics of economic processes and organisations, in particular, it was necessary to focus on the individual activity of problem-solving, innovation, creativity and routine generation. This was only possible by starting from a theory of mind that could explain how the agent acted in an interactive context. On the other hand, he also elaborated models of learning and organisational change reminiscent of the autopoietic and self-organising systems developed today in the connectionist school of cognitive sciences. Like Marshall, also Veblen (1994) and the other American institutionalists now see the identification of the mind model as a fundamental step to explain the dynamics of change and institutional development. Moreover, it served to advance the interpretation of the routines as codified knowledge and its application to the phenomena of technological change.

However, it is through the Austrian tradition of Menger (1963[1883]) and von Hayek (1952b) that theory of mind acquires an important role, albeit different from that later developed by Simon and cognitive economics. The mind is interpreted, from a psychobiological point of view, as an active elaborator of external information. The knowledge used by the agent is not only fixed by external parameters, but by the subjective and personal capacity to perceive and represent information. Knowledge therefore derives from the mind's ability to classify external stimuli actively using a *framework* of genetic and acquired origin. Having been genetically inherited, the neuronal structure is constantly moulded during the process of learning and information processing. The mental framework underlies the information processing that generates the knowledge which in turn guides the decision-making processes and individual action. Therefore, the characteristics of the human mind are fundamental to the genesis of institutions and their organisational peculiarities. Even if it might seem the opposite, this emphasis on the importance of the mind does not mean, according to von Hayek, that it is possible to explain institutions through reference to the mental mechanisms of action. Indeed, von Hayek and the Austrian tradition are all fiercely antipsychologist and contrary to Mill's epistemological programme (1866) of psychological reduction of social phenomena. From this point of view, von Hayek appears antithetical compared to the epistemological positions of methodological cognitivism, which is, in my opinion, a necessary condition for the cognitive explanation of economic action. Nonetheless, von Hayek's work allows decisive steps to be taken towards opening economics to the cognitive sciences and to the empirical study of behaviour in general.

9.2 Philosophical Origins of the Primacy of Reason

The history of economic thought shows that there was an inverse relationship between the articulated and empirical development of the economic agent's theory of mind and the attribution of rational capacity to the said agent. The greater the demand for rationality, the less the agent's psychological characterisation was developed. As the previous examples show, the maximum rational capacity now required by contemporary neoclassical economics (satisfaction of the computational requisites of Bayesian decision theory) mean that the agent has minimal psychological content. Instead, the opposite occurs in Hayekian subjectivism. This inverse proportionality appears to be a natural consequence of the relationship between reason and mind. Gifts of unlimited reasoning, like those ascribed to the neoclassical economic agent, are not combined with the empirical representation of a mind characterised by cognitive limits and weaknesses. The unlimited reason attributed, a priori, to the economic agent compresses and suffocates any space for human psychological expression. This dualism between reason and mind is not a novelty, but instead has deep, philosophical roots. It is linked to a precise tradition that can be seen as the progenitor of the model of rationality that was in vogue in economic science for two centuries.

What philosophical tradition are we referring to? In brief, we can distinguish two main schools of thought on rationality (Viale and Pozzali 2003, pp. 325–327): the first affirms the superiority of reason compared to intellect; the second asserts the opposite.

In the first, the classical philosophical tradition, reason is the strength that liberates us from prejudices, from myth, from established but false opinions, and from appearances, and which allows a universal or common criterion to be established for all areas of human conduct. In the tradition that spans from Heraclitus, Parmenides, Plato and Aristotle to St Augustine, Descartes, Spinoza, Leibniz and the Enlightenment, reason is man's fundamental and universal guide; it is what differentiates us from animals and allows us to tell truth from falsehood, because, as Seneca states, "Reason is nothing other than a part of the divine spirit descended (or sunk) into a human body". It is universal because it is present in all persons, who, as Descartes affirms, think differently only because they apply reason differently.

In opposition to this Olympic and universal vision of reason we find the second position. According to this minority tradition, expressed by Neoplatonism, St Thomas, medieval scholastics, Francis Bacon and, to a large extent, Kant, reason is subject to the primacy of intellect. Intellect should be regarded as superior because it is equipped with that intuitive and immediate character that allows it to gain a direct understanding of empirical reality, unlike reason which is limited by its discursive and a priori nature. While affirming the discursive nature of both, Kant also maintained that only that of the intellect was valid since its concepts are immediately derived from experience (Kant 1781/1787).

Although severely criticised by Kant, the primacy of reason and its discursive nature remains the dominant position in philosophy. This discursive and linguistic character, as summarised in Aristotle's syllogistic or in the Cartesian ideal of the chains of reasoning in geometry, leads to the formal development of the theory of rationality in the past century. The resulting logic of rationality will always maintain, as in Aristotle, the dual descriptive valency of its own procedures of reason, and normative valency in the sense of the rule for its correct use.

The theory of rationality inherited by the philosophical tradition and which underlies the theory of economic action in the nineteenth century is therefore characterised by unlimited, a priori and linguistic-intentionalist attributes. Its supposed descriptive property is based on the a priori presumption of the universal rationality of the human species and not on the a posteriori justification of people's real rational capacities.

Neoclassical economics and the model of rationality contained in von Neumann and Morgenstern's game theory are the realisation of this ideal (well represented by Laplace's metaphor of the demon endowed with unlimited computational rationality).

The broad concept of rationality has been always linked to epistemological normativity. The realm of a priori demonstrative proof, that is the things that people were absolutely certain about, remained the goal of epistemology and science until the beginning of the twentieth century. Scientific rationality fell into a definitive crisis with the failure of the neopositivist program and the emergence of relativism and socio-historical reductionism or, in other words, the dominance of the context of discovery over the context of justification. Likewise in the twentieth century the inclusive area of epistemological rationality had its radical change with the Naturalizing Epistemology Program of Willard O. Quine. There are no ways of analytically founding the truth. The only possibility is to discover the natural processes that humans follow in generating knowledge.

The realm of certainty and demonstrative proof had already experienced a strong downsizing during the seventeenth century with the acknowledgement of the irreducible uncertainty of human life and the emergence of the theory of probability. The impact of this revolution was at once directed to morality and human choice theory. Blaise Pascal and Pierre Fermat defined the border of reasonableness as the choice of the alternative that maximizes expected value. The various paradoxes from St. Petersburg to Allais and Ellsberg led to change the theory of reasonableness, attempting to resolve the discrepancy between description and normativity. This was made by tinkering with the utility or probability function while at the same time retaining the ideal of maximization or optimization. In any case, the concept of reasonableness, after a decline of interest during the end of the nineteenth and the beginning of the twentieth century, reemerged in the 50s and 60s in the form of the concept of "rationality" in economics, psychology and other social sciences. This rationality was assimilated to the calculation of probabilities, utilities and optimal decisions. The ideal of optimization entered not only the behavioral sciences but also animal biology (e.g. optimal foraging theory) and artificial intelligence (e.g. optimal artificial agents) (Gigerenzer and Selten 2001b).

As for the philosophy of science and also for the epistemology, the crisis of the a priori concept of rationality of choice began in the mid-twentieth century with the introduction by Herbert Simon of Bounded Rationality Theory. In Simon, I can dare say that the three naturalistic approaches find a common interpreter; beyond directly in the theory of rational choice, directly also in the philosophy of science where Simon, in opposition with Karl Popper, is the major supporter of the logic of discovery as psychology of discovery; indirectly, in epistemology where he contributed to the naturalistic theory of knowledge through his works on inductive reasoning and problem solving.

In conclusion, the original flaw in the philosophical concept of unlimited, a priori reason which is dominant over intellect has sacrificed the development of the theory of action in a "bed of Procustes" that leaves no space for empirical research on the intellect, on the real ways of reasoning and decision-making and on the non-intentional and non-conscious aspects of action.

9.3 Cognitive Limits of Human Reason and Bounded Rationality

As is well known, the theory of unbounded rationality has been subject to much criticism during the past few years resulting from empirical research in the cognitive field. These criticisms can be summarised by characterising the theory of action into its three main causal components of reasoning, judgment and choice (Shafir and LeBoeuf 2002, pp. 493–497):

(a) Reasoning

Empirical research over a number of years has documented systematic shortcomings in individuals' logical reasoning. It appears that certain connectives are easier to reason about than others; conjunctions (e.g. "and") are easiest, followed by conditionals (e.g. "if... then"), exclusive disjunctions (e.g. "A or B but not both"), and finally inclusive disjunctions (e.g. "A or B or both"). The mechanisms that account for this "illogical" behaviour can be explained using two opposite hypotheses: in logical reasoning the mind applies a limited number of abstract rules which only correspond to part of the rules of deductive logic; reasoning is not guided by any mental logic because it is based upon mental models that are constructed to represent the situation at hand.

(b) Judgment

People tend to express probability judgments that are correct where the relevance of simple probabilistic rules is made transparent. On the contrary, in richer contexts for judgment where the applicability of the normative rules is less apparent, people tend to produce errors of judgment. These errors are made using methods of thought known as *heuristics*. According to one such heuristic, the *representativeness* heuristic (see Kahneman et al. 1982) there is a tendency to evaluate the likelihood that a target belongs to a certain class based upon the degree to which the target resembles the prototypic class member.[1] This leads to a series of statistical-type errors, including the failure to appreciate regression phenomena and the fact that people are generally overconfident (when the evidence is remarkable but reliability is low) and occasionally underconfident (when the evidence is unremarkable but highly reliable).

(c) Choice

According to normative analyses of rationality, choice should be based on consistent preferences that depend on the subjective utilities of anticipated outcomes weighted by their probabilities. In addition, preferences must satisfy

---

[1] One example that illustrates the role of the representativeness heuristic in probabilistic judgments is the well-known Linda problem. It was posited as follows:

Linda is 31 years old, single, outspoken and very bright. She majored in philosophy. As a student, she was deeply concerned with issues of discrimination and social justice, and also participated in anti-nuclear demonstrations.

You should now rank the following statements in order of probability, using 1 for the most probable and 8 for the least probable.

These instructions were followed by eight statements about Linda's activities, including the following:

Linda is a bank teller (A)

Linda is active in the feminist movement (B)

Linda is a bank teller and is active in the feminist movement (A&B)

The description A&B is less probable than the others owing to the fundamental rule of probability whereby a conjunction of two attributes is less probable than either of the two attributes. Nonetheless, the majority of respondents considered it more probable than A because it was more representative of the characteristic of "being a feminist".

description and procedure invariance. Instead, people tend to construct their preferences on the basis of the nature and context of the decision, with the result that they are often unclear and inconsistent. Prospect theory (Kahneman and Tversky 1979b) posits that probabilities have non-linear impacts on decisions. Fundamental to the decision are changes in wellbeing, such as gains or losses based on a subjective point of reference rather than on the status quo. Individuals prefer to risk more when they have incurred losses and are risk-averse when they are in a situation of gains. This can have a compelling influence on decisions taken in the various contexts of choice. One need only change the "frame" from gain to loss, albeit with the same end result, to produce contradictory responses ("framing effect").

The results of studies on reasoning, judgment and choice have highlighted the limits of rational activity in the context of economic decision-making. The evidence of bounded rationality has given rise to new models of economic rationality. These have sought to build on the real characteristics, not the a priori ones, of economic action, namely on a theory of mind generated empirically. We can describe the main hypotheses that have emerged from cognitive criticism of unbounded rationality by following a criterion linked to two parameters, corresponding to the two blades of Simon's famous scissors of rationality (1990, p. 7):

1. The real constraints of the agent's computational capabilities
2. The real constraints of the structure of the task environment

The first hypothesis is that of *optimisation under constraints*. The search for information must be limited because the decision-makers only have a finite amount of time, attention and resources available. Stopping rules optimise the research, namely they calculate the costs and benefits of searching for each additional information and stop as soon as costs outweigh the benefits (Anderson and Milson 1989; Sargent 1993; Stigler 1961). This version of rationality sets the constraints either as the agent's decisions or in the arbitrary simplification of the environment. However, both constraints are represented by unrealistic norms, of an optimising type, at a psychological level (stopping rule) or in reality (arbitrary simplification of the environment). This version of rationality is still entirely subject to the original flaw of unbounded and a priori rationality.

The second hypothesis is the programme put forward by Tversky and Kahneman (1974) of *heuristics and biases*. These highlighted a series of inferential mechanisms responsible for fallacies (biases) in human reasoning given that they violate some rule of logic or of the calculation of probability. This is a model of bounded and empirically constructed rationality. A role is given to the unconscious components of judgment and choice (e.g. the "framing effect"). However, the resulting version of rationality is predominantly of the intentional kind (This version of rationality doesn't include the last theses of Kahneman on System 1 and System 2 (2003), that, on the contrary, recognize the strong role of intuition and emotion). The empiric study of human reasoning is compared to the classic canons of rationality, namely the rules for calculating probability, logic and Bayesian decision-making. In this way much of human inferential activity is treated as irrational without, on the contrary, showing concern for the success or otherwise of inferences in problem-solving and in giving responses that are adaptive to the environmental context in which they are generated. From this point of view, Kahneman and Tversky's model seems too preoccupied with preserving its reference to the a priori canons of unbounded rationality.

The third hypothesis is Herbert Simon's renowned theory of *bounded rationality* (2000). While, as an empirical theory par exellence, it is principally interested in both series of constraints, cognitive and environmental, its central focus is above all on the former, and indeed it is defined as procedural. Furthermore, it remains anchored to an intentionalist-type theory of action that leaves little room for the unconscious and tacit sphere of factors responsible for the action. The most recent hypothesis called programme of *fast and frugal heuristics* set forth by Gigerenzer and the Adaptive Behaviour and Cognition (ABC) research group (1999), is the natural development of Simon's theory. This broadens and extends the Simonian programme with the aim, above all, of identifying those heuristics which seem, on the one hand, to meet the requisites of bounded rationality, namely the limitation of cognitive capacities, and on the other those of *ecological rationality*, namely the ability to adapt inferences to the environment. As is well known, heuristics are a form of judgment that sacrifices the formal rigour and completeness of an algorithm in favour of speed and simplicity. Simon's "means-ends" heuristic is an example. In the case of *fast and frugal heuristics*, they offer even simpler rules for decision-making under pressure from time constraints.

This programme replaces the *coherence* criterion of inferential activities in relation to the laws of logic and probability with the *correspondence* criteria of decisions with the structure of the environment, using the principles of frugality, speed and accuracy.

The programme developed by Gigerenzer and the ABC group in 1999 appears to distance itself from the original flaw of unbounded and a priori rationality. In my view, however, it is still conditioned by it. Indeed, it appears to be preoccupied more with normative than with empirical issues. As in the case of Tversky and Kahneman, its greatest concern is a comparison between heuristics and the canonical models of unbounded and a priori rationality. Moreover, rather than being the inductive result of empirical research into human cognitive activity, Gigerenzer's heuristics are conjectures introduced on the basis of cues derived from human and animal psychology, and above all as the deductive consequences of principles assigned to human inferential activity, on an a priori basis, such as frugality, speed and simplicity. Lastly, alleged ecological rationality is a normative concern introduced more a priori than in empirical confirmation of the adaptive efficacy of heuristics.

To conclude, it does not seem possible to eliminate the original philosophical flaw completely, even in the theories of mind underlying the various versions of bounded rationality. The prevalence of the normative rather than the descriptive and empirical component guides the generation of theoretical hypotheses. If this proves an ineliminable constraint it follows that, in order to construct a psychological theory of human action, it is necessary to take a step backwards from rationality theory, which owing to its intrinsic and ineliminable nature is normative, a priori and intentionalist. As in the philosophical tradition of the superiority of the intellect compared to reason, this means questioning the various aspects of the mind responsible for action, without the constraint of their explicit and intentional character, their linguistic and computational essence and their normative value compared to a priori rules.

9.4 Bounded Rationality on a Large Scale

What is Bounded Rationality (Simon 1956; Gigerenzer and Selten 2001a)? Simon's metaphor of the pair of scissors is the best representation of the concept and of the connected naturalizing nature of the research program. One blade is the nature of our reasoning and decision making processes with all its limits in computation and time and the other blade is the nature of the environment, with all its complexity. The first blade is characterized by limited features compared to the ideal optimization model. The second is characterized by a changing complex structure. Sometimes the first blade fits with the second and those rational scissors work, but sometimes this does not happen. The rationality, that is the ability of the scissors to cut, is bounded by the fitting of one blade, that is reasoning and decision making, with the other blade, that is the environment. Fitting, in other words, means adaptive choices in a given environment. Bounded rationality is therefore a research program aiming to discover what are the natural specific decision rules that are adaptive in specific different environments. From this point of view the natural decision rules of bounded rationality are the only rules that can be labeled as rational in a prescriptive meaning. Their label of rational is obviously non universal but local to the specific environment or problem space where the rule is adaptive. In other words human beings are often, but not always, bounded rational. Actually sometimes they are also irrational, that is when their choice is not adaptive to the environment because they don't use the specific natural rule of bounded rationality that is suitable for the particular environment.

Economics and organizational studies have been mainly the dominion of the application of bounded rationality. Actually the application of bounded rationality is much more wide and inclusive. It covers any field that implies human choice. The adapting features of bounded rationality should deal with many disciplines that usually are outside the field, such as developmental psychology, social psychology, psychopathology, evolutionary psychology, and cognitive anthropology. These different areas could help deepen aspects of bounded rationality and might also be very useful in their application to the field of economics.

1. Since evolution by natural selection is an historical process the brain and body tend to perform functions that, in the past, *facilitated* reproduction. Whether they currently do so will depend on how closely the present resembles the past. If we can develop an accurate picture of a species' reproductive ecology – the set of physical transformations that had to occur over evolutionary time for individuals to reproduce – we can infer those properties the organism is likely to have in order to ensure that those transformations reliably took place. Evolutionary time,

the time it takes for reproductively efficacious mutations to arise and spread in the population, is often taken to be roughly 1,000–10,000 generations; for humans, that equals about 20,000–200,000 years. A major lesson of evolutionary approach to psychology is that if you want to understand the brain-mind, look deeply at the environment of our ancestors that is the *Environment of Evolutionary Adaptation (EEA)* as focused through the lens of reproduction. If the presumptions of *evolutionary psychology* are correct, the structure of our brain-minds should closely reflect our ancestral reproductive ecology. Evolutionary psychologists hold that behaviors or traits that occur universally in all cultures are good candidates for evolutionary adaptations. Evolved psychological adaptations (such as the ability to learn a language) interact with cultural inputs to produce specific behaviors (e.g., the specific language learned). Evolutionary psychologists contrast their approach with the standard social science model, according to which the mind is a general-purpose cognition device shaped almost entirely by culture.

Since an organism's adaptations were suited to its ancestral environment, a new and different environment can create a mismatch. Because humans are mostly adapted to Pleistocene environments, psychological mechanisms sometimes exhibit "mismatches" to the modern environment. One example is the fact that although about 10,000 people are killed with guns in the US annually, whereas spiders and snakes kill only a handful, people nonetheless learn to fear spiders and snakes about as easily as they do a pointed gun, and more easily than an unpointed gun, rabbits or flowers. A potential explanation is that spiders and snakes were a threat to human ancestors throughout the Pleistocene, whereas guns (and rabbits and flowers) were not. There is thus a mismatch between our evolved fear-learning psychology and the modern environment. This mismatch also shows up in the phenomena of the supernormal stimulus – a stimulus that elicits a response more strongly than the stimulus for which it evolved. The term was coined by Niko Timbergen to describe animal behavior, but Harvard psychologist Deirdre Barrett (2007, 2010) has pointed out that supernormal stimulation governs the behavior of humans as powerfully as that of animals. She illustrates junk food as an exaggerated stimulus for cravings for salt, sugar, and fats, and she describes how television is an exaggeration of social cues of laughter, smiling faces and attention-grabbing action. Magazine centerfolds and double cheeseburgers pull instincts intended for an EEA where breast development was a sign of health, youth and fertility in a prospective mate, and fat was a rare and vital nutrient.

From an EP perspective (Gaulin and McBurney 2003), cognition is not "general purpose," but uses heuristics, or strategies, that generally increase the likelihood of solving problems our ancestors routinely faced. From this point of view EP tries to single out the bounded rationality of our ancestors. For example, humans are far more likely to solve a logic problem that involves the detection of cheating (a common problem given our social nature) than the same logic problem put in purely abstract terms. Since our ancestors did not encounter truly random events, we may be cognitively predisposed to incorrectly identify patterns in random sequences. "Gamblers' Fallacy" is one example of this. Gamblers may falsely believe that they have hit a "lucky streak" even when each outcome is actually random and independent of previous trials. Most people believe that if a fair coin has been flipped nine times and Heads appears each time, that on the tenth flip, there is a greater than 50% chance of getting Tails. Humans find it far easier to make diagnoses or predictions using frequency data than when the same information is presented as probabilities or percentages, presumably because our ancestors lived in relatively small tribes (usually with less that 150 people) where frequency information was more readily available. Evolutionary psychology emphasizes the importance of kin selection and reciprocity in allowing for prosocial traits, such as altruism, to evolve. Like chimps, humans have subtle and flexible social instincts, allowing them to form extended families, lifelong friendships, and political alliances. Lastly EP underlines the evolutionary implications of some emotions (Eldakar et al. 2006, 2008). Some of them are universal and have a clear evolutionary meaning. For instance disgust has undoubtedly evolved to protect animals from toxins. Fear allowed animals to take flight and escape from predators.

The previous considerations show the importance of EP in the bounded rationality program. It helps in singling out the natural decision rules that could be adaptive in the ancestral time but that are no longer adaptive now. And, on the contrary, when there is no mismatch between the past and present environment it can be a precious heuristic discovery device to introduce potential natural decision rules that were effective in the past and now (for instance some simple heuristics as Take The Best or Recognition). It also helps to understand the particular role of emotions and of altruism in explaining the successful or unsuccessful adaptation of human decision making to contingent environment.

2. The importance of evolution is evident. What about development? The question is: are the developmental studies useful in outlining some stable cognitive processes in adult reasoning and decision making? Is it possible that what we discover about children's thought and rationality teaches us about what will go on in adult time? My considerations are that development might also be an important source of knowledge about bounded rationality. Let's think for example of the famous but now discredited theory of Jean Piaget on the genetic epistemology of the cognitive development of children. Knowing that children develop a competence for propositional calculus might have been very interesting in understanding deductive reasoning performances and biases among adults. As on the contrary, the current and actual knowledge that this is not the case. Nowadays the revolution in developmental psychology is showing data that can be very useful for the bounded rationality program. We know that infants are endowed with an innate set of principles that allow them to begin to interact with world. Principles of causal attribution; principles that allow them to characterize a living being from an artifact; principles that allow them to assume that external states of affairs may cause mental states and there is a causal chain from perception to beliefs to intentions to actions. Today with the mirror neurons theory we have also a possible neural explanation of mind reading and empathy in children. What can be the relevance for bounded rationality of these hypotheses?

Let's take the "Little scientist Thesis" of Gopnik and Meltzoff (1997). "*...There is strong empirical evidence that starting from their innate endowed principles, children propose abstract entities, coherently organized with causal relations among them. These entities serve to provide characteristic explanations, predictions and interpretations. Children initially ignore certain kinds of counter-evidence, then account for such evidence with auxiliary hypotheses, then use the new theoretical idea in limited contexts, and only finally reorganize their knowledge so that the new theoretical entities play a central role...*" This thesis can enlighten us about a stable effect on adult reasoning and decision making. One of the most important, also affecting scientists, is the confirmation bias that we find already in children. It has been considered a serious classical flaw by psychologists and philosophers of science in the rational image of scientists and humans. What are the suggestions coming from the developmental age? That in many cases the confirmation bias is a successful adaptive choice that allows children, like scientists and folks, to strengthen their theories by building, as Imre Lakatos pointed out, a protective belt of auxiliary hypotheses to make invulnerable the theoretical core. Therefore, in many cases it is bounded rational to commit the so called confirmation bias.

Some years ago I worked with a group of other scholars and tried to understand if children are good inductive thinkers (see part III of this volume). The result in category based induction seemed to show that children don't apply some of the most important inductive principles, such as the diversity principle, which states that with more diverse premises we have a stronger conclusion (Viale and Osherson 2006). The same seemed to happen also among the Itza Mayan adults of Guatemala (Lopez et al. 1997) and among the Vietnamese students (Viale and Osherson 2000) but not among American students (Nisbett et al. 2001). Also in this case a better reflection on the meaning of the results among children would have suggested that, as for the Itza Mayans, it is the ecological dimension of the problem that can stimulate the inductive reasoning and that the tests were totally artificial without any ecological meaning. In these kinds of tests only one blade of the scissors, the mind, was examined and not the fitting of the two blades that is the bounded rationality.

Many are the strange behaviors of children that are adaptive: from the presence of imaginary companions to the habit of cheating (Gopnik 2009). After all, children and their changeable adaptation towards the environment are an open sky laboratory of bounded rationality rules, heuristics, and behaviors that might help in understanding the final features of the adult decision maker.

3. Biological evolution seems to have selected behavioral modules or decision rules. Some of them are bounded rational in given environmental structures whereas others are not. Is cultural evolution and social interaction capable of affecting the inherited behavioral patterns? Let's take the example of the behavior of reciprocity and cooperation. There are no certainties about the predisposition to cooperate. Evolutionary psychology opts for the predisposition to cooperate/reciprocate with only kin and "close friends" (i.e. reciprocal altruism or repeated interaction with known individuals) as it is found also among

other primates. Others seem inclined towards a more inclusive cooperation (with kin, friends or anonymous people). In any case, evidence from cross-cultural experimental economics (Henrich 2000; Henrich et al. 2001) suggests that cultural differences can substantially affect the patterns of reciprocity and cooperation found in different social groups. Henrich has shown that the Peruvian Amazonian indios Machiguenga greatly deviate from the behavior of typical western subjects in both the ultimatum game and in a common pool resources game. The selfish behavior of the Machiguenga, confirmed also among Indios Mapuche of Chile, amounts to nearly half of the offer of westerners (average offer of 26% vs. 44%; modal offer of 15% vs. 50%) in the ultimatum game and less in the common pool resources game (mean contribution of 23% vs. 40%; modal contribution 0% vs. 60%). Individuals seem to be sensitive to socio-environmental cues which allow them to adjust or calibrate their degree of trust and their expectations of fairness and punishment in an adaptive way (Henrich et al. 2001). Such cues may be social or cultural. Social cues mean that individuals rapidly learn from small samples of either failed or successful interactions. Social learning is mainly based on imitation and other tools such as teaching and local enhancement. Rules such as "do-what-the-majority-do" or "do-what-the–successful-do" are plausible rules that are evident also in animal behavior. These rules are responsible for cultural transmission. The first conformist transmission causes individuals to preferentially copy the most common behavior in the population. Individuals use the frequency of a behavior as an indirect measure of the behavior's quality. The second prestige-biased transmission suggests that humans possess a tendency to copy prestigious individuals, i.e. those who receive the most displays of respect/deference and other sociolinguistic signals from others. Compared with the costly asocial learning via individual experience, this kind of social transmission allows the individual to more rapidly acquire a repertoire of fitness-enhancing or success-oriented traits and better-than-average solutions to the problems of life. To come back to the argument of cooperation, it seems that the same inherited character can be strengthened or not to become more adaptive, that is bounded rational to different environments. The cultural transmission is more effective than individual asocial learning in the bounded rational calibration of the behavioral pattern because it speeds up learning by skipping costly individual experimentation, sampling and data processing.

Cultural transmission seems to accumulate and stabilize cultural-evolutionary products that act as effective decision making algorithms, without the individual participants understanding how and why the particular system works. Systems of divination provide interesting examples of how culture provides adaptive solutions (Henrich et al. 2001; Dove 1993). Among the Kantu of Kalimantan, a tribe of Borneo, swidden farmers select a new garden location based both on the type of bird observed there, and the type of call the bird makes after it is first observed. They believe that birds actually supply supernatural information that foretells the future. This randomized selection diversified the types of garden across community members which spreads risk among households. This bounded rational cultural rule, based on superstition, suppresses errors that farmers make in judging the chance of a flood and reduces the chance of catastrophic failures across the entire group, decreasing the probability that many farmers will fail at the same time.

Hutchins and Hazlehurst (1991) suggest that gradual cultural transmission can accumulate effective mental models of complex problems that no individuals could solve on their own. In the past, inland-living native Californians evidently visited the coast to harvest nutritionally important shellfish. To facilitate this, these people acquired an effective bounded rational cultural model of the relationship between lunar phases and tides. Hutchins and Hazlehurst simulated the process where a small bit of individual learning and observation and the ability to transmit this information across individuals and generations, allows a population to produce an accurate, effective lunar-tide model.

The cultural transmission and socio-interactional processes can combine to give rise to adaptive group processes that distribute cognition, knowledge, skill, and labor. Decision making institutions like companies and markets, or governance structures like political systems, or government bodies aggregate information and processing powers distributed among group members in adaptive ways without individual participants necessarily understanding how and why the total system works. According to some authors (Boyd and Richerson 2001), cultural change through conformist and prestige-biased transmission can give rise to a high-level selective process called cultural group selection that can build increasingly adaptive and efficient systems at the group level that involve both distributed cognition and the complex division of labor.

It is well known that the bounded rationality approach can also help in understanding the adaptive emergence of conventions and social norms (March 1994). Conventions help in solving coordination problems. They can simplify decision making by creating "default choices" and "default choice rules". Moreover, they help communication because it is easier to convey ideas about conventional things. Social norms such as those incorporated into the social roles in family as in labor identified themselves in an interiorized and often automatic set of rules that frees people from evaluating the appropriateness of their behavior and permit them to direct attention to other matters.

Society also creates the environments where humans automatically behave in an irrational way. Following the metaphor of the scissors, it is as if one blade – the environment – does not allow the other – the mind – to slide. Social context has many different individual effects of this kind: it is arousing and arousal facilitates dominant responses; it boosts performance on easy tasks and hinders performance on harder tasks. Social interaction generates the loafing phenomenon, can interfere with automatic responses such as speaking, can intensify negative emotions such as shame and shyness and can increase harmful conformity, as in the case of Group Think or herd effect (Henrich et al. 2001). While these effects are not individually bounded rational, it is likely that sometimes they might have a positive adaptive meaning at a collective level.

Lastly there is a category of behaviors that are not bounded rational because it is the blade of the mind that does not slide on that of the environment. This is the case of many kinds of mental deviances and abnormalities, from neurosis to schizophrenia and cyclothymia, but also of many absences of mind in everyday life. This lack of bounded rationality can be described as a continuum from some common biases and errors in everyday life to the complete detachment from the environment and the impossibility of being attuned with its space-time coordinates. From the point of view of bounded rationality, it might be considered the separation between pathological and not pathological. For example, certain forms of magical thinking, as in the previous case of the Kantu or some deductive absurdities such as prelogic thinking or middle way logic or a steady risk-averse and fearful behavior, could be bounded rational because they are adaptive in given environments and consequently they should not be considered pathological. On the contrary, some so-called rational behaviors, such as stubborn and destructive falsificationism or a rigid, inflexible and pitiless bivalent moral reasoning or solipsistic and unrestrained, high-risk gambling or investing, can have serious unsuitable consequences at the individual and collective level and therefore might be considered pathological.

To conclude, I have shown some cues of emerging topics about bounded rationality that are outside economics, and organizational studies. We can discover a great deal of interesting data and theories in these fields that can endow with stronger credentials the concept of bounded rationality in economics.

9.5 Cognitive Economics: The Superiority of the Intuitive Mind

Gigerenzer's programme does contain a number of cues that appear to point in the right direction towards a naturalistic approach to bounded rationality (Gigerenzer and Selten 2001b). For example, he seems to acknowledge that often "people reach better judgments by using their intuition rather than by using reason" (Wilson and Schooler 1991) or that simple intuitive strategies are competitive with Bayesian inferences (McKenzie 1994). Indeed, according to Gigerenzer "...too much information and too much information-processing can hurt. Cognition is the art of focusing on the relevant and deliberating ignoring the rest." (Gigerenzer, Todd, and the ABC Group 1999, p. 21)

Moreover, Gigerenzer appears to attribute an important role to factors which do not form part of the intentional sphere, whether in searching for information or in decision-making. For example, "... emotions can also function as heuristic principles for guiding and stopping information search" (Gigerenzer, Todd, and the ABC Group 1999, p. 31). Their role seems important in decision-making processes, above all when they enable the mind to avoid the cognitive burden associated with the explicit acknowledgement of the norm, its evaluation, its choice and application.

In short, it is recognised that an important part of human cognition, responsible for decision-making, exists that cannot be represented by the accumulation of explicit information, the search for cognitive completeness and the conscious application of decision-making rules intentionally selected by the agent (Gigerenzer 2007).

It is precisely this awareness that marks out *cognitive economics* in the theory of economic action. On the contrary, in general, anyone who accepted the empirical results of cognitive sciences as anomalies of the theory of rationality in neoclassical economics was restricted to adding assumptions on cognitive limitations to the traditional model. These served to explain anomalies, such as exceptions to rationality. This monistic concept of rationality is questioned by cognitive economics. The normative dimension of this way of reasoning and judgment is not denied. It is apparent when the individual has time to reflect consciously and to work out probabilistic judgments, or make his or her own deductions from given premises. However, this only represents a minimal part of human decision-making activity. First, there are estimates and reasonings that cannot be normatively correct, even after careful and deliberate reflection. The underlying norms are too complex and "unfriendly" from a cognitive point of view. Secondly, most everyday cognitive activity occurs rapidly and intuitively, and is overwhelmingly influenced by emotional and affective variables. This type of cognitive activity does not usually produce correct judgments and decisions, from a normative point of view, but it does work for the practical purposes of everyday life. In this sense, it might be preferable to talk about a *dualistic model of rationality*: Type 1, the tacit type, is used in intuitive, everyday decisions; while Type 2, the explicit type, is used in analysis and normative judgments (Evans and Over 1996).

However, it is preferable to abandon the term rationality, owing to its ineliminable quality as the normative attribute of human decision-making capacities. Moreover, the word dualist can be replaced with double, because the two components are not in antithesis but integrated with one another. Instead of referring to the dualism of rationality, therefore, it would be better to refer to a *Cognitive Double-Mindedness*. This is composed of a first component, which corresponds to the tacit, intuitive activity modulated by context-dependent affective and emotional factors, and of a second component, representing the conscious activity of reasoning, dependent on rules but independent of context. The first component could also be termed the *Intuitive Mind*, and the second the *Reasoning Mind*. Many authors have expressed support for this double hypothesis. Epstein (1994) affirms that there is a coexistence between a system that is holistic, affective and guided by associationistic connections, and one that is analytic, logical and reason orientated. Likewise, Sloman (1996) proposes one system that is associative, and its computations reflect similarity and temporal structure, while the other is rule based, and it operates on symbolic structures and follows explicit computational principles. Even Kahneman (2003) reaffirms the thesis of a two-system cognitive architecture and refers to Stanovich's proposal (1999). The operations of the System 1 are fast, automatic, effortless, associative, and often emotionally charged; those of System 2 are slower, serial, effortful and deliberately controlled and rule-governed. The first system corresponds to intuition and shares many common characteristics with perception, while the second is associated with reasoning.

The thesis of a double system of mind is not new (Evans and Frankish 2010). In the 60s Reber in studying the implicit learning coined the term "cognitive unconscious" to refer to the idea that many cognitive processes occur outside of consciousness. "The acquisition of knowledge takes place largely independently of conscious attempts to learn and largely in absence of explicit knowledge about what was acquired" (Reber 1993, p. 5). During the 70s there was also the development of dual-process accounts of deductive reasoning (Wason and Evans 1975; Evans 1977). The theory came from two distinct origin. The first was the observation of a dissociation between behaviour and introspective reports. The behaviour in Wason selection task was biased whereas the participants gave rational-sounding explanations of their choices. The second origin was the observation that logical processes seemed to compete with non-logical biases, e.g. belief biases, in determining behaviour on various deductive reasoning tasks. In the 80s also social cognition develops models to explain the dissociation between explicitly stated attitudes and actual social behaviour (Nisbett and Wilson 1977). A number of dual-processing accounts have been developed. One was the distinction between automatic and controlled processing which has been developed into the theory of automaticity in social judgements (Bargh 2006). For example studies in automaticity show that stereotypes are powerful implicit knowledge structures that influence social behaviour in spite of contrary explicit attitudes.

As I wrote before the term duality seems to certify a separation and distinction between two minds. Stanovich (1999, Stanovich and Toplak 2012) is a great advocate of this position. He coined System 1 and System 2 to demarcate two different kinds of mental activity. On the contrary in the tradition of social judgment theory there is an account called *cognitive continuum theory* (Hammond 1996) that supports the continuity and not distinction between intuitive and analytic thinking. Also some philosophers are holding a similar monistic view. According to the virtual-system approach (Dennett 1991; Frankish 2004) the second system can be seen as emergent from the first, rather than distinct from it. This approach seems to be more evolutionary fitted, "showing how radically new forms of cognitive activity could develop without massive changes to neural hardware" (Evans and Frankish 2010, p. 22). The evolutionary perspective is also an argument to emphasize the idea that intuitive decision making can be highly effective and often superior to that based on analytical reasoning (Reyna 2004; Gigerenzer 2007). Table 9.1 summarizes the features attributed by various theorists to the two systems of cognition:

Cognitive economics fully encapsulates this double features of mind. No theory of economic action can be constructed without including the causal role of the factors indicated by the intuitive mind. On the other hand, for years theorists of decision-making using psychological techniques and neural imaging have recognised the intrinsic influence of these components. Damasio (1994) hypothesised that the best decisions need a somatic marker or a gut feeling which allows us to anticipate the pain or the pleasure resulting from the choice. Indeed, the images linked to positive or negative sentiments and emotions often guide decisions. The facility with which these images are represented in the mind gives them an alternative

Table 9.1 Features attributed by various theorists to the two systems of cognition (Evans and Frankish, 2010, p. 15)

System 1	System 2
Evolutionarily old	Evolutionarily recent
Unconscious, preconscious	Conscious
Shared with animals	Uniquely (distinctively) human
Implicit knowledge	Explicit knowledge
Automatic	Controlled
Fast	Slow
Parallel	Sequential
High capacity	Low capacity
Intuitive	Reflective
Contextualized	Abstract
Pragmatic	Logical
Associative	Rule-based
Independent of general intelligence	Linked to general intelligence

role in decision-making processes to judgments based on formal rules which are intentionally followed (Loewenstein et al. 2001). In this sense, we speak of "*affective heuristics*" (Slovic et al. 2001) as a way of explaining various phenomena, like the negative relationship between costs and benefits demonstrated under temporal pressure and for affective reasons. For example, contrary to economic reality where the relationship is, generally, positive, it was often found that, particularly when the judgments are made under time pressure, people who like a particular technology think it should be low-cost and bring widespread benefits (Finucane et al. 2000).

These findings are fundamentally important for any economic theory which sets out to explain how preferences are formed. Preferring one option to another is a process that is often determined by the greater mental *accessibility* of certain affectively loaded images linked to the choice. The intuitive mind is structured on the basis of accessibility, namely the facility with which certain mental contents come to mind. In choices based on intuition, which include most everyday economic choices made by ordinary people, it is above all those mental contents with greater emotional saliency that are most accessible, thereby determining the decision. From this point of view, the function of the intuitive mind allows us to explain, in general and simple terms, the activity of many heuristics discovered in the past few years, and in particular the representativeness heuristic. Why is it that many experiments (like in that on "Linda", described in note 1) reveal a low percentage of answers which conform to the principles of probability theory? Because in these instances, the decision-maker's mind tends to reduce the complexity of the calculation to simpler operations using a more accessible process of *attribute substitution* (Kahneman e Frederick 2002). In other words, the subject tends to evaluate the attribute of an event, such as, for example, the probability of Linda being a bank teller, or a feminist bank teller, by substituting another attribute, e.g. the similarity of Linda's description to that of a feminist, which is mentally more accessible.

Affective and emotional factors are the most important generator of attribute substitution owing to their capacity to make one property more mentally accessible than another.

This emotionally based accessibility phenomenon, typical of the intuitive mind, lies at the origin of a series of heuristics which are active in many economic decisions. These are referred to as *prototype heuristics* (Kahneman 2003), which share a common psychological mechanism, the representation of categories by their prototypes. Whenever we look at or think about a set of objects which is sufficiently homogeneous to have a prototype, information about the prototype is automatically accessible. There are various hypotheses as what constitutes a prototype. It could be defined in general terms as being characterised by the average values of the salient properties of the members of a given set or events. Clearly, affective factors are intrinsically linked to the formation and revision of a prototype, influencing the accessibility of the salient properties that make up the prototype. The greater the affective valence of a property, the greater its mental accessibility, and therefore the more probable it is that it will contribute to form the prototype. From this point of view, the prototype often does not represent the most intrinsic and relevant normative properties of a category, but only those which have a greater affective impact. This limited normative representativeness of the prototype means that when an event forming part of a category is judged, the judgment is based on the marginal properties of the prototype rather than on the basis of a more detailed analysis of the relevant properties of the event. For example, prototype heuristics frequently lead to a denial of the so-called *extensionality* of a category. In other words, when we add an element to a category we increase the overall value of the category. Therefore, an increase in the extension of a category will augment the value of its extensional attributes (e.g. if we add one or more businesses to a group of businesses in a sector, this will increase the overall turnover of the sector). This does not happen when we mentally use the prototype of a category, which by definition is based on the average properties of the set, not on their extensionality. This leads to counter-normative decisions. One example, selected from many, will serve to illustrate this phenomenon. A study by William H. Desvousges et al. (1993) on *WTP* (willingness to pay) highlighted a complete denial of the extension. A group of respondents were asked how much they would spend to prevent migratory birds being drowned in uncovered oil ponds. The number of birds to be saved changed depending on the various subsets. The amounts that the respondents were willing to pay were $80, $78, and $88, respectively, for saving 2,000 birds, 20,000 birds or 200,000 birds. In all the sub-sets, the emotionally charged prototype image of a single bird drowning in oil was the real target in the judgment regarding the economic value. This annulled the evidence of the different extension of the number of birds among the subsets of subjects.

Prototype heuristics are responsible for a larger number of commonplace judgments in economic life. It can be said that all the choices based on an analysis of sets and categories stimulates the activity of this type of heuristic. From evaluating the inductive support for an hypothesis provided by a set of data to estimating the economic worth of private and public goods, the predominance of choices are elaborated by the intuitive mind. In these cases judgments are reached using prototypes based on the dimensions of individual cases and lacking the dimension of the extension. To come to the point, it is not possible to construct a theory of economic beliefs and preferences without referring to the cognitive role of the intuitive mind in formulating these judgments.

The intuitive mind also underlies another fundamental characteristic of judgment and economic choice: the tacit nature of most mental processes implicated in economic action. This is at the heart of the well-known problem of "*tacit knowledge*" which has attracted the attention of many economists and social scientists, but which, above all, looks to the cognitive sciences for explicative solutions (Viale and Pozzali 2003).

The cognitive activity of subjects can, it is well known, be influenced not only by consciously perceived events, but also by those perceived unconsciously. It is also known that implicit memory mechanisms are present. Subjects affected by severe forms of amnesia still have the ability to perform particular tasks learned prior to the event. Moreover, there seems to be an asymmetry between the conscious acquisition of particular abilities and their effective implementation (Zeman 2001, p. 1278). This asymmetry appears to be confirmed by neurophysiological studies using neural imaging techniques. The tacit knowledge required to carry out a particular skill appears mainly to activate areas of the brain that are distinct from those activated when the skill is acquired knowingly. Data show how, in the presence of damage or inactivity in those areas of the brain responsible for the phenomena of perception and conscious memory, there are still signs of implicit memory and perception. This seems to open the way to the hypothesis of a separation between conscious and unconscious cerebral structures that may underlie the separation between the intuitive and the reasoning mind. This would also satisfy a principle of economy at a cognitive level: full awareness constitutes a cost in neurocognitive terms, since it implies the prolonged involvement of complex and high-level cerebral structures. In most everyday choices, which are frequently subject to standardisation and decision-making routines, the constant recourse to full consciousness and to intentional-type processes alone appears an unnecessary cognitive luxury.

Cognitive psychology also appears to support this thesis. The contributions by Nisbett and Wilson (1977), and by the research group coordinated by Ellen Langer (Langer 1978; Langer, Blank and Chanowitz 1978) were the first to pinpoint the presence of a net dissociation between explicit knowledge and the effective knowledge used to solve the tasks in hand. This was then confirmed by Reber (1993) in his studies on learning artificial grammars and on learning the probabilistic structure of event sequences where it was found that the capacity to know the structure underlying the stimuli was generally not acknowledged by the subjects.[2] Lastly,

[2] It was found that tacit mechanisms of knowledge can allow performances to be achieved that would normally be outside the range of the conscious cognitive faculties.

the research group coordinated by Broadbent (Berry and Broadbent 1988; Broadbent, Fitzgerald and Broadbent 1986) studied a series of tasks linked to the control of complex systems – for example, the problem of production control and social control – "the results showed that practice significantly improved ability to control the (. . .) production or personal interaction task, but had no effect on ability to answer post-task written questions" (Berry and Broadbent 1988, p. 253).[3]

In short, the tacit dimension of knowledge appears to play a major role in our decision-making processes and the intuitive mind is in charge of the cognitive processes that generate it. If tacit knowledge is generally important to decision-making processes in economic life, it is even more important in those requiring a *high level of knowledge*. At first glance, this might seem counterintuitive. In this sense, the tacit component of decision-making appears to be significant precisely in routine decisions, such as during everyday consumer behaviour in a supermarket or in repetitive office activities. Indeed, the conscious and explicit dimension of these is minimal, while most of the process is performed automatically and explicitly. On the contrary, in those activities requiring a high level of knowledge, such as those linked to research and technological innovation, the complexity of the problem-solving activity and the need for effortful cognitive action in order to achieve the results presupposes the activation of attention mechanisms and conscious inferential processes belonging to the superior cortical zones, corresponding to the area of the reasoning mind. Nonetheless, as it will be explained in Volume II it is precisely in situations involving the generation of technological knowledge and during the process of technology transfer and diffusion within the enterprise that tacit knowledge appears to play a crucial role in explaining the resulting economic dynamics. While being in the presence of conscious cognitive activities applied to relatively formalised forms of knowledge – such corresponding to science and technology – the individual cannot represent them all explicitly and completely owing to the complexity of the conceptual categories involved. This leaves an important residue of tacit knowledge that he or she cannot represent, communicate or transfer to others. To this we should add the tacit component linked to laboratory techniques, methodologies and practices. This bottleneck to technological change and diffusion is responsible for many institutional, organisational and economic aspects affecting the evolutive dynamics of industrial development. In a selective environment like industry, the system that is most able to generate, circulate and use innovative technological knowledge will have the greatest chance of building a reputation in the market. In short, the more an enterprise is capable of minimising the negative

[3] "In contrast, verbal instruction on how to reach and maintain the target value significantly improved ability to answer questions but had no effect on control performance. Moreover, there was no evidence for a positive association between task performance and question answering. Rather, individuals who were better at controlling the task tended to be worse at answering the questions." (Berry and Broadbent 1988, p. 253)

impact of tacit knowledge on the processes of generating, spreading and using technologies, the more its systems of innovation will be successful.[4]

In conclusion, economic action appears to be guided by psychological components that often belong more to the sphere of the intuitive mind than to that of the reasoning mind. Unlike other critical approaches to neoclassical rationality, cognitive economics is aware of this and moves the barycentre of the theory of mind for the economic agent away from the conscious, explicit, intentional and rational aspects of the reasoning mind towards the tacit, subconscious, intuitive and emotional aspects of the intuitive mind. As an empirical theory par excellence, cognitive economics does not reject the contribution of the reasoning mind to economic decision-making, in particular since, in many situations, its role cannot be denied. However, it is not the only cognitive reality responsible for economic choices. In this respect, by remaining within an intentionalist vision of cognitive activity, even the concept of bounded rationality loses much of its explicative capacity. In the case of the economic agent, rationality is not only constrained by the reduced computational and calculating ability of the conscious and intentional part of the human mind, it is also bound by the influence of intuitive, affective, emotional and tacit factors which characterise what we have dubbed the intuitive mind. The theory of mind of the economic agent is therefore based on a strongly integrated sense of *cognitive double-mindedness* in which the reasoning component or the intuitive one prevails depending on the situations and contexts of decision-making. However, there are few situations in which it can be said that the decision was taken by the reasoning component without the influence of the intuitive mind. The relationship between the two minds can be represented using the iceberg metaphor. The tiny fraction that appears on the surface is the reasoning mind, and this represents the surface image of the economic agent. However, it rests on the huge, submerged body of the iceberg, the intuitive mind, which remains invisible but is responsible for guiding the inferential pathways of *Homo oeconomicus*. *Cognitive economics* posits this double nature of the human mind and the primacy of the intuitive component to explain economic action.

[4] In today's reality, the success of America's innovation system depends on its institutional capacity to minimise the bottleneck of tacit knowledge. There are various means that are used, but the main one is the direct link between university and "corporate" laboratories through researchers and postgraduates able to move from one setting to the other. This form of "transfer by head" of technological knowledge avoids the distortions and filters created by communications and transfer between different parties because as bearers of different cognitive styles they are incapable of explaining the tacit components of knowledge.

Epistemological Pluralism and Economics 10

10.1 Epistemological Pluralism in Science

Is it possible to talk about many sciences or by doing so do we risk opening up dangerous gulfs in the principle of demarcation between science and non-science? If we identify specific epistemologies among the various empirical sciences, from Physics to Archaeology, is it possible to continue to assert the epistemological unity of scientific knowledge? And what is the position of economics in this classification?

This is one of the central issues of the philosophy of contemporary science. I will answer this question by tackling just the first half of the apple, i.e. the issue of epistemological pluralism, without touching on the much more difficult issue of the demarcation criterion. This is obviously subject to numerous epistemological misgivings, particularly from people who ask themselves how we can talk about differences in a sum of conceptual entities that have scientific attributes and are separated from others by a fence, without first establishing the characteristics of the boundary and of the passports that permit or forbid entry to the enclosure.

The 1970s appeared to mark the end of an intellectual process that had forcefully affected philosophy and the most important natural and social sciences in the twentieth century: the identification of the boundaries between scientific and non-scientific knowledge. An entire century of epistemological and logical meditation and confrontation with science historians and scientists about how to define a universal methodological rationality appeared to dissolve in the indistinct particulate of knowledge that was the fruit of the contingent situation. Relativism replaced the principle of the demarcation between science and non-science with the principle of continuity between all forms of knowledge. The rationalistic programme had tried to define analytical criteria in advance, in order to justify the label of scientificity, but was unable to avoid contradictions and tautology. On the other hand, the very history of science revealed various forms of methodological discontinuity, which were unable to provide a foundation for the universal principle of demarcation. The victory of relativism expressed in its philosophical, historical and sociological arguments seemed to definitively close the glorious page of the

R. Viale, *Methodological Cognitivism*,
DOI 10.1007/978-3-642-24743-9_10, © Springer-Verlag Berlin Heidelberg 2012

neo-positivist and demarcationist philosophy of science. From then on, this philosophy of science entered the books of the history of philosophy, but it no longer inspired future philosophical research. In fact, it seemed a kind of reckoning encapsulated in the world of philosophy, and therefore of little general significance. We did not immediately understand the perverse effects that a similar position would have on various aspects of cultural and social life. Social epistemology inspired by the principle of continuity was to question the primacy of official science in deciding the risks of a new technology, the priorities to give to funding for scientific research, the importance of teaching scientific method in schools and universities, the superiority of scientific medicine over alternative medicines, etc. Relativism would also be able to undermine the very epistemological identity of scientific disciplines, particularly the most vulnerable, like social sciences. All these perverse effects actually occurred and continue to emerge.

Recently, the need for a new epistemological approach to the specific nature of science has re-emerged to inspire the work of a growing group of intellectuals. For example, the book "Sciences de l'Homme et Sciences de la Nature" edited by sociologist Claude Grignon and biologist Claude Kardon (2009) can be considered one of the successful undertakings in this sense. All scientific disciplines have specific characteristics which set them apart from what is not science. However, these characteristics do not constitute a universal epistemology that can forge the unity of science. On the other hand, they do characterise regional or specific epistemologies. If one analyses the various disciplines, from physics and mathematics to musicology, including chemistry, evolutionary biology, epidemiology, archaeology, economics and sociology, one will note that they have an ontology and language of their own.

(a) Where its *ontology* is concerned, science has traditionally been broken down into three categories: *physical–chemical sciences*, *life sciences*, and *human sciences*. The ontology of the objects studied allows different languages to be used to represent them and to theorise. The ontology of particle physics makes it possible to use a formal, quantitative language to describe it. The ontology of life sciences (from molecular biology to histology) permits the use of languages that are symbolic (DNA), figurative (the cell) and verbal (the description of mitogenesis). The ontology of individual and aggregate facts of human history, on the other hand, allows them to be described in a natural and figurative language (rarely quantifiable in statistical terms). The reason for this lies in the very characteristics of the various ontologies. Whereas the objects of physics, like electrons, have a homogeneity that allows them to be generalised in quantitative categories, the opposite is true for the objects of human sciences, whose extreme variability often does not allow quantitative representations.

(b) The connection between the characteristics of representation and those of theory exists but it is not a foregone conclusion. For example, evolutionary biology uses a mathematical language to represent the evolution of the species, but refers to the theory of games and other metaphorical models for explicative purposes. Ophthalmology uses certain quantitative representations, such as intraocular pressure, but also provides qualitative and verbal explanations. Materials sciences use qualitative physical-chemical explanations at a micro level, linked to temperature and the molecular structure, but at a macro level they rely on empirical and experiential measurements and figures of the form, structure and vulnerability to torsion. The more a science tends to build quantitative natural laws, based on the abstract behaviour of homogeneous object classes, the more it will be theory driven. The more ontological non-homogeneity prevents effective abstraction, the more the theory will depend on the contingent facts noted. From this viewpoint, we can break sciences down into *nomothetic-deductive* and *historical-inductive*. Physics, as a nomothetic and deductive science, starts from theory to deduce facts. History, as an inductive science, starts from facts to induce hypotheses. However, physical-chemical sciences are not always only deductive, just as human sciences are not always inductive. This classification cuts transversely across the previous one. For example, although it is a physical-chemical science, cosmology also has historical characteristics (the history of the universe). And a human science like econometrics resembles nomothetic sciences (the dehistoricised laws of economics).

(c) What sets the former apart from the latter is above all the manner in which concepts such as *time*, *explanation* and *causality* are approached. In physics and in econometrics, laws are dehistoricised outside time. And in physics there is no causality because there can be no timing asymmetry between events (a characteristic of the relationship between cause and effect).

The epistemology of nomothetic sciences breaks with the notion of the irreversibility of time. The idea of a universal law eliminates the chronological dimension of phenomena, establishing an unchanging mathematical ratio between them. Explanation and forecast become the same thing. On the other hand, time is irreversible for historical sciences, there is timing asymmetry and therefore a causal relationship between antecedent and consequent. The explanation aims to identify the causal relationships between the phenomena and to open the black box of mathematical laws and statistical regularity. These categories also have numerous hybrids which have the attributes of both nomothetic sciences and historical sciences. For example, cosmology is both physical and historical. Its goal is to establish the history of an order of physical reality represented in a mathematical language. Or, at the other extreme, a science like economics tries to formalise a historical reality mathematically. Econometric models establish the limits to apply the nomothetic ideal to historical reality. Built on the model of universal physical laws, they are dehistoricised and eliminate the chronological and historical dimension of changes. "On reduit la variation à l'invariant, le changeant au constant de meme qu'on reduit le complexe au simple" (Grignon and Kardon 2009, p. 268).

(d) Another method for the transverse division of scientific disciplines is related to *data collection*. Experimental sciences like molecular biology generate control data that therefore express the limits of the available experimental methodologies (for example, the different optical power of microscopes). Observational sciences like astronomy or archaeology are also limited by observation technologies, but the data are those offered by nature or by history, with no possibility for human interference. However, the use of controlled experimentation plays a different cognitive role depending on the discipline. This role is linked to the greater or lesser trade-off between the empirical nature of the control and the generic nature of the controllable hypotheses. We have seen that the more homogeneous the ontology of objects the greater the possibility of generalising. Hypotheses can therefore have a certain generality without as a result generating abstractions that are too far removed from empirical reality. It is also a known fact that at a logical and epistemological level, the data collected in an experiment are comparable with infinite hypotheses and that at the other extreme, the more generic a hypothesis the more it is compatible with a larger number of experimental data. Therefore the correct standard in experimentation is to control hypotheses that are as non-generic as possible. In physics, chemistry and molecular biology, where ontology allows greater abstraction, represented numerically (in physics), symbolically (in chemistry) and figuratively or verbally (in molecular biology), experimentation can be based on fairly generic hypotheses. In these cases, the experimental control, which by its very nature cannot regard a large number of variables, manages to corroborate or falsify fairly generic hypotheses. In economics and social sciences, where ontology does not allow great abstraction and where potentially significant variables are more numerous, the control must be based on very circumscribed hypotheses.

(e) As we can see, various epistemologies characterise the various disciplines. This is certainly linked to the various *levels of reality* studied. However, this link is not exclusive. A single level of reality may present disciplines that have different epistemologies. For example, the biological level analysed by a nomothetic science such as molecular biology or by a historical science such as evolutionary biology. The economic phenomena can be analyzed by a nomothetic science such as econometrics or by an historical science such as economic history. The different epistemologies often derive from the different cognitive or practical-technological goals of the research. In materials science, the cognitive goal leads one to work in a limited scale of length, at an atomical and molecular level, in order to improve the micro bases of the design and the choice of materials. The practical goal on the other hands leads one to work on a broader length to examine the different phenomenal properties of the materials, like the steels used for railway tracks or the aluminium of aircraft wings. In economics the cognitive goals lead one to work on a limited scale of human behaviour in order to improve the micro foundation of economic phenomena. And, on the contrary, the practical goals lead the economist to work on a broader scale, such as econometrics, in order to give advices to political decision makers. This epistemological specificity of scientific disciplines reveals the impossibility of reductionist claims. It is not possible to simplify the various levels of reality only from a physical viewpoint and on the basis of its epistemology.

(f) At this point we must tackle the central problem of what the *demarcation principle* can be based on if there are various epistemologies that seem to refer to the different disciplines, and there does not seem to be any epistemological unity of science that distinguishes it from what is not science. The criterion that characterises the researcher's methodology most in the real practice of science is falsification. Even at the time of Sir Karl Popper, a number of scientists like Hans Adolf Krebs, John Eccles and Friedrich von Hayek entered the lists to support the principle of falsification against every philosophical, historical and sociological attempt to sink it. The same criterion, in its sophisticated version, has received empirical support from an epistemological analysis of the main scientific discoveries, undertaken by a group of historians coordinated by the philosopher Larry Laudan (Donovan et al. 1988). They noted that, contrary to the "new philosophy and sociology of science" and history of science as seen by Kuhn, one hypothesis flowed gradually into the other through the weapon of empirical confutation and logical contradiction.

In any case, from an epistemological viewpoint, there has not been much progress since Imre Lakatos' pronouncements on the theory of falsification. One formulation that is taking hold in the philosophy of science is that of the *theory of the severity of tests* (Mayo 1996) which combines a falsificationist approach with a Bayesian approach. She maintains that:

e indicates h if, and only if, the text conditions T are such that, in T, $P(e/h) > P(e/-h)$

In other words, a good experimental test procedure is one in which we have a high probability of observing the evidence e when the hypothesis h is true, and a low probability of observing it when the hypothesis is false (in this case we will observe $-e$).

10.2 The Epistemological Specificity of Economics

Analysis of economic issues can be traced back to Aristotle and the scholastic philosophers, but it was only with the physiocrats and Adam Smith's *Inquiry into the nature and causes of the wealth of nations* (1776), in the eighteenth century, that economics acquired its own identity as a topic for study and discipline. In those years, philosophical considerations were closely intertwined with economic considerations. Smith's objective, like that of David Hume (1739–40), was to build a science of society, on the model of Newtonian physics, founded on general laws of the mind and of action. Both Smith and David Ricardo had an inclusive conception of the economic motives of human action. The individual's search for wealth and happiness pervaded all of human life and was not confined only to economic behaviour, as it would be after Mill.

Only with the work of John Stuart Mill (1836) do we find a clear identification of the epistemological problems that characterised the new discipline of economics. They can basically be divided into three components: (1) method, i.e. the definition of how to generate and justify the hypotheses in the economic field; (2) rationality, i.e. how the principles at the basis of the action are characterised; (3) wellbeing, i.e. what it is right to pursue for the individual and for society.

1. *Method.* Discussion about method and in particular the role of empirical observations in the discovery and testing of economic theory, was made possible primarily by Mill. For the fathėr of the inductive method, the complexity of the economic phenomena and the presence of many combined causes does not allow the application of *a posteriori* methods typical of natural sciences, based on the generalisation of the causes starting from observation of the empirical effects. Mills, on the other hand, proposes an *a priori* method which overturns the relationship between cause and effect. First of all the individual causes of economic phenomena must be identified. This may be achieved through *introspection* for fundamental principles, such as the desire for wealth or to satisfy present pleasures and the aversion to work. From causal laws we can deduce the economic effects that are then compared with empirical reality. If the effects do not tie up with the phenomena this does not question the primary causal principles, which are considered true, but only our exactness in having taken all the relevant factors or minor and disturbing causes into consideration. Mill's position has been criticised from opposing fronts. Some, from a *realist* position, have accused him of refusing the role of empirical research both in the identification of the theory and in its falsification. On the other hand there are those from an instrumentalist position who challenge his concern with the causal and realistic nature of explicative principles.

Terence Hutchinson (1938) belongs to the former current, and he challenges the non-falsifiable nature of introspectively introduced theoretical principles. On the other hand, if one wishes to maintain the empirical nature of economic theory, these principles must also be subjected to observational control, for example using psychological research methodologies. Recently the use of experiments in the economic field seems to be going in this very direction. What is more, even the vague nature of the causes of disturbance always salvages the theory in the face of this empirical anomaly. On the contrary, according to Daniel Hausman (1992), the *ceteris paribus* clause should clearly identify which significant factors of disturbance must be called on to justify any empirical counter-examples. This current includes the economic methodologists who follow the teachings of Karl Popper and Imre Lakatos. They are concerned that economists pretend to be falsifiers, while in fact they never worry about defining an empirical base with which to test the theory or different competing theories. What is more, many exponents of this current reveal a philosophical concern with constructing theories that correspond to the reality of the causal mechanisms responsible for economic phenomena. In this regard we should remember the recent cognitive and neuro-economic turnaround that is motivated by the epistemological goal of discovering the mental and neuronal functioning of the processes of economic reasoning and decision.

The second, *instrumentalist*, current emerges from a series of epistemological premises. If, as Duhem-Quine maintains, it is true that the theories cannot be falsified because it has not been defined which part of them (hypotheses, laws, principles, etc.) or of auxiliary hypotheses (hypotheses about the functioning of tools, data collection, the specification of parameters, etc.) the anomaly addresses, and if the theories are under-determined by empirical data, i.e. infinite theories can explain the data themselves, then there is no sense in having realistic concerns regarding the assumptions of the theories. As Milton Friedman said in 1953, economic models must only be predictive tools. Good economic theories (like a good snooker player) are those that generate correct forecasts regarding prices and quantities (they make correct shots) *as if* they were true (as if the player knew the complex physical and mathematical formulae that decide the optimal trajectory of the ball). It does not matter how theoretical assumptions have been introduced, whether at a hypothetical, introspective or inductive level, nor whether they correspond to reality or not, provided they act as a predictive black box (but it is not clear what to do with the black box if it systematically generates incorrect forecasts). Instrumentalism seems to inspire much of the theoretical activity of neoclassical economics. The goal is to construct models that can represent an economic world that is simplified and therefore not real, and which for their mathematical and cognitive ease of handling allow us to prepare forecasts regarding economic phenomena. The negation of the empirical and realistic nature of method in economics reaches its peak in Deirdre McCloskey's *rhetorical* approach (1986). There is no longer any methodological criterion to evaluate theories, because what counts is only the rhetorical capacity of persuasion.

2. *Rationality*. As we have seen in the previous chapter, in philosophical tradition it is possible to find two major currents related to rationality. One sustains the primacy of reason over the intellect, while the other sustains the opposite. In the former, the classical philosophical tradition, reason is the force that sets one free from prejudice, allowing one to distinguish what is true from what is false, and separating man and animal. As in Aristotle, it will maintain the dual character of the procedures inherent in reason that is both descriptive and prescriptive, in the sense that it provides the rules for its correct use. As Descartes maintains, men have different opinions only to the extent that they apply reason differently. The Olympic and universal vision contrasts with the second position as expressed by New Platonism, Thomas Aquinas, mediaeval scholastics, Francis Bacon and, to a great extent, Kant. The intellect must be considered superior to reason because it has that intuitive and immediate character that enables it to understand empirical reality directly. Rationality that is taken as the basis of the theory of choice in economics in the nineteenth century, right up to modern neoclassical economics, belongs to the first current. It is Olympic, universal and has the dual normative and descriptive character. The theory is normative to the extent that it defines what type of choice must be made on the basis of specific preferences and rational beliefs. Preferences are rational if they are comprehensive and transitive. Beliefs are rational if they satisfy the axioms of the calculation of probability. Choices are rational if they maximise utility. It is therefore irrational to choose one alternative from various options if another one maximises utility. The theory is descriptive because it states that in reality an economic agent will never choose an alternative from various possibilities if a second one is available that does maximise utility. This theory of rational choice has its roots in Mill's definition of the *homo*

œconomicus as man's sphere of action, separate and limited to economic contexts according to the principle of the pursuit of maximum wellbeing. Starting from this premise, which is also common to other authors like Nassau Senior, classical and neoclassical economics have developed the rational principles of choice that underpin the model of the economic agent at a formal level. This has led to the transformation of what were only vague rules and behaviour precepts in Mill's time, into real, proper formal models like those created by the equations of the theory of Bayesian decision.

The theory of rationality has been the target of a great deal of criticism. The first comes from contemporary epistemology and regards the prescriptive and *a priori* character of rationality. According to the *internalist* theories of rationality (Goodman 1965; Goldman 1986; Stich 1990), the normative source of reason must stem from man's intuitive and cognitive capabilities. There can be no genesis or justification of the principles of rationality other than what is generated within the human mind. This criticism of the normative aspect is easily linked to criticism of the descriptive component of rationality. As Hutchinson had already pointed out in 1938, the empirical nature of economics cannot regard only the 'protective belt' of auxiliary hypotheses (like those of the type of assets, the function of costs, economic institutions, etc.) that surrounds the principle of maximisation. Even the fundamental assumptions of rationality must have an empirical weight. Herbert Simon's concept of *bounded rationality* (1957, 1982, 2000) starts from this descriptive purpose. Faced with the complexity of the environment, the economic player who possesses limited cognitive abilities is unable to make complicated calculations to maximise utility, but is content with taking satisfactory decisions (*satisficing principle*). In these years, the empirical criticism of the theory of optimising rationality present in neoclassical economics has acquired various aspects, which recently seem to converge (see Viale (ed.) 2005a). Starting with Vernon Smith (1962), *experimental economics* concentrates on a series of experimental trials on human behaviour, and on the institutions of the market and of business. *Behavioural economics* and *cognitive economics*, from Simon's work right up to that of Daniel Kahneman and Amos Tversky (Kahneman 2003; Kahneman and Tversky 2000; Kahneman et al. 1982) and Gerd Gigerenzer (Gigerenzer, Todd, and ABC Group 1999), have analysed the processes of economic reasoning and judgement, highlighting the systematic errors and heuristics used to reason and to decide. Recently, particular attention has also been focused on the emotional and intuitive aspects that play an important part in directing decision-making processes. And finally, *Neuroeconomics* (Camerer et al. 2005) uses brain function detection technologies (like functional magnetic resonance) to verify cognitive hypotheses and to identify stable neuronal activation configurations in relation to the various types of economic decision. It is clear from what is illustrated above that the new currents of economic research have moved the goals of epistemological realism and that the reductionist attempt to explain economic action by the neuropsychological causal mechanisms of the human mind is taking hold.

3. *Wellbeing*. Starting from Adam Smith's work, economics have taken the pursuit of individual wellbeing to be the fundamental assumption of his theory of action. From this viewpoint, the descriptive component of the theory of action of contemporary economics has been accused of conforming to an ethic of selfishness. Only individual utility, substantiated by a greater wealth of tangible assets, seems to characterise the choice of the economic player. In fact, this criticism is also extended, and wrongly so, to the normative component of the theory of rationality. This does not seem correct because the normative part of rationality is purely formal, and makes no claims about the content of preferences and choice, but only specifies their logical structure. In fact the egoism or altruism of a choice depends only on the content of preference. As Amartya Sen (1992) maintains, they can be designed to increase one's economic wellbeing or, on the contrary, they can also be designed to promote other people's well-being. One may pursue the maximisation of individual utility by sacrificing oneself for other people instead of only thinking of oneself. Unlike the neoclassical conception that considers the individual to be driven only by egoistic interests, experimental economics has highlighted how the economic agent is also moved by dispositions that focus on other people's social and economic conditions. The search for the optimum in strategic interaction between several individuals can no longer occur with the premise that the various actors share the same motivational structure of self-interest, i.e. oriented to maximise their own gain. On the contrary one must take into account a motivational heterogeneity that is also characterised by altruism, fairness, solidarity, reciprocity or opposing negative sentiments, but in any case oriented to other people. From the concept of *homo œconomicus* we progressed to one of *homo reciprocans* (Fehr and Gachter 1998). From this viewpoint the ontological characterisation of the economic assets that are the objective of both individual choices and collective choices also changes. They are no longer only *tangible* assets like finance or real estate. Or *intangibles* like information and knowledge (see Foray 2000). Even *relational assets*, i.e. happiness in relations with other people, the satisfaction of feeling loved and of returning the attentions and help of other people, become the objective of economic analysis (Frey 2008; Sacco and Zarri 2005; Zamagni 2005).

10.3 Experiments in Economics

Experimental economics has been successful in opening new areas of economic research, as in the case of the economics of happiness. Experimental economics has particular epistemological features and problems by comparison with cognitive economics. How can we sum up the differential characteristics of the regional epistemology of experimental economics?

(a) First of all, the ontological dimension of behaviour and its neuro-cognitive causes allows a representation that is above all analogical, figurative and verbal. In some cases, it is possible to make a numerical generalisation of uniform categories of behaviour. Even the explicative and causal hypotheses can only be quantitative on rare occasions and when the *ceteris paribus* clause is included in non-problematic background knowledge. Most explanations must be based on models that are analogical, figurative and verbal. From this viewpoint, experimental economics must emerge from the *numerical paradox* for which only what is quantitative is relevant and only what is relevant may be quantitative.

(b) The goal of experimentation is to *control* hypothesis. For us to say this, the control data must show us clearly and unambiguously that this hypothesis is not false, i.e. that the probability of observing these data if the hypothesis were false is very low. In other words, the data must correspond to a strict control of the hypothesis. For this to occur in the field of behavioural sciences, the hypothesis must be very *circumscribed,* i.e. it must allow experimentation to be able to manipulate all the relevant causal variables. In the event of poorly circumscribed hypotheses, the quantity of potential and not manipulable causal variables is so large that the evidence would not be able to determine a strict control of the hypothesis. The construction of very general hypotheses remains outside the epistemological constraints of experimentation on man's economic behaviour.

(c) One of the accusations made against a certain experimental economics is that of being *neoclassical economics masked* by conventional devices. The experiments would be used to give neoclassical economics an increasingly complicated, intricate protective belt based on ad hoc hypotheses. If experimental economics were to take this direction, it might also generate some interesting data regarding marginal external aspects of economic behaviour, but, as Hutchinson said, it would abandon the attempt to develop circumscribed hypotheses that might converge on a new theory of economic action. One obviously must not think that the new theory could include all economic behaviour. Nor should one think that a general and simplified theory of economic action, like the neoclassical, is still possible. There are various components of economic behaviour that must be developed in addition to a new theory of the utility that could derive from the development of the prospect theory. Here are some examples: a *theory of learning* necessary to explain how previous successes and mistakes affect decision-making processes, and how information is transformed into cognitive patterns that guide decisions; a *theory of relational assets* or altruism, outside the theory of utility, that is able to model the effect of empathy, of sharing one's actions with others, of sharing common decisions, of the pooling resources etc.; a *theory of time* that is able to explain how we represent time, what are the external factors that influence a different ponderation of time, how the value of time changes in relation to the different propensity to risk (weak will, time discounting, short-sightedness); a *theory of the representation of uncertainty and of risk* that is not based on simplistic mental arithmetic.

(d) Economics is proposed as a *de-historicised science* that tends to create universally valid laws. Experimental economics must not fall into this physicalist error, which is also typical of a large part of cognitive science. On the contrary, it must realise that reasoning and decision-making processes are guided by the pragmatic schemes and semantic structure of knowledge, which has a fundamentally contextual and historical dimension. One strong temptation of experimental economics is that of considering the reasoning and decision-making processes dictated by mental logic as impermeable to factors of context and learning. Instead, as numerous research projects have highlighted, like Johnson Laird's theory of mental models, Cheng and Holyoak's theory of pragmatic schemes, reasoning and decision-making are guided by our schemes, and by the significance that we give to the external objects and actions on which our learning is based. If this is true, then the historical context must enter deliberately among the initial conditions of every experimental setting.

(e) Experimental economics must avoid falling into the *double dualistic fallacy* of considering mental entities as ontologically separate from neural entities, and behaviour entities as separate from mental entities. Ontologically, brain, mind and behaviour are all one. For practical and cognitive purposes, research has focused on paths that are often separate and distinct. And different epistemologies have also been created, i.e. different languages have been used to represent and theorise, different methodologies to collect data, and to create and justify hypotheses. But today, the relationship between neuroscience and psychology is converging increasingly, even from an epistemological viewpoint. This is evident in both professional change and in the new manuals of cognitive psychology. There is growing integration between neural imaging work and the psychologist's experimental activities and empirical research. Generally, the role of neural imaging is above all to exert empirical control on the common or distinct neural mechanisms that underpin cognitive or emotional functions. A typical contribution of neural imaging is to show that there is the same neural substratum at the basis of separate cognitive functions and that the hypothesis in question could therefore be unlikely because it is superfluous. Or, at the other extreme, that a single psychological function is generated by different neural substrata and the hypothesis could therefore be unlikely because it is too simple. The semantic slippage between psychological and neural languages that many look forward to has not been developed yet. Feyerabend's eliminative materialism will be difficult to achieve for reasons that are, in my opinion, related more to pragmatic language than to the irreducible property dualism. In any case, experimental economics will always have to refer to mechanisms that give a causal explanation of external behaviour, detected by mind-brain experiments. Otherwise it will be reduced only to producing accidental generalisations without any theoretical capacity and with a not-replicable predicative field (without affecting the recommendations regarding the severity of controls stated earlier).

(f) One fundamental tool to empirically control the realism of behavioural hypotheses is *simulation*. In addition to the classic simulation of individual cognitive processes expounded by Simon, there is growing interest in the simulation of agents and CAS-Complex Adaptive Systems. These are a formidable micro-meso instrument to represent the emergence of social phenomena. The risk in some cases is to mould the simplified mind of the agents after the event and ad hoc in relation to the output that one wishes to achieve. Another risk is that of hypostatizing emerging phenomena as realities that overcome the ontological confines of interactive individual behaviour. In spite of this, it is clear that it would be interesting to develop a new regional epistemology of the sciences of complexity, in relation to that of cognitive economics.

Neurocognition and Financial Behaviour 11

An emerging field in economics is that of behavioural finance. It is the result of the collection of many kinds of data coming from experimental, behavioural, cognitive economics and neuroeconomics. Financial behaviour is relatively almost easily studied in natural settings and artificial experiments. The results of these studies are allowing the control of hypotheses in cognitive economics and the generation of new insights in the economic behaviour. The following is a short outline of these contributions (the reference is to Hilton 2001; Attia and Hilton 2011; Viale 2011).

11.1 The Forecasting Superiority of Dart-Throwing Monkeys

Anyone who has had any experience investing on the Stock Exchange will remember how much disappointment and anger a financial consultant can cause. When the Stock Market was bullish, his arsenal of formulas and tricks to interpret stock movements seemed to be just right. Sometimes you could even catch sight of a touch of elegance in his inductions and inference of stock trends curves. However, the miracles of his magic wand were soon transformed into a sort of curse as soon as the markets began to contract, never mind the catastrophe of 2008. One might think that in fact one could expect no more from bank clerks with some routine decision-making powers but without the technical skills of great financial analysts. Unfortunately things do not seem any better even among the so-called gurus of finance. And anyone who has observed the dynamics of the markets and analysts' forecasts over the years, will also be aware of how many blunders they make.

Analyses often cloaked with an array of data, inferences and mathematical models have been revealed in most cases as not only marginally but completely incorrect. The Economist, which draws extensively on the financial analyses in question every week, occasionally demonstrates its mental independence by

The present chapter is a revised version of Viale, R. (2008). Per un'economia 'brainful', Foreword to Camerer, C., *La neuroeconomia*, Il Sole 24 Ore, Milan, and Viale, R. (2011). Soros e l'Effetto Gregge. foreword to Attia, C., & Hilton, D.J. (2011). *Decidere in Finanza.* Milano: Il Sole 24 Ore.

R. Viale, *Methodological Cognitivism*,

DOI 10.1007/978-3-642-24743-9_11,

proposing heterodox articles or inquiries. In 1994, for example, the magazine asked four professional groups (four former Finance Ministers from OECD countries, four Chairmen of multinational companies, four students of Economics at Oxford University, and four London dustmen) to predict the economic prospects for the next decade, analysing their forecasts for four indices: the average growth rate of OECD countries; average inflation; the price of petrol in 1994; the year when Singapore's GDP would overtake Australia's. Who made the worst forecasts? Not the dustmen, but the former Finance Ministers. The dustmen and the company managers actually identified the most correct scenarios.

The results of these tests, and those of many others, should certainly make us sit up. Our savings, and the economic policies of governments and large companies depend on analyses and forecasts that prove unreliable. Goldman Sachs, Credit Suisse, UBS, City Group, Morgan Stanley, JP Morgan Chase, Deutsche Bank, Bank of America and numerous other institutions in the world employ hoards of analysts to predict the future, who are systematically proved wrong by reality. We can take some recent examples. In 2009, Morgan Stanley predicted that inflation would be low in China, and instead it reached a peak of 5% in 2010. Goldman Sachs guaranteed that China would grow by just 6% in 2009, and instead it reached 9.3%. For the United States, low interest rates were forecast for 2011, as an effect of quantitative easing, i.e. the increased money supply decided by the Fed. Instead, so far this very measure has brought an increase in the rates of 10-year bonds of 2.5–3.5%.

What is more striking about the incorrect forecasts is the impudent way that analysts glibly adjust their mistakes after the event, as if nothing has happened. In October 2010 Goldman Sachs forecast that the American economy would slow down from 2.6% to 1.8%. In December they had already changed their estimate, increasingly it by 40%. They now predict that the United States will grow by 2.5% at the beginning of the year, up to an average for the year of 4%. Financial forecasts seemed to be absolutely useless. Philip Tetlock, a psychologist at Berkeley, analysed 82,361 forecasts by 284 professional analysts. The forecasts contained in this study were so inadequate that they were surpassed by the casual forecasts made by "dart-throwing monkeys", i.e. by the darts thrown at a blackboard by a group of monkeys.

11.2 Semantic and Pragmatic Anchoring

Financial analysts and all "forecasters" generally have an impossible task. As Karl Popper said, while natural science forecasts never have a sure inductive basis and are therefore just conjecture, those regarding society do not even have the minimal coordinates of an inductive basis. Social reality is too complex, there are too many initial conditions to take into consideration and above all, there is never any regularity in the phenomena. So all "forecasters" can do is extrapolate arbitrary regularities from contingent trends and project them into the future. This is what financial analysts do all the time, cloaking their products behind the label of scientific analysis. The forecasts mentioned are the product of this fallacious methodology.

But the error is magnified if we consider a recurring bias that forecasters fall into systematically. When they select the data on which to base their projections, they are unconsciously conditioned by what is known as the anchoring and adjustment heuristic. This describes the individual's tendency to perform a numerical estimate in two steps. First he anchors himself to some initial value, which is then corrected in the most plausible direction, up or down. This heuristic produces a chain reaction: the saver is anchored to the forecasts of the bank analysts, who are themselves influenced by the news from economic journalists, who are conditioned by the numbers of the analysts of the large merchant banks, which are influenced by the forecasts of the rating agencies or the assessments of international financial institutions, themselves anchored to present and immediately past stock values and prices. The anchoring effect is produced very subtly and unconsciously. Some experiments have shown that even non-pertinent data such as a telephone number or social security number can influence the numerical evaluations of completely different topics like the evaluation of a house or a consumer product.

What is more, the way the data are presented also has a powerful effect. Tversky and Kahneman (1974) asked two questions about the trend of the Dow-Jones Index which were semantically the same but differed in the manner of their presentation, and obtained different results. The framing of the second question, which contained numerical information, acted as an anchor which automatically influenced the reply, hooking onto the numbers read. This phenomenon emerges in many financial decisions, like the choice of a form of financing or insurance cover, because most financial and welfare products focus attention on specific threshold values.

Another phenomenon studied in recent years which influences anchoring, is the order in which data are presented. Generally speaking, it seems that the first data have greater weight in terms of the formulation of a judgement (*priority effect*) while the last are remembered better (*recency effect*). But it appears that in some cases the recency effect prevails as an anchorage. The problem is that the prevalence of one of the two effects seems to depend on the complexity of the task, the amount of information provided and when the opinion is formulated (if it is formulated after the data are communicated or gradually as they are presented).

In any case, there is a logic upstream of the selection of the data to consider. In general, when faced with a range of information, the individual follows conversational and epistemological maxims of interpretation. Conversational maxims were introduced some time ago in the studies of Paul Grice (1993) and subsequently developed by other scholars like Dan Sperber and Deirdre Wilson. One of the basic principles is that of cooperation. When one speaks elliptically, omitting some passages and leaving areas of shadow, the listener will complete the semantic gaps with inferences known as *conversational implicatures*. For example, if one person says: "The Monsanto share is growing strongly, but it is a technological share", the listener will assume from the "but" that the speaker intends to underline that in these times of financial crisis and recession, the fact that it is a share in a company with a high intensity of biotechnological research, may make it more fragile compared to shares in less cyclic or more stable sectors like foods. Apart from these pragmatic conversational maxims, according to some epistemologists like Donald Davidson and Daniel Dennett, we apply other logical and epistemological principles to our interpretation. For example, we try to give logical consistency when we are faced with muddled and disjointed expressions, phrases and texts. We also assume, if there is no evidence to the contrary, that whoever is speaking to us is telling the truth when he makes statements that at first sight appear unrealistic. Davidson writes (1970, p. 253):

> We must develop a theory of what he intends, simultaneously giving content to his attitudes and his words. Because we need to give meaning to his words, we will propose a theory that recognizes him as a coherent person, who believes in truth and loves good.

Conversational maxims and principles of consistency and truth help us to construct a story with causal links to the text we are reading or that is communicated to us. Recent research shows that constructing a consistent and comprehensive story is necessary to take decisions. The problem is that the individual is not always able to make a complete reconstruction and sometimes remains anchored to the way information is presented. For example, if two different presentations are made of a company – one orderly and historical from the past to the latest results, and the other muddled – and a sample is asked to predict its performance on the Stock Exchange, only the first report allows the important element of performance to be used fully. In the case of the muddled reconstruction the individual is more influenced by variables other than the results. What does this tell us? That if one tries to anticipate the actions of investors, analysts and savers, it is not enough to know what information they have but also how this was communicated to them, and therefore the "story model" that they have constructed mentally. Depending on the model, some variables are more important in determining an opinion and the consequent decision.

11.3 Dostoevsky's Gambler

The importance of the order in which information is presented, and the pragmatic dimension of communication are linked to another powerful effect linked to the way data are presented. Classic experiments carried out by Kahneman and Tversky (1979a) (Kahneman 2007) have highlighted the fact that in tests that present the same monetary value of the stakes, if the question is posed as a gain, the answer tends to present an aversion to risk, whereas if the question is perceived as a loss, the individual decides with a propensity to risk. This phenomenon, known as the *framing effect*, leads to an inversion of the preferences when the same problem is framed differently. This inversion, called the *reflection effect*, proves to be a very powerful phenomenon in economic behaviour. People decidedly increase their propensity to risk when they interpret the situation in terms of loss, while they are averse to risk if the situation is presented as a gain.

As Fyodor Mikhailovich Dostoevsky asked in *The Gambler*, when is the irrational escalation behaviour that takes a gambler to bankruptcy manifested? Towards the end of the evening, when the gambler perceives that the day is closing at a loss and he wants to overturn the result by increasingly risky behaviour. The same attitude was noted in a series of studies of the banking and financial world of Wall Street and other international stock markets. When the Stock Exchange adds up the gains and losses at the end of the day, there will be a greater trend on the part of traders to take risky decisions if negotiations have not gone well during the day. The same also happens when the Stock Market opens the following day; focusing on the losses and overlooking the gains will also generate risky investment behaviour.

The different psychological impact of a loss as opposed to a gain is represented by *prospect* theory (Kahneman and Tversky 1979b). The value function of this theory abstracts this aversion to loss. The value of this coefficient is equal to two: in other words, to put it simply, one has to gain approximately Euro 2,000 to compensate for the annoyance of having lost 1,000. This value function which differs from that of neoclassical economics which presumes a coefficient of one, explains much economic behaviour that violates the forecasts of economic theory. First of all, it explains the difficulties of negotiation between the purchaser and the buyer (Pietroni and Rumiati 2008): the seller who deprives himself of an asset, values it much higher than his counterpart who purchases it, who must deprive himself of his money. In addition to which, each of the parties perceives the concession made to the other as a loss, thus attributing greater weight to it than to a potential gain.

An aversion to loss also produces the well-known *disposition effect*, i.e. the tendency to sell shares whose prices has risen too soon but to hold on to shares that have lost value. In some analyses by American and Israeli fund managers, we can note a systematic tendency to the disposition effect, which damages their performance. The best managers are those that have shown the greatest ability to realise losses. Is it only aversion to loss that is responsible for this behaviour? No, various studies seem to show that anticipated regret for the loss of possible future earnings prevails, determining the disposition effect. In other words, as often happens in our decision-making processes, we usually reason counterfactually, asking ourselves what could or should have happened if we had taken a different decision. In this case, the alternative hypothesis that a share sold at a loss might regain value triggers regret that prompts us not to sell. Anticipated regret for a possible loss has a value several times higher than the annoyance due to an actual loss caused by remaining inactive.

11.4 Does "Affect" Guide the Markets?

The regret illustrated in the previous example opens the discussion of an increasingly important chapter of economic psychology and behavioural finance: the role of affection and emotion in judgement, choice and decision (Gigerenzer 2007; Bonini and Hadjichristidis 2009). The issue has been overlooked for many years by cognitive psychology due to the methodological difficulties of studying it. Today, on the other hand, it is becoming central in most fields of psychology. Daniel Kahneman himself, in his *Nobel Lecture* of 2002, clearly underlines that it is important to refer to two types of cognitive processes. There is System 1 – or the emotional and intuitive mind – which thinks rapidly, without effort, in an associative, tacit, automatic and parallel manner, while System 2 – or the reasoning mind – thinks more slowly, in a serial, conscious way, expending energy and respecting the rules (Viale 2005b, p. 244; see Chap. 9 of this volume).

The first System is proving increasingly to be the submerged part of the iceberg. Its "pervasiveness" is expressed in all aspects of human behaviour and even more so of economic and financial behaviour. If we wish to conventionally break down the components of behaviour into judgement, decision and action, we can see that many past hypotheses in the explanation in each of these stages have been revised in the light of the affect and emotion variable. This has led some people, like Paul Slovic, to introduce the concept of an "affect heuristic" (Slovic et al. 2001) and Antonio Damasio (1994) to talk of "somatic markers" in decision-making. For example, affect plays a role in the value function (utility) and the pondering of probabilities. Subjective probabilities are not independent of the affective nature of outcomes. A 1% probability is greater when the outcome has a significant affective component rather than a poor affective component. The subjective perception of probability depends on the affective value that the individual associates with the expected results. While the theory of utility maintains that utility and probability are independent, the results of some research show that they are not. The low probabilities have a greater weight when the expected positive or negative results trigger sentiments of hope or fear. This phenomenon has obvious consequences for the judgement that lies at the basis of one's economic and financial choices, between options with different probabilities and expected utilities. As we have seen earlier, even loss aversion, regret and the *endowment effect* (i.e. attributing greater value to an asset when one owns it) have a strong affective base. This is displeasure, the negative emotion of losing or of depriving oneself of an asset which conditions the value function, increasing the utility of the asset itself.

Another effect of affect on judgement is linked to the relationship between risk and utility. Generally speaking, in economic theory there is a direct link between the two variables: the more a choice embodies risks, the greater the apparent utility of the outcome. On financial markets, the riskier the share, the greater the premium paid as a result; we can think of the bonds of risky countries like Argentina and Greece compared to those of Germany and the United States. Obviously in everyday life, reality is often different. There are large risks that have no utility, except that of having run them. I can walk for no reason on the cornice outside my flat on the twentieth floor just to show everyone how brave I am. Or I can drive at top speed when I am drunk just to entertain my friends. In these cases large risks are associated with low utility. In fact, at a psychological level, we tend to apply a trade-off between risk and affective evaluation. For example, when we positively value a share for its past history, for the company's good communicative image, for its pleasant managing director, etc. we are attributing a low risk of negative outcomes to it. Take the effect on investors of adding ".com" to the name of shares, at the peak of the Internet bubble, between June 1998 and July 1999. In a study undertaken a few years ago (Cooper et al. 2001) out of 95 shares analysed, the "dotcom effect" caused their value to increase by an average of 74% in the 10 days following the announcement of the name change. Financial bubbles seem to owe a great deal to the value of the affect component in judgement.

The affect component is crucial in the representativeness and availability heuristics, and the emotional salience of an example is the basis for the generalisation for an entire category. The error of extrapolation made by investors, when they tend to consider that the past performance of a share is representative of its future performance, is typical. And the emotionally more salient events are those recalled most easily at a mnemonic level. According to many authors, it is thanks to this mechanism that in periods of expansion many financial institutions relax the risk standards and make gross forecasting errors. As Galbraith said in 1954, it is our mnemonic skills that make us forget past crises and only remember present successes, which takes us gradually towards a new crisis. Of course *prototype heuristics* (Kahneman 2003) are a hypothesis developed recently to introduce emotional salience into various types of judgement. For example, various experiments carried out in the past have shown that it is the emotional accessibility of a prototype (for example, a share in a sector that has enjoyed strong growth on the Stock Market, promoted in all the media) that determines the judgement of the entire category(for example a growth forecast for the entire sector).

There is another way that System 1 of the mind affects judgement. If we go back to the initial example of The Economist, it does not seem that the quantity of data and analyses is a guarantee of analytical and forecasting success. Often too many data reduce our capacity to judge. As Gigerenzer underlined successfully (2007), intuitive, gut feelings are often better than elaborately structured judgements. There are various simple and frugal heuristics that give better decision-making results than those achieved with the algorithms of economic rationality.

And finally, affectivity comes into play not only at the judgement stage, but also at the downstream stage of decision-making and action. As neuroeconomics has shown (Camerer et al. 2005), affective components, conveyed by cortical and subcortical structures like the amygdala or the insula, underpin risk behaviour and the perception of trust in one's own actions and those of others.

11.5 How to Avoid the Flock

What is surprising after the various financial crisis or the scandals that have involved several industrial giants, is that they have not taken into consideration the explanations and possible remedies that behavioural and cognitive economics has for years been proposing to decision-makers to avoid or attenuate this disaster (Bazerman 2009). Take the case of the LTCM (Long Term Capital Management), a hedge fund created in 1994 which was increasingly successful until its disastrous collapse in 1998. It adopted "brilliant" models to price shares and measure risks, elaborated by brilliant economists and mathematicians like Fisher Black, Myron Scholes and Robert Merton, who won the Nobel Prize for Economics in 1997 (after Black's premature death in 1995). In the first 2 years the fund doubled its capital. It had assets of $125 billion and off-balance sheet positions of $1,250 billion (the United States budget!). These resources were the result of the uninhibited use of the leverage between indebtedness and capital. While most hedge funds had leverage of 2:1, the LTCM leverage was as high as 50:1 and in some cases 250:1. The entire system was based on supposed risk management that made it possible to establish a given value for the shares and was based on a hypothesis of normality (as if the fluctuations and risks followed a Gaussian curve). For example, it envisaged that the maximum loss in 1 day could not exceed $35 million. We know what happened. The managers were unable to correct the estimates, even if since 1997 they had seen many signs of anomalous turbulence on the Asian and South American markets. At the peak of the Russian crisis, daily losses amounted to $553 million, which forced the Fed to intervene to bail it out. Various emotive and cognitive components, as well as the adoption of an incorrect model, allowed a predicted disaster to occur: hyper security and pathological risk propensity; egocentricity and organisational narcissism; the illusion of control and a confirmation bias; conformism to the flock effect. What is surprising is that the same formula that brought disaster in the case of LTCM – also known as the Black-Scholes case – remained popular until it finally contributed to the great crisis of 2008!

The LTCM disaster highlights a whole range of problems that were later responsible for the 2008 crisis. Some of them are related to the organisational and social dyscrasia that underpins risk evaluation and management in financial organisations. Two are particularly important. First of all, at an organisational level, risk managers are actually subordinate to traders. A company's purpose is to make deals, so if we are talking of risks, it tends to undervalue them and to take them. When a deal is presented, social pressure inside the company tries to communicate the positive aspects and opportunities, and to minimise the risks. So risk managers are seen as disturbances, something that often leads them to adopt attitudes that are not critical but conventional. And secondly, there is a cultural subservience to the rating agencies (which continues today). Their forecasts are considered oracles and represent a conscious or unconscious anchorage for a company's internal assessments. It is a shame that, as numerous cases show, they often make dreadful errors of judgement, and there is a serious problem of a conflict of interest between companies to be rated and rating agencies. How can we think that an agency rating can be objective if the company is paying and might not renew the contract the following year; if the agency often provides organisational consultancy inside the company itself; and if there is often an exchange of personnel between the agency and the company?

Many of the problems of social behaviour in the financial field could be neutralised, at least in part, by standards, rules and laws that induce the saver or finance operator to take care to avoid situations in which it is easy to make errors of judgement. The *libertarian paternalism* of Thaler and Sunstein (2008) tends to gently "NUDGE" the individual to protect his interests better and to prevent institutional mechanisms, like those of the rating agencies, from damaging the saver. How can this be done? A few examples: we can help the individual to grasp the difference between real utility and perceived utility, by forcing him to consider, as in the case of some mortgage agreements in France, what he would have to pay if interest rates were to rise in future while the value of the property falls; we forbid mortgages with rates like those of hybrid American "2–28" and "3–27" mortgages (behind the *subprime* mortgages crisis), which trap borrowers with a very low initial rate, known as a "teaser", which then rises over the years; we do not allow conflicts of interest between rating agencies and companies, forbidding consultancy contracts with the same company being renewed more than once; we combat misleading advertising and make contract information cognitively and emotively "friendly"; starting at school, we systematically provide a financial education based on knowledge of behavioural and cognitive finance, introducing the techniques of "debiasing" and metacognitive control of our judgement and decision-making processes.

To conclude, we must ask one question: what are financial forecasts for if, as we have shown, they are not generally reliable? We suspect that their role may be to create that imitative behaviour that is gradually transformed into herd behaviour from which careful speculators can make enormous profits. Many years ago George Soros, in a private conversation, told me that when he invests he does not look at analysts' numbers, but tries to empathetically interpret what the other small, medium and large investors who read those numbers will do. Interpreting what the herd is thinking, trusting analysts' estimates and prone to fall into the many cognitive traps, has enabled smart financiers like George Soros to make their fortunes. By empirically anticipating the hypotheses of behavioural finance!

11.6 The Contribution of Neuroeconomics

Early in the 1990s, Giacomo Rizzolatti and his colleagues in a neuroscience laboratory at Parma University, made a revolutionary discovery which many scientists claim was as important for our understanding of the brain as DNA was for the cell (see Chap. 4 of this volume). They identified the "mirror neuron", a particular type of motor neuron of the brain that has a dual function, being responsible both for our actions and for our understanding of other people's actions. The discovery is a classic case of serendipity (a term coined by British diplomat Horace Walpole in 1754, who referred to a Persian fairy tale in which three princes from the kingdom of Serendip – the Arab name for Sri Lanka – made unexpected and lucky discoveries). In the laboratory where Rizzolatti's group were studying the motor neurons of macaque monkeys, there were some peanuts:

> Sometimes the monkeys used them to perform tasks, and at other times they were the reward for a task performed with another object. But everyone liked the peanuts, not only the primates. And at a certain point, between recordings, someone watching the experiments "stole" some from the container prepared for the animals. When one of

> these "thefts" occurred, just as the researcher on duty was putting a handful of nuts into his mouth, the oscilloscope recording the monkey's neuron activity let out a very strange *tac-tac-tac* sound. The monkey had stopped and was not interacting with any other object (Rizzolatti and Vozza 2008, pp. 30–31).

The very neurons that were activated when the macaque took the peanuts, were stimulated when the monkey saw the researcher do the same thing. These neurons have the ability to be activated to reflect the actions of others, as well as permitting our own.

This is an important discovery. For the first time we understand the brain mechanisms that allow the individual to understand the behaviour of others. In experiments also carried out successfully on humans, it has been shown that, to understand someone else's action, when we observe it, it needs to be reproduced by the network of neurons that is active when we perform the same action ourselves. The amazing fact is that mirror neurons are differentiated for the purpose of the action taken. Neurons that are activated when we grasp something, are different from those excited when we hold or drop or tear something, and so on.

Why is it important to start from the discovery of mirror neurons to introduce the issue of neuroeconomics? Because one of the most important cognitive functions of economic behaviour is the attempt to understand what we can expect from other people. In negotiation, competition, cooperation and economic organisation, we act in relation to what we think other people will do. We try to understand what other people are thinking (mindreading) and to enter their way of thinking, in order to predict how they will act. And how do we do this? From the latest research, it appears that we do it by mirroring the significance of other people's behaviour, activating neuronal circuits that are responsible for our behaviour to an equal degree (Rizzolatti and Sinigaglia 2006). This mindreading mechanism lies at the heart of economic thought. The concept of *equilibrium* demands that agents correctly predict what other people will do. This is made possible both by constructing hypotheses about other people's minds, and by learning processes based on imitation that seem to be caused by the same type of mirror neuron networks.

Today's neuroscientific discoveries are opening up the black box of economic behaviour. It looks as if we will be able to challenge the pessimism shown by Jevons in 1871, when he expressed his scepticism about the possibility of directly measuring the sentiments that determine human behaviour. This is the goal of neuroeconomics: to use the new techniques of neuroscience to identify the brain mechanisms responsible for the violation or confirmation of the theory of traditional economic action. From this viewpoint, neuroeconomics and *behavioural cognitive economics* develop their hypotheses in parallel. Psychological analysis of economic behaviour allows us to identify the errors or confirmations of traditional economic theory, and neuroeconomics tries to corroborate or refute these hypotheses, identifying the brain mechanisms that are responsible for them.

In its relationship with the explanation of economic phenomena, the neuroeconomic approach may be *weak* or *strong*. When it is *weak*, it is prepared to gradually reform standard economic theory in the light of experimental changes from psychological inquiry, confirmed by neuroscientific analysis techniques. The weak approach is based on a *dualistic* theory of mind-body problem (see Chap. 2 of this volume), which sustains the irreducibility of the mentalist language (like that of economics based on preferences, desires and action). Between the languages and models of the brain and the mind there can only be coordination but not identity or, worse still, the *elimination* of the latter, the mental languages, over the brain languages. The goal of the *strong* position, on the other hand, is to refound economics on the basis of neural concepts. The theory of mind-body problem underpinning this position is of the radical *monistic* type. For it, we have to eliminate any reference to a mental language, which is inherited from a past of ignorance about how the brain functions. The only causal reality of man's visible behaviour is the nervous system and the concepts that explain it can only derive from it.

Neuroeconomists (Camerer et al. 2005) embrace a weak or incremental approach to neuroeconomics above all (although at times they seem to wish for a less moderate position of neuroeconomic re-establishment of economic functions and concepts). Like behavioural economics, this does not intend to contrast the theory of rational choice, but wishes to extend its horizons, taking into examination variables considered not measurable by traditional economics. We could say that it supports the position of Glimcher and Rustichini (2004), according to whom the goal of neuroeconomics is to provide a "mathematical, behavioural and mechanistic" explanation for choices. For neuroeconomics, the problem is showing whether the discovery of the *mechanistic* basis (i.e. of cerebral causal models) "is able to improve the ability to explain and predict choices, while maintaining mathematical discipline and continuing to employ behavioural data".

The challenge of neuroeconomics is therefore to demonstrate that it is possible to identify this mechanistic basis and to show that it increases our ability to explain and to predict. Until a few decades ago, neuroscientists had very limited tools at their disposal to study the brain. They were based primarily on analysis of the influence of pathological conditions on limited areas of the brain (traumatic, vascular and degenerative lesions). It was possible to extrapolate (using the inductive principle of the difference) which mental function was altered by a lesion to a specific area of the brain. Numerous cases can be found in neuropathological literature. One of the most studied pathologies is that of the "split brain", where the connections between the left and right hemispheres of the brain are cut. The right hemisphere enables the patient to interpret language, but not to speak, which is what the left hemisphere does. For example, in a case described by LeDoux (1996), the right hemisphere was invited to make a sign with the hand, based on an invitation projected onto the left part of a screen, so that it would only be processed by the right hemisphere. The left hemisphere saw the hand make a sign but was not aware of the instructions given to the right hemisphere. When the patient was asked to explain the reason for his behaviour, the left hemisphere tended to invent a rational reason such as: "I saw a friend so I waved to him" (behaviour that reflects the brain's egocentric tendency to rationalise). Another type of technique used in the past was the electroencephalograph (EEG), which measures the electrical activity related to stimuli or behaviour through electrodes applied to the scalp. Both technique provide a great deal of information, but the former depends too much on chance detection of available pathologies, while EEG has a low resolution and can only detect activity in surface regions.

A powerful and easy-to-use technique has recently been introduced, which scans even deep regions of the brain: fMRI (*functional Magnetic Resonance Imaging*), which determines the blood flow to the brain, starting from changes noted in magnetic properties due to the oxygenation of the blood. These techniques – with numerous others that employ electrical, magnetic or pharmacological stimulation, and psychophysical analysis (heartbeat, blood pressure, sweat, behavioural activity, etc.) – literally made it possible to open the black box of the brain and to build up increasingly realistic hypotheses about the causes of human behaviour.

One of the most important results of this neurocognitive revolution is to have obtained observational proof of the prevalence of the *affective and automatic component* over the *cognitive and controlled component* in psychological activity. This is something that psychologists had maintained for decades, particularly psychoanalysts. But today we have empirical visual proof of this psychic architecture. This discovery has an important falsifying effect on the psychology implicit in the theory of economic rationality, all focused on the conscious and deliberative capacity of the economic operator. As Camerer says (see Table 11.1), mental activity can be represented by a diagram with four quadrants related to cognitive and affective variables on one hand and controlled and automatic processes on the other. Each quadrant corresponds to a part of the brain responsible for the specific psychological activity. The controlled cognitive and affective processes (quadrants I and II) are located in particular in the front areas of the brain; the automatic cognitive processes (quadrant III) particularly in the occipital (corresponding to the rear part of the brain), parietal (upper part) and temporal (lateral) areas of the brain. A structure under the cortex, known as the amygdala, seems to be responsible for a conspicuous part of automatic affective processes (quadrant IV).

Most mental life is caused by the automatic processes. Controlled processes come into play at particular moments, when something unexpected happens, because we have to take a decision we have never taken before, or we must concentrate to understand a text. Quadrant I (Table 11.1) corresponds to the pondered and conscious reasoning and decision-making processes that lie behind traditional models of economic activity. When we have to calculate the costs and benefits of a limited number of options, with few evident variables, we use this quadrant in particular. I say "in particular" because it is difficult for the affective and emotional component not to be involved in this type of choice. When we buy a car, but even if we buy apples, we make a rational calculation of our needs (for example, the price, the functional characteristics, etc.) but we are also consciously or subconsciously influenced by emotional and affective variables. For example, the memory we have removed of an accident we have witnessed, involving a certain type of car could, unconsciously, cause us to value that model negatively. Or the mental link between the colour bright red and physical wellbeing ("his colouring is good so he is well"), and the opposite connection between a pale colour and

Table 11.1 Two dimensions of neural functioning (Camerer et al. 2005)

	Cognitive	Affective
Controlled processes		
Serial		
Effortful		
Evoked deliberately	I	II
Good introspective access		
Automatic processes		
Parallel		
Effortless		
Reflexive	III	IV
No introspective access		

sickness ("he is as pale as a corpse") can prompt us to prefer apples with a nice bright red colour, even if they are more expensive and less healthy (because they have been treated chemically), than yellow or grey apples. In these cases quadrant IV (Table 11.1) comes into play. These are automatic affective processes that are conveyed by structures under the cortex, like the amygdala, which seem to be independent of our conscious control. For example, once we have learned to associate an affective sensation, like disgust or fear, with a given object like a food or an animal, it is very difficult for us to cancel this memory rationally. This is very important to understand how an economic operator deals with *risk*. It appears that in most cases, risk aversion behaviour is guided by an immediate response of fear. The amygdala is responsible for this response: it is the centre responsible for assessing the stimuli from the environment or from memory and for grasping the signs of potential danger. It is activated both when stimuli are perceived consciously and when we are not aware of the danger signs. With our will and reasoning, i.e. by making the cortex work, we manage to attenuate some sensations of fear. This is the way we can explain how psychotherapy can be successful in reducing manic attitudes and unmotivated fears. However, recent research seems to show that it is always a question of control and attenuation, but not of suppression of the fear. In fact, as LeDoux showed in his study (1996), when the nervous connections between the cortex and the amygdala are cut, our old fears return, because the amygdala has maintained a memory of them latent. It also appears that different thresholds of amygdala activation may be innate. If the threshold is high, in other words if it takes more intense stimuli to activate the sensation of fear, the individual will have a higher propensity to risk and will take decisions that envisage a greater probability of failure. Compulsive gamblers, irrational speculators, delinquent and self-destructive behaviour could be explained by this insensitivity to the stimuli of fear. We could even suppose that risky behaviour in adolescence could derive from an immaturity of the cortex-amygdala system.

Other important affective phenomena are also caused by different nervous structures. Indignation, envy and trust have been studied in depth to find the cerebral correlation. An interesting discovery by Zak et al. (2003) is the correlation between the oxytocin hormone and trust. It was found in various games based on cooperation that an increase of this hormone is generated in the player who trusts the other player. In negotiations there is a greater probability of success when the negotiators meet face to face, because physical contact, looking each other in the eye, and feeling that the other is physically present in front of you, increases the oxytocin level, which stimulates certain areas of the brain. This does not happen when communications mediators like writing, the telephone and to a certain extent even videoconferences, are used.

As neuroeconomics has shown (Camerer et al. 2005), affective components, conveyed by cortical and subcortical structures like the amygdala or the insula, underpin risk behaviour and the perception of trust in one's own actions and those of others. Let us see how. According to some authors, one area that specialises in trust is the *prefrontal cortex* (Brodmann's area 10). Neuroscientific research has analysed the way the brain functions in behavioural experiments that imply the attribution of trust. Above all, they used strategic interaction games in which the decision of one of the two players is influenced by the existence or lack of a relationship built on trust. There are various *trust games*. In them one player may, if he wishes, trust the other, who may reciprocate or defect. The main result common to many of them is the presence of cooperative decisions guided by trust, which are contrary to the rational prescriptions of the game theory, according to which a player should not trust and the other should defect. The explanation of this behaviour is the presence in the subjects of rules of *fairness* which prompts them to behave in a manner contrary to their economic utility. The brain areas activated in unfair situations seem to be the *dorsolateral prefrontal cortex*, for cognitive processes like the evaluation of offers, the *insula*, which is associated with negative emotions (like indignation or pain), and the *frontal cingulate gyrus* which has executive functions. Some hormones also seem to play an important role in the mechanisms of trust. In various types of games an increase in oxytocin has been noted in the player who is prompted to stimulate the trust of the other player. This increase occurs when the contact is direct, face-to-face and not mediated by communications technologies. Looking in the eye someone who has cooperated with us also seems to activate the ventral striate areas that generate gratification. The presence of neurocognitive mechanisms of trust seems to be explained by its fundamental role from an evolutionary viewpoint. The success of the human species seems to be based on strong interdependence between its members. Trust allows the cooperative behaviour and reciprocity that strengthen interdependence to develop.

Neuroscience seems to recognise the growing importance of the emotions in decision-making and risk. The frontal lobe is responsible for reasoning and decision-making processes. The orbitofrontal cortex seems to play an essential role in the rapid evaluation of emotional information in decision-making processes. For example, in the presence of a stimulus (for example, walking in front of a dog) it could be responsible for assessing the reinforcement properties (for example, fear of being bitten by the dog, which had tried to attack him the week before) and the consequent action (for example, avoiding the dog). When this region is damaged, the representations necessary to guide an action enter the working memory, but without their emotive content. For example a person with this type of lesion, who encounters the same dog when it is sitting quietly in front of the house, manages to describe its potentially threatening features, but without elaborating in emotional terms the affective memories linked to his past experience with the animal.

Bechara and his colleagues (1997) verified how this lesion can influence risk behaviour. Participants were given four decks of cards, two of which were "bad" in the long terms (high gains alternating with even higher losses) while the other two were "good" in the long term (low earnings and even lower losses). The results have shown that the normal subjects, after having suffered a few losses, began to choose from the "good" decks (aversion to risk), while the patients with orbitofrontal lesions continued to choose from the "bad" decks (propensity to risk). Using the Skin Conductance Response (SCR) which measures the state of excitement of the autonomous nervous system (in particular sweating, a sign of fear), the authors noted an anticipatory SCR in normal subjects every time they were about to choose a card from a "bad" deck, while this response was not noted in patients with an orbitofrontal lesion. Unlike the subjects without orbitofrontal lesions, patients did not show the emotional experience of the fear of losing, linked to the previous negative choice. In other words, they do not anticipate the possible negative effect of their actions, persisting in choosing decks that potentially trigger future regret.

Learning and emotional memory therefore seem to be fundamental in configuring individual behaviour in relation to risk. The orbitofrontal cortex does not seem alone in performing this function. It interacts primarily with the *amygdala*, another neural structure that triggers emotional memory. The mnemonic role of the amygdala is evident in a paradigmatic experiment carried out by LeDoux (1996) on the cortical suppression of the activation of the amygdala. When a rat, trained to fear an electric discharge after it hears a particular sound, hears the sound several times not followed by the discharge, the fear response is rapidly "extinguished". But if the neural connections between the cortex and the amygdala are cut, the original response of fear to the sound returns. This shows that the conditioning to fear is not cancelled by "extinction", but is suppressed by the cortex, remaining latent in the amygdala. This and other experiments show that the function of the orbitofrontal cortex is to modulate emotions *top-down* to the sub-cortical structures, and the amygdala in particular. In LeDoux's experiment, it suppresses the activation of the amygdala. In other studies, the representation of possible negative results at cortex level, is linked to the emotional memories contained in the amygdala, stimulating the fear that induces risk-averse behaviour (while in the opposite case of orbitofrontal patients, the lack of representation of possible negative results leads to behaviour reflecting a propensity to risk). In fact, risk-averse behaviour is guided by a fear response, and it looks as if fear itself can be traced back to the amygdala. The amygdala continually evaluates incoming stimuli to grasp the signs of potential danger. The stimuli are noted both when they emerge at a conscious level and when they are at an unconscious level. A recent study shows that the framing effect, one of the most important phenomena to explain risk behaviour, is associated with the activity of the amygdala. The propensity to risk when one notes a loss frame (as described by the prospect theory) is correlated to an increase in amygdala activity to elaborate the emotional information of fear implicit in the negative decision-making context. And finally, in subjects that reveal pathological risk propensity, like compulsive gamblers and irrational speculators, the sensitivity to fear of the negative effects of their actions seems reduced.

What do these studies have to say about economics? That the economic activity generated by the conscious and rational capacity for calculation envisaged by traditional economics, is often overcome by emotional and affective factors. Moreover, innate components sometimes exist that determine a particular style of refusal of or propensity for certain types of behaviour, as in the case of risky behaviour.

Quadrant IV is closely linked to quadrant III (Table 11.1). This quadrant oversees our capacity to conceptually classify and label objects. It is related to automatic cognitive processes. When we see a known object, for example a red apple, quadrant III enables us to identify it as belonging to the category of red apples. This takes place automatically, without our realising it. But this identification is not just cognitive because, as various research projects show, starting with Zajonc's work (1998), each phenomenon and object also has affective labelling that presents itself automatically and is linked to quadrant IV. In fact, as we saw earlier, the red apple also evokes sensations of wellbeing, as well as sinful sensations linked to biblical symbolism. When we reflect deliberately on why a red apple evokes sinful images, we realise that it is related to the episode of Adam, Eve and the serpent in the Bible, which we have heard so many times. At the exact moment that we are conscious of this link, we have activated the last quadrant, no. II (Table 11.1), i.e. controlled affective processes.

Dividing mental activity into four in this way, justified by the discoveries of the new "geography" of the brain, has profound implications for economic theory. For example, think of an important element of neoclassical economics and its application to the economics of wellbeing, in other words the theory that choices reveal preferences that cannot be observed. If we choose a red apple instead of a yellow one, this shows that we prefer one to the other. But if this theory is to be predictive, we must suppose that our preference remains constant in time, i.e. that we always prefer a red apple to a yellow one. To be realistic, this assumption must be based on understanding of the causes of the preference. For example, a preference for a red apple might be contingent and reversible, because after we witness a road accident with a number of bloody bodies, we might develop an automatic aversion (quadrant IV) to anything that reminds us of blood. Or what once appealed to us because of its connections to sin, could produce the opposite controlled effect (quadrant II) today, in the middle of a religious crisis. And so on.

There are various traditional concepts that neuroeconomics questions and redefines, from intertemporal choice to the indirect utility of money, decision-making in a state of risk and uncertainty, and behaviour in the game theory. One of the strongest criticisms of neuroeconomics is voiced by Gul and Pesendorfer (2005), who accuse it of not providing an exact example of precise empirical application, i.e. in which it is possible that "a parameter of choice – such as the coefficient of aversion to risk or the discount factor – can be observed by visualising brain activity". Camerer (2005, 2007) retorts that this is not true and refers to a series of experiments that link parameters of choice to neural processes. This was obtained for the degree of aversion to ambiguity, aversion to loss, the discount rate and many other means of economic choice.

Another attempt to save the theory of traditional rationality is the insidious attempt to try to demonstrate that brain behaviour incorporates the principles of economic rationality. For example, it has been said that there are neurons that codify expected gratification or that the nervous system uses Bayesian probabilistic models during motor sense learning. If this can be justified for primary and elementary tasks, common to other forms of life, it is not true for the most important aspects of economic behaviour, which envisage complex calculations and interaction with a scarcely predictable environment.

To conclude, neuroeconomic research is changing the way economic research is performed. First of all, it is a powerful aid to cognitive and experimental research into decision-making models and economic action. Secondly, it poses new problems and issues, like those of the prevalence of automatic affective processes, which will profoundly change the same economic concepts. One example of the overpowering force of neuroscience, which digresses a little but is particularly intriguing, is the redefinition of the concept of *free will* in the light of some data obtained from EEG recordings of brain activity. As we know, free will is a theological expression, introduced by St. Augustine in the fifth century and the subject of his bitter disputes with Pelagius and subsequently of the violent clashes between Luther and Erasmus in the sixteenth and seventeenth centuries. It basically represents the freedom of choice and human will. There are very well articulated philosophical arguments that develop and define the concept. One of these is the *deterministic* argument, which starts from the assumption that every event in nature is determined by its causal precedents and that it is therefore impossible for human choice not to follow the same rule. This negative vision is questioned not only by great philosophers like Kant, but also by our common psychological experience. At the moment that we choose, we have the feeling that nothing has prompted our choice. It seems that there is an infinitesimal moment that generates out decision, but that it is not caused by anything at all. Neuroscience seems to explain this sensation today with a structural characteristic of the human brain, the *cognitive inaccessibility* of much of its activity. The brain works and produces psychic activity and we do not realise it. For example, through research with EEG, it has been demonstrated (Libet 1985) that the moment when we have a feeling that we are about to take a decision is preceded by 300 milliseconds by the wave of brain activity associated with that decision. After another 200 milliseconds from the moment in which we feel that we are about to decide, the behavioural response manifests itself. So the brain has already started to act before we have the sensation that we want to act. Because this brain activity is not accessible to us on a cognitive level, we have the feeling that we have decided freely, that no cause has preceded our decision, but that is not the case. What is more, this sensation of free will is reinforced by the awareness that our previous decision has produced our subsequent behaviour. The issue is a complex one and there could be many objections: for example, that free will anticipates the first wave of brain activity. This is not the time or place to go into this problem in detail. What I wanted to underline is the impact that neuroscientific studies have on problems that are apparently a long way from its goals.

The gradual opening of the black box of the brain will provide more surprises that will help to change the old concepts of human sciences.

Part III

Mind, Culture and Epistemological Universals

Subjective Rationality and Cultural Diversity

12

If social theory has to be policy-relevant, it has to use a not too unrealistic "model of man", even though any model represents a drastic simplification of the real world. In practice, however, even simple beliefs or the most familiar types of behavior that we observe in everyday life can only be explained with difficulty by the two dominant models to which the familiar labels of *Homo sociologicus* and *Homo oeconomicus* are attached respectively. Redressing this situation may be one of the most challenging problems facing contemporary theory.

Taken at their highest level of generality, current sociological explanations of behaviour are often irrational (of the form "the subject x had no reason for doing y, but he had internalized the norm N"). In general terms, current economic explanations of behavior are often rational in a narrow sense (of the form "the subject x had objectively valid reasons for doing y, since he preferred g to g' and y was objectively the best way of getting g").

Many sociologists often feel uncomfortable with the usual sociological explanations for behavior: they may be valid, but they can also be circular, merely verbal, and ad hoc (e.g. "x had no reasons for doing y, but he had internalized the view that y is good"). Other sociologists feel uncomfortable with the typical economic explanation of behavior, notably because it cannot account for a number of collective phenomena. For instance, it is hard to see how magical rituals could be analyzed along economic lines. Olson (1965) himself, who made a major contribution to drawing sociologists' attention to the economic interpretation of behavior, clearly indicated that the behavioral axiomatics used in his much quoted book were not universal.

The point we would like to develop in a sketchy fashion is that sociological analysis needs a third model. We call it the rational model in the broad sense (RBS): it takes the form "the subject x had good, though possibly objectively invalid reasons for doing y, since ...". According to Simon (1982), the rationality of the subject can be qualified as subjective when the reasons are objectively invalid.

The present chapter is a modified version of Boudon, R., & Viale, R., (2000). Reason, cognition and society. published in Mind & Society, 1,vol. 1.

DOI 10.1007/978-3-642-24743-9_12,

When the reasons are objectively valid, we return to the economic model, a particular version of the RBS. The core notion - subjective rationality – of the RBS model is methodologically crucial, because it fills a wide gap between irrational actions ("x had no reasons for doing y, but...") and narrowly rational ones ("x had objectively valid reasons for doing y, since...").

Note that, although it was not christened by classical sociologists, it was often used implicitly by Max Weber, Emile Durkheim, and Vilfredo Pareto as well as Karl Marx. In other words, classical sociology reminds us that a major methodological problem of the social sciences consisted of developing the open theory of rationality sketched by Weber when he started from the basic postulate that even the strangest religious beliefs should be considered meaningful, being in principle *verstaendlich*, i.e. (this is the only clear interpretation of this attribute) explainable by reasons.

When the reasons of the actor and/or believer are objectively sound, we have little trouble understanding why they are perceived as good by the subject as well as by the observer: they are good because they are objectively grounded. It is more intriguing when the reasons are not objectively grounded, but are still perceived by the subject as well as the observer as being "good" reasons.

While this point is not always sufficiently recognized, the findings of modern cognitive psychology confirm the importance of the Weberian postulate that reasons can be objectively ungrounded and still good. In many cases, it is impossible to understand the inferences of subjects placed in a problem-solving situation without this category: their answers are false, yet they are *verstaendlich*; they can be explained by the fact that the subjects have good reasons for believing that they are valid.

This concept is not only indispensable to sociological analysis, it allows the sociologist to avoid the Scylla and Charybdis of homo sociologicus and homo oeconomicus. This was well understood by the founding fathers: it is very easy to draw examples from the works of Marx, Durkheim, Pareto, or Weber in which the notion of subjective rationality is implicitly introduced and plays a crucial role in their analyses. In these examples, behavior and/or beliefs are interpreted as inspired by what we call good reasons, even if these beliefs are false, strange, or detrimental to the subject.

12.1 Subjective Rationality in Durkheim, Marx, and Weber

It is interesting to start with an example borrowed from Durkheim, since he is seldom seen as a writer who would have insisted on explaining actions and beliefs rationally. But, while this is true of his theoretical writings, in his empirical analyses he often offers explanations of social behavior using the RBS model.

When Durkheim (1897) tries to explain in his *Suicide* why economic booms appear to be associated with higher suicide rates, he effectively introduces an explanation of the subjective rationality type. Suicide rates appear to be high in the ascending phase of the cycle, contrary to natural expectations, because this is when anomie is high. But this correlational analysis is grounded in a psychological analysis which Durkheim conducts in a sketchy fashion, probably because it is contradictory to his methodological principles. His assumption is that the anticipations and expectations of the social players are grounded on good reasons: in a stable economic situation, they tend to start from the principle that they can expect, say, for the coming year, the same gains as the year before, while in a expanding economic cycle, when many people's financial position appears to be improving, they will change their expectations regarding the goals that can be aimed at and attained.

At this point Durkheim implicitly introduces a brilliant hypothesis, namely that people would extrapolate from the tangent to the curve at each point of time. Thus, in the first part of the ascending phase, before the inflection point, their expectations would tend to be under-optimistic, while in the second part, they would be over-optimistic. At least, this is one way of explaining why Durkheim predicts an increase in disillusionment and consequently in suicide rates in the second part of the ascending phase of the business cycle, but not in the first (see Boudon 1981).

This classical analysis is an excellent illustration of the notion of subjective rationality and its effectiveness. Being in an uncertain situation, Durkheim's economic subjects have good reasons to try to reduce the uncertainty by using the most current method of prediction-extrapolation from the present to the future. Also, Durkheim's analysis shows that the notion of subjective rationality can play a crucial role even in explaining apparently irrational behavior. His theory explains why economic subjects tend to have normally invalid expectations about the future: they tend to be *under-and-over-optimistic* in the ascending phase of the cycle, *under-and-over-pessimistic* in the descending phase. These invalid expectations are grounded on good reasons, however, as are the invalid inferences observed by cognitive psychologists.

The validity of Durkheim's data on the correlation between suicide rates and business cycles has been much discussed and one need not to take this correlation at face value. In the same fashion, nobody needs to believe in the Marxian theories of exploitation and surplus value. Nevertheless, it is interesting to see that, when Marx tries to understand why workers accept exploitation, as well as in many of his other analyses, he proposes a subjective-rational interpretation.

This goes against the famous principles he developed, namely in the opening pages of the *German Ideology*. In this classic, Marx supposes that unknown, unobservable factors can produce distorted pictures of the world in the social subject, without his being aware of it. In other words, Marx suggests that unobservable causes rather than reasons should be evoked to explain beliefs. This is a typical "sociological" irrational explanation. (They have no reasons of accepting exploitation, but they have internalized the view that . . .).

Contradicting this general theory of beliefs, Marx explains at one point in *Das Kapital* (1867) why workers have good reasons to accept exploitation so readily. Behavior running against an actor's own interests is typically explained in most cases in an irrational fashion. Against his own principles, Marx sketches a rational explanation, however, which we reconstruct in the following way (see Elster 1985):

in order to discover whether they are exploited, the workers should calculate the difference between their salaries and the value of their work. But to determine the value of their work, they would have to master a complex economic theory they are unlikely to be aware of, as well as a series of empirical information to which they do not have access. As they still want to know whether their salaries are fair or not, they turn toward a natural substitute: comparing their salaries to the salaries of individual producers. Suppose then that a craftsman working alone needs the same number of hours to produce one pair of shoes as the baker needs to produce x loaves. If he sells his pair of shoes for the price of x loaves, he will be satisfied. So also will the workers in a shoe factory, suggests Marx. They will tend to consider that the natural fair price of one pair of shoes is x loaves. By doing so, they introduce a bias in their estimation, since an individual producer uses more time to produce a pair of shoes than the average worker in a shoe factory. So they will underestimate the value of their own work, but they will develop this illusion with good reasons. On the whole, according to this analysis, the workers will agree with good reasons to leave to the capitalist the gain resulting from the division of labor without counterpart. Again, one need not endorse the theory of surplus value in order to admire the ingenuity with which Marx explains how and why the social actor can use good reasons to act against his own interest.

Another classic example can be used to illustrate the crucial importance of the notion of subjective rationality for analysing social behavior: the discussion concerning the interpretation of magic. In fact, magic is a crucial phenomenon for any discussion of rationality because belief in magic is often perceived as a canonical example of irrationality: "How is it possible to believe in such causal relationships?" is the typical reaction of any observer confronted with magical beliefs. So, in most cases, magical beliefs are explained using the Homo sociologicus model: the social actors passively endorse the norms and beliefs of their group.

Again, the theory of magic that Durkheim (1912) develops sketchily in *The Elementary Forms of Religious Life* appears to be far removed from the basic methodological principles generally associated with his name. In fact, his theory is very close to Weber's (1922) and it illuminates both the content of the notion of subjective rationality itself and its scientific fruitfulness.

According to this theory, one should first take seriously the fact that those who believe in magic have no knowledge of a number of theories that Westerners have developed over the centuries. Secondly, everyday action needs theories, and magic is a theory that provides guidelines for the actor. According to Durkheim, magical theories are applied theories derived more or less directly from religious theories exactly as many of our technical devices are inspired by scientific theories. Of course, these guidelines are not as efficient as those of science. But showing that magic is inefficient requires the mobilization of methods of causal analysis, which were developed by science.

Of course, as they are false, magical beliefs are often contradicted by reality. But, writes Durkheim, we often observe that scientists keep their faith in a theory even when it appears to be contradicted by facts. Anticipating very precisely the ideas developed by classic and modern philosophers of science, such as Duhem, Kuhn and Lakatos, Durkheim (1897, pp. 508–528) suggests that scientists have good reasons for doing so. They can always hope that minor changes in the theory will make it compatible with facts, or doubt whether the facts contradicting the theory are genuine or artifacts, and so on. Moreover, a long time will often elapse before it can be ascertained which of these typical situations is created by the discovery of facts contradicting the theory. Therefore, in most cases it is as rational to try to save the theory as to replace it.

For the same reasons, magicians retain confidence in their theories even though they do not always work. Exactly like scientists, they will also devise auxiliary hypotheses to explain why the theory has failed: the rituals have not been conducted in the proper way; some unknown factors have thwarted the influence of the rituals, and so on.

On the other hand, even in our world where methods of causal analysis are well mastered, many people (including many scientists) appear to believe all kinds of unconfirmed causal relations. Many people see a causal link between all kinds of practices and health or long life simply because in such cases collinearity is often so powerful that it is practically impossible to check seriously whether or not x really has an effect on y. Thus, after many years, it was recently discovered that idea that stress was a main cause of stomach ulcers is a magical belief, one might say. This magical belief was endorsed by many people, however, including many scientists.

A subtle argument explicitly developed by Durkheim (1897, p. 527) can be added to this. Ethnologists have observed that rain rituals are celebrated during the rainy season. So, says Durkheim, the confidence of the primitive in the effectiveness of the rituals is reinforced by the fact that rain is actually more frequent in that period when crops start growing and need rain, and when, consequently, the people celebrate these rituals. Durkheim's hypothesis is in other words that collinearity would - at least occasionally – reinforce the magical causal beliefs of primitive societies and that their causal assumptions are confirmed by genuine observable correlations.

On the whole, Durkheim suggests that magical beliefs in primitive people are of the same nature as many of our own beliefs, the difference being that, because of the development of science, a number of old beliefs have become obsolete. Consequently, when we see other people still believing in these old beliefs, we have a strong feeling of irrationality. But as soon as we evoke the causal relationships in which we ourselves believe on such existential problems as health or long life, for instance, we become conscious of the fact that magical and scientific knowledge coexist as easily in our societies as technical and magical knowledge do in primitive societies.

Weber (1922, pp. 227–228) wrote that, to the primitive, "the actions of the rainmaker are exactly as magical as the actions of the firemaker." By this aphoristic statement he meant that primitive man has no reasons to introduce the asymmetry between rain and firemaking which we introduce ourselves, precisely because the process by which kinetic energy is transformed into thermal energy is familiar to us.

Reciprocally, the primitive man to whom this process is unfamiliar has no reason to see a basic difference between fire and rainmaking.

So, both Weber's and also Durkheim's implicit diagnosis of magic is that primitive societies should not be considered as less rational than our own. When confronted with existential problems they develop theories and conjectures, which they derive from the body of knowledge available socially. They are ready to forget them as soon as better theories are proposed, but as long as these alternative theories are not available, they have good reasons for believing – as do scientists – even in theories which repeatedly fail. Moreover, reality can only reinforce rather than contradict their beliefs, even when these beliefs are false, as Durkheim has noted in one of the most brilliant parts of his analysis of magic.

12.2 Cultural Differences in Reasoning

Weber's and Durkheim's diagnosis of magic parallels some interesting results in cognitive anthropological studies of reasoning and belief formation. Also according to these studies there are no important differences between the civilized mind of Western people and the primitive mind of tribal people.

There are two main ways of making comparative studies on reasoning.

The first approach compares the reasoning performances in different cultures to some normative model of reasoning, for example to the canon of probabilistic calculus.

Evans-Pritchard in his classic volume on Azande magic notes that "the logic of therapeutic treatment consists in the selection of the most prominent external symptoms, the naming of the disease after some object in nature it resembles (e.g., the physical movements of bush monkeys resemble epileptic seizures; ringworm resembles fowl excrements) and the utilization of the object as the principal ingredient in the drug administered to cure the disease" (1937, p. 487). Contrary to the main theories in anthropology, Azande magical thinking is not an irrational symbolic attempt to influence uncontrollable events (Malinowski 1954) or a persuasive rhetoric, designed to arouse sentiments (Tambiah 1973). Rather, according to some cognitive anthropologists, it shows an inclination to rely on resemblance between events to estimate correlation among the same events (Shweder 1977, p. 447).

According to Shweder this inclination is not a peculiar feature of Azande or other primitive cultures. Magical thinking "is an expression of a *universal disinclination* of normal adults to draw correlational lessons from their experience coupled with a *universal inclination* of normal adults to seek symbolic and meaningful connections (resemblances) among objects and events" (Shweder 1977, p. 447).

This perspective overcomes Weber and Durkheim's positions: primitive thinking does not seem different from our way of reasoning because magical thinking, as a practice, is not a mode that distinguishes one culture from another. Resemblance, not probabilistic correlation, is a fundamental conceptual tool of the normal reasoner. The universality of resemblance stems from peculiar cognitive constraints of the human mind. In fact, it is well known that chance and probability are non-intuitive concepts, difficult to learn and absent from the thinking of normal adults. And correlation is a statistical second order concept expressing the relation between two relations. As Tversky and Kahneman (1973) pointed out, people apparently estimate the degree to which items go together in behavior by the ease (availability) with which they can bring to mind a higher order symbol of a behavioral type in which the items compatibly fit as parts of the imagined whole. They appear to substitute one type of relationship for another. Resemblance and correlation become merged in everyday thought.

The comparison of everyday reasoning to other normative models often seems to confirm the results obtained on magical thinking. Various biases in probabilistic and deductive reasoning reveal a worrying picture of the rational performance of human beings. But one question is unavoidable. Are the irrational outcomes of experimental tests on reasoning a reliable indicator of the cognitive abilities of the reasoners? Or is the abstract and unrealistic format of most tests not a good indicator of the real human ability for reasoning and decision making? Moreover, it may be too pretentious to use normative models of reasoning as a reference to compare different styles of reasoning among Western and non-Western reasoners. Consequently, it might be preferable and less demanding to make transcultural analyses comparing descriptive models of reasoning. For example comparing reasoning performances to some descriptive model of reasoning, as the model of category-based induction, studied by Osherson and colleagues (Osherson et al. 1990).

An important example of this approach is a series of studies (Lopez et al. 1997) that aim to identify the universal cultural features of folk-biological inductions. The aim of the investigation was to determine whether industrialized Americans and traditional Itzaj-Mayans readily use their taxonomies of mammals to make inductions about those mammals, and whether those inductions are comparable across both cultures and whether they are also comparable to scientific inductions. Itzaj are Mayan Amerindians living in the Peten rainforest region of Guatemala. They were the last independent native polity in Mesoamerica to be conquered by the Spaniards and have preserved all the ethnobiological knowledge recorded for lowland Maya. The studies tested three of 13 empirical phenomena regarding category-based inductions, introduced by Osherson et al. (1990), the most important of which are presented in Table 12.1. The three phenomena tested were similarity, typicality and diversity in general arguments.

A general inductive argument is one in which the category in the conclusion properly includes the categories in the premises. For example the conclusion category MAMMAL in argument (a) below includes the premise category HIPPO and HAMSTER:

(a) Hippos have ulnar arteries
(b) Hamsters have ulnar arteries
(c) All mammals have ulnar arteries

An argument is strong if belief in the premises causes people to believe the conclusion. The experiments use blank properties (properties regarding which lay

Table 12.1 Summary of nine inductive phenomena in Osherson et al. (1990)

Phenomenon	Description and example
Specific arguments	
Similarity	The more similar the premise(s) to the conclusion, the more stronger the argument: ROBIN/SPARROW > PENGUIN/SPARROW
Diversity	The more diverse the premises, the stronger the argument: LION, GIRAFFE/RABBIT > LION, TIGER/RABBIT
Monotonicity (number)	The more premises, the stronger the argument: FOX, PIG, WOLF/GORILLA > PIG,WOLF/GORILLA
Non monotonicity (heterogeneity)	An argument gets weaker if a premise from a different category is added: FLY/BEE > FLY, ORANGUTAN/BEE
General arguments	
Typicality	The more typical the premise(s), the stronger the argument: ROBIN/BIRD > PENGUIN/BIRD
Diversity	The more diverse the premises, the stronger the argument: HIPPO, HAMSTER/MAMMAL > HIPPO, RHINO/MAMMAL
Monotonicity (number)	The more premises, the stronger the argument: HAWK,SPARROW,EAGLE/BIRD > SPARROW,EAGLE/BIRD
Non-monotonicity (heterogeneity)	An argument gets weaker if a premise from a different category is added: CROW, PEACOCK/BIRD > CROW, PEACOCK, RABBIT/BIRD
Conclusion-specificity	The more specific the conclusion, the stronger the argument: BLUEJAY, FALCON/BIRD > BLUEJAY, FALCON/ANIMAL

people do not have substantial prior knowledge) in order to minimize the role of properties in induction, and instead maximize the role of categories.

For both Americans and Itzajs, similarity and typicality predicted patterns of induction. Very different mammals qualify as typical among Americans and Itzajs, but they perceived arguments with typical premises as stronger. Moreover, for both Americans and Itzajs, similarity relations embodied in the folk taxonomy prompt the pattern of induction. On the contrary, Lopez et al. (1997) found a striking difference between Americans and Itzajs with respect to diversity-based reasoning. Americans preferred arguments with more diverse premises. In sharp contrast, the Itzajs did not.

Does this result indicate the return of a new form of magical thinking?

Other studies tried to control the evidence of the previous investigation. In one of these (Viale and Osherson 2000), a comparative analysis was made between Italian university students and Vietnamese university students. Like the Americans in the previous study, Italians preferred arguments with more diverse premises. Instead the Vietnamese did not. Does this result mean that this supposed new form of magical thinking also applies to oriental, well-educated Vietnamese students?

The diversity phenomenon seems to be a stable feature in category-based reasoning among Western people, not only for university students, but also in office-workers and workers (Viale and Osherson 2000). And it is also true that this kind of induction seems to be an important part of scientific rationality. Newton's theory commands such wide assent because it accurately predicts heterogeneous, diverse phenomena, such as the trajectories of balls thrown into the air, the behavior of gyroscopes, and the orbit of celestial bodies. Most theories in the philosophy of science agree on the importance of the diversity principle in theory choice. And the history of some of the main scientific discoveries confirms the importance of this principle as a guide to scientific change (Donovan et al. 1988).

12.3 Universality of Thinking Between Cultures

Nonetheless there are some critical reflections to be made on the empirical differences among Western and non-Western reasoners present in these and other experimental studies (see Chap. 13 for a detailed analysis).

Firstly, the normative character of the diversity principle is problematic. For example, according to the Bayesian perspective of scientific inquiry (Myrvold 1996), there is no direct relation between confirmation by conjunctive evidence and the diversity of the evidence. In some cases the combined evidence will have a diminished confirmatory, and even a falsifying effect on the hypothesis (Viale and Osherson 2000).

Secondly, the results on non-Western reasoners are not stable. For example 63% of the Korean sample in a study by Choi et al. (1997) prefer heterogeneous evidence to homogeneous. Contrary to those of Mayan and Vietnamese samples, these data are reinforced by recent discoveries in evolutive psychology. In a study by Lopez et al. (1997) even American 8-year-old second graders judge a general argument to be stronger the more diverse its premise categories. Korean and second graders data show that difference phenomenon in category-based induction is not exclusive to adult Westerners and therefore it may not be Western culture dependent.

Thirdly, Lopez et al. (1997, p. 288) write that "Itzaj participants had extensive knowledge of the habits, characteristics, and ecological proclivities of Peten mammals; this ecological knowledge appears to have blocked diversity-based reasoning by rendering premises implausible on the basis of what the Itzaj know to be true. Cultural knowledge available to the Itzaj may have rendered the diversity strategy irrelevant". Moreover in a study on American tree experts, Medin et al. (1997) discovered that diversity-based reasoning involving local trees and novel diseases is stronger in taxonomists, less strong in landscapers and very weak in maintenance personnel. Categories at a higher rank than genus (and family) are more salient and inductively useful to taxonomists than to maintenance personnel. As in the case of Itzaj, maintenance personnel seem to have rejected the diversity principle in favor of ecology-based reasoning. Therefore it is the different scientific expertise and knowledge that seems to play the major role in diversity-based reasoning. Therefore within-culture differences in expertise and scientific knowledge may correspond to cross-cultural differences. Culture might be a problem of expertise.

Fourth, the context dependency seems to play a major role in cross-cultural differences. For example in the Itzaj follow-up 4 (Lopez et al. 1997, p. 284) the researchers tested the Itzaj's reasoning about real-world scenarios. The tests were about saving money, inspecting farmland and buying corns. Results show that most of the Itzaj responses on these items were diversification responses, indicating that the Itzaj follow the diversity principle when reasoning about everyday life and problem solving.

In cross-cultural studies it is well known that familiarity with the materials about which one is asked to reason is important if people are going to apply their cognitive skills (Cole 1977, p. 476). An example might be provided by Gladwin's (1970) description of Puluwat navigators, who use an abstract star compass to help them get from island to island, but who fail to respond with sufficient abstractness to a Piagetian seriation task.

Moreover, cognitive skills developed in a practical experience are not easily transferred to other domains of activity. A concrete example is shown by the work of Greenfield and Childs (1974) about whether or not learning to weave one of the traditional Zinacantenan cloth patterns influenced a general ability to represent patterns. The results show very little influence of weaving experience on any generalized ability to represent patterns.

> Practical experience develops specific component cognitive skills whereas ... other more general cultural influences, economic activity for instance, develop generalized cognitive performance (Greenfield and Childs 1974, p. 29).

Finally, there is another way to reaffirm the diversity between Western and non-Western thinking. Specific structures of particular languages, far from the Western culture, might strongly influence both semantic and conceptual development and therefore produce quite different modes of thinking. This thesis is linked to the Whorfian hypothesis according to which each language both embodies and imposes upon the culture a particular world view, making certain semantic distinctions obligatory and others optional or marking certain distinctions with clear morphological variations, while others can only be expressed by complex and indirect means. According to Choi and Bowerman (1991) in Korean, for example, there are no terms like English "in" and "out" and the related concepts. Therefore it cannot be represented the action of putting an object in a container or on a surface. Korean spatial terms distinguish only between "tight fit" relationships (a finger in a ring, a picture on a wall) and "loose fit" ones (a ring in a box, an umbrella leaning on the wall).

According to Levinson (1994) in some Mayan languages all spatial terms mark absolute distinctions (like "north" and "south") rather than marking spatial relations between objects and the speaker (like English "left" and "right").

How can we communicate and discuss rationally if, as it is emphasized by the Whorfian tradition, we cannot share fundamental concepts representing the world, as in the case of various American Indian languages, like the Apache, in which there are no things or actions, but only events, where there are no agents and acts, no separate space and time (e.g., in Apache "It is a dripping spring" is expressed by "As water, or springs, whiteness moves down-ward")?

Does this evidence express insurmountable differences in the world view of cultures brought about by differences in natural languages?

The answer seems negative, and a piece of negative evidence just comes from a, at first sight, striking example of linguistic relativity: the case of colour. Colour is a continuous physical variable which can be easily designated by objective measures which are independent of the colour terms in any given language. Then it should be a field little influenced by cultural variables. Nevertheless there is a great variability of colour terms among the different languages. The anthropological literature reports this variability. For example there are cultures which have only one word to describe the colours which English distinguishes as "green" and "blue", or cultures whose word for "orange" includes much of what we would classify as "red". Moreover, people like the Dani of West Irian (Indonesian New Guinea) only have a two-term colour language (Rosch 1972), while Western people use a multi-term colour language. This kind of evidence might appear to confirm the Whorfian thesis that a language could arbitrarily cut up the colour space into quite different categories. If this were the case it would support the thesis on radical differences in thinking between cultures, including category-based induction. But prima facie cultural variability does not appear to be so worrying to the opponents of cultural relativism. First, in a study (1972) Heider discovered that Dani, as well Americans, recognized the main colours (the focal colours) better than others, although they had no words to name them. Second, Berlin and Kay (1969) and others researchers in a number of more recent studies have shown that there is an evolutionary sequence that correlates the number of basic level colour terms and a society's level of technological development. The various stages occur in unrelated languages and in geographically distant parts of the world. This sequence develops from the first stage, relative to a primitive agricultural society, that has only two basic colour terms (black and white) to the seventh stage of industrialized society that has 11 basic colour terms (black, white, red, yellow, green, blue, brown, purple, pink, orange, grey). The development of new terms stems from the practical needs and task-dependency of an increasingly complex society, but nevertheless primitive man has the perceptual ability to discriminate the basic colours without having the words to name them. Therefore, the linguistic relativity between cultures in naming colours hides a strong universality in the perception of colours.

In conclusion, primitive thinking and modern thinking, non-Western cultures and Western cultures resemble each other much more than is shown by superficial evidence. There is a negative similarity between them in sub-optimal performances compared to normative canons of reasoning. But these canons and the experimental tests that incorporate them are often too abstract and too, computationally, demanding compared to the kind of real problems that human reasoners face in everyday life. Moreover, the cultural differences found in non-Western thinking do not appear to be deeply rooted in the skills of the reasoners. Instead they are motivated by the different kinds of problem solving and pragmatic contexts that shape and drive the reasoning processes. Western education, culture and everyday problem-solving (e.g., the economic decision-making of a customer; the rational choice made by an elector; technical skill in using everyday machines; scientific knowledge in taking care of his own health and the environment; etc.) shape particular kinds of reasoning more inclined to abstractness and pattern recognition. But we can observe the same kind of thinking in non-Western cultures. The difference is that it is less widespread in everyday reasoning, but it is only present in particular tasks (as in the case of the use of abstract star compass by Puluwat and the weaving patterns of Zinacantenan). Moreover Western culture and education teach us to deal with arbitrary problems (e.g., games, puzzles, tests, mathematical and logical problems, etc.), while in more primitive cultures people are trained to deal, mainly, with concrete and real problems linked to survival. This difference may explain their inclination not to assume, hypothetically, the premises of the cognitive tests, but to deal with them in a realistic way. Obviously if this is the case the results of the tests do not stem from different reasoning processes, but from a different understanding and interpretation of the premises.

Therefore the poverty and oddity of thinking emphasized by these results is, often, an artifact of the cognitive tests not a prelogical feature of primitive reasoners.

12.4 Good Reasons and Decision Making

There are good reasons to explain the different ways of thinking in cultures different from ours. It is very likely that Westerners in the same situation - of education, culture and everyday problem solving – would reason in the same way. There are good reasons for Itzaj Mayans to rely on ecological knowledge in dealing with the premises of category-based induction tests. They are the same reasons that differentiate the results of the taxonomists compared to maintenance personnel in the same kind of test. There are good reasons for Puluwat or Zinacantenan people not to accept the abstract and arbitrary tests of cognitive anthropologists. They are very far from the concrete meanings of their everyday life.

The presence of good reasons to explain odd way of reasoning in cultures that are different from ours provides strong support for the methodological thesis of RBS (Rational model in Broad Sense). The reconstruction of the good reasons to explain beliefs and actions would have been impossible if the competence of non-Western reasoners had been completely different from ours. Without common inferential principles even the RBS model would not work. We cannot explain any social action without presupposing some common way of reacting to the situations or some common reasoning and decision-making processes. The universality of ways of thinking is, therefore, a necessary condition for any rational explanation of social action.

What can cognitive science tell us about decision making and action based on good reasons? With its help can we achieve some more intersubjective way of dealing with the problem of good reasons or are we condemned to the idiosyncratic methodology of *verstehen*?

Main stream cognitive psychology has followed the formal modelling approach. It associates a numerical value – stemming from normative models like expected utility theory (von Neumann and Morgenstern 1947) or a descriptive theory such as prospect theory (Kahneman and Tversky 1979b) – to each option and characterizes choice as the maximization of value. This approach has been used in experimental studies of consumer behavior and rational economic choice. It is well known that many biases and errors are made by the decision-makers when answering experimental tests. According to this approach, the human image is of an irrational animal.

An alternative approach, less popular in economics and decision research, but more widespread in history and political science, employs an informal, reason-based analysis. As is pointed out in Shafir et al. (1993, p. 12) "this approach identifies various reasons and arguments that are purported to enter into and influence decision, and explains choice in terms of the balance of reasons for and against the various alternatives". Using this approach it is possible to understand the various failures of the principles of rational choice theory. The only difficulty is to avoid the trap of ex-post rationalization. The subjects often find reasons for their actions that were not present in the decision process. Some interesting studies, which try to overcome the problem of ex-post rationalization, compare rational decision-making and reason-based choice. These studies show that many failures of rational choice theory, such as expected utility maximization, can nevertheless be explained rationally using a wider theory of rationality like RBS. Two brief examples are given.

1. *Failure of procedure invariance*: in a binary choice situation it should not matter whether people are asked to choose or to reject one of two options. What matters is not the way in which the options are described, but the content of the options themselves. If people prefer the first they will reject the second, and vice versa. On the contrary, a recent study (Shafir 1993) has shown that the positive features of options will have more weight when choosing, while the negative features of options will be weighted more heavily when rejecting. This result is rooted in subjective good reasons. They are likely to focus on reasons for choosing an option when deciding which to choose, and to focus on reasons for rejecting an option when deciding which to reject. But one of the most basic assumptions of the rational choice theory is the principle of procedure invariance, according to which we must use an equivalent procedure to choose, strategically, the best option. And the choose-reject asymmetry represents a clear failure of procedure invariance and value maximization. It, nevertheless, can be justified and explained rationally by a subjective good reasons-based choice: reasons for choosing are more compelling when we choose than we reject, and reasons for rejecting matter more when we reject than when we choose.

2. *Failure of the principle of independence of irrelevant alternatives*: according to this principle the preference ordering between two options should not be altered by the introduction of additional alternatives. Instead there is strong evidence that the addition and removal of options from a given set of options can influence the choice made by the agent. In particular, the tendency to prefer option x over y can be increased by adding a third alternative z that is clearly inferior to x, but not to y. This phenomenon is called asymmetric dominance (Huber et al. 1982) and it is explained by Simonson and Tversky (1992) in terms of "tradeoff contrast". That is, the tendency to prefer an option is increased or decreased according to the favorable

or unfavorable tradeoff to that option. The failure of the principle of independence of irrelevant alternatives is, obviously, a violation of value maximization. But it can be explained by reason-based choice. When an agent has to choose between two options, x and y, and x is of higher quality whereas y is better priced, he may find it hard to decide if quality differences outweigh the price differences. If a third alternative z is introduced and if z is clearly inferior to y but not to x, the decision-maker has clearly good reasons to choose y over x (Shafir et al. 1993, p. 26).

In conclusion, what do these and other similar results mean? They mean that in a given context of choice, subjective good reasons drive reasoning processes towards typical decisions and actions. In the same kind of circumstances conscious decision-making based on good reasons by many agents will give similar outputs. This behavior may be regarded as irrational according to a narrow concept of rationality, like expected utility maximization, but it may be assessed as rational according to the RBS model.

The knowledge that comes from this kind of study strengthens the RBS model. We can establish regularities about inferential rules, generalizing individual decision-making based on good reasons. Reason-based choice is responsible for the constancy of inferential inclinations that drive decision-making towards results that violate the normative model of rationality.

Discovering regularities in the inferential principles that are driven by good reasons strengthens the tools used by the social scientist to explain the social action. He can appeal to some intersubjective model of reason-based choice in order to explain the social action. Therefore he should not only rely on an idiosyncratic methodology of "understanding" and *verstehen.* The effect of this shift of methodological individualism towards *methodological cognitivism* is evident. The RBS model in social sciences meets that of cognitive science and its epistemology is closer to that of natural sciences. The social scientist is no longer alone when he is trying to mentally simulate the situation of choice faced by the agent. Now he can rely on some general condition-action rules that can increase his explanatory power.

Hempel vindicated?

Biology and Culture of Human Inference 13

13.1 Innate Principles of Reasoning

In the past philosophers used to put infants and children on the opposite side from science in the spectrum of cognitive rationality. Their supposed cognitive immaturity did not allow them to approach the ideal image of rational beings. Two psychologists Alison Gopnik and Andrew Meltzoff declared, at the end of the introduction to their book:

> Ultimately, our reason for watching and talking to children is the same as Socrates'. The most central questions in cognitive science are questions that only they can answer (Gopnik and Meltzoff 1997, p. 9).

One of the questions that children seem to answer in their book is about the analogy of the child as a little scientist. The central idea of the book is that "the processes of cognitive development in children are similar to, indeed perhaps even identical with, the processes of cognitive development in scientists" (Gopnik and Meltzoff 1997, p. 3).

Infants are endowed with an innate set of principles that allows them to begin to interact with the world. Among these principles, one of the most important allows a causal attribution to relations between physical events. At around the age of 6 months, the infant is able to apply the principle of cohesion – a moving object maintains its connectedness and boundaries – the principle of continuity – a moving object traces exactly one connected path over space and time – and the principle of contact – objects move together if and only if they touch (Spelke et al. 1995).

This chapter is a modified version of Viale, R. (2006). "Local or Universal Principles of Reasoning", and Viale, R., & Osherson, D. (2006). "Cognitive development, Culture, and Inductive Judgment" previously published in Viale, R., Andler, D., & Hirschfeld, L. Biological and Cultural Bases of Human Inference. Reproduced by permission of Taylor and Francis Group, LLC, a division of Informa plc.

DOI 10.1007/978-3-642-24743-9_13, © Springer-Verlag Berlin Heidelberg 2012

Moreover, there is the theory of biology and the theory of psychology. These theories show that infants individuate some theory-specific causal mechanisms to explain interactions among the entities in a domain. A child has an intuition of what characterises a living being from an artefact or an object. Between the ages of 2 and 5, the child assumes that external states of affairs may cause mental states and that there is a causal chain from perception to beliefs to intentions and to actions (see Sperber et al. 1995). According to Viale (1999) these results on causal cognition in infants seem to justify the anti-Humean thesis of causal inferences based on synthetic a priori principles.

What are the features of these principles? Data from developmental studies and a certain universality of causal perception in cross-cultural studies seem to support the hypothesis that we are endowed with early-developed cognitive structures corresponding to maturational properties of the mind-brain. They orient the subject's attention towards certain types of clues, but they also constitute definite presumptions about the existence of various ontological categories, as well as what can be expected from objects belonging to those different categories. Moreover, they provide subjects with "modes of construal" (Keil 1995), different ways of recognising similarities in the environment and making inferences from them. Moreover and more surprisingly, contrary to the Piagetian theory according to which the notion of causality is domain-general and gradually modified by experience, "different conceptual domains are structured by different principles which (1) carry information about the types of stimuli that are likely to correspond to particular ontological categories, (2) convey expectations about non-obvious properties of objects in different domains, (3) constrain the manner in which spontaneous inductive inferences are made about objects from different domains" (Boyer 1995, p. 623).

The previous Piagetian notion of formally defined stages, characterised by principles which apply across conceptual domains, has been replaced by a series of domain-specific developmental schedules, constrained by corresponding domain-specific principles. These principles constitute a core of probably innate "intuitive theories" which are implicit and constrain the later development of the explicit representations of the various domains. As Gelman highlights, "different sets of principles guide the generation of different plans of action as well as the assimilation and structuring of experiences" (1990, p. 80). They establish the boundaries for each domain which single out stimuli that are relevant to the conceptual development of the domain.

The three main intuitive theories individuated by cognitive science are the theory of physical objects, the theory of biology and the theory of psychology. These theories allow that infants individuate some theory-specific causal mechanisms to explain interactions among the entities in a domain. A child has an intuition of what characterises a living being from an artefact or an object. Between the ages of 2 and 5, the child assumes that external states of affairs may cause mental states and that there is a causal chain from perception to beliefs to intentions to actions.

The intuitive theory of physical causality is the least controversial and very rich in empirical data. Intuitive physical principles orient the child's understanding of the physical environment from infancy. Principles specifying that solid objects are cohesive and continuous and are not susceptible to action at a distance seem to emerge before 4 months (Leslie 1988; Baillargeon and Hanko-Summers 1990; Spelke 1990). At around 6 months the infant is able to apply the principle of support – i.e., that objects fall if they are not supported (Spelke 1990). The specific patterns of movements allow him to make ontological distinctions between self-generated and non-self-generated movement (Massey and Gelman 1988). This distinction gives an initial skeleton to the differentiation between animate and inanimate kinds of objects, which has important consequences for causal reasoning in the biological and psychological domain.

Research on causal cognition has shown that there are perceptions of causality that are not affected by previous experiences, whether of the same specific kind of relations or of an analogous kind. Besides, there is a great amount of empirical data showing that there is, in many cases, a strong cognitive tendency to infer a priori the effect of observing a cause without any dependence on previous experienced regularity. These empirical data seem to meet Hume's challenge, i.e. to show examples of perception and of a priori inference of a non-experienced causal relation (Viale 1999).

Starting from these data Gopnik and Meltzoff introduce "The Little Scientist Thesis":

> There is strong empirical evidence that starting from their innate endowed principles, children propose abstract entities, coherently organised with causal relations among them. They make ontological commitments and hold counterfactuals. These entities serve to provide characteristic explanations, predictions and interpretations. Children initially ignore certain kinds of counter-evidence, then account for such evidence with auxiliary hypotheses, then use the new theoretical idea in limited contexts, and only finally reorganise their knowledge so that the new theoretical entities play a central role. When the new theory is under construction, they engage in extensive experiments relevant to the theory and collect empirical generalisations (Gopnik and Meltzoff 1997).

The innate theories function as a start-up of the conceptual development, but, while innate, they would be defeasible. They are later modified and revised by new evidence: "Innate theories are like the Neurath boat that pushes off from the pier. The boat you start out in may have considerable effect on the boat you end up with, even if no trace of the original remains" (Gopnik and Meltzoff 1997, p. 51).

Children resemble scientists in their method of theory change. One theory can substitute another when it fits the empirical evidence better and allows one to make better predictions. Counter-evidence to a theory is ignored unless it manifests itself persistently. The methodological criteria of theory change in little scientists are not the guarantee of truth and representational success. Many false hypotheses are generated using these criteria. But nonetheless they seem to be a guarantee of conceptual learning from errors to generate theories that fit the world better.

13.2 Are Children Rational?

As agents of abductive inference, children have an enviable reputation. It rests upon the remarkable transition from benighted neonate to savvy and enterprising 5-year-old. During this period, children acquire a grammatical system, discover the boundaries of tolerated behavior, and begin to discern the biological and physical kinds encountered in their environment. It is no wonder that developmental psychologists often compare children's achievements to that of professional scientists embarked on their own voyage of discovery. If the analogy can be sustained, it suggests that the study of cognitive development might offer clues to the successful implementation of computerized scientific activity, by simulating the child's successful strategy.

Conceiving the child as scientist, however, requires more than recording her impressive achievements. Intellectual development must also be shown to derive from the kind of theory construction attributed to professional scientists. Assimilation of development to rational inquiry is precisely the view of an influential school of developmental psychology, recently defended in (Gopnik and Meltzoff 1997). Abstracting away from differences in background knowledge and startup funds, children (like scientists) are claimed to develop a succession of theories that evolve adaptively under the impact of data. At each step the child is supposed to have an organized corpus of belief that amounts to a scientific doctrine. And the transition between theories is supposed to depend on their respective, predictive success – as well as on simplicity criteria familiar from the history of adult science. This attractive picture of cognitive growth is meant to apply to knowledge of the physical and social world, as well as to word meaning, to mental events in other minds, and so forth.

The opposing view is Chomsky's triggering model. According to this conception, it suffices for children to come into contact with a few key data in order for an articulated and stable theory to leap to mind. The claim is that the child's theory enjoys not the slightest justification of a sort that makes sense to professional scientists. The process is typically described in terms of parameter setting, as is well known. Let us try to isolate the different commitments of the two perspectives on development, namely, the "little scientist" view versus the triggering model of the Chomsky. On the former account, we expect each advance in cognitive development to issue in the kinds of theories announced by scientists, for example, involving hypothetical variables related to each other in some deductive way. Such is the synchronic commitment of the little scientist view. But notice that the triggering model is equally compatible with the child having scientifically respectable theories throughout development. It needs only be imagined that each parameter flip brings to the fore a pre-stored body of mature, scientific belief.

The two views of development are more easily distinguished diachronically, in terms of the kinds of experience that nudge the child from one theory to the next. The triggering model conceives this process in the same way that visual stimuli trigger imprinting in baby ducks. In contrast, the little scientist view assimilates the child's use of experience to theory selection on the part of a rational agent.

Clearly, the little-scientist perspective is more joyous than that of the triggering model. Whereas parameter setting imposes tight limits on the kinds of theories that ordinary folk can construct about their world, little scientists can help themselves to everything accessible to modern science. Preferences notwithstanding, we must try to evaluate which of the rival perspectives is closer to the truth – or closer with respect to some particular domain of knowledge.

Norms and criteria of theory change and conceptual development in children give a positive representation of the rational attitude of humans. On the contrary, there is a dark side of the coin. Little scientists seem not to satisfy elementary canons of correct reasoning. For example, one candidate principle of inductive reasoning concerns the diversity of evidence in support of a general hypothesis. It is widely claimed that greater diversity entails greater support (e.g.: Hempel 1966, pp. 33–38; Franklin and Howson 1984). Why did Newton's theory end up commanding so much assent? One reason is that in the presence of various background assumptions, the theory accurately predicts heterogeneous phenomena, such as the trajectories of balls thrown into the air, the behaviour of gyroscopes, and the orbit of celestial bodies. At the end of the seventeenth century, these phenomena appeared very diverse, which forced respect for the theory despite reservations about the reliance on occult, non-mechanical entities like gravity.

The diversity principle has been the object of psychological investigation. Osherson et al. (1990) have discovered that it is one of the phenomena present in category-based induction tasks.

A general inductive argument is one in which the category in the conclusion properly includes the categories in the premises. For example, the conclusion category MAMMAL in argument (1) below includes the premise category HIPPO and HAMSTER:

(1) Hippos have ulnar arteries.
    Hamsters have ulnar arteries.
    ____
    All mammals have ulnar arteries.

An argument is strong if belief in the premises causes people to believe the conclusion.

American adults seem to support a general or a specific conclusion more when the premises are more different than when they are more similar. On the contrary, studies made by López et al. (1992) and Gutheil and Gelman (1997) among 6-year-olds and 9-year-olds show an opposite attitude. For example, 6-year-olds prefer the argument (2):

(2) Cows have ulnar arteries.
    Buffalos have ulnar arteries.
    ____
    All animals have ulnar arteries.

to the alternative argument (3):

(3) Cows have ulnar arteries.
Cats have ulnar arteries.

All animals have ulnar arteries.

Moreover, both 6-year-olds and 9-year-olds prefer more homogeneous premises to more diverse premises in arguments with specific conclusions like (4):

(4) ______________________________
Kangaroos have ulnar arteries

Children seem not to apply a fundamental norm of inductive reasoning. Therefore the little scientist hypothesis might be weakened.

The diversity principle is a genuine feature of rational inquiry, hence part of the meaning of the "little scientist" hypothesis? Viale and Osherson (2006) argue against the use of the diversity principle as a normative standard of inductive reasoning. The diversity variable is not related in such a simple fashion to argument strength, even at the prescriptive level. This is because so-called "blank" predicates (that is, predicates that are indefinite in their application to given categories, but clear enough to communicate the kind of property in question) often retain enough meaning to open the door to legitimate reasoning that violates the diversity principle. An example is provided by the predicate *often carry the parasite Floxum.* It counts as blank since the parasite *Floxum* is unfamiliar, so nothing can be divined about which mammals are more or less likely to suffer from it. Now, consider the following arguments:

(5) Housecats often carry the parasite Floxum.
Fieldmice often carry the parasite Floxum.

All mammals often carry the parasite Floxum.

(6) Housecats often carry the parasite Floxum.
Tigers often carry the parasite Floxum.

All mammals often carry the parasite Floxum.

It seems undeniable that housecats resemble tigers more than they resemble fieldmice. Yet it appears perfectly defensible to judge argument (6) to be stronger than (5), on the grounds that housecats might catch Floxum from fieldmice (their prey) whereas they have little contact with tigers. In this case, reasonable judgements about strength run counter to the advice offered by the diversity principle. Hence, the latter is discredited as a basis for evaluating inductive intuition. Of course, the example does not show that diversity always gives the wrong advice, only that it sometimes does. But this is enough to undermine its claim to normative status.

If we accept the Bayesian probability theory as a normative account of scientific inference, as most contemporary philosophy of science is doing (Howson and

Urbach 1993), we may propose that it is the probability of premises prior to accepting the conclusion that governs its strength (Horwich 1982)[1]. Under these conditions argument strength stands in a simple relation to premise-probability as it is expressed by the following principle:

Premise Probability Principle (PPP)

Suppose that arguments A,B / C and A1,B1 / C are given, where C logically implies A, A1, B, and B1. Then the strength of the first argument is greater than the strength of the second if and only if $P(A \wedge B) < P(A1 \wedge B1)$.[2]

---

[1] To get the analysis off the ground, it is necessary to give a probabilistic interpretation of argument strength. Recall that an argument is strong to the extent that its premises give reason to believe its conclusion. Thus in a strong argument, the probability of the conclusion given the premises should be greater than the probability of the conclusion alone. An argument with premises A,B and conclusion C should therefore be strong to the extent that $P(C/A \wedge B) > P(C)$. Recall that $P(C/A \wedge B)$ denotes the conditional probability of C given A and B. The symbol "$\wedge$" denotes conjunction. The unconditional probability of the conclusion C (namely, without assuming A and B), is denoted by P(C). Many authors have measured argument strength by comparing the prior probability of the conclusion with its probability given the premises, e.g., Good (1960) and Hintikka (1968).

There are many ways to quantify the extent to which $P(C/A \wedge B)$ exceeds P(C). Following other authors, like Myrvold (1996), we rely on the ratio of the conditional to the unconditional probability. Officially:

Definition: Let argument A,B//C be given. Its strength is defined to be

$$\frac{P(C/A \wedge B)}{P(C)}$$

Premises confirming a conclusion thus yield strength greater than 1, and premises weakening a conclusion yield strength less than 1.

The arguments figuring in the present discussion are all general, and therefore have the particularity that the conclusion logically implies each premise (since the same predicate occurs in all statements, and the conclusion category includes the premise categories). Under these conditions, argument strength stands in a simple relation to premise-probability.

[2] PREMISE PROBABILITY PRINCIPLE (PPP): Suppose that arguments A,B / C and A1,B1 / C are given, where C logically implies A, A1, B, and B1. Then the strength of the first argument is greater than the strength of the second if and only if $P(A \wedge B) < P(A1 \wedge B1)$.

Proof: By definition, the strength of the first argument is greater than the strength of the second if and only if

$$\frac{P(C/A \wedge B)}{P(C)} > \frac{P(C/A1 \wedge B1)}{P(C)}$$

By familiar properties of conditional probability, the latter inequality holds if and only if

$$\frac{P(C \wedge A \wedge B)}{P(C) \text{ x } P(A \wedge B)} > \frac{P(C \wedge A1 \wedge B1)}{P(C) \text{ x } P(A1 \wedge B1)}$$

The less probable the premises, the stronger the argument. Diversity of premises is often (but not systematically) associated with low premise probability. For example, it seems less likely that Cows and Cats have ulnar arteries than that Cows and Buffalos do. Based on this assumption, PPP accounts for the greater strength of (3) compared to (2). Likewise, given their unrelated habitats, housecats and tigers seem less likely to carry common parasites than do housecats and mice. For anyone sharing the latter judgement, PPP rules (6) to be stronger than (5).

From the proof of PPP it can be seen that the principle applies to arguments with any predicate, blank or not. Its normative status is thereby enhanced since inductive reasoning almost invariably involves meaningful predicates. Observe also that PPP is a consequence of no more than the axioms of probability along with our definition of argument strength.

Some experiments on PPP (Lo et al. 2002) were designed to collect judgements about argument strength versus premise probability in two-premise general arguments with blank predicates. The crucial items were arguments evaluated at separate times for strength and premise probability. In Experiment 1, American preschoolers showed reliable (albeit imperfect) conformity to PPP. Indeed, they showed more conformity to PPP than to the diversity principle. In Experiment 3, it was seen that Taiwanese children showed as much conformity to PPP as their American counterparts.

The premise probability principle (PPP) has better credentials as inductive model since it follows from the axioms of probability and a plausible definition of argument strength. The experiments reveal detectable conformity to PPP on the part of young children in different cultures. If these findings are supported and extended by further experimentation, they provide one clear sense in which young children's inductive methodology can be interpreted as properly scientific.

Furthermore, these studies show how, prior to environmental conditioning resulting from different latitudes and longitudes, there is cognitive uniformity that appears to be based on a common hereditary endowment of the same principles of reasoning.

Since C implies A, A1, B, and B1, the last inequality holds if and only if

$$\frac{P(C)}{P(C) \times P(A \wedge B)} > \frac{P(C)}{P(C) \times P(A1 \wedge B1)},$$

which holds if and only if

$$\frac{1}{P(A \wedge B)} > \frac{1}{P(A1 \wedge B1)},$$

thus if and only if
$P(A \wedge B) < P(A1 \wedge B1)$,
which proves the claim.

13.3 Reasoning Biases or Experimental Errors?

If the studies on biases and errors during developmental age do not generate great concern about the image of human rationality, on the contrary, the enormous amount of empirical evidence collected over the past 40 years on sub-optimal ways of human reasoning and decision-making has provoked great bewilderment. "How can we go to the Moon with so many constant errors of judgement?" was the question asked by a colleague to Nisbett and Ross after having read the proofs of the first 8 chapters of their book *Human Inference: Strategies and Shortcomings of Social Judgement* (1980). The image of man that is portrayed in the book is of a person unable to use formal criteria of reasoning and decision-making like those that scientists use in their activity. Man chooses samples that are biased by systematic tendencies; he is not able to assess the co-variation between events; he is biased in the causal attribution; he makes predictions ignoring base rate and regression towards the mean; he tends to confirm the theory instead of falsifying it.

Nevertheless, man goes to the moon, that is, he is quite able to adapt to his social and natural environment. He is able to understand, predict and control many aspects of his life and his environment. He is able to plan his career, to make diagnoses from his symptoms, to discuss rationally many problems. There are two important aspects of human irrationality that can find a moderate interpretation.

The first concerns sub-optimality in assessing co-variation among events, that is a crucial ability for generating hypotheses. Outside the laboratory, in real life, there are many circumstances that allow good performance in co-variation:

(a) Because, sometimes the stimuli are well perceived, evident, close, and, motivationally, relevant.
(b) Because, when co-variation is very strong, a single prototypical case can offer a reliable representation of the general relation.
(c) Because, most of our theories are founded on co-variations made by experts (scientists, advisers, consultants) in particular fields.

The second and most important concern about human rationality is the "perseverance bias". People tend to persevere in their beliefs even when faced with data that falsify them. This phenomenon seems to undermine the dynamic image of theory change of the little scientists thesis. Actually, the dynamics of theory change of the child compared to the adult is much stronger. In fact, the "little scientist" metaphor finds its justification in the greater analogy between child and scientist than child and adult. Adults, for many acceptable and unacceptable reasons, are more conservative in maintaining their theories of the world. They prefer stability of their system of thought and find it difficult to integrate, in the quick flow of contemporary life, empirical counter evidence into new alternative theories. Nevertheless (Viale 2001b, p. 225):

(a) The maintenance of a theory in front of anomalies, until we are sure that it is systematic, seems a sound methodological rule also in the scientific community.
(b) The adult seems more close to the model of the technologist rather than the scientist. He needs to apply theories in everyday problem-solving. He has no time to worry about the truth of the theory. What is important is that it functions

in solving practical problems. He fears more a casual error in applying the theory in a given pragmatic context than a systematic error that would need the generation of an alternative theory. Nevertheless, as in technology, the solution works if the embodied theory is valid. Therefore, sooner or later, even the adult is obliged to change ill-functioning theories.

On the other hand, not all people accept a picture of man as being naturally inclined to systematic errors and bias. Following the tradition of studies on probabilistic judgement, the main stream, represented by Kahneman et al. (1982), sees in natural heuristics the "strategies of simplification that reduce the complexity of judgement tasks, to make them tractable for the kind of mind that people happen to have" (p. XII). Availability heuristic and representativeness heuristics are an example of these inferential tools used by the human mind and based on the limits of memory. Their activation appears to be responsible for probability judgements that do not comply with the canons of Bayesian theory. These results have been criticised by Gigerenzer (1991, 1994) and Cosmides and Tooby (1996) who, following evolutionist psychology, regard probabilistic reasoning as based on observed frequencies, sequences of events and limited samples. Contrary to the frequentist approach, the Bayesian method adopted by Kahneman and Tversky uses probability expressed in percentages that are a highly processed cultural product and consequently do not seem to be a natural representation to study probabilistic reasoning. As a result, many errors and biases identified in the experiments undertaken in the past few years appear not to be an expression of irrationality in human cognition but rather the effect of an unnatural method of studying probabilistic reasoning. This offers contrast between two opinions on the natural dimension of probabilistic reasoning: the first focuses on the limitations of the mind and the use of heuristics, whereas the second stresses the categorisation of events through sequences and frequencies. According to Macchi and Bagassi (2006) this characterisation is inadequate. In fact, both approaches fail to take account of an important explanatory element for the formation of errors and biases: the pragmatic effect of context-dependent variables activated by the formulation of a problem. The difficulties and sub-optimal features of many tests on probabilistic reasoning are related more to the structure of the text than to the heuristic factors or the statistical format in which the probabilities are expressed. And this consideration is true irrespective of the use of "cultural percentages" or "natural frequencies".

13.4 Cultural Differences in the Styles of Reasoning

When we analyze the cognitive rationality stemming from the cognitive tests on everyday reasoning, one important question concerns the cultural variability of the styles of reasoning. Are cognitive abilities universal or context-dependent? Can we discover common patterns of thinking among different cultures or does each socio-cultural environment shape its system of thought?

An answer to this question comes from Nisbett and Masuda (2006), Nisbett et al. (2001) and Nisbett (2003) on the differences between Asian and American thinking. They rely on an impressive number of cognitive tests that try to compare the way of reasoning of North Americans, mainly university students, and East Asians – Korean, Chinese and Japanese – mainly university students. The East Asians and the Americans respond in qualitatively different ways to the same stimulus situation in many different tests.

For example, American participants showed large primacy effects in judgements about co-variation, whereas Chinese participants showed none. "Control illusion" increased the degree of co-variation seen and the reported accuracy of Americans but tended to have the opposite effects on Chinese. Koreans were greatly influenced in their causal attribution by the sort of situational information that has no effect for Americans. Koreans showed great hindsight bias effects under conditions where Americans showed none. Finally, Americans responded to contradiction by polarising their beliefs, whereas Chinese responded by moderating their beliefs.

The results can be summarized as follows.

The *American* vs. *East Asian style of thinking* (Nisbett et al. 2001).

1. *Explanation*: East Asians tend to explain events, both social and physical, more with respect to the field and Americans tend to explain events more with respect to a target object and its properties.
2. *Prediction* and "*postdiction*": East Asians tend to make predictions with reference to a wider variety of factors than Americans do. Consequently, they are less surprised by any given outcome and they are more prone to "hindsight bias", or the tendency to regard events as having been inevitable in retrospect.
3. *Attention*: since East Asians locate causality in the field instead of the object, they tend to be more accurate at "co-variation detection", that is the perception of relationship within the field.
4. *Control*: Americans are more subject to the "illusion of control", that is, a greater expectation of success when the individual is involved in interaction with the object – even when that interaction could not logically have an effect on the outcome.
5. *Relationships and similarities* vs. *rules and categories*: East Asians tend to group objects and events on the basis of their relationships to one another, for example, "A is a part of B". Americans would be expected to group them more on the basis of category membership, for example, "A and B are both Xs". Americans are inclined to learn rule-based categories more readily than East Asians and to rely on categories more for purposes of inductive and deductive inference.
6. *Logic vs. experiential knowledge*: East Asians are more influenced by prior beliefs in judging the soundness of a formal argument. Americans are more able at setting aside prior beliefs in favour of reasoning based on logical rules.
7. *Dialectics vs. the law of non-contradiction*: East Asians are inclined to seek compromise solutions to problems ("Middle Way") and to reconcile contradictory

propositions. Americans tend to seek solutions to problems in which a given principle drives out all but one competing solution, to prefer arguments based on logic, and to reject one or both of two propositions that could be construed as contradicting one another.

These differences are reflected in the different kind of errors and biases that affect East Asians and Americans. We cannot say that one culture is normatively better than another. East Asians are better at causal co-variation and less prone to "illusion of control". Americans are better at deductive reasoning in category-based induction and less prone to "hindsight bias". Obviously, better does not mean that they satisfy, absolutely, the normative canons of rational reasoning. It is well known that the tradition of investigation into deductive and probabilistic errors and biases started in American colleges.

Therefore, we can say that we are faced with two different mixes of rational and irrational reasoning. But the crucial thesis of Nisbett et al. (2001) and Nisbett and Masuda (2006) is that the different ways of reasoning are not a contingent and superficial feature, but they are rooted in two completely different systems of thinking, that is, in different metaphysical and epistemological principles that shape the American and East Asian cognition differently. These two different systems of thinking originated causally from two different socio-cultural environments: the old Greek trading society and classical philosophy on one hand and the old Chinese agricultural society and Confucian philosophy on the other.

Different social and economic variables gave birth to different styles of thought that we can summarise under the heading of "holistic" and "analytic" thought. Nowadays, these different styles of thought continue to be effective in differentiating the reasoning processes of contemporary Americans and East Asians.

Norenzayan (2006) also confirms the results of Nisbett and Masuda (2006), Nisbett (2003) and Nisbett et al. (2001). The cultural differences between Western and Asiatic populations are examined in a variety of cognitive tasks that involve formal and intuitive reasoning. Formal reasoning is rule-based, emphasises logical inference, represents concepts by necessary and sufficient features, and overlooks sense experience when it conflicts with rules of logic. Intuitive reasoning is experience-based, resists decontextualising or separating form from content, relies on sense experience and concrete instances, and overlooks rules and logic when they are at odds with intuition. The reasoning of European American, Asian American, and East Asian university students was compared under conditions where a cognitive conflict was activated between formal and intuitive strategies of thinking. The central hypothesis was that European Americans would be more willing to set aside intuition and follow rules than East Asians (Norenzayan 2006). The results of the experiments (Norenzayan 2006) confirm the starting hypothesis that European American students have a much stronger tendency to ignore intuition and follow the rules of reasoning when the latter conflict with the former.

13.5 The Apparent Diversity of Tribal and Civilised Styles of Reasoning

The first consideration about this anti-universal conception of cognition comes from the supporters of the universal endowment of cognitive abilities. If the innate theories of physics, of biology and of mind are true, then these theories form a common universal cognitive basis for the thought of every human in the world. Other investigators are even more radical. There are even common essential beliefs about the nature of the social world (Hirschfeld, 1996) and even religious conceptions, such as spirits and superhuman agents, are remarkably similar from one culture to another (Boyer 1993).

In my opinion, this position may be consistent with the anti-universal thesis of Nisbett et al. The little scientist hypothesis can explain why. We know that conceptual and theory change in the developmental age does not start from nothing, but from an innate endowment of theory about causality, the physical world and so on. The change towards new theories is triggered by empirical evidence and informative inputs that come from the environment. These evidential and informative inputs obviously are variable in relation to the particular developmental contexts. Therefore, they drive the generation of different theories on how to interpret and understand the world. They are the metaphysical and epistemological theories representing the implicit premises of our reasoning and thinking. In conclusion, it is very likely that such different socio-cultural contexts as the East Asian and American ones are able to lead, in the developmental age, to the generation of different metaphysical and epistemological theories that have a different effect on ways of reasoning.

Norenzayan (2006) agrees with the previous consideration. The human mind is equipped with basic cognitive primitives and possesses cognitive processes that carry out many tasks, such as exemplar-based categorisation, deductive reasoning, causal attribution, and so on. However, this basic endowment does not rule out differentiated development in response to cultural and environmental stimuli. These differences are manifested in various ways. Firstly, different cultural practices can make a given cognitive process, which is universally available in principle, accessible in a differentiated way. Asians appear to have a greater propensity than Westerners for exemplar-based categorisation, and a lesser propensity to decontextualise deductive arguments and more to explain behaviour by referring to the situational context. Secondly, through discoveries and inventions, societies often introduce artificial and complex new ways of thinking which differentiate one culture from another. One need only think of the statistic and probabilistic revolution in the seventeenth century and its impact on Western rationality and decision-making models. Or the development and influence of the ancient Taoist notion of yin and yang in the contemporary Chinese way of reasoning in relation to modal concepts like change, moderation and relativism.

The second consideration about the thesis proposed by Nisbett et al. relates to the implicit support of a kind of cognitive relativism. This is the natural consequence of the socio-economic determinism present in their thesis. In fact, according to them, social organisation and economic structure are the major determinants of the causal chain metaphysics-epistemology-cognition. Different socio-economic configurations generate fixed irreversible different causal chains. The world seems shaped with different and incommensurable causal chains related to the different socio-economic structures.

One of the results that Nisbett et al. bring to support their thesis seems to go in the opposite direction. It deals with the difference principle that we mentioned before in a previous paragraph. According to them:

> Koreans make less use of categories for purposes of inductive inference than do Americans and therefore are not able to follow the difference principle in an argument with a specific conclusion. (Nisbett et al. 2001)

Faced with two arguments (7) and (8), they prefer (7) because they are less able than Americans to generate from the category in the conclusion RABBIT, the inclusive category MAMMALS and therefore to estimate that LIONS and TIGERS have a minor coverage of the category MAMMAL than LIONS and GIRAFFES (Choi et al. 1997).

(7) Lions have ulnar arteries.
Tigers have ulnar arteries.
____
Rabbits have ulnar arteries.

(8) Lions have ulnar arteries.
Giraffes have ulnar arteries.
____
Rabbits have ulnar arteries.

On the contrary, if the category MAMMAL is made salient by changing the conclusion to:

(9) ________________________
Mammals have ulnar arteries.

the principle of difference is satisfied.

Data that seem more severe about the ability to use categories come from a study that has been carried out in Vietnam at the University of Ho Chi Min City (Viale and Osherson 2000). The sample seems to show that even using arguments with a general conclusion, and not only with a specific conclusion, the East Asian students are unable to apply the difference principle. Does this mean that there are fixed wired-in limitations in the cognitive processing of categories in some people – e.g. East Asians – but not in others – e.g. Americans? I don't think so as I showed before introducing the Premise Probality Principle.

Anther answer comes from the studies carried out among traditional Itzaj-Mayans from the Peten region of Guatemala (Lopez et al. 1997; see Atran et al.

2006) in order to identify the universal cultural features of folk-biological inductions on mammal categories. They discover that, as in the previous case of Vietnam, Itzajs did not follow the diversity principle with general and specific conclusions. These data were very different from those found in many American Colleges where the diversity principle was always followed. They tried to explain, through a number of follow-up studies, what the reasons were for this difference. The conclusion was not one of radical cognitive differences but rather an ecology-based reasoning stemming from the particular pragmatic context where they were living. "Itzaj participants had extensive knowledge of the habits, characteristics, and ecological proclivities of Peten mammals; this ecological knowledge appears to have blocked diversity-based reasoning by rendering the premises implausible on the basis of what the Itzaj know to be true. Cultural knowledge available to the Itzaj may have rendered the diversity strategy irrelevant" (Lopez et al. 1997, p. 288).

In fact, they tried to control the hypothesis of ecology-based reasoning in two following studies. One was made on Itzajs, using arguments stemming from real world scenarios and not from natural taxonomy. The tests were about saving money, inspecting farmland and buying corn. It showed that they were able to follow the diversity principle when reasoning about everyday life and pragmatic problem solving. One of the tests was the following:

> Imagine you want to buy several bags of corn from a given person. Before buying them, this person will show you only two cobs of corn to check whether all the corn is good. Do you prefer him to show you two cobs from one and the same bag (non-diversification response), or do you prefer him to show you one cob from one bag and another cob from another bag (diversification response)? (Lopez et al. 1997, p. 284)

The majority of Indios choose the diversification response because, according to their theory based on real life experience, they had good reasons to widen the sample.

The other study was made on American tree experts. They discovered that the less expert the individuals were – for example, maintenance personnel – the more subject they were to ecology-based reasoning and the less they followed the diversity principle. On the contrary, expert taxonomists were able to extrapolate the inclusive categories more easily and to follow the diversity principle. Scientific knowledge enables the taxonomists to generate more salient categories at a rank higher than genus and family. When an individual, as in the case of the maintenance personnel, has knowledge based on concrete examples of trees at the genus level, he is not able to reason using categories at a higher rank, and, consequently, cannot follow the diversity principle. On the contrary, the taxonomist can generate more generalised theories about the same object of everyday experience – e.g. the trees – therefore he is able to categorise at a more abstract level. These more abstract theories enable him to generate and use inclusive categories and therefore to satisfy the diversity principle.

13.6 Lay Folks Reasoning

These tests appear capable of demonstrating that cognitive styles from other cultures, like those used by the Indios, for example, which seem so different, in terms of performance, from Western ones, in fact present similar cognitive skills. The data presented above are reported in Atran et al. (2006) which tackles various topics linked to *folk biology*. The first set of experiments was carried out with Yukatek Maya and urban American children and showed how the former, but not the latter, were able to reason on the members of the biological world without using analogies with humans. American children, on the other hand, show an anthropocentric bias that can be explained by their different experience and interaction with animals and plants compared to the Indios children, who have lived in the rain forest since birth. Therefore, it would seem that "humans are not the prototype that organises the domain of animals".

The second set of experiments was carried out with 4 and 5-year-old children belonging to the Maya Indios tribe and on Brazilian and American children living in cities. Both appear to use "concepts of innate species potential, or underlying essence, as an inferential framework for projecting known and unknown biological properties to organisms in the face of uncertainty". Together with the first set of experiments, these studies confirm the hypothesis that folk biology does not come from folk psychology. Children from different cultures relied on the concept of underlying essence and not on the properties of human beings to reason on the properties of animals and plants.

The third set of experiments was carried out with adult Maya Indians and Americans living in the Mid West. Both sample populations showed a common tendency to prefer the generic species level – the level of robin and oak – as the taxonomic rank to reason and make inductive inferences. This result appears to be counter-intuitive among American adults owing to their scant knowledge and culture of individual animal and plant species. One would have expected that, for reasons of experience and similarity reasoning, the preferred level would be that of life-forms – the level of tree and bird. Instead, also among the Americans the level of generic species is preferred to make inductions on the distribution of biological properties and for "predicting patterns in the face of uncertainty". This result is a further confirmation of the presence of concept of underlying essences, the "generic-species level as a partitioning of the ontological domains of plant and animal into mutually exclusive essences".

The fourth set of experiments was carried out with adult Mayas, American college students and various groups of biological experts (landscapers, park workers, birdwatchers, professional taxonomists). It showed that all groups tend to categorise generic species spontaneously into taxonomies with higher and lower levels. "People from diverse societies build topologically-similar biological taxonomies that guide inferences about the distribution of biological and ecological properties". As we have seen before only the students and, for the great part, the taxonomists use diversity-base reasoning. Instead the other groups use ecology-base reasoning and the "taxonomy constrains the likely operational range of ecological agents and causes".

We saw earlier that Atran et al. (2006) present data that appear to falsify the thesis that folk biology is parasitic on folk psychology. On the contrary, according to other authors, the propensity to attribute human psychological properties to non-human agents appears much more pervasive than that to animals alone. Since the concept of person seems to be a primitive concept that is applied to all non-human intentional agents, like animals (Carey 1985), but also to ghosts (Boyer 1990) and gods (Barrett and Keil 1996), these non-human intentional agents are represented with human psychological properties, including intentional, emotional and affective forms. There even appears to be a tendency to treat the computer as a conversational partner, attributing it with human psychological properties and regarding it as a much more real intentional agent than we might otherwise imagine (Moon and Nass 1996). There appears to be a fundamental level, that of personhood, on which all the other levels depends. When intentional agency appears in other domains – animal, ghost, or inanimate object – it is a result of conceptual inheritance from person.

However, how does this mind-reading function occur? There are two main conflicting theories on the subject. According to the first theory, also known as "Theory Theory", people have *folk-psychological* knowledge of what goes on in other people's minds and how that makes them act in particular situations. This kind of knowledge can be defined as a "theory" of other people's mental activity (Churchland 1981; Fodor 1987; Gopnik 1993). According to the second theory, also known as "Simulation Theory", individuals try to identify with other people's mental activities, their beliefs and aims, and therefore they can infer their consequent actions and behaviour (Heal 1986; Gordon 1986; Goldman 2006). Perner and Kühberger (2006) ask how we can decide which of these two mind-reading models is genuinely active. One possibility is the different result produced by the simulation model compared to the Theory Theory when elaborating prediction. If we examine the predicted behaviour of an individual faced with two options, the simulation model only allows one option to be analyzed at once, whereas the Theory Theory, in principle, also allows both conditions to be placed alongside. Whereas empathic simulation literally means getting into the other person's mind and elaborating the choice by examining the options one at a time and then comparing them, the theory regarding the behaviour of the other person can blend and juxtapose the two conditions.

In any case, understanding the behaviour of other humans through the attribution of desires, beliefs and intentions appears essential to the constitution of human society itself. Reading other people's minds in order to interpret their behaviour is a crucial aspect of man's adaptation to evolutionary challenges (Tomasello 1999). As will be seen later with regard to the role of testimony and argumentation (Sperber 2006), the complexity of networks and social ties in human communities makes the possibility of mind-reading, getting inside other people's minds, an essential tool to detect and track failures to co-operate and to avoid the costs of cheating. This human capacity, termed by some authors the Theory of Mind (ToM), appears to emerge very early on and can already be found at the age of 9 months when the movement of a human hand is interpreted as intentional, but not that of an artefact

(Woodward 1998). As the child learns language, he tends to follow the mother's gaze to understand what is the referent for the word, therefore attributing it the intention to refer to the denotate of the term (Baldwin 1991). Lastly, as Hirschfeld affirms (2006) a ToM milestone in the developmental age "is the capacity to grasp that other people hold beliefs that one knows to be false".

The importance of ToM to our understanding of the social world appears to be demonstrated by the social maladjustment found in autistic children who appear to lack the ability to represent others as having beliefs and desires independent of one's own (Baron-Cohen 1996). The fundamental level of folk psychology is also manifested in a form of *folk ontological holism* which is found when we attribute intentionality to social aggregates. As Hirschfeld writes (2006) "traffic jams, stampedes, riots, folie a deux (trois ou beaucoup), and other forms of 'groupthink' are aggregate phenomena that are best understood without appeal to individual persons' mental states" but ascribing to them intentions as if they had a mind of their own. According to most authors, this attribution of intentions is parasitic on folk psychology and does not constitute an independent *folk sociology*. Hirschfeld (2006) disputes both the thesis that social understanding is largely concerned with the interactions of individual persons and their mind and the thesis that only individual persons (and other complex living organisms) are genuine intentional agents. The understanding of the social dimension may also occur without understanding other persons' minds as postulated by ToM. We can understand another's behaviour by identifying the social category to which he belongs and by foreseeing the standard and stereotypical forms of behaviour resulting from this categorisation. For example, if we meet an old retired general who is queuing to buy a ticket with us, we would expect him to show a low tolerance threshold to anyone failing to respect the order of precedence. Or if we meet a priest in the street, we would expect him to show verbal or non-verbal irritability with dissolute or shameless behaviour. But, as exemplified by the case of Temple Grandin, mentioned by Hirschfeld (2006), even definite cases of autism can understand the collective behaviour of groups of agents (Sacks 1995). Grandin was an autistic scientist who specialised in understanding animal psychology and raising and treating herds of domestic animals under stress. However, she was incapable of penetrating the human mind, and therefore did not possess a ToM with which to transfer intentional and affective activities to non-human agents like pets; her "extraordinary ability comes from her capacity to 'see' the nature of animal social experience without anthropomorphising it". Some studies on autistic children presented by Hirschfeld (2006) appear to show that, even "with significant impairment in their ability to interpret the behavior of others with respect to mental states, [they] were virtually unimpaired in their ability to interpret the behavior of others in terms of the groups of which they were members". They were able to do this by utilising the social stereotypes and in this way their capacity of group reasoning were independent of the capacity for person-based reasoning about behaviour. This capacity for group-based reasoning independent of ToM person-based reasoning seems to emerge very early in human development. It is based on a number of cognitive and perceptive characteristics. Studies of geometric figures (Berry and Springer 1993; Springer et al. 1996) show that perceptual figures are crucial to intentional attributions. Specific patterns of motion invite people to attribute intentions to geometric figures without making any use of ToM. "Coordinated movement plus a version of spatial contiguity would thus seem an important determinant of perception of corporate individuality", namely the attribution of intentional individuality to groups, sets, aggregates of persons without any anthropomorphisation process. To these aspects, we can add others concerning the common characteristics that supervise the social categorisation of a group of individuals compared to others. For example, physical characteristics, like skin colour, hair colour or stature, or behavioural traits, like a sub cultural type of dress and aesthetic identity. Therefore, the attribution of intentional individuality to groups and social aggregates is unrelated to the attribution of human psychological characteristics, such as desires, beliefs and emotions.

To sum up, for Hirschfeld it is a question of recognising that together with ToM and the person as a primitive cognitive, there is another primitive cognitive represented by the social entity. Therefore, alongside folk psychology and folk biology, we must introduce a new level of lay folks reasoning, that of folk sociology.

13.7 Evolution of Social Practices to Avoid Falsity

As we have seen above, one of the evolutionary explanations of folk psychology and the capacity for mind-reading represented by ToM is the possibility of foreseeing and intercepting untruthful behaviour that pretends to co-operate. The creation of social networks and organisations and even institutions themselves appear to be fostered by the ability to avoid the social costs of cheating behaviour.

Alvin Goldman's Social Epistemology (1999) supports this veritistic aim. It identifies two goals: first, to criticise the Cartesian image of the knowledge generated by isolated thinkers with no connections; second, to launch a critical attack on those epistemological concepts of a relativistic and constructivist type that reject any truthful criterion of knowledge generation and evaluation. On the contrary, according to Goldman (1999), social practices like communication, testimony and argumentation are developed to help the individual pursue the goal of truth in the furthering of knowledge. This goal seems to be an epistemological universal.

Unfortunately, this truthful function of social procedures is not univocal, but, as Sperber affirms (2006), Goldman fails to point out that a "significant proportion of socially acquired beliefs are likely to be false beliefs and this not just as a result of the malfunctioning, but also of the proper functioning of social communication". If we analyze two means of communication, testimony and argumentation, we find that truth was not the evolutionary factor that led to the stabilisation of communications. It is the causing of desirable effects on the audience that makes communication advantageous to the communicator. From this point of view "Communication produces a certain amount of misinformation in the performance of its function, more specifically, in the performance of those aspects of its function that are beneficial to the communicator". Also when analyzed using game theory, there is no stable solution to the game between a true or false communicator and the listener who has or does not have faith in what the communicator says. Even if, in theory, the condition of the truthfulness of the communicator and the faithfulness of the listener is convenient to both, there is no stable solution to the game. Rather, it is through argumentation that evolution has developed ways of defending itself against the risk of falsehood. Contrary to animals, humans do not just communicate information, they also argue it. According to Sperber (2006) argumentation has neither the general function of providing the reasons for accepting a given argument nor that, affirmed by evolutionary psychology, of "domain- and task-specific inferential mechanisms corresponding to problems and opportunities met in the environment in which a species has evolved".

Instead, in Sperber's view, "there are evolutionary reasons to expect a kind of seemingly general reasoning mechanism in humans, but one that is in fact, specialised for processing communicated or to be communicated information" (Sperber 2000). This mechanism does not seem to be linked to individual cognitive activity but instead is functional to communicative activity. Communicating does not just mean testimony, as in the case of animals, but trying to cite reasons and arguments to support your own thesis. In this sense, the listener has developed various instruments to gauge the trust of the speaker. As Sperber points out (2006), the two instruments – the capacity to distinguish between behavioural signs of sincerity or insincerity and trust in relation to benevolence to the speaker – are not specifically applicable to an assessment of the argument. Above all, "coherence checking", namely focusing on the internal and external coherence of the message and what you believe in, serves as a marker for possible lies passed on by the communicator.

To be more persuasive, in their cultural evolution humans have developed a form of argument that uses various logical terms like "if", "and" "or", and words like "therefore", "but" and so on. This explains, for example, as Nisbett and Masuda affirm (2006), the development of rhetoric and logic in ancient Greeks compared to the lack of this development in China. This development stemmed from the need of the Greeks, a society of merchants and individuals, to persuade their partners through the discussions and confrontations that occurred for commercial, political, religious and later philosophical reasons. Whereas the contemporary inhabitants of China, as part of an organic society whose purpose was above all harmony and social balance, did not feel the need to affirm their reasons and tended to prefer the Middle way logic in discussions and comparisons.

The communicator develops the argumentative capacity to persuade, even if he does not always succeed; the listener develops coherence checking to assess the reliability of the communicator's arguments, even if he is often wrong. The communicator develops the capacity to be considered honest and reliable in testimony, even if he isn't; the listener develops fallible psychological instruments to identify whether the communicator is lying. In evolution, truth and rationality, falsehood and irrationality blend and the evolution of the social practice of communication are less univocally marked by the truthful ideal of what Goldman thinks.

13.8 Universal and Local Cognitive Styles and Their Normative Consequences

From the experiment described by Atran et al. (2006) it emerges that genetically inherited cognitive universals, represented by "universal taxonomic structures, centred on essence-based generic species", are likely to be present. These innate concepts could have been selected at an evolutionary level in order to represent important and recurrent aspects of nature.

These data seem to support the image of a human being genetically endowed with concepts and universal principles of inference. It is likely that there are not fixed irreversible cultural differences in cognition that stem from relative cultural different and fixed metaphysical and epistemological theories about the world. On the contrary, the cognitive abilities develop from universal type inferential principles that are genetically inherited. They can follow different paths of development, depending on different cultural contexts. However, their diversity is reversible and the cognitive styles are dependent on knowledge, expertise and on pragmatic needs. These factors are able to reduce and, in some cases, to neutralise the cultural diversity of the cognitive abilities.

This conclusion is well known in cognitive anthropology. Education can quite easily shape cognitive attitudes making them trans-culturally similar. And the problem-solving ability is much stronger in real world scenarios linked to particular pragmatic contexts and practical needs than it is in abstract tasks. The need for practical problem-solving can trigger cognitive abilities that were hidden in abstract and uninteresting tasks (Boudon and Viale 2000). Moreover, as we have seen before (Macchi and Bagassi 2006), the pragmatic dimension of the discourse involved in solving the problems of the experiments seem to strongly influence the answers. For example, many biases seem to be caused by the structure of the text than by a natural or cultural propensity to errors.

Also the analysis reported earlier on the normative aspects of probabilistic reasoning in children (see Viale and Osherson 2006) appears consistent with these remarks. By adopting a different normative principle of inductive judgement as the Probability Premise Principle – which seems to fit with the Bayesian theory of probability – it was seen that children from two different cultures, for example American and Chinese-Taiwanese, do not show any significant differences in their replies which conform to the normative standards of PPP. Before environmental differences start to influence cognitive styles, children appear to show the same inductive style, irrespective of latitude and longitude.

Even Nisbett (2003) acknowledges that reversibility exists in the cognitive style of East Asians and Americans. Chinese people who have lived for a few years in America tend to adopt American cognitive styles and vice versa. In the experiments, adequate priming can significantly reduce cultural inclinations in cognitive styles. In tests of causal attribution carried out by the developmental psychologist Miller (1984, quoted in Nisbett 2003), similar behaviour can be seen between Hindu East Indian children and American children. Not until the adolescence did Indian and Americans begin to diverge in causal attribution. Instead, when adult, Indians tend to explain behaviour in term of contextual factors while Americans reason in terms of individual dispositions.

If, as seems to be shown by Viale and Osherson (2006), Lo et al. (2002), Lopez et al. (1997), and Atran et al. (2006), there do not appear to be differences in the cognitive style concerning some forms of inductive reasoning between people from different cultures, this has an important consequence for the normative justification of belief formation and revision.

The presence or otherwise of cultural differences in the cognitive style of reasoning and decision-making is, according to Weinberg et al. (2006), a fundamental epistemological fact when understanding which epistemological strategy to adopt in justifying knowledge. Why? One of the epistemological theories most in vogue over the past few years is the *internalist* theory. It affirms that the sole source of normative legitimation for our beliefs is internal, inside us. With a proper process of self-exploration we can discover the correct epistemic norms for belief formation and revision. By analogy with Romanticism in literature, Weinberg, Nichols, and Stich call this approach Epistemic Romanticism (2006). In fact, as in the case of Romanticism, only by exploring within ourselves can we make the real essence of our selves emerge, and also in Epistemic Romanticism we are the normative source of the epistemic principles. But in what way? One of the most debated solutions is that which identifies epistemic intuitions as the main cause, namely the spontaneous judgement about the epistemic properties of some cases. There are various examples of Intuition Driven Romanticism (IDR). The best known is the reflective equilibrium strategy of Goodman (1965) in which "a [normative] rule is amended if it yields an inference we are [intuitively] unwilling to accept [and] an inference is rejected if it violates a [normative] rule we are [intuitively] unwilling to amend".

The balance may occur in various forms. It may be "narrow" if we restrict the rules and inferences, for example, only to those of philosophical interest. It may be "expert" if we restrict the creation of a reflexive balance to the category of professionals of knowledge – the epistemologists, for example. Many researchers, including Laudan (1984) and Goldman (1986), support Intuition Driven Romanticism. Rules of justification are required to justify one's own beliefs. These rules will specify permissible ways in which cognitive agents may go about the business of forming and revising their beliefs. How can we decide that a rule is correct? By appealing to a higher level, "a criterion of rightness". But how can we decide what this criterion is? Goldman affirms that the correct criterion of rightness is the one that comports with the conception that is "embraced by everyday thought and language" (Goldman 1986, p. 58).

"A criterion is supported to the extent that implied judgements accord with such intuitions and weakened to the extent that they do not" (Goldman 1986, p. 66).

Now, the validity of IDR, in its various versions, is based on a condition: that universal intuitions exist which can be used to determine universal norms for the formation and revision of beliefs. If, on the contrary, for the same type of events and cases the intuitions were different in relation to cultural, ethnic and social contexts, then it would not be possible not to admit some form of epistemic relativism.

This would reveal the impossibility of IDR strategies to generate a normative theory of knowledge.

We saw earlier that Nisbett and Masuda (2006) appear to show that a difference exists between the cognitive styles of Westerners and Far Easterners. However, Viale and Osherson (2006) and Atran et al. (2006) put forward data and arguments that seem to weaken the cognitive relativism outlined by Nisbett and Masuda's thesis. Weinberg et al. (2006) start from Nisbett's results and from what might be termed the moral relativism of Haidt et al. (1993) to verify empirically whether IDR is false and whether we are faced with a situation of epistemic relativism. To do this, they undertake a series of tests involving persons from different cultural, ethnic and social extractions. They wanted their intuition probes – the cases that they ask subjects to judge – to be similar to cases that have actually been used in the recent literature in epistemology.

For example, a category of examples that was widely used in epistemology was the "Gettier cases" (Gettier 1963) "in which a person has good (though, as it happens, false, or only accidentally true, or in some other way warrant-deprived) evidence for a belief which is true".

As appears to emerge from Nisbett and Masuda (2006) and Norenzayan (2006) the East Asians have a tendency to make categorical judgements on the basis of similarity. Instead, Westerners are more inclined to focus on causes when they have to classify things. The intuition probe that was used to explore cultural differences on Gettier cases was the following:

> Bob has a friend, Jill, who has driven a Buick for many years. Bob therefore thinks that Jill drives an American car. He is not aware, however, that her Buick has recently been stolen, and he is also not aware that Jill has replaced it with a Pontiac, which is a different kind of American car. Does Bob really know that Jill drives an American car, or does he only believe it?
>
> REALLY KNOWS ONLY BELIEVES
>
> The striking finding in this case is that a large majority of Ws give the standard answer in the philosophical literature, viz. 'Only Believes'. But amongst EAs this pattern is actually *reversed*! A majority of EAs say that Bob really knows.

The results from this and the other intuition probes seem to prove that East Asians and Westerners are sensitive to different features of the situation, different epistemic vectors as Weinberg, Nichols, and Stich call them (2006). East Asians are much sensitive to communitarian, contextual factors, while Westerners respond to more individualistic, dispositional ones. The conclusion is that since IDR relies upon epistemic intuitions that are not universal but local to one's own cultural and socio-economic group, it is not able to lead to genuine normative conclusion.

13.9 Conclusion: Outside the Relativist Cages

The conclusion put forward by Weinberg et al. (2006) appears to reinforce the thesis of epistemological relativism. If it is not possible to find an inner and universal foundation for normative principles and if we are prisoners within our local contexts, how can we not give in to relativism? However, are we really certain that no universal principle exists on which we can base the justification for our knowledge of the world?

Earlier we saw that while cultural difference do exist in cognitive styles, these are not irreversible and tend to narrow when they involve pragmatic and existential problems rather than abstract and artificial ones. The greater the adaptive meaning of a problem is, the greater the uniformity of the reply adopted. It seems likely that our conceptual cages, used in cultural learning and socialisation processes, can be questioned in relation to different social and adaptive contexts.

Irrespective of the culture to which we belong, at birth we all receive the same innate endowment of principles of reasoning. The cultural differences that subsequently emerge in individuals are mainly in response to metaphysical and ontological theories and schemes for representing and interpreting the world (Gopnik and Meltzoff 1997; Nisbett and Masuda 2006). Both the metaphysical theories that dominate our cognitive styles and the physical theories on the empirical nature of the world can be altered in the light of new cultural contexts and new empirical evidence. The relative plasticity of cognitive abilities in different cultures reflects the dynamics of theory change in the "little scientist" hypothesis. Human cognitive abilities depend on a person's theories about the world. But these theories are not fixed, irreversibly, by his or her local socio-cultural condition. They can be changed in relation to pragmatic feedback, empirical evidence and new information derived from the environment. The relative theory change is driven by methodological norms that are effective during childhood (and we meet it again, in a similar fashion, inside the scientific community). The methodological norms of theory change appear, to a large extent, universal.

It is true that humans often fall into errors of deduction, statistical assessment, causal attribution, inductive support, and so on. These errors both in scientific enterprise and in everyday life seem not to have a great effect on the growth of knowledge and on economic and social development. The reason for the scarce effect of biases, errors and irrational reasoning might rely solely on the meta-inferential norms of theory change. Children, scientists, adults make mistakes and generate false theories or empirical generalisations about the world; they produce beliefs that do not correspond to reality. However, at the same time, they are able to accept information, empirical evidence or pragmatic feedback from the world about the reliability, legitimacy and pragmatic utility of their hypotheses. If the theory does not work, soon or later it will be changed and another theory will be generated. Therefore, the synchronic consequences of errors stemming from irrational reasoning are diachronically neutralised by the application of the norms of theory change.

Weinberg et al. (2006) are right when they write that any epistemological internalist justification of knowledge has to cope with the cultural diversity of thinking. Boudon (1995) tackled the same problem in a different manner. If we wish to avoid both the dangers of cultural relativism and of ethnocentrism, we should be able to find trans-cultural and trans-contextual reasons for beliefs and actions. If every reason that justifies a belief or an action is relative to a given local socio-cultural context and cannot be judged by others living in different contexts, then rationality will shatter into a dispersed multitude of different and incommensurable reasons. If the reasons are relative to local socio-cultural contexts but they can be judged by the inhabitants of other ethnic niches, then we can speak of transcultural reasons. An example, taken from Boudon (1995), may help to explain this point. The Papago Indios of Arizona explain any social and natural events by the will of a god living on the top of Boboquivari mountain. The place is visible to anyone in the tribe. Why does nobody see the god of the mountain? The reason is because the ants inform him when humans are coming and he hides himself. Can we accept their reasons? Obviously, according to our beliefs, knowledge and theories of the world, their reasons seem to us completely unacceptable. But if we try to represent the theories and beliefs of the Indios, which function as the premises of their reasons, then we can justify their reasons according their theories of the world. It might be thought reasonable that they propose the ant hypothesis to justify the impossibility of seeing the god of the mountain. If this is the interpretation of the Indios' reasons, then what are the differences between this position and the relativistic one? The same exercise used in relation to the Indios' reasons can be replicated for a multitude of other ethnic niches.

The crucial point that distinguishes a normative position from a relativistic one relies, in my opinion, on using the methodology of theory change (Viale 2001b, p. 233). As a thought experiment, think of a variation of the previous story. The same person that told us the story of the god of the mountain informs us that the Indios believing in the ant story are professional scientists and engineers working at the nearby nuclear power station. At this point, it is likely that our chances of justifying the believers' reasoning would greatly decrease. And the justification would become almost null if, talking with them, we discovered that they share with us all our metaphysical and epistemological principles about the world. In this case, their reasons for believing the ant theory would become very unsound. A likely hypothesis is that the reason for our judgement of their irrationality relies on the following principle (that is an application of the methodology of theory change characteristic of the "little scientist" hypothesis): *A given theory is maintained if a better alternative theory is not available. A theory is better when it has more empirical content and is able to solve the problems of the old one plus some others. When one has a better theory he should use it instead of the previous one.*

Faced with a new and better theory, its negative utilisation can present different situations (Viale 2001b, p. 234). The subject may not accept the new theory that increases his ability to explain the empirical phenomena. The maintenance of the old theory may rely on traditional habits, emotional factors, theoretical support, and so on. He can accept the new theory and put it in his knowledge base. But at the same time he can continue to use the old one to generate his beliefs about the world. If the two theories are inconsistent, his cognitive behaviour relies on an inconsistent set of beliefs. If the two theories are consistent, but the old one is implied by the new one, his cognitive behaviour relies on a theory that has less empirical content or problem-solving ability. He acquires the new theory and puts it into his knowledge base, but his previous beliefs continue to be triggered in an automatic and reflex way. They are not based on conscious reasons. They are a kind of traces of the old theory and they do not stem from any intentional act of reasoning.

When the traditional Indios had only beliefs and knowledge stemming from their tradition, their belief in the ant theory might be judged to be reasonable because no better alternative theories were available. But when "nuclear" Indios have at their disposal alternative hypotheses to explain the behaviour of the god and these hypotheses are able to explain other aspects of the world, we can suppose that their belief in the ant theory might be judged as rationally unjustified.

As in the case of the Arizona Indios, also in relation to the diversity principle analyzed by Atran et al. (2006) we can say that the knowledge and beliefs of the taxonomists would not justify their preference for an argument with more homogeneous premises that does not satisfy the diversity principle. Using the same argument, we might say that, hypothetically, the Itzajs, with an education on abstract taxonomy about mammals, ceteris paribus, would not be justified in still relying on ecology-based reasoning and not satisfying the diversity principle.

On the basis of the previous arguments, we can hold the following procedural normative principle:

> There is reason to justify a belief of a subject that is the effect of given theories on the world when the subject has no knowledge of alternative theories that are better for their empirical content and problem-solving ability.

It might be objected that there is no reason to try to establish normative criteria for the rational justification of beliefs. The world will go on without the need for any general normative constraint. In reality, there are many fields of human life where implicit normative criteria are applied. Education and science are important examples. Often the criteria are ad hoc and lack transparency. Other times, they rely on a priori canons of rationality that find their justification in some kind of narrow social consensus by some elite set of experts. Consequently, it may be worthwhile trying to develop some general norms of epistemological justification that stem from our best real procedures of knowledge acquisition – i.e. science and developmental age. The positive features of the proposed epistemological procedural principle may be the fulfilment of the following two conditions (Viale 2001b, p. 235).

It seems to meet our intuition about the reasons for accepting a belief given the actual knowledge of the subject.

It seems to be coherent with the "internalist epistemology" programme: extrapolating the norms of justification from the internal cognitive procedures of theory generation and application.

In conclusion, the cultural variability of inferential styles and the errors and biases of human reasoning and decision-making appear to outline an epistemological picture characterised by relativism and irrationality. This picture is countered by a number of normative factors, following the internalist theory and linked to the "little scientist" hypothesis: the universal endowment of inferential principles that are both innate and adaptive in the sense of evolutionary psychology; the presence from birth of a method of theory and conceptual change based on empirical falsification, pragmatic consequences and problem-solving which also appears to be explained, in evolutionary terms, by its capacity to promote successful environmental adaptation.

These innate principles of reasoning and the method of theory change are universal and characterise man's shared capacity, irrespective of any cultural context. They allow the man to create hypotheses, to learn from mistakes and to correct his theories in order to make them empirically and pragmatically successful.

Cognitive Diversity in Western and Eastern Thinking 14

...It is precisely because the Chinese mind is so rational that it refuses to become rationalistic and ...to separate form from content.
Shun-Hsien Liu (1974)
To argue with logical consistency...may not only be resented but also be regarded as immature.
Noburo Nagashima (1973)

14.1 Language, Pragmatics and Representation of Knowledge

The transmission of knowledge at a written or verbal level relies on various non-intentional factors. These factors, which constitute the pragmatics of the communication and understanding of knowledge, are not universal but vary with education, the cultural context, and the level and type of cultural preparation and professional expertise.

In a linguistic relationship between two individuals, the person speaking usually tends to adopt elliptical expressions that do not completely represent what he intends to communicate. He does this because he envisages that the person receiving the message will fill in the empty spaces, adding the missing information. The recipient generates "conversational implicatures" (Grice 1989) that give meaning to the information received.

The communicator will obviously calibrate his message and the quantity of missing information on the basis of his expectations regarding the pragmatic-linguistic agreement of the receiver. If he thinks that the receiver belongs to his own pragmatic-linguistic community, he will expect that certain information gaps will be filled according to models of conversational implicature shared by the members of the group. This expected automatism will induce him to use elliptical

This chapter is a modified version of Viale, R. (2008). Diversità culturale e cognizione. In R. Caterina (a cura di) (ed.), *I fondamenti cognitivi del diritto*. Pearson Paravia Bruno Mondadori SpA.

R. Viale, *Methodological Cognitivism*,
DOI 10.1007/978-3-642-24743-9_14, © Springer-Verlag Berlin Heidelberg 2012

forms without worrying about the completeness of the information. If, on the contrary, he thinks that the receiver is not part of his own community, then he will try to modulate the information in proportion to the supposed distance from the conversational implicature models he uses. It is clear that there is a *continuum* of concentric circles of pragmatic-linguistic micro-communities. Take, for example, the elliptical language used within a family, or that used by a group of friends, or in a working environment, etc. It is clear that the further one goes from the focal point represented by the individual speaking (whose linguistic-pragmatic context is linked to cultural, professional, ethnic and psychological factors), the more the message must be calibrated when only a limited amount of information about the receiver is available.

There is a sort of "paradox of inversion of concentric circles", similar to the one introduced by David Hume for empathy and loyalty (1911, vol. II, p. 437). The farther we go from our nuclear into kinship, community, town, state, nation and so on, the more loyalty and empathy (or affection, as the stoics described it) or, in our case, the pragmatic-linguistic harmony of the individual in relation to other people will decrease.

This effort to fine tune the message tries to intercept the largest possible number of crucial factors that determine the pragmatic-linguistic behaviour of the receiver. The farther one travels from the focal point, the greater the lack of information available to complete the message. Take the extreme case of a receiver affected by psychopathological schizophrenic disorders. In this case, unless he is the psychiatrist treating him, the speaker does not have any information about the pragmatic-linguistic models he uses to receive and interpret the message. In these conditions, our defensive strategy is to try to provide exhaustive, detailed and simplified information, well aware that this does not guarantee the formation of conversational implicatures, which are as unpredictable as they are original and bizarre, on the part of the psychotic patient. Without going to these extremes, we only have to imagine the communication problems that arise between people of different cultures and languages. This is not due entirely to the obvious case of the inaccurate use of the terms of a foreign language or to limited knowledge of idiomatic expressions and the contexts in which a particular word is used to obtain a desired meaning.

There is also a more structural difficulty that seems to relate precisely to the organisation of knowledge and to inferential activities. It seems evident, in general terms, that a language can influence the organisation of knowledge in different ways. The type of alphabet can stimulate different ways of representing knowledge. For example, it seems that Chinese, that most ideogrammic of languages, tends to generate a representation based more on images, while Indo-European languages seem to generate comparatively more linguistic propositions. Even the more or less intense use of nouns or verbs influences the representation of knowledge. A language that contains more nouns will tend towards an organisation based on conceptual categories and focused on objects, while one with a greater density of verbs will focus more on relational aspects.

Research carried out in recent years into the diversity of thought in the Far East and in the West has revealed that differences in the way language is organised in the two cultural areas is at the origin of the different organisation of knowledge. As we will see later in detail, Asians – particularly Chinese, Korean and Japanese – show less interest than Westerners – particularly Anglo-Americans – in creating abstract categories of objects, learning new categories by applying rules to properties and using categories in inductive activities (Nisbett 2003, p. 248). On the other hand, they are more interested in highlighting relationships and interactions than Westerners are.

How can these differences be explained on a linguistic basis? Categories are denoted by nouns (which refer to groups of objects that share the same properties) and relations by verbs (which usually denote an action that connects two objects). So we can presume that the languages that give more importance to nouns will be the ones in which the representation of knowledge is based more on conceptual categorisations of objects and phenomena. Generally speaking, a noun denoting an object or a phenomenon is introduced into a language after the crucial variables that characterise its field of application have been defined. This can be explicit – for example when technical terms are introduced, like computer or cell phone – or implicit, when a noun enters linguistic practice, for example 'Made in Italy' (the Italian products linked to Italian Style of Life and Design) or hooligan. In both cases, the end result is achieved by a process of conceptual categorisation. On the other hand, languages that attribute more importance to verbs reflect an organisation of knowledge that is based less on categorisation and on an ontology of discreet, definite objects, and more on functional, relational and contextual aspects and on a continuous relationship between objects.

When we refer to the importance of nouns or verbs, it is not intended as a judgement based only on quantitative factors, for example the higher number of nouns present in a language, but also on qualitative factors, for example the position of nouns and verbs in a sentence. In Chinese, Japanese and Korean, verbs are placed primarily at the beginning and end of a sentence. These positions are more important and evident than others, because they act as stimuli to attention mechanisms. In European languages on the other hand, and English in particular, verbs are hidden in the middle of the sentence and this decreases their cognitive salience.

The greater importance of nouns in English than in Asian languages is reflected in children's education, as the developmental psychologists Anne Fernald and Hiromi Morikawa pointed out in 1993. Western parents are obsessed by nouns and spend much more time than East Asian parents showing objects to children and teaching them to pronounce and remember their names. East Asian mothers, on the other hand, are more prone to teach them social standards and rules, and the functions of the objects.

As Nisbett wrote (2003, p. 150), we might hear the following conversation between an American mother and her son about a model car:

> That's a car. See the car? Do you like it? It's got nice wheels.

A Japanese mother, on the other hand, would speak differently to her child:

> Here! It's a vroom vroom. I give it to you. Now give this to me. Yes! Thank you.

The parents' different educational style is reflected in an element highlighted by Gopnik and Choi (1990): East Asian children learn to categorise objects later than Western children. This delay can be explained by the limited training in categorisation that East Asian parents give their children. A number of studies (Smith et al. 2002) seem to confirm that children, taught to create categories of objects on the basis of a number of characteristics like the typical shape of a cup, show a greater ability to use the names of new objects.

As Nisbett observed (2003, pp. 157–158), Indo-European languages' preoccupation with and focus on nouns and categories is underlined by another typical feature of Anglo-Saxon languages and, to a lesser extent, even Latin languages: the prominence of the subject. A sentence in English is always polarised on a subject that represents an object or an event. Even phrases that describe situations like a snow fall or rain begin with a subject: "It is snowing". The opposite is true of Far Eastern languages. Instead of being subject-prominent, they are oriented towards the issue and the context. In general, sentences in Japanese, Chinese and Korean have a space at the beginning to introduce the topic or context that gives meaning to the rest of the sentence. This verbal behaviour has been confirmed in numerous studies. In an experiment conducted by Masuda and Nisbett (2001), Americans and Japanese were shown underwater scenes including fish and aquatic plants. The Americans began with the description of an object ("There was a large fish, maybe a trout, that was moving to the left"), whereas the Japanese started with the context ("It looked like a pond"). For a Westerner, it is the Self that acts, whereas for the East Asian what acts is something that is undertaken in agreement with others or that is "the consequence of an individual action in a field of forces" (Nisbett 2003, p. 158).

This is clearly reflected in the language. The grammar of Western languages is "agentive" in the sense that it highlights the role of the subject in determining the action. East Asian languages on the other hand focus on the context. For example, there are different words for "I" in Japanese that reflect different types of relationships with other people. As Nisbett noted (2003, p. 158) there is one "I" in relation to my colleague, another "I" in relation to my wife, etc.. The subject expressed by the word "I" depends on the context of environmental interaction.

Is the effect of language on the representation and therefore the communication of knowledge so strong and profound? What is said above seems to indicate that language plays a profound role in determining the communication of knowledge. Some linguistic anthropologists (Whorf 1956) claim that it is language itself that determines the metaphysics with which we convey and structure our cognitive information. Different languages generate distinct metaphysics. It is language that determines the structure of the world, the boundaries between objects that our thought represents. Every language is a different grid that structures the cognitive activity of its speakers in order to make their universe of meanings occasionally mutually incommensurable (Boudon and Viale 2000).

This linguistic reductionism seems to be exaggerated. On the contrary, there are studies that reveal an effect of culture on thought that is independent of language (for example, see Ji et al. 2002). We do not intend to question the effect of language in the structuring of knowledge. But its effect is rather that of accentuating the focalisation and stabilisation of a different propensity to relations, in the case of East Asians, or to objects and categories in the case of Westerners, which is taught and learned during parental education processes. It is true that different languages are associated with different systems of representation. Chinese, Japanese and Korean languages are highly contextual and words have multiple meanings, given by the context of the phrase. The education of East Asian children, however, aims to highlight the relations and the context for reasons that are upstream and have a historical original (as we will see) in East Asian culture. We could say that language reflects thought and at the same time influences its structure in a recursive process of dynamic and diachronic exchange and interchange between the two dimensions. In English, the meaning of words is less tied to the context (although various polysemic terms do exist). At the same time, however, it is education itself that seems to influence the propensity to use words for objects, isolated from the context. As Shirley Brice Heath pointed out (1982), middle-class American parents try to accustom their children to decontextualise words as much as possible. They try to teach the meaning of terms independent of the context in which the denoted object tends to position itself. For example, instead of teaching the word dog, describing the relations or the context in which the dog acts – kennel, bone, cat, master – they concentrate on its independent and "structural" characteristics, such as four paws, barking, tail, etc., which are valid in all contexts. The above is also valid for Anglo-Saxon languages. The historical reasons for the polarisation on categories and objects, independent of the context, in the development of Western thought, is reflected in and influences changes in language in a recursive process of dynamic retroaction between the two dimensions.

Language seems to be a powerful component in determining the variety of the structure of thought, while on the other hand the structure of language tends to correspond to the representation of knowledge based on categories and objects. This different cognitive structure, which is present in the individual mind, conveys forms of knowledge that have different levels of understanding in people who belong to different linguistic communities. The greater the conceptual difference expressed by the language, the greater the diversity of the cognitive content and the smaller the capacity of the person receiving the message to understand and represent the knowledge.

14.2 Cultural Differences in Logical Reasoning

However, the difficulty of transmitting knowledge is not determined only by language. Together with language there are cultural factors that play an obvious role in generating knowledge and the standards for its justification and acceptability. Different styles of generating and justifying knowledge determine different propensities to acknowledge it, accept it and understand it.

In recent years, Richard Nisbett and a group of psychologists and cognitive anthropologists working with him (Nisbett et al. 2001; Nisbett and Masuda 2006;

Nisbett 2003) have carried out a systematic study of the cultural differences in attention, perception and reasoning processes between Westerners and Asians. Their results are based on a large number of cognitive tests that compare the way in which Koreans, Chinese and Japanese on one hand, and North Americans on the other, tackle reasoning and decision problems. The Asians and the Americans respond in qualitatively different ways to the same type of stimulus conveyed in different types of tests.

The first consideration to make regards logical reasoning. Chinese tradition is somewhat lacking in contributions to logic. In the fifth century BC, the Chinese philosopher Mo Tzu tried to develop a study of a number of important principles of logic like the idea of necessary and sufficient conditions, the principle of non-contradiction and the law of the excluded middle. However he never formalised his system and after him logical thought in China vanished. India had a strong logical tradition, but because of the mistakes and imprecise interpretation they contained, the Chinese translations of the texts had no impact on Chinese culture. As a consequence, China did not have a tradition of logical thought (for example it never developed the principle of non-contradiction) and this also influenced the poor development of geometry, because its demonstrations are based on formal logic and in particular on the principle of contradiction. However, this cultural deficiency cannot explain the peculiar Asian style of logical reasoning in full. As we will see later, there are reasons linked to background knowledge that can motivate it.

A number of studies carried out in recent years have revealed that:

(a) The Chinese seem more comfortable with contradictions than Westerners are. In tests that proposed conflicting assertions, East Asians tended to accept a much higher number of them than Westerners did. A test was carried out presenting proverbs that contained contradictions. In this case too, the Chinese showed a clear preference for the proverbs that contained inconsistencies. This inclination to accept contradictions is a long way from the Western style which, on the contrary, sets out to avoid them. Unlike bivalent Western logic, East Asians seem to be guided by a "middle way logic". Between two contradictory values, they do not try to find the true one and exclude the false one, but to highlight intermediate values, or to value both horns of the dilemma. We can understand that this logical attitude has important implications for various aspects of cognitive and social life: seeking intermediate solutions in bargaining; in the choice of a product they will focus less on the presence or absence of specific attributes; when evaluating a scientific or everyday hypothesis, they will be less concerned by inconsistencies and falsification; in discussion and argument they will not tend to use logical instruments like *reductio ad absurdum* or the simple search for contradiction; in legal reasoning rhetorical arguments will be stronger than syllogistic arguments, and so on.

The propensity to accept contradictions more easily is also revealed in the recurrence of a mistake that Westerners also display: that of judging as acceptable conclusions that are incorrect from a deductive viewpoint, but preferable from an emotional viewpoint.

(b) East Asians tend to classify objects and events on the basis of family relations and resemblances, while Americans tend to classify them on the basis of categories based on rules. In an experiment, Liang-Hwang Chiu (1972) showed a group of Chinese and American children three types of pictures, a cow, a hen and some grass and asked them to indicate which pair of objects could go together. The American children chose the cow and the hen, while the Chinese children put the cow and the grass in the same group. The former justified their choice by saying that "both are animals", while the latter motivated their choice by the fact that "the cow eats the grass". Similar experiments were carried out among the adults with other triplets, with the same results. It emerges clearly from these and other studies, that the Chinese are guided by factors linked to the relationship between the objects (the grass is eaten by the cow), while the Westerners' reasoning mainly seems to follow rules that define the category they belong to (cow and hen are part of the animal world). In this regard there is extensive literature about "category-based induction" in children (Viale and Osherson 2006) and in adults (Viale and Osherson 2000), which shows that it is more difficult for East Asians, particularly Koreans and Vietnamese, than it is for Americans and Europeans, to generate inclusive categories, and that the inductive justification of conclusions on the basis of premises, tends to follow criteria of family resemblance and functional or spatial relations.

For example, between topics (1) and (2), Koreans and Vietnamese tend to prefer topic (1) as the most convincing at an inductive level, because they are less able than the Americans to generate the inclusive category MAMMALS from the category RABBITS present in the conclusion. This leads them not to estimate that more homogeneous categories like LIONS and TIGERS generate a weaker semantic cover than LIONS and GIRAFFES (Viale and Osherson 2006).

(1) Lions have an ulnar artery
Tigers have an ulnar artery
Rabbits have an ulnar artery

(2) Lions have an alnar artery
Giraffes have an ulnar artery
Rabbits have an ulnar artery

The surprising result (Viale and Osherson 2000) is that the application of this principle, known as the "diversity principle", did not change the Vietnamese' replies when the conclusion was

(3) Mammals have an ulnar artery

14.3 Cultural Differences in Causal Reasoning

(a) Westerners have a tendency to give causal explanations of phenomena, based on the properties of the object and, in the case of human action, on internal dispositions. East Asians, on the other hand, are not obsessed with providing causal explanations and when they are, give greater significance to contextual factors and to the causal field between objects, and less to the properties of the individual object and, in the case of human action, to dispositional factors. One example among many is the one analysed by Morris and Peng (1994). It regards a murder that took place at the University of Iowa in 1991. After losing an award competition for a university position and failing in his appeal against the decision, a Chinese student returned to his department and killed the consultant who had handled his appeal, several fellow students and finally himself. Morris and Peng, who were studying at the University of Michigan at the time, analysed the interpretations given by the American press, in particular the New York Times, and by the Chinese press, in particular the World Journal, to the reasons for this murder. While the American press concentrated on the individual dispositional factors ("bad-tempered", "propensity to use weapons", "incapable of facing up to competition and challenges", etc.), the Chinese focused on the situational aspects ("isolated from the Chinese community", "rivalry with the murdered students", "ease of finding weapons in the United States"). We could motivate this different polarity between individual and contextual attributions by a defensive and justificationist attitude of the Chinese press toward one of their compatriots. However, this doubting hypothesis is falsified by many other cases in which the murderer was American but the American and Chinese press maintained a similar approach.

In the past, a number of psychologists had already noted the tendency on the part of individuals to attribute other peoples' actions to personal inclinations and not to external influences. This error was defined by Lee Ross (1977) as a "*fundamental attribution error*". An experiment conducted by Edward E. Jones and Victor A. Harris (1967) first drew attention to this phenomenon. A group of people was involved in a situation in which one of them was taught to sustain a particular political theory with his companions, for example, to support Castro's regime in Cuba. Subsequently the trained subject presented the arguments in favour of Castro and his political system to his companions. Amazingly, most of the students questioned about the reasons for their colleague's position, although they were aware of their origin, attributed them to genuine convictions and not to the conditioning undertaken to prepare for the test. There was no difference in the errors of attribution made by Americans and East Asians in this test. However, the replies of the East Asians and Americans changed drastically when the subjects identified empathetically with the situation of the target subject. For example, Choi and Nisbett (1998) asked participants in the test to first write an essay about a particular topic, for example to support the liberalisation of marijuana, taking a definite position and using a combination of four topics. With this new angle to the test, the responses of the East Asians also changed in relation to those of the Americans. While the latter were blocked in their error of attribution, the former were able to attribute the positions of the target subject to the conditioning carried out previously.

(b) The differences in causal reasoning between East Asians and Westerners seem to have characteristics that go beyond the preferences between a causal field or a causal subject. This is revealed, for example, in the way History is taught in

American and Japanese schools. Masato Watanabe (1998) has studied exactly how historical events are explained in American and Japanese schools. The style of Japanese teachers could be defined as situational empathy. They try to stimulate students to consider the context in which a given historical action took place, and to identify the reasons that caused a particular historical figure to behave in a particular way (even in the case of an enemy of Japan). They are basically interested in explaining "how" a certain event has taken place rather than "why". On the other hand, when history is taught in American schools, instead of starting from the context of the factors that have produced a historical fact, teachers start from the event itself (the French Revolution took place in 1789) and work backwards, introducing explanatory causes. They try to reconstruct the causal chain that generated it, starting from the final effect. The questions that students and teachers ask themselves are linked to "why" rather than "how". As we will see later, this style of causal reasoning, which also underpins the explanation of natural sciences, seems, according to Nisbett (2003), to have its roots in the different original historical-social conditions which have characterised the West, starting from the Greek civilisation, and the East, starting from the ancient Chinese civilisation. In any case, this tendency to create causal chains induces Westerners to consider far fewer factors than East Asians. As we see in science, the attempt is to abstract only the relevant causes and to overlook the rest.

(c) A study undertaken by Choi et al. (2000) found that while the Koreans identified as irrelevant just 1/3 of the information given to explain the murder by the physics student described earlier, the Americans found that more than half of the information was not significant. This type of propensity, which differs from causal reasoning, may help to explain a recognised error of judgement known as "hindsight bias". When we have to assess the inevitability or predictability of historical events, like the Second World War or the Korean War, we tend to overestimate the probability of their happening compared to our ability to predict the same phenomenon before we knew the outcome. This was highlighted by Fischhoff (1975) in a series of tests that compared probability estimates of its outcome before a historical event and subsequent evaluations.

"It was inevitable that Hitler would lose to the Allies" or "If I had all the information, I would have forecast that the Cuban missile crisis would end with Khrushchev backtracking". These are some frequent opinions that we hear in an analysis of historical events. Choi and Nisbett (2000) analysed the differences between Westerners and Asians in committing "hindsight bias". Their hypothesis was that differences in causal reasoning between the two cultures would generate differences in that context. Westerners, who are more prone to explicitly abstracting causal links of ordinary historical events, should have been less prone to make facile forecasts. In fact, definite and limited causal antecedents can only generate a few final outcomes. East Asians, on the other hand, who use less explicit models of causal reasoning that consider a much larger number of factors as potential causes, are more likely to find some event that is responsible for the end result. This hypothesis was confirmed in the experiments carried out. The East Asians tended to be less surprised by events that they had previously considered improbable. They tended to rationalise them easily, unlike the American students.

These results highlight a fundamental difference in the implicit and explicit aspects of the representation of knowledge between East Asians and Westerners. In daily life, Westerners tend to adopt an almost scientific cognitive style. They abstract a few relevant factors and generate causal models. This allows them to maintain the component of tacit knowledge fairly low, and simplifies the transfer of information and communication. On the other hand, the models are hazier and more complex in East Asians, and the components of the model are less definite. The tacit part is therefore significant, with obvious consequences for the exchange of information in mutual understanding and in collaboration on issues with a significant cognitive component.

14.4 Cultural or Perceptive Differences?

The cognitive tendency of East Asians to attribute significance to the causal field, rather than the causal object, and of Westerners to attribute it to the object rather than the causal field, seems related to what happens in the perceptive sphere. In psychology of perception experiments we can see that East Asians tend to focus attention on a large number of contextual factors, while for Americans the focus is primarily on the objects in the foreground and not on those in the background. It is not clear if the component represented by the world's different interpretative schemes is responsible for the different perceptive attitude, or if the causal relationship is the reverse. In the second case, we should suppose a different genetic base between East Asians and Westerners, responsible for the neurophysiological structure that can generate different perceptive performances. This hypothesis seems to go against the results of many studies (see, for example, those contained in Viale et al., eds., 2006) which underline that there is universality of inferential principles between new-borns and young children; that the differentiation between Westerners and East Asians takes place after the processes of acculturation and socialisation; that the answers of adults of East Asian and Western origin, who have been resident for some time in the United States and China respectively, to psychology of reasoning and decisions tests tend to converge with the performance of individuals from the host country. If the results of these studies were confirmed, it would exclude the possibility that a different genetic base may be responsible for the different perceptive attitudes, which in turn are responsible for the different cognitive performances.

Various forms of evidence are provided in psychology of perception:

(a) Ji et al. (2000) found that the Chinese were better at identifying co-variations between events than the Americans. This seems to indicate that the Chinese pay more attention to the field or to the interdependence between objects.
(b) Witkin et al. (1954) identified a perceptive aptitude known as "field dependence". It makes it possible to separate or not separate an object from the field that it belongs to. The background or the frame in which the object is positioned

influences the way it is identified and brings it into focus. Ji et al. (2001) have discovered that the Chinese are more subject than the Americans to the "field dependence" phenomenon. For the Chinese, the field and background have a greater influence on the way a subject is perceived (for example, a vertical shaft perceived as oblique in relation to a change in the frame).

(c) When they showed various underwater scenes to Japanese and American participants, Masuda and Nisbett (2001) recorded their observations. The first statement was classified in relation to the focus on specific salient objects (defining salience as being larger, moving faster, or having more brilliant colours than other fish), or on the context (for example, the colour of the water, the base of the scene, objects in the background). The Americans mentioned salient objects much more frequently than the Japanese, who concentrated more on the context and on relations between objects.

(d) Simons and Levin (1997) and other perceptual psychologists have highlighted a phenomenon known as "change blindness". In order to maintain a consistent view of the world, the central nervous system tends to minimise changes between two very similar scenes, transforming them into one highly consistent image. They discovered that the individual did not distinguish between two images presented one after the other that were very similar but with marginal differences (but he did manage to recognise the change if the figures are observed simultaneous). On the basis of this phenomenon, Nisbett and Masuda (2006) suggested and verified that Westerners, who are more aware of salient objects, are more capable of detecting changes in them, while East Asians, who pay more attention to the background and to relations between objects, find it easier to recognise differences in the field and contextual factors.

(e) One indirect proof of this different perceptive propensity lies in a human activity that tends to simulate perceptive experience: figurative art. When an artist represents a landscape or a portrait in a painting, a sculpture or a photograph, he will express in the work of art the peculiar way in which he sees and interprets the object. These are the mental models he has in mind, which derive from the history of his perceptions, filtered and piloted by his expectations, and conceptual schemes that will orient his aesthetic expression. So the different propensity to focus on the salience of individual objects rather than on the background and the context that is typical of the perceptive aptitude of Westerners and East Asians, should be reflected in their artistic activity. In fact, as Nisbett and Masuda noted (2006), landscape painters in the West generally paint low horizons, as if the landscape was seen by an observer on the ground, which restricts the dimension and quantity of the objects contained in it. On the other hand, East Asians tend to place the horizon higher, as if the landscape were seen by a bird flying in the sky. This opens up the space and increases the number of objects it contains.

Another phenomenon is evident in portraits. In the West there is a tendency to put the figure portrayed in the forefront so that it almost entirely fills the canvas. In portraits by Asian painters, on the other hand, the figure is smaller, in the background and set in the surrounding environment.

14.5 Background Knowledge and Cognitive Differences

It has been shown (Viale and Pozzali 2007; Pozzali and Viale 2007) that the inferential component of tacit knowledge, defined as "Implicit Cognitive Rules", seems to depend directly on the principles contained in "Background Knowledge", which include moral and social values, and ontological, metaphysical and epistemological principles that are the background to our interpretation of reality. This direct relationship seems important, for example, to explain significant differences in tacit knowledge that limit the transfer of knowledge between the world of academic research and that of industrial research.

Even the cognitive and perceptive differences outlined earlier seem to be linked to a radical difference where "Background Knowledge" is concerned. I will concentrate above all on the differences in East Asian Background Knowledge.

First of all, Asian thought, and Chinese thought in particular, can be described as *dialectical*. It concentrates on the contradictions and on how to transcend them, or to find elements of truth in them. Peng (1997) outlined a number of principles that could underpin dialectical thought, set out in order of their general and implied importance.

The Principle of Change. The world is not static but dynamic and constantly changing. Being in one state is only an indication that it is about to change. Because constant events do not exist, and reality is in a constant flow, even the concepts that should characterise reality are not fixed objectively and universally, but are subjective, fluid and flexible. This metaphysical principle explains the difficulty, highlighted earlier, that the Chinese have in using rules to characterise objects. Because they do not view reality as a compound of discrete objects, characterised by stable properties that define their individuality, objects and events can only be classified on the basis of "family" resemblance relations.

The Principle of Contradiction. Because the world is changing constantly, it is full of oppositions, contradictions, inconsistencies and anomalies. At the moment that a thing exists, it is already becoming something else. If a thing is beautiful, young or good, the process is already underway within it that will make it become ugly, old and bad. Health and sickness identify with each other like all other mutually interdependent attributes. This principle is at the heart of Taoism: "Tao is conceived as both 'being' and 'non-being'." These contradictions are evident in linguistic representation which, for its very nature, is unable to conceptualise the flow of reality, but tries to fix the properties of an object artificially at a given moment. This principle explains the different cognitive style of East Asians in facing contradictions. The middle way logic that tends to consider contradictions not as an anomaly to be overcome, but as the distorted and simplistic representation of the complexity of reality, is justified by this principle. In the Chinese, this produces a hazier attitude to negotiation, the search for compromise, and a cognitive style that is less inclined, when it controls a hypothesis, to focus on conceptual inconsistencies or empirical falsification.

Holism or the Principle of Relativity. As a result of the principles of change and of contradiction, nothing can exist in isolation and independently. Every object and event is connected to numerous others inter-dependently. To understand something we have to understand all the relations that link that object to other objects and the various parts of the object with itself. This principle explains the propensity, illustrated earlier, to reason causally not on the basis of a link between individual factors but by identifying the causal field, i.e. the complex context of several objects in which the object is immersed. If the world is created by continuous flows of substances and if every event cannot be separated from the complex reality in which it is placed, this explains why the illusion of control is much weaker than in Western subjects. And finally this dependence on the field, on background and on the context is manifested at a cognitive and perceptive level.

This classification of "Background Knowledge" lies behind the peculiar "Implicit Cognitive Rules" that differentiate East Asian and Western thought. This different style of thought is manifested in numerous professional and daily activities. Here are a few examples. Asian medical tradition is of the Holistic type, opposed to radical intervention whether pharmacological or surgical. Health is the result of a balance between a very broad, variegated causal field of endogenous and exogenous factors. Illness cannot be identified analytically with a single agent or pathogenic event as it is in the West. As a result, therapies such as antibiotics, hormones or surgery that aim to neutralise a specific pathogenic target are not considered valid.

The peculiar type of logical inference known as "middle way logic" seems to influence the cognitive and epistemological style present in science. Western scientific methodology tends to argue according to the "principle of non-contradiction" and the "excluded middle" which translates into logical procedures such as "reductio ad absurdum", syllogism, "modus tollens", etc. This type of logical inference has generated a scientific style founded on confrontation, criticism, empirical attempts at control and falsification, the search for formal contradictions that have made Western scientific thought dynamic, open to change and innovative. There was no similar trend in East Asian countries, including Japan to a certain extent, where there was stagnation and conservatism due to a lack of critical attitude and spirit of contradiction.

Similar comments could be made regarding East Asian hostility to the contradictory and argumentative oppositions in trade, politics, legal activities and daily life. The difficulty of defining net incontrovertible contract terms that represent an irreversible commitment is well-known. In East Asia, a contract is generally only an opaque, hazy outline for the development of commercial relations between the two parties. What is more, in the case of damage to people or property, instead of taking legal action to try to demonstrate that a certain type of behaviour contravenes a legal standard, in East Asia they prefer to look for compromise solutions by mediation between the two parties. This also happens because in East Asia there is no clear, straightforward representation of what is right or wrong. There seem to be religious reasons behind this moral perception. In East Asia it is customary to embrace different religious credos, even if they contradict each other. People may be Confucian, Taoist, Buddhist and Christian at one and the same time. This situation reverberates in widespread tolerance and opposition to the clear, categorical statement of what is right or wrong, which is not what happens in the monotheistic Abrahamic religions. And finally, according to Asian holistic principles, the universe is a single whole composed of interconnected and not separate parts. This is reflected in the role attributed to the individual in politics, in society and in law. He cannot be represented ontologically as a person with a personal heritage of "positive" and "negative" rights in relation to other people and to social institutions. On the contrary, because he is ontologically comparable to the social-natural whole he is a part of, no justification or foundation of individual rights can be extrapolated. This explains the despotic approach of many East Asian regimes to civil rights, and the dialogue between deaf people between the West and the East about these issues.

Adaptive Theory Change as Epistemological Universal

15

Human beings often accept beliefs and reasons in ways that are considered irrational because they do not conform to given canons of rationality. These conventional canons stem, generally, from the main formal models of deduction and induction. There is a great deal of dissatisfaction in accepting this kind of normative judgement. The acceptance of a particular formal canon seems arbitrary and its foundation generates the well known "trilemma of Münchausen"[1] (Albert 1968). This uneasiness has produced two different reactions. The first is the nihilist one. There is no need to establish any normative account of rationality because "anything goes" and every reason should be accepted. The second is what can be labelled, to a great extent, as a "naturalizing epistemology" programme (Quine 1969). According to it, the normative account of rationality should be generated by the descriptive account of how individuals reason and generate their beliefs.

In this chapter I wish to analyze four dimensions of human cognition – science, developmental age, adult age and different cultures. This chapter is mainly based on parts of the previous three chapters. The arguments and data of the previous three chapters will be used as summarizing premises supporting a general principle of rational justification based on theory change.

The analysis is focused on a fundamental aspect of human cognition: the generation of empirical beliefs about the world. Humans generate empirical generalizations and theories that represent general or particular aspects of the world. These beliefs can be maintained or can be substituted with others. In general the change is driven by the inadequacy of the old belief in representing some empirical aspects of the world or in satisfying pragmatic goals in some context of

[1] The "trilemma of Münchausen" according to Hans Albert (1968) is about the foundation of a theory. A theory is founded either on first propositions that are not founded, and on propositions that are founded on other propositions that must be founded on others and so on according to a "*regressum* ad infinitum" process, and on propositions that are their own logical consequences.

The present chapter is a modified version of Viale, R. (2000). Reasons and Reasoning: What comes First? In R. Boudon, P. Demeulenaere & R. Viale (eds.). *L'explication des normes sociales*, Presses Universitaire de France. With kind permission from the Publishers.

DOI 10.1007/978-3-642-24743-9_15,

problem solving. Moreover, the generation of new beliefs that are able to fit our empirical and pragmatic desiderata is accompanied by many kinds of errors and biases according a-priori standards of inductive and deductive rationality. Nevertheless, even if human reasoning seems biased, human ability in adapting to the world is almost successful by generating truthful representations of empirical reality. The epistemological ability of humans seems little affected by errors and biases in reasoning. The generation of new beliefs to better fit empirical phenomena seems to be made not casually but according to given general rules of theory change. The results of these changes from previous beliefs to new beliefs, according the rules of theory change, seem to be overcoming, diachronically, the synchronic effect of errors and biases in inductive and deductive reasoning.

If this is the case, the thesis of the chapter is that the norms of theory change – that we discover in the best examples of the growth of knowledge – can represent a naturalistic methodological criterion to assess the reasons for generating a belief and consequently a naturalistic criterion of rationality.

15.1 Shared Norms of Theory Choice and Biases in Reasoning Among Professional Scientists

Methodological rationality has been the main target of the destructive analyses of both the "new philosophy of science" and the contemporary sociology of science. Instead of the traditional image of the scientist as a "truth pursuer", he appears to be painted as a "utility pursuer". Pursuing pragmatic goals seems to be the only norm shared by the members of the scientific community. No room seems to be left for shared rational criteria of choice.

The conclusion of the new philosophy of science and the sociology of science stems mainly from a historical analysis and from an anthropological understanding of scientific behaviour. The "ideological" prejudices of contemporary philosophical and social studies of science have made them forget an interesting empirical aspect of the methodological attitude of scientists: their beliefs in the methodological norms of choice.

The empirical study of methodological norms of theory choice has been the aim of a study carried out on a sample of 120 applied scientists, working at the European Union Joint Research Centre of Ispra in Italy (Viale and Cerroni 2002). According to a common sociological stereotype, applied scientists should be the farthest from a model of scientist as rational truth pursuer. They are too constrained by practical needs and by short-term logic. Consequently, they should be driven to develop methodological rules "à la carte", able to satisfy local contingent pragmatic goals. Therefore, any result of the empirical investigation showing an opposite image to the methodological beliefs of applied scientists – that is, the presence of rational criteria of theory choice – is, a fortiori, more meaningful for the overall image of science.

The test was made checking some of the main theses formulated in the contemporary philosophy of science. The first result is that the data do not show any relevant correlation between social variables – status, expertise, gender, nationality, and discipline – and methodological style.

Table 15.1 Viale and Cerroni (2002)

Give your evaluation of the following criteria in order to prefer one hypothesis rather than another one	Values[a]
Allows to solve theoretical problems not solved by other theories	71.9
Solves problems already solved and others emerging subsequently	37.7
Allows the possibility of making predictions outside its initial domain	37.4
Allows correct predictions with less additional hypothesis	20.3
Is capable of offering a visual image of phenomena	17.3
Offers a better data fitting	7.4
Is better confronting crucial experiments	7.3
Allows to make analogies with theories successful in other domains	−11.9
Is elegant and simple	−14.9
Solves problems outside its initial domain	−33.3
For the expertise matured while using it	−42.4
Has a higher computational handiness	−48.1
Obtains a higher consensus inside the scientific community that uses it	−51.1

[a]Values are evaluated adding all the scores (1–100) assigned to the option, with a suitable normalization

As regards the evaluation of hypotheses (Table 15.1), the scientists show a preference for rational criteria linked to empirical scope and problem solving.

The first three choices are well established in the philosophy of Lakatos (1978, pp. 66–70) and Laudan (1984, p. 100). On the contrary, the criteria that received less support in the test are those linked to pragmatic or conventional reasons: simplicity, computational ease, social consensus inside the scientific community.

As for the selection of the criteria of choice in front of empirical anomalies (Table 15.2) the scientists seem inclined not to adopt a dogmatic falsificationism.

They prefer to check the correctness of the methods and if the anomaly continues to persist they take it seriously into account. It is meaningful that the least selected criterion is the most conventionalist one: introducing hypotheses which are not testable in order to save the theory.

Moreover, they answer the other questions in the following way:

(1)

80% of scientists think that the evaluation of a hypothesis cannot be made without comparing it to others.

(2)

71% of scientists believe that the aim of science is to produce theories that are true representations of the world and only 29% think that the aim is to generate fictions that are useful for their application.

Table 15.2 Viale and Cerroni (2002)

Confronting several experiments that do not validate a hypothesis, which are the methodological criteria to be adopted?	Values[a]
To verify the adequacy in having followed the experimental protocol	110.8
To consider anomalies relevant only if they manifest themselves persistently	61.7
To refuse to abandon the basic hypothesis falsified by experiments	7.1
To abandon the hypothesis	7.0
To ignore anomalies as long as the hypothesis continues to successfully predict new phenomena	−23.2
To consider our incapacity rather than the inadequacy of the hypothesis	−28.1
To abandon temporarily the unsolved problems and return to them subsequently	−43.3
To attach importance to anomalies only if there is already a rival hypothesis that explains them	−45.0
To introduce additional hypotheses not yet justified in order to save the general scientific assumptions	−48.5

[a]Values are evaluated adding all the scores (1–100) assigned to the option, with a suitable normalization

(3)

70% of scientists believe that the truth of a hypothesis is founded on the reliability of the experimental methods used to justify it, while 18% believe in the certainty, and only 12% in the probability of the theory.

The rationality emerging from these results seems to have particular features: it is comparative, realist and procedural. Moreover the results of this test are coherent, to a great extent, with the results of the historical-methodological test contained in the volume of Donovan et al. (1988), that represents the methodological behaviour of the upper level basic scientists of the past.

The conclusion is that we can claim that in this sample of applied science, the methodological beliefs seem, to a great extent, similar to those of the best basic science of the past.

Contrary to the previous example there are other empirical data that support a disturbing image of the rational ability of scientists. One of my concerns stems from a study of the conjunction fallacy carried out with the same sample of scientists as the previous example. The scientists read the following item:

(4) (Viale and Osherson 2000)

Suppose we have learned that in a secret location near Archangel in Siberia, the Russians have built an advanced installation for energy production. From confidential sources it has been determined that the installation produces an average of 100 megawatts.

Our respondents then were asked to rank order eight possibilities in terms of likelihood. Two of these possibilities were the following:

(5)

(a) The installation uses turbo-gas technology (A).

(b) The installation uses turbo-gas technology for the co-generation of steam and electricity (A & B).

70% of the scientists ranked the second, conjunctive possibility as more likely than the first. This is a probabilistic fallacy, discussed at length by psychologists. Other items, like the replication of the famous Linda's test (6), yields similar rates of fallacious responding by the same respondents.

(6) (see Hertwig and Chase 1998)

Linda is 31 years old, not married, she is extrovert and brilliant. She studied philosophy. When a student, she was a political militant and took part in anti-nuclear sit-ins.

Please rank order the following statements by their probability, using 1 for the most probable, and 8 for the least probable.

Three of the possibilities were:

1) Linda is a bank teller (A)
2) Linda is a militant feminist (B)
3) Linda is a bank teller and is a militant feminist (A & B)

They rank 3 before 1, but this choice is fallacious. In fact, as everyone of us knows:

(7)

$p\ (A) > p\ (A\ \&\ B)$

It must thus be asked whether even professional scientists are consistently guided by probabilistic principles when reasoning about technical matters related to their specialization. The answer seems negative.

Many tests on probabilistic and deductive reasoning show an image of scientists that commit probabilistic fallacies, even if they are professional statisticians, as the previous one, and deductive fallacies, as the confirmation bias.

In conclusion, we face a double image of the professional scientists. On one hand they tend to follow shared norms of theory choice that, to a great extent, fit the normative canons of scientific rationality. But on the other, the same scientists are tend to fall into the traps of probabilistic and deductive reasoning.

15.2 Good Theory Formation and Inductive Fallacies Among "Little Scientists"

In the past philosophers used to put infants and children on the opposite side from science in the spectrum of cognitive rationality. Their supposed cognitive immaturity did not allow them to approach the ideal image of rational being. Recently two psychologists Alison Gopnik and Andrew Meltzoff declared, at the end of the introduction of their book.

(8) *Words, Thoughts, and Theories* (Gopnik and Meltzoff 1997, p. 9)

"Ultimately, our reason for watching and talking to children is the same as Socrates'. The most central questions in cognitive science are questions that only they can answer".

One of the questions that children seem to answer in their book is about the analogy of the child as a little scientist. The central idea of the book is that

(9) (Gopnik and Meltzoff 1997 p. 3)

"the processes of cognitive development in children are similar to, indeed perhaps even identical with, the processes of cognitive development in scientists".

Infants are endowed with an innate set of principles that allows them to begin to interact with the world. Among these principles, one of the most important is the one that allows a causal attribution to the relations among physical events. At around the age of 6 months, the infant is able to apply the principle of cohesion – a moving object maintains its connectedness and boundaries – the principle of continuity – a moving object traces exactly one connected path over space and time – and the principle of contact – objects move together if and only if they touch (Spelke et al. 1995). Moreover, there is the theory of biology and the theory of psychology. These theories show that infants individuate some theory-specific causal mechanisms to explain interactions among the entities in a domain. A child has an intuition of what characterizes a living being from an artefact or an object. Between the ages of 2 and 5, the child assumes that external states of affairs may cause mental states and that there is a causal chain from perception to beliefs to intentions and to actions (Viale 1999).

(10) *The Little Scientist Thesis* (Gopnik and Meltzoff 1997)

There is strong empirical evidence that starting from their innate endowed principles, children propose abstract entities, coherently organised with causal relations among them. They make ontological commitments and hold counterfactuals. These entities serve to provide characteristic explanations, predictions and interpretations. Children initially ignore certain kinds of counter-evidence, then account for such evidence with auxiliary hypotheses, then use the new theoretical idea in limited contexts, and only finally reorganise their knowledge so that the new theoretical entities play a central role. When the new theory is under construction, they engage in extensive experiments relevant to the theory and collect empirical generalisations.

The innate theories function as a start-up of the conceptual development, but, while innate, they would be defeasible. They are later modified and revised by new evidence.

(11) (Gopnik and Meltzoff 1997, p. 51).

"Innate theories are like the Neurath boat that pushes off from the pier. The boat you start out in may have considerable effect on the boat you end up with, even if no trace of the original remains."

Children resemble scientists in their method of theory change. One theory can substitute another when it fits the empirical evidence better and allows one to make better predictions. Counter-evidence to a theory is ignored unless it manifests itself persistently. These criteria remind me of those selected in the previous questionnaire submitted to adult scientists.

The Methodological criteria of theory change in big and little scientists are not the guarantee of truth and representational success. Many false hypotheses are generated using these criteria. But nonetheless they seem to be a guarantee of conceptual learning from errors to generate theories that fit the world better.

Norms and criteria of theory change and conceptual development in children give a positive representation of the rational attitude of humans. On the contrary, as in the case of big scientists, there is a dark side of the coin Little scientists seem not to satisfy elementary canons of correct reasoning. For example, one candidate principle of inductive reasoning concerns the diversity of evidence in support of a general hypothesis. It is widely claimed that greater diversity entails greater support (e.g., Hempel 1966, pp. 33–38; Franklin and Howson 1984). Why did Newton's theory end up commanding so much assent? One reason is that in the presence of various background assumptions, the theory accurately predicts heterogeneous phenomena, such as the trajectories of balls thrown into the air, the behaviour of gyroscopes, and the orbit of celestial bodies. At the end of 17th century, these phenomena appeared very diverse, which forced respect for the theory despite reservations about the reliance on occult, non-mechanical entities like gravity.

The diversity principle has been the object of psychological investigation. Osherson et al. (1990) have discovered that it is one of the phenomena present in category-based induction tasks.

A general inductive argument is one in which the category in the conclusion properly includes the categories in the premises. For example the conclusion category MAMMAL in argument (12) below includes the premise category HIPPO and HAMSTER:

(12)

Hippos have ulnar arteries
Hamsters have ulnar arteries

All mammals have ulnar arteries

An argument is strong if belief in the premises causes people to believe the conclusion.

American adults seem to support a general or a specific conclusion more when the premises are more different than when they are more similar. On the contrary, studies made by Lopez et al. (1997) and Gutheil and Gelman (1997) among 6 year olds and 9 year olds show an opposite attitude. For example 6 year olds prefer the argument (13):

(13)

Cows have ulnar arteries
Buffalos have ulnar arteries

All animals have ulnar arteries
to the alternative argument (14):

(14)

Cows have ulnar arteries
Cats have ulnar arteries

All animals have ulnar arteries
Moreover both 6 year olds and 9 year olds prefer more homogeneous premises to more diverse in arguments with specific conclusions like (15):

(15)

Kangaroos have ulnar arteries
Children seem not to apply a fundamental norm of inductive reasoning. Therefore the little scientist hypothesis might be weakened.

In a recent paper, it was argued against the use of the diversity principle as a normative standard of inductive reasoning (Viale and Osherson 2000). If we accept the Bayesian probability theory as a normative account of scientific inference, as most contemporary philosophy of science is doing (Howson and Urbach 1993), we may propose that it is the probability of premises prior to accepting the conclusion that governs its strength (Horwich 1982). Under these conditions argument strength stands in a simple relation to premise-probability.

(16) Premise Probability Principle (PPP)

Suppose that arguments A,B/C and A,B'/C are given where C logically implies A,B and B'. Then the strength of the first argument is greater than the strength of the second if and only if P(A & B) < P(A & B').

In a study made in Texas by Lo et al. (2002), among fourth and fifth graders – 10 and 11 year olds – the results show that children recognise the different probability of copies of propositions, and they show reliable (albeit imperfect) conformity to the Premise Probability Principle. They prefer arguments with less probable premises to those with more probable premises. Therefore children seem to be able to conform to shared canons of induction in scientific inferences.

In conclusion, little scientists seem to suffer from a mild schizophrenia similar to that of big scientists. They seem to follow sound criteria of conceptual and theory change, but at the same time, they lack an important inferential principle of induction such as the diversity principle but not another such as the PPP.

15.3 Problem Solving Ability and Biases in Reasoning Among "Naive Scientists"

If the studies on biases and errors during developmental age don't generate great concern about the image of human rationality, on the contrary, the great amount of empirical evidence collected in these last 40 years on sub-optimal ways of human reasoning and decision making has provoked great bewilderment. "How can we go to the Moon with so many constant errors of judgement"? was the question asked by a colleague to Nisbett and Ross (1980, It. transl. 1989) after having read the proofs of the first 8 chapters of their book "*Human Inference: Strategies and Shortcomings of Social Judgement*" (1980, Italian transl. 1989). The image of man that is portrayed in the book is of a person unable to use formal criteria of reasoning and decision making like those that scientists use in their activity. Man chooses samples that are biased by systematic tendencies; he is not able to assess the co-variation between events; he is biased in the causal attribution; he makes predictions ignoring base rate and regression towards the mean; he tends to confirm the theory instead of falsifying it.

Nevertheless, man goes to the moon, that is, he is almost able to adapt to his social and natural environment. He is able to understand, predict and control many aspects of his life and his environment. He is able to plan his career, to make diagnoses from his symptoms, to discuss rationally many problems. There are two important aspects of human irrationality that can find a moderate interpretation.

The first concerns sub-optimality in assessing co-variation among events, that is a crucial ability for generating hypotheses. In reality, outside the laboratory, in everyday life, there are many circumstances that allow good performance in co-variation:

(17) Satisfactory Co-Variations

Because, sometimes the stimuli are well perceived, evident, close, and, motivationally, relevant.

Because, when the co-variation is very strong, a single prototypical case can offer a reliable representation of the general relation.

Because, most of our theories are founded on co-variations made by experts (scientists, advisers, consultants) in particular fields.

The second and most important concern about human rationality is the "perseverance bias". People tend to persevere in their beliefs even when faced with data that falsify them. This phenomenon seems to undermine the dynamic image of theory change of the little scientists thesis. Actually the dynamics of theory change of the child compared to the adult is much stronger. In fact, the metaphor of little scientist finds its justification in the greater analogy between child and scientist than child and adult. Adults for many acceptable and unacceptable reasons are more conservative in maintaining their theories of the world. They prefer stability of their system of thought and find it difficult to integrate, in the quick flow of contemporary life, empirical counter evidence into new alternative theories. Nevertheless,

(19) *The Adult Technologist Thesis*

a) *The maintenance of a theory in front of anomalies, until we are sure that it is systematic, seems a sound methodological rule also in the scientific community.*
b) *The adult seems more close to the model of the technologist rather than the scientist. He needs to apply theories in everyday problem solving. He has no time to worry about the truth of the theory. What is important is that it functions in solving practical problems. He fears more a casual error in applying the theory in a given pragmatic context than a systematic error that would need the generation of an alternative theory. Nevertheless, as in technology, the solution works if the embodied theory is valid. Therefore even the adult is obliged to change, sooner or later, ill-functioning theories.*

15.4 Cognitive Relativism or Universality Among "Exotic Scientists"?

When we analyse the cognitive rationality stemming from the cognitive tests on everyday reasoning, one important question concerns the cultural variability of the styles of reasoning. Are cognitive abilities universal or context-dependent? Can we discover common patterns of thinking among different cultures or does each socio-cultural environment shape its system of thought? The answer to these questions is crucial, because in the case of the variability of the styles of reasoning, the refusal to adopt a priori prescriptive standards of rationality would oblige us either to fall into a socio-cultural relativism or to try to maintain a rational approach by relying on a naturalistic rule of belief generation – as the methodological rules of theory change present in science and infants.

An answer to this question comes from a recent article of Nisbett et al. (2001) on the differences between Asian and American thinking. They rely on an impressive amount of cognitive tests that try to compare the way of reasoning of North Americans, mainly university students and East Asians – Korean, Chinese and Japanese – mainly university students. The East Asians and the Americans respond in qualitatively different ways to the same stimulus situation in many different tests.

For example, American participants showed large primacy effects in judgements about co-variation, whereas Chinese participants showed none.

"Control illusion" increased the degree of co-variation seen and reported accuracy of Americans but tended to have the opposite effects on Chinese.

Koreans were greatly influenced in their causal attribution by the sort of situational information that has no effect for Americans.

Koreans showed great hindsight bias effects under conditions where Americans showed none.

Finally Americans responded to contradiction by polarising their beliefs, whereas Chinese responded by moderating their beliefs. We can summaries the results in (20).

(20) THE AMERICAN versus. EAST ASIAN STYLE OF THINKING (Nisbett et al. 2001)

1) *EXPLANATION: East Asians tend to explain events, both social and physical, more with respect to the field and Americans tend to explain events more with respect to a target object and its properties.*
2) *PREDICTION and "POSTDICTION": East Asians tend to make predictions with reference to a wider variety of factors than Americans do. Consequently they are less surprised by any given outcome and they are more prone to "hindsight bias", or the tendency to regard events as having been inevitable in retrospect.*
3) *ATTENTION: since East Asians locate causality in the field instead of the object they tend to be more accurate at "co-variation detection", that is the perception of relationship within the field.*
4) *CONTROL: Americans are more subject to the "illusion of control", that is, a greater expectation of success when the individual is involved in interaction with the object – even when that interaction could not logically have an effect on the outcome.*
5) *RELATIONSHIPS AND SIMILARITIES vs. RULES AND CATEGORIES: East Asians tend to group objects and events on the basis of their relationships to one another, for example, "A is a part of B". Americans would be expected to group them more on the basis of category membership, for example, "A and B are both Xs". Americans are inclined to learn rule-based categories more readily than East Asians and to rely on categories more for purposes of inductive and deductive inference.*
6) *LOGIC vs. EXPERIENTIAL KNOWLEDGE: East Asians are more influenced by prior beliefs in judging the soundness of a formal argument. Americans are more able at setting aside prior beliefs in favour of reasoning based on logical rules.*
7) *DIALECTICS vs. THE LAW OF NONCONTRADICTION: East Asians are inclined to seek compromise solutions to problems ("Middle Way") and to reconcile contradictory propositions. Americans tend to seek solutions to problems in which a given principle drives out all but one competing solution, to prefer arguments based on logic, and to reject one or both of two propositions that could be construed as contradicting one another.*

These differences are reflected in the different kind of errors and biases that affect East Asians and Americans. We cannot say that one culture is normatively better than another. East Asians are better at causal co-variation and less prone to "illusion of control". Americans are better at deductive reasoning, in category-based induction and less prone to "hindsight bias". Obviously, better does not mean that they satisfy, absolutely, the normative canons of rational reasoning. It is well known that the tradition of investigation into deductive and probabilistic errors and biases started in American Colleges.

Therefore, we can say that we are faced with two different mixes of rational and irrational reasonings. But the crucial thesis of Nisbett et al. is

(21)

that the different ways of reasoning are not a contingent and superficial feature, but they are rooted in two completely different systems of thinking, that is, in different metaphysical and epistemological principles that shape differently the American and East Asian cognition. These two different systems of thinking originated causally from two different socio-cultural environments: the old Greek trading society and classical philosophy on one side; the old Chinese agricultural society and Confucian philosophy on the other side.

Different social and economic variables gave birth to different styles of thought that we can summarise under the heading of "holistic" and "analytic" thought. Nowadays these different styles of thought continue to be effective in differentiating the reasoning processes of contemporary Americans and East Asians.

The first objection to this anti-universal conception of cognition comes from the supporters of the universal endowment of cognitive abilities. If the innate theory of physics, of biology, of mind are true, then these theories form a common universal cognitive basis for the thought of every human in the world. Other investigators are even more radical. There are even common essential beliefs about the nature of social world (Hirschfeld 1996) and even religious conceptions such as spirits and superhuman agents are remarkably similar from one culture to another (Boyer 1993).

According to me, this position is not able to weaken the anti universal thesis of Nisbett et al.. The little scientist hypothesis can explain why. We know that conceptual and theory change in the developmental age does not start from nothing, but from an innate endowment of theory about causality, the physical world and so on. The change towards new theories is triggered by empirical evidence and informative inputs that come from the environment. These evidential and informative inputs, obviously are variable in relation to the particular developmental contexts. Therefore, they drive the generation of different theories on how to interpret and understand the world. They are the metaphysical and epistemological theories representing the implicit premises of our reasoning and thinking. In conclusion, it is very likely that so different socio-cultural contexts as the East Asian and American ones are able to lead to, in the developmental age, the generation of different metaphysical and epistemological theories that affect differently the ways of reasoning.

The second objection relates to its implicit support of a kind of cognitive relativism. It is the natural consequence of the strong socio-economic determinism present in their thesis. In fact, according to them, social organization and economic structure are the major determinants of the causal chain metaphysics-epistemology-cognition. Different socio-economic configurations generate fixed irreversible different causal chains. The world seems crowded, in principle, with different and incommensurable causal chains related to the different socio-economic structures.

My criticism starts from one of the results that Nisbett et al. bring to support their thesis. It deals with the difference principle that we saw before. According to them:

(22) (Nisbett et al. 2001)

"Koreans make less use of categories for purposes of inductive inference than do Americans and therefore are not able to follow the difference principle in an argument with a specific conclusion."

Faced with two arguments (23) and (24) they prefer (23) because they are less able than Americans to generate from the category in the conclusion RABBIT, the inclusive category MAMMALS and therefore, to estimate that LIONS and TIGERS have a minor coverage of the category MAMMAL than LIONS and GIRAFFES.

(23) Choi et al. (1997)

Lions have ulnar arteries
Tigers have ulnar arteries

Rabbits have ulnar arteries

(24)

Lions have ulnar arteries
Giraffes have ulnar arteries

Rabbits have ulnar arteries

On the contrary, if the category MAMMAL is made salient changing the conclusion into

(25)

Mammals have ulnar arteries

the principle of difference is satisfied.

Data that seem more severe about the ability to use categories come from a study that we have carried out in Vietnam at the University of Ho Chi Min City (Viale and

Osherson 2000). Our sample seems to show that even with arguments with a general conclusion, and not only with a specific conclusion, the East Asian students are not able to apply the difference principle. Does this mean that there are fixed wired-in limitations in the cognitive processing of categories in some people – e.g. East Asians – , but not in others – e.g. Americans? I don't think so.

The answer comes from an interesting study carried out among traditional Itzaj-Mayans of Peten of Guatemala by Lopez et al. (1997) to identify the universal cultural features of folk-biological inductions on mammal categories. They discover that, as in the previous case of Vietnam, Itzays did not follow the difference principle with general and specific conclusions. These data were very different from those found in many American Colleges where the diversity principle was always followed. They tried to explain with some follow-up studies what the reasons were for this difference. The conclusion was not that of radical cognitive differences but of an ecology-based reasoning stemming from the particular pragmatic context where they were living.

(26) Lopez et al. (1997, p. 288)

"Itzaj participants had extensive knowledge of the habits, characteristics, and ecological proclivities of Peten mammals; this ecological knowledge appears to have blocked diversity-based reasoning by rendering premises implausible on the basis of what the Itzaj know to be true. Cultural knowledge available to the Itzaj may have rendered the diversity strategy irrelevant".

In fact, they tried to control the hypothesis of ecology-based reasoning in two following studies. One was made on Itzajs, using arguments stemming from real world scenarios and not from natural taxonomy. The tests were about saving money, inspecting farmland and buying corn . It showed that they were able to follow the diversity principle when reasoning about everyday life and pragmatic problem solving.

The other was made on American tree experts. They discovered that the less expert the individuals were – for example, maintenance personnel – the more subject they were to ecology-based reasoning and the less they followed the diversity principle. On the contrary, expert taxonomists were able to extrapolate the inclusive categories more easily and to follow the diversity principle. Scientific knowledge enables the taxonomists to generate more salient categories at a rank higher than genus and family.

These data seem to support a thesis contrary to that of Nisbett et al. It is likely that there are not fixed irreversible differences in cognition that stem from relative different and fixed metaphysical and epistemological theories about the world. The cognitive abilities are dependent on knowledge, expertise and on pragmatic needs. These factors are able to reduce and, in some cases, to neutralise the cultural diversity of the cognitive abilities.

This conclusion is well known in cognitive anthropology. Education can quite easily shape cognitive attitudes making them, trans-culturally, similar. And the problem solving ability is much stronger in real world scenarios linked to particular pragmatic contexts and practical needs than it is in abstract tasks. The need for practical problem solving can trigger cognitive abilities that were hidden in abstract and uninteresting tasks (Boudon and Viale 2000).

What does this remark mean in my discourse?

(27) *The Exotic Scientist Thesis*

The relative plasticity of cognitive abilities in different cultures reflects the dynamics of theory change of the little scientist hypothesis. Human cognitive abilities depend on his theories about the world. But these theories are not fixed, irreversibly, by his local socio-cultural condition. They can be changed in relation to pragmatic feedbacks, empirical evidence and the new information coming from the environment. The relative theory change is driven by methodological norms that are effective during childhood, and we meet it again, in a similar fashion, inside the scientific community. The methodological norms of theory change seem, to a great extent, universal.

15.5 Conclusion: Theory Change as a Criterion of Rationality

"Big scientists", "little scientists", "adult technologists" and "exotic scientists" seem to share a common schizophrenia about their rationality or irrationality. The study of their reasoning behaviour is full of empirical evidence regarding biases and errors according given normative canons of rationality. On the contrary, their ability to adapt to the world, to solve problems in given pragmatic contexts, to increase their empirical knowledge is well grounded from every day experience and from empirical studies. Moreover they are inclined to rely on methodological norms of theory and conceptual change that, to a great extent, seem universal. Therefore irrational inferential behaviour seems to go along with rational meta-inferential norms.

There are some remarks on this representation.

Humans often fall into errors of deduction, statistical assessment, causal attribution, inductive support and so on. These errors both in the scientific enterprise and in everyday life seem not to have a great effect on the growth of knowledge and on economic and social development. My thesis is that the reason for this scarce effect of biases, errors and irrational reasoning might rely just on the meta-inferential norms of theory change. Children, scientists, adults make mistakes, generate false theories or empirical generalizations about the world, they produce beliefs that do not correspond to reality. However, at the same time, they are able to accept from the world the information, empirical evidence or pragmatic feedback about the reliability, the legitimacy, the pragmatic utility and the truth of their hypotheses. If the theory does not work, it, soon or later, will be changed and another theory will be generated. Therefore

(28)

the synchronic consequences of errors stemming from irrational reasoning are, diachronically, neutralized by the application of the norms of theory change.

If an analysis of rationality wishes to have relevance, it has to cope with the cultural diversity of thinking. Boudon is right when he writes (1995) that if we wish to avoid cultural relativism and ethnocentrism, we should be able to find trans-cultural and trans-contextual reasons for beliefs and actions. If every reason that can justify a belief or an action is relative to a given local socio-cultural context and cannot be judged by others living in different contexts, then rationality will shatter into a dispersed multitude of different and incommensurable reasons. If the reasons are relative to local socio-cultural contexts but they can be judged by inhabitants of other ethnic niches, then we can speak of trans-cultural reasons.

An example, coming from Boudon (1995), can explain my point. The Indios Papago of Arizona explain any social and natural events by the will of a god living on the top of Boboquivari mountain. The place is visible to anyone in the tribe. Why does nobody see the god of the mountain? The reason is because the ants inform him when humans are coming and he hides himself. Can we accept their reasons? Obviously, according to our beliefs, knowledge and theories of the world, their reasons seem to us completely unacceptable. But if we try to represent the theories and beliefs of the Indios, that function as the premises of their reasons, then we can justify their reasons according their theories of the world. It might be judged as reasonable that they propose the ant hypothesis to justify the impossibility to see the god of the mountain.

If this is the interpretation of the Indios' reasons, then what are the differences between this position and the relativistic one? The same exercise made for Indios' reasons can be replicated for a multitude of other ethnic niches.

The crucial point, that distinguishes a rational position from a relativistic one, relies according to me on the application of the methodology of theory change. As an example, think of a variation of the previous story. The same person that has told us the story of the god of the mountain informs us that the Indios believing in the ant story are professional scientists and engineers working at the nearby nuclear power station. At this point, it is likely that our possibility of justifying the reasons of the believers would greatly decrease. And the justification would become almost null if, talking with them, we discovered that they share with us all our metaphysical and epistemological principles about the world. In this case their reasons for believing the ant theory would become very unsound.

A likely hypothesis is that the reason for our judgement of their irrationality relies on the application of the methodology of theory change that we develop in the developmental age (and we find again in science):

(29) Methodological Norm of Theory Change of Children and Scientists

A given theory is maintained if a better alternative theory is not available. A theory is better when has more empirical content and is able to solve the problems of the old one plus some others.

When the traditional Indios had only beliefs and knowledge stemming from their tradition, their belief in the ant theory might be judged as reasonable because no better alternative theories were available. But when "nuclear" Indios have at their disposal alternative hypotheses to explain the behaviour of the god and these hypotheses are able to explain other aspects of the world, we can suppose that their belief in the ant theory might be judged as rationally unjustified.

The previous argument does not apply only to substantive theories, but also to different styles of reasoning. Let's come back to the study of Lopez et al. (1997) of the Itzajs Mayans. We saw before that they had good reasons for refusing arguments with diverse premises that did not fit their ecology-based knowledge. At the same time, they grasp the diversity principle in topics involving real world scenarios like the following:

(30) Lopez et al. (1997, p. 284)

"Imagine you want to buy several bags of corn from a given person. Before buying them, this person will show you only two cobs of corn to check whether all the corn is good. Do you prefer him to show you two cobs from one and the same bag (non-diversification response), or do you prefer him to show you one cob from one bag and another cob from another bag (diversification response)?"

The majority of Indios choose the diversification response because according to their theory based on real life experience, they had good reasons to widen the sample. Also in the case of the American tree experts, the previous argument is valid. When one, as in the case of the maintenance personnel, has a knowledge based on concrete examples of trees at the level of genus, he is not able to reason using categories at a higher rank, and, consequently, cannot follow the diversity principle. On the contrary, when one, as in the hypothetical case of the maintenance man that become a taxonomist, he can generate more generalized theories about the same object of everyday experience – e.g. the trees – therefore he is able to categorize at a more abstract level. These more abstract theories enable him to generate and use inclusive categories and therefore to satisfy the diversity principle.

As in the case of Arizona Indios, we can say that the new theory would not justify the taxonomist's preference for an argument with more homogeneous premises and not satisfy the diversity principle. With the same argument we might say that, hypothetically, the Itzajs, with an education on abstract taxonomy about mammals, ceteris paribus, would not be justified in still relying on ecology-based reasoning and not satisfying the diversity principle.

On the basis of the previous arguments, we can formulate an epistemological principle of rational justification based on theory change:

(31) Epistemological Principle of Rational Justification

There is reason to justify a belief of a subject if it is the effect of given theories on the world and the subject has not the knowledge of alternative theories that are better for their empirical content and problem solving ability.

Faced with a new and better theory, its negative utilisation can present different situations that seem not to find a rational justification. (1) The subject may not accept the new theory that increases his ability to explain the empirical phenomena. From the point of view of the epistemological principle of rational justification, the maintenance of the old theory seems not to rely on good reasons, and therefore it may be unjustified. (2) He can accept the new theory and put it in his knowledge base. But at the same time he can continue to use the old one to generate his beliefs about the world. If the two theories are inconsistent his cognitive behaviour is not justified, because it relies on an inconsistent set of beliefs. If the two theories are consistent, but the old one is implied by the new one, his cognitive behaviour is not justified because, according to the epistemological principle of rational justification, it relies on a theory that has less empirical content or problem-solving ability. (3) He acquires the new theory and puts it into his knowledge base, but his previous beliefs continue to be triggered in an automatic and reflex way. They will not be justified because they are not based on conscious reasons. They are a kind of traces of the old theory and they do not stem from any conscious act of reasoning.

In conclusion, it might be objected that there is no reason to try to establish normative criteria of rational justification of beliefs. The World goes ahead without the need for any general normative constraint. In reality there are many fields of human life where implicit normative criteria are applied. Education and science are important examples. Often the criteria are ad-hoc and lack transparency. Other times, they rely on a-priori canons of rationality that find their justification in some kinds of narrow social consensus by some elite set of experts. Consequently, it may be worthwhile trying to develop some general norms of rational justification that stem from our best real procedures of knowledge acquisition – i.e. science and developmental age.

The positive features of the proposed epistemological principle of rational justification may be the fulfillment of the following two conditions:

(a) It seems to meet our intuition about the reasons for accepting a belief given the actual knowledge of the subject.
(b) It seems to be coherent with the "naturalizing epistemology" programme: extrapolating the norms of rationality from the situations where there is a better growth of knowledge – that is science and developmental age.

Obviously this solution, pretending to avoid the "trilemma of Münchausen", is aware that it may fall into the trap of "naturalistic fallacy".

References

Agassi, J. (1973). Methodological individualism. In J. O'Neill (Ed.), *Modes of individualism and collectivism*. London: Heinemann.

Albert, H. (1968). *Traktat uber Kritische Vernung*. Tubingen: Mohr.

Allison, G. T. (1971). *The essence of decision*. New York: Harper Collins Publishers.

Allport, G. (1985). The historical background of social psychology. In G. Lindzey & E. Aronson (Eds.), *Handbook of social psychology*. New York: Random House.

Anderson, J. (1983). *The architecture of cognition*. Cambridge, MA: Harvard University Press.

Anderson, J. A., & Rosenfeld, E. (1988). *Neurocomputing: Foundations of research*. Cambridge, MA: MIT Press.

Anderson, J. R., & Milson, R. (1989). Human memory: An adaptive perspective. *Psychological Review, 96*, 703–719.

Antiseri, D. (1996). Trattato di Metodologia delle Scienze Sociali. Torino: UTET.

Anscombe, G. E. M. (1957). *Intentions*. Oxford: Basil Blackwell.

Armstrong, D. H. (1968). *A materialist theory of the mind*. London: Routledge and Kegan Paul.

Arrow, K. (1951). *Social choice and individual values*. New York: Wiley.

Arrow, K. J. (1971). Economic welfare and the allocation of resources for invention. In F. Lamberton (Ed.), *Economics of information and knowledge*. London: Penguin Books.

Asendorpf, J., & Baudonniere, P. M. (1993). Self-awareness and other-awareness: Mirror self-recognition and synchronic imitation among unfamiliar peers. *Developmental Psychology, 29*, 88–95.

Atran, S., Medin, D., & Ross, N. (2006). Thinking about biology: Modular constraints on categorization and reasoning in the everyday life of Americans, Maya, and scientists. In R. Viale, D. Andler, & L. Hirschfeld (Eds.), *Biological and cultural bases of human inference* (pp. 1–31). Mahwah, NJ: Lawrence Erlbaum Associates.

Attia, C., & Hilton, D. J. (2011). *Decidere in Finanza*. Milano: Il Sole 24 Ore.

Augoustinos, M., Walker, I., & Donaghue, N. (2006). *Social cognition*. London: Sage.

Baillargeon, R., & Hanko-Summers, S. (1990). Is the object adequately supported by the bottom object? Young infants' understanding of support relations. *Cognitive Development, 5*, 29–54.

Baldwin, D. A. (1991). Infants' contribution to the achievement of joint reference. *Child Development, 62*(5), 1875–1890.

Bargh, J. A. (Ed.). (2006). *Social psychology and the unconscious*. New York: Psychology Press.

Baron-Cohen, S. (1996). *Mindblindness: An essay on autism and theory of mind*. Cambridge, MA: MIT Press.

Barrett, D. (2010). *Supernormal stimuli: How primal urges overran evolutionary purpose*. New York: Norton.

Barrett, D. W. (2007). *The R/evolutionary science behind our weight and fitness crisis*. New York: W.W. Norton.

Barrett, J. L., & Keil, F. C. (1996). Conceptualizing a non-natural entity: Anthropomorphism in god concepts. *Cognitive Psychology, 31*(3), 1219–1247.

DOI 10.1007/978-3-642-24743-9,

Barry, B. M. (1970). *Sociologists, economists and democracy*. London: Macmillan.
Bazerman, M. (2009). *Quanto sei (a)morale?* Milan: Il Sole 24 Ore.
Beach, L. R., & Mitchell, T. R. (1978). A contingency model for the selection of decision strategies. *Academy of Management Review, 3*, 439–449.
Bechara, A., Damasio, H., Tranel, D., & Damasio, A. (1997). Deciding advantageously before knowing the advantageous strategy. *Science, 275*, 1293–1295.
Becker, G. S. (1981). *A treatise on the family*. Cambridge, MA: Harvard University Press.
Berlin, B. O., & Kay, P. D. (1969). *Basic color terms*. Berkeley, CA: University of California Press.
Berry, D. C., & Broadbent, D. E. (1988). Interactive tasks and the implicit-explicit distinction. *British Journal of Psychology, 79*, 251–272.
Berry, D. S., & Springer, K. (1993). Structure, motion, and preschoolers' perceptions of social causality. *Ecological Psychology, 5*(4), 273–283.
Bhargava, R. (1992). Individualism in Social Science: Forms and Limits of a Methodology. Oxford: Clarendon Press.
Binmore, K., Morgan, P., Shaked, A., & Sutton, J. (1991). Do people exploit their bargaining power? An experimental study. *Games and Economic Behaviour, 3*, 295–322.
Binmore, K., Shaked, A., & Sutton, J. (1985). Testing non-cooperative bargaining theory: A preliminary study. *American Economic Review, 75*, 1178–80.
Birch, S. A. J., & Bloom, P. (2003). Children are cursed: An asymmetric bias in reasoning. *Psychological Science, 14*, 283–286.
Black, D. (1958). *The theory of committees and elections*. Cambridge, UK: Cambridge University Press.
Blakemore, S. J., & Decety, J. (2001). From the perception of action to the understanding of intention. *Nature Reviews Neuroscience, 2*, 561–67.
Blaug, M. (1980). *The methodology of economics*. Cambridge, UK: Cambridge University Press.
Bonini, N., & Hadjichristidis, C. (2009). *Il sesto senso*. Milan: Il Sole 24 Ore.
Boudon, R. (1981). *The logic of social action*. London: Routledge.
Boudon, R. (1984). *La place du désordre. Critique des theories du changement social*. Paris: Presses Universitaires de France. It. Translation (1985), *Il posto del disordine*, Bologna: Il Mulino.
Boudon, R. (1990). *L'art de se persuader des idées douteuses, fragiles ou fausses*. Paris: Fayard.
Boudon, R. (1993a). Towards a synthetic theory of rationality. *International Studies in the Philosophy of Science, 7*(1), 5–19.
Boudon, R. (1993b). More on 'good reasons'. *International Studies in the Philosophy of Science, 7*(1), 87–102.
Boudon, R. (1994). *The art of self persuasion*. London: Polity Press.
Boudon, R. (1995). *Le juste et le vrai. Etudes sur l'objectivité des valeurs et de la connaissance*. Paris: Fayard.
Boudon, R., & Viale, R. (2000). Reasons, cognition and society. *Mind & Society, 1*, 41–56.
Bourdieau, P. (1977). *Outline of a theory of practice*. Cambridge, UK: Cambridge University Press.
Bower, G. H., & Glass, A. L. (1976). Structural units and the redintegrative power of picture fragments. *Journal of experimental psychology, 2*, 456–466.
Boyd, R., & Richerson, P. J. (2001). Norms and bounded rationality. In G. Gigerenzer & R. Selten (Eds.), *Bounded rationality: The adaptive toolbox*. Cambridge, MA: MIT Press.
Boyer, P. (1990). *Tradition as truth and communication: A cognitive description of traditional discourse*. New York: Cambridge University Press.
Boyer, P. (1993). *The naturalness of religious ideas*. Berkeley, CA: University of California Press.
Boyer, P. (1995). Causal understandings in cultural representations: Cognitive constraints on inferences from cultural input. In D. Sperber, D. Premack, & A. Premack (Eds.), *Causal cognition: A multidisciplinary debate* (pp. 615–649). New York: Oxford University Press.
Broadbent, D. E., Fitzgerald, P., & Broadbent, M. H. (1986). Implicit and explicit knowledge in the control of complex systems. *British Journal of Psychology, 77*, 33–50.
Bunge, M. (1980). *From neuron to behaviour and mentation*. New York: Raven press.

Camerer, C. (2007). The case for a 'mindful' economics. In A. Caplin & A. Schotter (Eds.), *Handbook of economic methodology*. Oxford: Oxford University Press.
Camerer, C., Loewenstein, G., & Weber, M. (1989). The curse of knowledge in economic setting: An experimental analysis. *Journal of Political Economy, 97*, 1232–54.
Camerer, C., Loewenstein, G., & Prelec, D. (2005). Neuroeconomics: How neuroscience can inform economics. *Journal of Economic Literature, XLIII*(1), 9–64.
Campbell, D. T., & Cook, T. D. (1979). *Quasi-experimentation*. Chicago: Rand-McNally.
Carey, S. (1985). *Conceptual change in childhood*. Cambridge, MA: MIT Press.
Carlson, S. M., & Moses, L. J. (2001). Individual differences in inhibitory control and children's theory of mind. *Child Development, 72*, 1032–1053.
Carnap, R. (1950). *Logical foundations of probability*. Chicago: Chicago University Press.
Carr, L., Iacoboni, M., Dubeau, M.-C., Mazziotta, J. C., & Lenzi, G. L. (2003). Neural mechanisms of empathy in humans: A relay from neural systems for imitation to limbic areas. *Proceedings National Academy of Science, 100*, 5497–5502.
Cartwright, N. (1983). *How the laws of physics Lie*. Oxford: Oxford University Press.
Carver, C. S., & Scheier, M. F. (1981). *Attention and self regulation: A control theory approach to human behavior*. New York: Springer Verlag.
Chapman, L. J., & Chapman, J. P. (1959). Atmosphere effect re-examined. *Journal of Experimental Psychology, 58*, 220–6.
Cheng, P. W., & Holyoak, K. J. (1985). Pragmatic reasoning schemas. *Cognitive Psychology, 17*, 391–416.
Cheng, P. W., & Holyoak, K. J. (1989). On the natural selection of reasoning theories. *Cognition, 33*, 285–313.
Cherniak, C. (1986). *Minimal rationality*. Cambridge, MA: MIT Press.
Chiu, L.-H. (1972). A cross-cultural comparison of cognitive styles in Chinese and American children. *International Journal of Psychology, 7*, 235–242.
Choi, S., & Bowerman, M. (1991). Learning to express motion events in English and Korean: The influence of language-specific lexicalization patterns. *Cognition, 41*, 83–121.
Choi, I., & Nisbett, R. E. (1998). Situational salience and cultural differences in the correspondence bias and in the actor-observer bias. *Personality and Social Psychology Bulletin, 24*, 949–960.
Choi, I., & Nisbett, R. E. (2000). The cultural psychology of surprise: Holistic theories and recognition of contradiction. *Journal of Personality and Social Psychology, 79*, 890–905.
Choi, I., Dalal, R., & Kim-Prieto, C. (2000). *Information search in causal attribution: Analytic vs. holistic*, Unpublished manuscript, Seoul National University.
Choi, I., Nisbett, R. E., & Smith, E. E. (1997). Culture, categorization and inductive reasoning. *Cognition, 65*, 15–32.
Churchland, P. M. (1979). *Scientific realism and the plasticity of mind*. Cambridge, UK: Cambridge University Press.
Churchland, P. M. (1981). Eliminative materialism and the propositional attitudes. *Journal of Philosophy, 78*, 67–90.
Churchland, P. M. (1989). *A neurocomputational perspective. The nature of mind and the structure of science*. Cambridge, MA: MIT Press.
Churchland, P. M. (1995). *The engine of reason, the seat of the soul: A philosophical journey into the brain*. Cambridge, MA: MIT Press.
Churchland, P. M. (1998). The neural representation of the social world. In P. A. Danielson (Ed.), *Modelling rationality, morality and evolution*. Oxford: Oxford University Press.
Churchland, P. S. (1986). *Neurophilosophy, toward a unified science of the mind/brain*. Cambridge, MA: MIT Press.
Churchland, P. S., & Sejnowski, T. (1992). *The computational brain*. Cambridge, MA: MIT Press.
Cohen, J. L. (1981). Can human irrationality be experimentally demonstrated? *The Behavioural and Brain Sciences, 4*, 318–20.

Cole, M. (1977). An ethnographic psychology of cognition. In P. Johnson-Laird & P. C. Wason (Eds.), *Thinking*. Cambridge, UK: Cambridge University Press.

Coleman, J. (1990). *Foundations of social theory*. Cambridge, MA: Harvard University Press.

deCondorcet, M. J. A. (1785). *Essay sur l'application de l'analyse à la probabilité des decisions rendues à la pluralité des voix*. Paris de l'Imprimerie Royale.

Cooley, C. H. (1902). *Human nature and the social order*. New York: Scribner.

Cooper, M. J., Dimitrov, O., & Rau, P. R. (2001). A rose.com by any other name. *Journal of Finance, 56*(6), 2371–2388.

Cosmides, L., & Tooby, J. (1996). Are humans good intuitive statisticians after all? Rethinking some conclusions from the literature on judgment under uncertainty. *Cognition, 58*, 1–73.

Craig, A. D. (2002). How do you feel? Interoception: the sense of physiological conditions of the body. *Nature Reviews Neuroscience, 3*, 655–666.

Damasio, A. (1994). *Descartes' error: Emotion, reason, and the human brain*. New York: Avon.

Davidson, D. (1970). Mental events. In L. Foster & J. Swanson (Eds.), *Experience and theory*. Amherst, MA: University of Massachusetts Press.

Davidson, D. (1980). *Essays on action and events*. Oxford: Oxford University Press.

Davidson, D. (1984). *Inquiries into truth and interpretation*. Oxford: Oxford University Press.

de Finetti, B. (1931). Sul significato soggettivo delle probabilità. *Fundamenta Mathematicae, 17*, 298–329.

Dennett, D. (1978). *Brainstorms*. Montgomery: Bradford Books.

Dennett, D. (1981). Three kinds of intentional psychology. In R. Healey (Ed.), *Reduction, time and reality*. Cambridge, UK: Cambridge University Press.

Dennett, D. (1987). *The intentional stance*. Cambridge, MA: MIT Press.

Desvousges, W., Johnson, F., Desvousges, W., Johnson, F., Dunford, R., Hudson, S., Wilson, K., & Boyle, K. (1993). Measuring natural resource damages with contingent valuation: Tests of validity and reliability. In J. Hausman (Ed.), *Contingent valuation: A critical assessment*. Amsterdam: North Holland.

Deutsch, D., & Feroe, J. (1981). The internal representation of pitch sequences in tonal music. *Psychological Review, 88*, 503–522.

Di Nuoscio, E. (1996). *Le ragioni degli individui*. Soveria Mannelli: Rubbettino.

Dilthey, W. (2002). *Selected works volume 3: The foundation of historical world in the human sciences*. Princeton, NJ: Princeton Universtity Press.

Doise, W. (1986). *Levels of explanation in social psychology*. Cambridge, UK: Cambridge University Press.

Donovan, A., Laudan, L., & Laudan, R. (Eds.). (1988). *Scrutinizing science. Empirical studies of scientific change*. Dordrecht: Kluwer Academic Publishers.

Dove, M. (1993). Uncertainty, humility, and adaptation in the tropical forest: The agricultural augury of kantu. *Ethnology, 32*(2), 145–167.

Downs, A. (1957). *An economic theory of democracy*. N.Y: Harper nad Row (trad. it., 1988), *Teoria economica della democrazia*. Bologna: Il Mulino.

Duhem, P. (1969). *To save the phenomena*. Chicago: University of Chicago Press.

Dummett, M. (1982). Realism. *Synthese, 52*, 55–112.

Durkheim, E. (1897). *Suicide, a study in sociology*. New York: The Free Press. 1962.

Durkheim, E. (1912). *Le formes élementaires de la vie religieuse*. Paris: Presses Universitaires de France. 1979.

Eddy, D. M. (1982). Probabilistic reasoning in clinical medicine: Problems and opportunities. In D. Kanheman, P. Slovic, & A. Tversky (Eds.), *Judgment under uncertainty: Heuristics and biases*. Cambridge, UK: Cambridge University Press.

Edwards, W. (1968). Conservatism in human information processing. In B. Kleinmuntz (Ed.), *Formal representation of human judgement*. New York: Wiley.

Edwards, D., & Potter, J. (1992). *Discursive psychology*. London: Sage.

Egidi, M. (1992). Il dilemma 'as if'. *Sistemi Intelligenti, IV*(3), 461–487.

Egidi, M., & Rizzello, S. (2003). Economia cognitiva: Fondamenti ed evoluzione storica. *Sistemi Intelligenti, XV*(2), 221–246.
Eldakar, O. T., Wilson, D. S., & O'Gorman, R. (2006). Emotions and actions associated with altruistic helping and punishment (PDF). *Evolutionary Psychology, 4*, 274–286.
Eldakar, O. T., & Wilson, D. S. (2008). Selfishness as second-order altruism. *Proceedings of the National Academy of Sciences of the USA, 105*(19), 6982–6986.
Elster, J. (1983). *Explaining technical change*. Cambridge, UK: Cambridge University Press.
Elster, J. (1985). *Making sense of Marx*. Cambridge, UK: Cambridge University Press.
Enelow, J. M., & Hinich, M. J. (1984). *The spatial theory of voting*. Cambridge, UK: Cambridge University Press.
Epstein, S. (1994). Integration of the cognitive and the psychodynamic unconscious. *American Psychologist, 49*, 709–24.
Evans, J. (1977). Toward a statistical theory of reasoning. *Quarterly Journal of Experimental Psychology, 29*, 297–306.
Evans, J., & Frankish, K. (Eds.). (2010). *In two minds*. New York: Oxford University Press.
Evans, J., & Over, D. E. (1996). *Rationality and reasoning*. Hove, UK: Psychology Press.
Evans-Pritchard, E. E. (1937). *Witchcraft, oracles and magic among the azande*. Oxford: Clarendon.
Fehr, E., & Gachter, S. (1998). Reciprocity and economics: The economic implications of homo reciprocans. *European Economic Review, 42*, 845–859.
Fernald, A., & Morikawa, H. (1993). Common themes and cultural variations in Japanese and American mothers' speech to infants. *Child Development, 64*, 637–656.
Field, A. (1977). Logic meaning and conceptual role. *Journal of Philosophy, 74*, 379–408.
Finucane, M., Alhakami, A., Slovic, P., & Johnson, S. (2000). The affect heuristic in judgments of risks and benefits. *Journal of Behavioral Decision Making, 13*, 1–17.
Fischhoff, B. (1975). Hindsight=foresight: The effect of outcome knowledge on judgment under uncertainty. *Journal of Experimental Psychology. Human Perception and Performance, 1*, 288–299.
Fodor, J. (1975). *The language of thought*. New York: Cromwell.
Fodor, J. (1987). *Psychosemantics*. Cambridge, MA: MIT Press.
Fodor, J. (1990). *A theory of content and other essays*. Cambridge, MA: MIT Press.
Foray, D. (2000). *L'économie de la connaissance*. Paris: Le Découverte.
Foucalt, M. (1972). *The archeology of knowledge*. London: Tavistock.
Franklin, A., & Howson, C. (1984). Why Do scientists prefer to vary their experiments? *Studies in History and Philosophy of Science, 15*, 51–62.
Frege, G. (1982). Uber Sinn und Bedeutung in *Zeitschrift fur Philosophie und Philosopische Kritik*.
Frey, B. (2008). *Happiness: A revolution in economics*. Cambridge, MA/London, England: MIT Press.
Friedman, M. (1953). *Essays in positive economics*. Chicago: University of Chicago Press.
Frith, C. D. (2003). Neural Hermeneutics: How brains interpret minds. Keynote Lecture. *9th Annual Meeting of the Organization of Human Brain Mapping*. New York.
Gadamer, H. G. (1960). *Wahrheit und Methode, Grundzuge einer philophischen Hermeneutik*. Tubingen: J. C. B. Mohr; Italian Translation (1972), *Verità e Metodo*. Milano: Fabbri.
Gallese, V., & Goldman, A. (1998). Mirror neurons and the simulation theory of mind-reading. *Trends in Cognitive Sciences, 12*, 493–501.
Gallese, V., Keysers, C., & Rizzolatti, G. (2004). A unifying view of the basis of social cognition. *Trends in Cognitive Science, 8*(9), 396–403.
Ganel, T., & Goodale, M. A. (2003). Visual control of action but not perception requires analytical processing of object shape. *Nature, 426*, 664–667.
Gaulin, S. J. C., & McBurney, D. H. (2003). *Evolutionary psychology*. Upper Saddle River, NJ: Prentice Hall.

Gazzaniga, M. S., Ivry, R. B., & Mangun, G. R. (2002). *Cognitive neuroscience*. New York: Norton & Company.
Geertz, C. (1973). *The interpretations of cultures*. New York: Basic Books.
Gelman, R. (1990). First principles organize attention to and learning about relevant data: Number and the animate/inanimate distinction as examples. *Cognitive Sciences, 14*, 79–106.
Gergen, K. J. (1994). *Realities and relationships: Soundings in social construction*. Cambridge, UK: Cambridge University Press.
Gettier, E. (1963). Is justified true belief knowledge? *Analysis, 23*, 121–123.
Gigerenzer, G. (1991). How to make cognitive illusions disappear: Beyond "heuristics and biases". In W. Stroebe & M. Hewstone (Eds.), *European review of social psychology* (Vol. 2, pp. 83–115). Chichester, UK: John Wiley and Sons.
Gigerenzer, G. (1994). Why the distinction between single-event probabilities and frequencies is important for psychology (and vice versa)? In G. Wright & P. Ayton (Eds.), *Subjective probability*. Chichester, UK: Wiley.
Gigerenzer, G. (2007). *Gut feelings: The intelligence of the unconscious*. New York: Viking Press.
Gigerenzer, G., & Selten, R. (2001a). Rethinking rationality. In G. Gigerenzer & R. Selten (Eds.), *Bounded rationality: The adaptive toolbox*. Cambridge, MA: MIT Press.
Gigerenzer, G., & Selten, R. (Eds.). (2001b). *Bounded rationality: The adaptive toolbox*. Cambridge, MA: MIT Press.
Gigerenzer, G., Todd, P., & The ABC Research Group. (1999). *Simple heuristics that make us smart*. New York: Oxford University Press.
Gilbert, D. T., Fiske, S. T., & Lindzey, G. (Eds.). (1998). *The handbook of social psychology* (4th ed.). New York: McGraw Hill.
Gilbert, D. T., Gill, M. J., & Wilson, T. D. (2002). The future is now: Temporal correction in affective forecasting. *Organizational Behavior and Human Decision Processes, 88*(1), 430–444.
Giocoli, R. (2003). *Modelling rational agents*. Cheltenham: Edward Elgar.
Gladwin, T. (1970). *East is a big bird*. Cambridge, MA: Harvard University Press.
Glimcher, P. W., & Rustichini, A. (2004). Neuroeconomics: The consilience of brain and decision. *Science, 306*, 447.
Goffman, E. (1963). *Stigma: Notes on the management of spoiled identity*. Englewood Cliffs, NJ: Prentice Hall.
Goldman, A. (1986). *Epistemology and cognition*. Cambridge, MA: Harvard University Press.
Goldman, A. (1993). *Philosophical application of cognitive science*. Boulder: Westview Press.
Goldman, A. (1999). *Knowledge in a social world*. Oxford: Clarendon Press.
Goldman, A. (2006). *Simulating minds*. New York: Oxford University Press.
Goldstein, L. J. (1958). The two theses of methodological individualism. *The British Journal for the Philosophy of Science, IX*(33), 1–11.
Goldstein, L. J. (1974). Social sciences, ontology, and explanation: Some further reflections. *Philosophy of the Social Sciences, 4*(3), 359–368.
Good, I. J. (1960). Weight of evidence, corroboration, explanatory power, information and the utility of experiments. *Journal of the Royal Statistical Society, B, 22*, 319–331.
Goodman, N. (1965). *Fact fiction and forecast*. Indianapolis: The Bobbs-Merril.
Gopnik, A. (1993). How we know our minds: The illusion of first-person knowledge of intentionality. *The Behavioral and Brain Sciences, 16*, 1–14.
Gopnik, A. (2009). *The philosophical baby*. New York: Farrar, Straus and Giroux.
Gopnik, A., & Choi, S. (1990). Do linguistic differences lead to cognitive differences? A cross-linguistic study of semantic and cognitive development. *First Language, 10*, 199–215.
Gopnik, A., & Meltzoff, A. N. (1997). *Words, thoughts and theories*. Cambridge, UK: Cambridge University Press.
Gordon, R. (1986). Folk psychology as simulation. *Mind & Language, 1*, 158–171.
Gordon, R. (1995). Simulation without introspection or inference from me to you. In T. Stone & M. Davies (Eds.), *Mental simulation*. Oxford: Blackwell.

Greenfield, P. M., & Childs, C. (1974). Weaving, color terms and patterns representation: cultural influences and cognitive development among Zinacantecos of southern Mexico. In J. Dawson & W. Lonner (Eds.), *Reading in cross-cultural psychology. Proceedings of the first international conference of the international association for cross-cultural psychology*. Hong Kong: University of Hong Kong Press.

Grice, P. (1993). *Logica e conversazione*. Bologna: il Mulino.

Grice, H. P. (1989). *Studies in the way of words*. Cambridge, MA: Harvard University Press.

Grignon, C., & Kardon, C. (2009). *Sciences de l'homme e sciences de la nature*. Paris: Edition de la Maison de les sciences de l'homme.

Gul, F., & Pesendorfer, W. (2005). The case for mindless economics. In A. Caplin & A. Schotter (Eds.), *Handbook of economic methodology*. Oxford: Oxford University Press.

Gutheil, G., & Gelman, S. (1997). Children's use of sample size and diversity information within basic level categories. *Journal of Experimental Child Psychology, 64*, 159–174.

Hacking, I. (1983). *Representing and intervening*. Cambridge, UK: Cambridge University Press.

Haidt, J., Koller, S., & Dias, M. (1993). Affect, culture and morality. *Journal of Personality and Social Psychology, 65*(4), 613–628.

Halpern, D. F. (1985). *Thought and knowledge*. Hillsdale, NJ: Erlbaum.

Hamilton, D. L., & Sherman, S. J. (1996). Perceiving persons and groups. *Psychological Review, 103*, 336–355.

Hammond, K. R. (1996). *Human judgement and social policy*. Oxford: Oxford University Press.

Hauser, M. (2006). *Moral minds*. New York: Prentice Hall.

Hausman, D. M. (1992). *Essays on philosophy and economic methodology*. New York: Cambridge University Press.

Hausman, D. M., & McPherson, M. S. (1993). Economics, rationality, and ethics. In D. M. Hausman (Ed.), *The philosophy of economics*. Cambridge, UK: Cambridge University Press.

Heal, J. (1986). Replication and functionalism. In J. Butterfield (Ed.), *Language, mind, and logic*. Cambridge, UK: Cambridge University Press.

Heath, S. B. (1982). What no bedtime story means: Narrative skills at home and school. *Language in Society, 11*, 49–79.

Heider, E. R. (1972). Universals in color naming and memory. *Journal of Experimental Psychology, 93*, 10–20.

Heider, F. (1958). *The psychology of interpersonal relations*. New York: Wiley.

Hempel, C. (1965). *Aspects of scientific explanation*. New York: The Free Press.

Hempel, C. (1966). *Philosophy of natural sciences*. Englewood Cliffs, NJ: Prentice-Hall.

Henrich, J. (2000). Does culture matter in economic behavior? Ultimatum game bargaining among the machiguenga. *American Economic Review, 90*(4), 973–979.

Henrich, J., et al. (2001). Group report: What is the role of culture in bounded rationality? In G. Gigerenzer & R. Selten (Eds.), *Bounded rationality: The adaptive toolbox*. Cambridge, MA: MIT Press.

Hertwig, R., & Chase, V. M. (1998). Many reasons or just one: How response mode affects reasoning in the conjunction problem. Thinking and Reasoning, 4, 319–352.

Hey, J. D. (1991). *Experiments in economics*. Oxford: Basil Blackwell.

Higgins, E. T. (1997). Beyond pleasure and pain. *American Psychologist, 52*, 1280–1300.

Higgins, E. T., & Bargh, J. A. (1987). Social cognition and social perception. *Annual Review of Psychology, 38*, 369–425.

Hilton, D. (2001). The psychology of financial decision-making: Applications to trading, dealing, and investment analysis. *Journal of Behavioral Finance, II*(1), 37–53.

Hintikka, J. (1968). The varieties of information and scientific explanation. In B. Van Rootselaar & J. F. Staal (Eds.), *Logic, methodology and philosophy of science III*. Proceedings of the third international congress for logic, methodology and philosophy of science, Amsterdam 1967 (pp. 311-331). Amsterdam, North-Holland.

Hirschfeld, L. (1996). *Race in the making: Cognition, culture, and the child's construction of human kinds*. Cambridge, MA: MIT Press.

Hirschfeld, L. (2006). Who needs a theory of mind? In R. Viale, D. Andler, & L. Hirschfeld (Eds.), *Biological and cultural bases of human inference* (pp. 1–31). Mahwah, NJ: Lawrence Erlbaum Associates.

Hogarth, R., & Reder, M. (1987). Introduction: Perspectives from economics and psychology. In R. Hogarth & M. Reder (Eds.), *Rational choice*. Chicago: The University of Chicago Press.

Holland, J. M., Holyoak, K. J., Nisbett, R. E., & Thagard, P. R. (1986). *Induction*. Cambridge, MA: MIT Press.

Homans, G. C. (1967). *The nature of social nature*. New York: Harcourt, Brace & World.

Homans, G. C. (1970). The relevance of psychology to the explanation of social phenomena. In R. Borger & F. Cioffi (Eds.), *Explanation in the behavioural sciences*. Cambridge, UK: Cambridge University Press.

Horwich, P. (1982). *Probability and evidence*. Cambridge, UK: Cambridge University Press.

Howson, C., & Urbach, O. (1993). *Scientific reasoning: The Bayesian approach*. Chicago: Open Court.

Huber, J., Payne, J. W., & Pluto, C. (1982). Adding asymmetrical dominated alternatives: Violations of regularity and similarity hypothesis. *Journal of Consumer Research, 9*, 90–98.

Hull, C. L. (1943). *Principles of behaviour. An introduction to behaviour theory*. New York: Appletan Century.

Hume, D. (1739/1740). *A treatise of human nature*. Oxford: Clarendon Press. 1978.

Hume, D. (1911). A treatise of human nature. In E. Rhys (Ed.), *Everyman's library*. London/New York: J. M. Dent & Sons Ltd/E.P. Dutton.

Hutchins, E., & Hazlehurst, B. (1991). Learning in the cultural process. In C. G. Langton, C. Taylor, J. D. Farmer, & S. Rasmussen (Eds.), *Artificial life II: SFI studies in the sciences of complexity* (Vol. X, pp. 689–706). Redwood City, CA: Addison-Wesley.

Hutchinson, T. W. (1938). *The significance and basic postulates of economic theory*. New York: August M. Kelley.

Iacoboni, M. (2008). *Mirroring people. The new science of how we connect with others*. New York: Farrar, Straus & Giroux.

Iacoboni, M., Lieberman, M. D., Knowlton, B. J., Molnar-Szakacs, I., Moritz, M., Throop, C. J., & Fiske, A. P. (2004). Watching social interactions produces dorsomedial prefrontal and medial parietal BOLD fMRI signal increases compaing to a resting baseline. *NeuroImage, 21*, 1167–73.

Iacoboni, M., Molnar-Szakacs, I., Gallese, V., Buccino, G., Mazziotta, J. C., & Rizzolatti, G. (2005). Grasping the intentions of the other with one's own mirror neuron system. *PLoS Biology, 3*, 529–535.

Jacob, P., & Jeannerod, M. (2005). The motor theory of social cognition. A critique, Trends in Cognitive Science, 9, 1, 21–25.

Janis, I. L. (1982). *Groupthink*. Boston: Houghton Mifflin.

Jervis, R. (1992). Political implications of loss aversion. *Political Psychology, 13*, 187–204.

Jevons, W. S. (1871). *The principles of political economy*. London: Macmillan & co.

Ji, L., Peng, K., & Nisbett, R. E. (2000). Culture, control, and perception of relationships in the environment. *Journal of Personality and Social Psychology, 78*, 943–955.

Ji, L., Su, Y., & Nisbett, R. E. (2001). Culture, prediction, and change. *Psychological Science, 12*, 450–456.

Ji, L., Zhang, Z., & Nisbett, R. E. (2004). Is it culture or is it language? Examination of language effects in cross-cultural research on categorization. Journal of Personality and Social Psychology, 87, 57–65.

Johnson Laird, P. (1983). *Mental models*. Cambridge, UK: Cambridge University Press.

Johnson Laird, P. (1988). *The computer and the mind*. London: William Collins Sons & Co. Italian Translation, Il Mulino, Bologna, 1990.

Johnson Laird, P., & Byrne, R. M. J. (1990). *Deduction*. Hillsdale: Erlbaum.

Johnson-Laird, P. N., & Steedman, M. (1978). The psychology of syllogisms. *Cognitive Psychology, 10*(1), 64–99.

Jones, E. E., & Harris, V. A. (1967). The attribution of attitudes. *Journal of Experimental Social Psychology, 3*, 1–24.

Kahneman, D. (2003). Maps of bounded rationality: Psychology for behavioural economics. *American Economic Review, 93*(5), 1449–1475.

Kahneman, D. (2007). *Economia della felicità*. Milan: Il Sole 24 Ore.

Kahneman, D., & Frederick, S. (2002). Representativeness revisited: Attribute substitution in intuitive judgment. In T. Gilovich, D. Griffith, & D. Kahneman (Eds.), *Heuristics and biases: The psychology of intuitive judgment*. New York: Cambridge University Press.

Kahneman, D., & Tversky, A. (1972). Subjective probability: A judgment of representativeness. *Cognitive Psychology, 3*, 430–454.

Kahneman, D., & Tversky, A. (1973). On the psychology of prediction. *Psychological Review, 80*, 237–351.

Kahneman, D., & Tversky, A. (1979a). Intuitive prediction. Biases and corrective procedures. *Management Science, 12*, 313–327.

Kahneman, D., & Tversky, A. (1979b). Prospect theory: An analysis of decision under risk. *Econometrica, 47*, 263–291.

Kahneman, A., & Tversky, D. (1987). Rational choice and the framing of decisions. In R. Hogarth & M. Reder (Eds.), *Rational choice*. Chicago: The University of Chicago Press.

Kahneman, D., & Tversky, A. (2000). *Choices, values, and frames*. Cambridge, UK: Cambridge University Press.

Kahneman, D., Slovic, P., & Tversky, A. (Eds.). (1982). *Judgement under uncertainty: Heuristics and biases*. Cambridge, UK: Cambridge University Press.

Kant, I. (1781/1787). *The critique of pure reason, the Cambridge edition of the works of Immanuel Kant (1998)*. Cambridge, UK: Cambridge University Press.

Keil, F. C. (1995). The growth of causal understandings of natural kinds. In D. Sperber, D. Premack, & A. Premack (Eds.), *Causal cognition: A multidisciplinary debate* (pp. 234–267). New York: Oxford University Press.

Kelley, H. H. (1967). Attribution theory in social psychology. In D. Levine (Ed.), *Nebraska symposium on motivation* (Vol. 15, pp. 192–238). Lincoln, NE: University of Nebraska Press.

Keynes, J. M. (1936). *The general theory of employment, interest and money*. London: Mac Millan.

Keynes, J. N. (1917). *The scope and method of political economy* (4th ed.). London: Mc Millan.

Kim, J. (1998). *Mind in a physical world*. Cambridge, MA: MIT Press.

Kitcher, P. (1989). Explanatory unification and the causal structure of the world. In P. Kitcher & W. C. Salmon (Eds.), *Scientific explanation* (pp. 410–505). Minneapolis, MN: University of Minnesota Press.

Kolmogorov, A. N. (1950). *A foundation of probability*. New York: Chelsea.

Kosslyn, S. (1981). *Image and mind*. Cambridge, MA: Harvard University Press.

Kripke, S. A. (1980). *Naming and necessity*. Oxford: Blackwell.

Lakatos, I. (1970). Falsification and the methodology of scientific research programmes. In I. Lakatos & A. Musgrave (Eds.), *Criticism and the growth of knowledge*. Cambridge, UK: Cambridge University Press.

Lakatos, I. (1978). *The methodology of scientific research programmes* (Philosophical Papers, Vol. 1). Cambridge, UK: Cambridge University Press.

Langer, E. (1975). The illusion of control. *Journal of Personality and Social Psychology, 32*, 311–328.

Langer, E., (1978). Rethinking the role of thought in social interaction. In J. Harvey, W. Ickes, & R. Kidd (Eds.), *Proceedings of the 13th annual conference of the Cognitive Science Society*, Erlbaum, Hillsdale.

Langer, E., Blank, A., & Chanowitz, B. (1978). The mindlessness of ostensibly thoughtful action: The role of "placebic" information in interpersonal interaction. *Journal of Personality and Social Psychology, 36*, 635–642.

Langley, P., Simon, H. A., Bradshaw, G. L., & Zytkow, J. M. (1987). *Scientific discovery*. Cambridge, MA: MIT Press.

Laudan, L. (1984). *Science and its values.* Berkeley, CA: University of California Press.
LeDoux, J. E. (1996). *The emotional brain: The mysterious underpinnings of emotional life* (It. trans. *Il cervello emotivo. Alle origini delle emozioni*, Baldini and Castoldi, Milan 1998). New York: Simon & Schuster.
Leslie, A. M. (1988). The necessity of illusion: Perception and thought in infancy. In L. Weizkrantz (Ed.), *Thought without language.* Oxford: Clarendon Press.
Levins, R. (1968). *Evolution in changing environment.* Princeton, NJ: Princeton University Press.
Levinson, S. C. (1994). Vision, shape and linguistic description: Tzeltal body part terminology and object description. *Linguistics, 32*, 791–885.
Lewis, D. K. (1983). New work for a theory of universals. *Australasian Journal of Philosophy, 61*, 109–43.
Libet, B. (1985). Unconscious cerebral initiative and the role of conscious will in voluntary action. *Behavior and Brain Sciences, 8*, 529–566.
Liu, S.-H. (1974). The Use of analogy and symbolism in traditional Chinese philosophy. *Journal of Chinese Psychology, 1*, 313–338.
Lo, Y., Sides, A., Rozelle, J., & Osherson, D. (2002). Evidential diversity and premise probability in young children inductive judgment. *Cognitive Science, 26*, 181–206.
Loewenstein, G., Weber, E., Hsee, C., & Welch, N. (2001). Risk as feelings. *Psychological Bulletin, 127*, 267–86.
Lopez, A., Atran, S., Coley, J. D., Medin, D. L., & Smith, E. E. (1997). The tree of life: Universal and cultural features of folkbiological taxonomies and inductions. *Cognitive Psychology, 32*(3), 251–295.
López, A., Gelman, S. A., Gutheil, G., & Smith, E. E. (1992). The development of category-based induction. *Child Development, 63*, 1070–1090.
Lucas, R. E. (1981). *Studies in business cycle theory.* Cambridge, MA: MIT Press.
Macchi, L., & Bagassi, M. (2006). Probabilistic reasoning and natural language. In R. Viale, D. Andler, & L. Hirschfeld (Eds.), *Biological and cultural bases of human inference* (pp. 1–31). Mahwah, NJ: Lawrence Erlbaum Associates.
Mackie, J. L. (1974). *The cement of the universe.* Oxford: Clarendon Press.
Malinowski, B. (1954). *Magic, science and religion.* New York: Doubleday.
March, J. G. (1994). *A primer of decision making.* New York: Free Press.
Markus, H., & Kitayama, S. (1991). Culture and the self: Implications for cognition, emotions, and motivation. *Psychological Review, 35*, 63–78.
Markus, H., & Kunda, Z. (1986). Stability and malleability of the self concept. *Journal of Personality and Social Psychology, 51*, 858–866.
Marr, D. (1982). *Vision.* San Francisco, CA: Freeman.
Marshall, A. (2002). Ye Machine. In T. Raffaelli (Ed.), *Marshall's evolutionary economics.* London: Routledge.
Martelli, P. (1989). Teorie della scelta razionale. In A. Panebianco (a cura di), L'analisi della politica (pp. 159–192). Bologna: Il Mulino.
Marx, K., (It. transl.,1971). *Per la critica dell'economia politica.* Roma: Editori Riuniti.
Marx, K. (1867). *Das Kapital.* Hamburg/New York: O. Meissner/L.W. Schmidt.
Massey, C., & Gelman, R. (1988). Preschoolers' Ability to decide whether pictured unfamiliar objects can move themselves. *Developmental Psychology, 24*, 307–317.
Masuda, T., & Nisbett, R. E. (2001). Attending holistically vs. Analitically: Comparing the context sensitivity of Japanese and Americans. *Journal of Personality and Social Psychology, 81*, 922–934.
Matlin, M., & Strang, D. (1978). *The Pollyanna principle: Selectivity in language, memory and thought.* Cambridge, MA: Schenkman.
Mayo, D. G. (1996). *Error and the growth of experimental knowledge.* Chicago: University of Chicago Press.
McCloskey, D. N. (1986). The rhetoric of economics. In D. M. Hausman (Ed.), *The philosophy of economics.* Cambridge, UK: Cambridge University Press.
McGee, V. (2005). Inscrutability and its discontent. *Nous, 39*, 397–425.

McKenzie, C. R. M. (1994). The accuracy of intuitive judgment strategies: Covariation assessment and Bayesian inference. *Cognitive Psychology, 26*, 209–239.
Medin, D. L., Lynch, E., Coley, J. D., & Atran, S. (1997). Categorization and reasoning among tree experts: Do all roads lead to Rome? *Cognitive Psychology, 32*(1), 49–96.
Mellor, D. H. (1971). *The matter of chance*. Cambridge, UK: Cambridge University Press.
Menger, C. (1963). *Investigations into the method of the social sciences with special reference to economics*. New York: New York University Press.
Mill, J. S. (1836). *On the definition of political economy and the method of investigation proper to it, in collected works of john Stuart mill* (Vol. 4). Toronto: University of Toronto Press. 1967.
Mill, J. S. (1st edition, 1843; 8th edition, 1956). *A system of logic ratiocinative and inductive*. (It. trans., 1968, *Sistema di Logica Raziocinativa ed Induttiva*. Roma: Ubaldini Editore).
Mill, J. S. (1848). *Principles of political economy*. London: Parker.
Mill, J. S. (1866). *A system of logic*. London: Macmillan.
Miller, J. G. (1984). Culture and the development of everyday social explanation. *Journal of Personality and Social Psychology, 46*, 961–978.
Montesano, A. (1998). Rationality in economics: A general framework. In G. Preyer, G. Peter, & A. Ulfig (Eds.), *After the received view. Developments in the theory of science* (Protosociology, Vol. 12, pp. 290–296).
Moon, Y., & Nass, C. (1996). How "real" are computer personalities? psychological responses to personality types in human-computer interaction. *Communication Research, 23*(6), 1651–1674.
Morris, M. W., & Peng, K. (1994). Culture and cause: Americans and Chinese attributions for social and physical events. *Journal of Personality and Social Psychology, 67*, 949–971.
Moscovici, S. (1984). The phenomenon of social representations. In M. Farr & S. Moscovici (Eds.), *social representations*. Cambridge, UK: Cambridge University Press.
Mukamel, R., Ekstrom, A. D., Kaplan, J., Iacoboni, M., & Fried, I. (2007). *Mirror neurons of single cells in human medial frontal cortex*. Paper presented at the program n. 127.4, 2007 Abstract.
Myrvold, W. C. (1996). Bayesianism and diverse evidence: A reply to Andrew Wayne. *Philosophy of Science, 63*, 661–665.
Nagashima, N. (1973). A reversed world: Or is it? In R. Horton & R. Finnegan (Eds.), *Modes of thought*. London: Faber and Faber.
Neale, M. A., & Bazerman, M. H. (1991). *Cognition and rationality in negotiation*. New York: Free Press.
Newell, A. (1990). *Unified theory of cognition*. Cambridge, MA: Harvard University Press.
Newell, A., & Simon, H. (1972). *Human problem solving*. Englewood Cliffs, NJ: Prentice Hall.
Nisbett, R. E. (2003). *The geography of thought: How Asians and Americans think differently...and why*. New York: The Free Press.
Nisbett, R. E., & Masuda, T. (2006). Culture and point of view. In R. Viale, D. Andler, & L. Hirschfeld (Eds.), *Biological and cultural bases of human inference*. Mahwah, NJ: Lawrence Erlbaum Associates.
Nisbett, R. E., & Ross, L. (1980). *Human inference: Strategies and shortcomings of social judgement*. Englewood Cliffs, NJ: Prentice-Hall (Italian Translation, 1989, Bologna: Il Mulino).
Nisbett, R. E., & Wilson, T. D. (1977). Telling more than we know: Verbal reports on mental processes. *Psychological Review, 84*, 231–259.
Nisbett, R. E., Peng, K., Choi, I., & Norenzayan, A. (2001). Culture and systems of thought: Holistic vs. analytic cognition. *Psychological Review, 108*, 291–310.
Norenzayan, A. (2006). Cultural variaiton in reasoning. In R. Viale, D. Andler, & L. Hirschfeld (Eds.), *Biological and cultural bases of human inference* (pp. 1–31). Mahwah. NJ: Lawrence Erlbaum Associates.
Olson, M. (1965). *The logic of collective action*. Cambridge Mass: Harvard University Press. (Trad. it., 1983), *La logica dell'azione collettiva*. Milano: Feltrinelli.
Olson, M. (1982). *The rise and decline of nations*. (trad. it., 1984), *Ascesa e declino delle nazioni*. Bologna: Il Mulino.
Olson, M. (1994). *Logica delle istituzioni*. Milano: Edizioni della Comunità.

Osherson, D., Smith, E., Wilkie, O., López, A., & Shafir, E. (1990). Category-based induction. *Psychological Review, 97*(2), 185–200.

Panebianco, A. (Ed.). (1989). *L'analisi della politica*. Bologna: Il Mulino.

Pappalardo, A. (1989). L'analisi economica della politica. In A. Panebianco (a cura di), L'analisi della politica (pp. 193–216). Bologna: Il Mulino.

Pareto, V. (1944). *Trattato di Sociologia Generale*. Milano: Ed. di Comunità.

Parisi, D. (2003). Economia o economia? *Sistemi Intelligenti, XV*(2), 185–220.

Parsons, T. (1954). *Essays in sociological theory*. Glencoe, Ill: Free Press.

Peng, K. (1997). *Naive dialecticism and its effects on reasoning and judgment about contradiction*. Unpublished Ph.D. thesis, University of Michigan, Ann Arbor, MI.

Perner, J., & Kühberger, A. (2006). Framing and the theory-simulation controversy: Predicting People's decisions. In R. Viale, D. Andler, & L. Hirschfeld (Eds.), *Biological and cultural bases of human inference* (pp. 1–31). Mahwah, NJ: Lawrence Erlbaum Associates.

Petroni, A. (1989). L'individualismo metodologico. In A. Panebianco (a cura di), L'analisi della politica (pp.135–158). Bologna: Il Mulino.

Pietroni, D., & Rumiati, R. (2008). *La mente che negozia*. Milan: Il Sole 24 Ore.

Pfeiffer, J., Iacoboni, M., Mazziotta, J. C., & Dapretto, M. (2008). Mirroring other emotions relates to empathy and interpersonal competence in children. *NeuroImage, 39*, 2076–85.

Popkin, S. (1979). *The rational peasant*. Berkeley, CA: University of California Press.

Popper, K. (1959). *The logic of scientific discovery*. London: Hutchinson.

Popper, K. (1960). *The poverty of historicism*. London: Routledge and Keegan Paul.

Popper, K. (5th edition, 1966). *The open society and its enemies* (It. transl, 1974, *La società Aperta ed i Suoi Nemici*. Roma: Armando). London: Routledge.

Popper, K. (1972). *Objective knowledge*. Oxford: Clarendon Press.

Popper, K. R., & Eccles, J. C. (1977). *The self and its brain*. New York: Springer International.

Pozzali, A., & Viale, R. (2007). Cognition, types of "tacit knowledge" and technology transfer. In B. Walliser (Ed.), *Cognitive economics: New trends*. Oxford: Elsevier.

Premack, D., & Woodruff, G. (1978). Does the chimpanzee have a theory of mind? *The Behavioral and Brain Sciences, 1*, 515–526.

Quattrone, C., & Tversky, A. (1988). Contrasting rational and psychological analysis of political choice. *American Political Science Review, 82*, 719–736.

Quine, W. O. (1960). *Word and object*. Cambridge, MA: MIT Press.

Quine, W. O. (1969). Epistemology naturalized. In W.O. Quine (Ed.), *Ontological relativity and other essays*. New York: Columbia University Press.

Quine, W. O. (1985). Epistemology naturalized. In H. Kornblith (Ed.), *Naturalizing epistemology*. Cambridge, MA: MIT Press.

Robbins, L. (1935/1983). An Essay on the Nature and Significance of Economic Science. 3rd edition. London: Macmillan.

Ramsey, F. P. (1931). *The foundations of mathematics*. London: Routledge.

Reber, A. S. (1993). *Implicit learning and tacit knowledge. An essay on the cognitive unconscious*. Oxford: Oxford University Press.

Reichenbach, H. (1949). *The theory of probability*. Berkeley, CA: University of California Press.

Reyna, V. F. (2004). How people make decisions that involve risk: A dual-process approach. *Current Directions in Psychological Science, 13*, 60–6.

Rips, L. J., & Marcus, S. L. (1977). *Supposition and the analysis of conditional sentences*. Hillsdale, NY: Erlbaum.

Rizzolatti, G., & Sinigaglia, C. (2006). *So quel che fai. Il cervello che agisce e i neuroni a specchio*. Milano: Cortina.

Rizzolatti, G., & Vozza, L. (2008). *Nella mente degli altri*. Bologna: Zanichelli.

Rizzolatti, G., Fogassi, L., & Gallese, V. (2001). Neurophysiological mechanisms underlying the understanding and imitation in action. *Nature Reviews Neuroscience, 2*, 661–670.

Robbins, L. (1935/1983). An Essay on the Nature and Significance of Economic Science. 3rd edition. London: Macmillan.

Rock, I. (1983). *The logic of perception*. Cambridge, MA: MIT Press.

Rosch, E. (1972). The structure of color space in naming and memory for two languages. *Cognitive Psychology, 3*, 337–354.

Rosenberg, A. (1983). If economics isn't science, what is it? In D. M. Hausman (Ed.), *The philosophy of economics*. Cambridge, UK: Cambridge University Press.
Rosenberg, A. (1988). *Philosophy of social science*. Oxford: Clarendon Press.
Ross, L. (1977). The intuitive psychologist and his shortcomings. In L. Berkowitz (Ed.), *Advances in experimental social psychology* (Vol. 10, pp. 173–220). New York: Academic Press.
Ryle, G. (1949). *The concept of mind*. London: Hutchison.
Sacco, P. L., & Zarri, L. (2005). Teoria dei giochi comportamentali e preferenze sociali. In R. Viale (Ed.), *Le nuove Economie. Dall'economia evolutiva a quella cognitiva: oltre i fallimenti della teoria neoclassica*. Milano: Editrice Il Sole 24 Ore.
Sacks, O. W. (1995). *An anthropologist on mars: Seven paradoxical tales* (1st ed.). New York: Knopf.
Salmon, W. (1984). *Scientific explanation and the causal structure of the world*. Princeton, NJ: Princeton University Press.
Samson, D., Apperly, I., Kathirgamanathan, U., & Humphreys, G. W. (2005). Seeing it my way: A case of a selective deficit in inhibiting self-perspective. *Brain, 128*, 1102–111.
Samuelson, P. A. (1966). *The collected scientific papers of Paul A. Samuelson*. Cambridge, MA: MIT Press.
Sargent, T. J. (1993). *Bounded rationality in macroeconomics*. Oxford: Oxford University Press.
Sartori, G. (1987). *The theory of democracy revisited*. Chatham, NJ: Chatham House.
Schelling, T. (1966). *Arms and influence*. New Haven, CT: Yale University Press.
Schleiermacher, F. D. E. (1998). In A. Bowie (Ed.), *Hermeneutics and criticism and other writings*. Cambridge, UK: Cambridge University Press.
Schreiber, D., & Iacoboni, M. (2005). *Monkey see monkey do: Mirror neurons, functional brain imaging, and lloking at political faces*. Washington, DC: American Political Science Association Meeting.
Sellars, W. (1963). *Science, perception and reality*. London: Routledge and Kegan Paul.
Sen, A. (1970). *Collective choice and social welfare*. San Francisco, CA: Holden Day.
Sen, A. (1992). *Inequality re-examined*. Cambridge, MA: Harvard University Press.
Senior, N. (1836/1965). *The outline of the science of political economy*. New York: A.M. Kelley.
Shafir, E. (1993). Choosing versus rejecting: Why some options are both better and worse than others. *Memory & Cognition, 21*, 546–556.
Shafir, E., & LeBoeuf, R. (2002). Rationality. *Annual Review of Psychology, 53*, 491–517.
Shafir, E., Simonson, I., & Tversky, A. (1993). Reason-based choice. *Cognition, 49*, 11–36.
Shepsle, K. A., & Weingast, B. (1982). Institutionalizing majority rule: A social choice theory with policy implications. *American Economic review, Papers and Proceedings, 72*, 367–371.
Shweder, R. A. (1977). Likeness and likelihood in everyday thought: Magical thinking and everyday judgments about personality. In P. N. Johnson-Laird & P. C. Wason (Eds.), *Thinking*. Cambridge, UK: Cambridge University Press.
Simon, H. A. (1956). Rational choice and the structure of the environment. *Psychology Review, 63*, 129–138.
Simon, H. A. (1957). *Models of man*. New York: Wiley.
Simon, H. A. (1982). *Models of bounded rationality*. Cambridge, MA: MIT Press.
Simon, H. A. (1985). *Causalità, razionalità, organizzazione*. Bologna: Il Mulino.
Simon, H. A. (1986). Rationality in psychology and economics. In R. Hogarth & M. Reder (Eds.), *Rational choice*. Chicago: The University of Chicago Press.
Simon, H. A. (1990). Invariants of human behavior. *Annual Review of Psychology, 41*, 1–19.
Simon, H. A. (1997). *An empirically based microeconomics*. Cambridge, UK: Cambridge University Press.
Simon, H. A. (2000). Bounded rationality in social sciences: Today and tomorrow. *Mind & Society, 1*(1), 25–41.
Simon, H. A., Egidi, M., Marris, R., & Viale, R. (Eds.). (1992). *Economics, bounded rationality and the cognitive revolution*. Aldershot: Edward Elgar.

Simons, D. J., & Levin, D. T. (1997). Change blindness. *Trends in Cognitive Sciences, 1*, 261–267.
Simonson, I., & Tversky, A. (1992). Choice in context: Tradeoff contrast and extremeness aversion. *Journal of Marketing Research, 29*, 281–295.
Singer, T., Wolpert, D., & Frith, C. (2003). Introduction: The study of social interactions. In C. Frith & D. Wolpert (Eds.), *The neuroscience of social interaction*. Oxford: Oxford University Press.
Skinner, B. F. (1953). *Science and human behaviour*. New York: Mac Millan.
Sloman, S. (1996). The empirical case for two systems of reasoning. *Psychological Bulletin, 119*, 3–22.
Slovic, P., Finucane, M., Peters, E., & Mac Gregor, D. G. (2001). The affect heuristic. In T. Gilovich, D. Griffin, & D. Kahneman (Eds.), *Heuristics and biases: The psychology of intuitive thought*. New York: Cambridge University Press.
Smith, A. (1776). *Inquiry into the nature and causes of the wealth of nations*. The Modern Library, 1937, New York. Random House, Inc.
Smith, E. E., & Kosslyn, S. M. (2007). *Cognitive psychology. Mind and brain*. Upper Saddle River, NJ: Pearson-Prentice Hall.
Smith, L. B., Jones, S. S., Landau, B., Gershkoff-Stowe, L., & Samuelson, L. (2002). Object name learning provides on-the-job training for attention. *Psychological Science, 13*, 13–19.
Smith, V. (1962). An experimental study of market behaviour. *Journal of Political Economy, 70*, 274–279.
Soya, N., Carey, S., & Spelke, E. (1991). Ontological categories guide inductions of word meaning: Object terms and substance terms. *Cognition, 38*, 179–211.
Spelke, E. S. (1990). Principles of object perception. *Cognitive Science, 14*, 29–56.
Spelke, E. S., Phillips, A., & Woodward, A. L. (1995). Infants' knowledge of object motion and human action. In D. Sperber, D. Premack, & A. Premack (Eds.), *Causal cognition: A multidisciplinary debate*. New York: Oxford University Press.
Sperber, D. (2000). Metarepresentations in an evolutionary perspective. In D. Sperber (Ed.), *Metarepresentations: A multidisciplinary perspective* (pp. 117–137). New York: Oxford University Press.
Sperber, D. (2005). The varieties of human social cognition. www.interdisciplines.org/mirror/papers/3/1/3_1.
Sperber, D. (2006). An evolutionary perspective on testimony and argumentation. In R. Viale, D. Andler, & L. Hirschfeld (Eds.), *Biological and cultural bases of human inference* (pp. 1–31). Mahwah, NJ: Lawrence Erlbaum Associates.
Sperber, D., Premack, D., & Premack, A. (Eds.). (1995). *Causal cognition: A multidisciplinary debate*. New York: Oxford University Press.
Springer, K., Meier, J. A., & Berry, D. S. (1996). Nonverbal bases of social perception: Developmental change in sensitivity to patterns of motion that reveal interpersonal events. *Journal of Nonverbal Behavior, 20*(4), 1199–1211.
Stanovich, K. (1999). *Who is rational? Studies of individual differences in reasoning*. Mahwah, NJ: Erlbaum.
Stanovich, K., & Toplak, M. (2012). Defining features versus incidental correlates of Type 1 and Type 2 processing. Mind & Society, 11, 1. DOI 10.1007/s11299-011-0093-6.
Sternberg, R. J. (2009). *Cognitive psychology*. Belmont, CA: Wadsworth.
Stich, S., & Nisbett, R. (1980). Justification and the psychology of human reasoning. *Philosophy of Science, 47*, 188–202.
Stich, S. (1983). *From folk psychology to cognitive science*. Cambridge, MA: MIT Press.
Stich, S. (1990). *The fragmentation of reason*. Cambridge, MA: MIT Press.
Stigler, S. (1961). The economics of information. *Journal of Political Economy, 69*, 213–225.
Tajfel, H., & Turner, J. C. (1986). The social identity theory of intergroup relations. In S. Worchel & W. G. Austin (Eds.), *Psychology of intergroup relations*. Moterey, CA: Brooks/Cole.

Tajfel, H. (1981). *Human groups and social categories: Studies in social psychology*. Cambridge, UK: Cambridge University Press.

Tambiah, S. J. (1973). Form and meaning of magical acts: A point of view. In R. Horton & R. Finnegan (Eds.), *Models of thought*. London: Faber and Faber.

Taylor, C. (1985). *Philosophy and the human sciences: Philosophical papers 2*. Cambridge, UK: Cambridge University Press.

Tetlock, P. (2005). *Expert political judgement*. Princeton, NJ: Princeton University Press.

Thaler, R., & Sunstein, C. (2008). *Nudge*. London: Penguin Books.

Thaler, R. (1987). The psychology and economics. In R. Hogarth & M. Reder (Eds.), *Rational choice*. Chicago: The University of Chicago Press.

The Economist. (1994). Garbage in, garbage out. April 23, p. 86.

The Economist. (1994). Mind over matter, 23 April, pp. 79–81.

Tomasello, M. (1999). *The cultural origins of human cognition*. Cambridge, MA: Harvard University Press.

Turner, V. (1974). *Dramas, fields, and metaphors: Symbolic actions in human society*. Ithaca, NY: Cornell University Press.

Tversky, A., & Kahneman, D. (1973). Availability: A heuristic for judging frequency and probability. *Cognitive Psychology, 5*, 207–232.

Tversky, A., & Kahneman, D. (1974). Judgement under uncertainty: Heuristics and biases. *Science, 185*, 1124–1131.

Tversky, A., & Kahneman, D. (1980). Causal schemas in judgements under uncertainty. In M. Fishbein (Ed.), *Progress in social psychology*. Hillsdale, NJ: Erlbaum.

Tversky, A., & Kanheman, D. (1986). Rational choice and the framing of decision. *Journal of Business, 59*, S51–S278.

Uleman, J. S. (1999). Spontaneous versus intentional inferences in impression formation. In S. Chaiken & Y. Trope (Eds.), *Dual-process theories in social psychology* (pp. 141–160). New York: Guilford.

Ullman, S. (1979). *The interpretation of visual motion*. Cambridge, MA: MIT Press.

van Boven, L., & Loewenstein, G. (2003). Social projection of transient drive states. *Personality and Social Psychology Bulletin, 29*(9), 1159–1168.

van Boven, L., Dunning, D., & Loewenstein, G. (2000). Egocentric empathy gaps between owners and buyers: Misperceptions of the endowment effect. *Journal of Personality and Social Psychology, 79*, 66–76.

van Fraassen, Bas. (1980). *The scientific image*. Oxford: Oxford University Press.

Veblen, T. B. (1994). *The collected works of Thorstein Veblen*. London: Routledge.

Vermazen, B., & Hintikka, M. B. (1985). *Essays on Davidson: Actions and events*. Oxford: Clarendon Press.

Viale, R. (1989). Epistemologia, cognizione e razionalità deduttiva. In R. Viale (Ed.), *Mente umana mente artificiale*. Milano: Feltrinelli.

Viale, R. (1991). *Metodo e società nella scienza*. Milano: Franco Angeli.

Viale, R. (1992/2008). Cognitive constraints of economic rationality. In H. Simon, M. Egidi, R. Marris, & R. Viale (Eds.), *Economics, bounded rationality and the cognitive revolution*. Aldershot: Edward Elgar.

Viale, R., et al. (1993). Cognizione e razionalità delle credenze nelle scienze sociali. In R. Boudon (Ed.), *Teoria della razionalità*. Roma: Borla.

Viale, R. (1994a). Dans la Boîte noire: les mécanismes cognitifs de la décision scientifique. In R. Boudon & M. Clavelin (Eds.), *Le rélativisme est-il résistible?* Paris: Presses Universitaires de France.

Viale, R. (1994b). Oltre l'individualismo metodologico: il cognitivismo metodologico. *Sociologia e Ricerca Sociale, 43*, 89–95.

Viale, R. (1995). Alcune considerazioni epistemologiche e cognitive sul rapporto tra scienza ed arte, *Ricerca scientifica ed educazione permanente*, 102.

Viale, R. (1997a). Some methodological aspects of Herbert Simon's bounded rationality theory. In S. Herbert (Ed.), *An empirically based microeconomics*. Cambridge, UK: Cambridge University Press.
Viale, R. (1997b). From neoclassical to cognitive economics: The epistemological constraints of feasibility and realism. In R. Viale (Ed.), *Cognitive economics* (Quaderni lascomes 1, lascomes series). Torino: La Rosa Editrice.
Viale, R. (1999). Causal cognition and causal realism. *International Studies in the Philosophy of Science, 13*(2), 151–167.
Viale, R. (2001a). Truth, science, and politics: An analysis of social epistemology. In R. Viale (Ed.), *Knowledge and politics*. Heidelberg: Physica-Verlag.
Viale, R. (2001b). Reasons and reasoning: What comes first? In R. Boudon, P. Demeulenaere, & R. Viale (Eds.), *L'Explication des normes sociales*. Paris: Presses Universitaires de France.
Viale, R. (Ed.). (2005a). *Le nuove Economie. Dall'economia evolutiva a quella cognitiva: oltre i fallimenti della teoris neoclassica*. Milano: Editrice Il Sole 24 Ore.
Viale, R. (2005b). Quale mente per l'economia cognitiva. In R. Viale (Ed.), *Le nuove economie*. Milano: Il Sole 24 Ore.
Viale, R. (2006). Local or universal principles of reasoning? In R. Viale, L. Hirschfeld, & D. Andler (Eds.), *Biological and cultural bases of human inferences*. Mahwah, NJ: Erlbaum.
Viale, R. (2011). Soros e l'Effetto Gregge. foreword to Attia, C. and Hilton, D. J. (2011). *Decidere in Finanza*. Milano: Il Sole 24 Ore.
Viale, R. (forthcoming). *Epistemology, cognition, and innovation*, second volume of *Methodological cognitivism*. Heidelberg: Springer.
Viale, R., Andler, D., & Hirschfeld, L. (Eds.). (2006). *Biological and cultural bases of human inference*. Mahwah, NJ: Lawrence Erlbaum Associates.
Viale, R., & Cerroni, A. (2002). Methodological criteria of choice in science: The case study of Ispra's joint research center. Quaderni Lascomes 7/2002, *Lascomes Series*
Viale, R., & Osherson, D. (2000). The diversity principle and the little scientist hypothesis. *Foundations of Science, 5*(2), 239–253.
Viale, R., & Osherson, D. (2006). Cognitive development, culture, and inductive judgment. In R. Viale, D. Andler, & L. Hirschfeld (Eds.), *Biological and cultural bases of human inference*. Mahwah, NJ: Lawrence Erlbaum Associates.
Viale, R., & Pozzali, A. (2003). Al di qua della razionalità: la conoscenza tacita. *Sistemi Intelligenti, XV*(2), 325–346.
Viale, R., & Pozzali, A. (2007). Cognitive aspects of tacit knowledge and cultural diversity. In L. Magnani & P. Li (Eds.), *Model-based reasoning in science and medicine*. Berlin Heidelberg: Springer.
Vogeley, K., Bussfeld, P., Newen, A., Hermann, S., Happe, F., Falkai, P., Maier, W., Shah, N. J., Fink, G. R., & Zilles, K. (2001). Mindreading: Neural mechanisms of theory of mind and self-perspective. *NeuroImage, 14*, 170–81.
von Hayek, F. A. (1952a). *The counter revolution in science*. New York: Free Press.
von Hayek, F. A. (1952b). *The sensory order. An inquiry into the foundations of theoretical psychology*. London: Routledge.
von Hayek, F. A. (1973). From scientism and the study of society. In J. O'Neill (Ed.), *Modes of individualism and collectivism*. London: Heinemann.
von Mises, R. (1957). *Probability, statistics and truth*. London: Allen & Unwin.
von Neumann, J., & Morgenstern, O. (1947). *Theory of games and economic behavior*. Princeton, NJ: Princeton University Press.
von Wright, G. H. (1971). *Explanation and understanding*. Ithaca, NY: Cornell University Press.
Wason, P. C., & Evans, J. (1975). Dual processes in reasoning? *Cognition, 3*, 141–154.
Watanabe, M. (1998). Styles of reasoning in Japan and the United States: Logic of education in two cultures. Paper presented at the American Sociological Association, San Francisco, CA.

Watkins, J. (1973). Methodological individualism. In J. O'Neill (Ed.), *Modes of individualism and collectivism*. London: Heinemann.

Weber, M. (1922). *Wirtschaft und Gesellschaft*. Tubingen: Mohr.

Weber, M. (1949). *The methodology of the social sciences*. Glencoe: Free Press.

Weber, M. (1978). *Economy and society*. Berkeley, CA: University of California Press.

Weinberg, J., Nichols, S., & Stich, S. (2006). Normativity and epistemic intuitions. In R. Viale, D. Andler, & L. Hirschfeld (Eds.), *Biological and cultural bases of human inference* (pp. 1–31). Mahwah, NJ: Lawrence Erlbaum Associates.

Whorf, B. L. (1956). *Language, thought and reality*. New York: Wiley.

Wilson, T. D., & Schooler, J. W. (1991). Thinking too much: Introspection can reduce the quality of preferences and decisions. *Journal of Personality and Social Psychology, 60*, 181–192.

Wimsatt, W. (1981). Robustness, reliability and multiple-determination in science. In M. Brewer & B. Collins (Eds.), *Knowing and validating in social sciences*. San Francisco, CA: Jossey-Bass.

Witkin, H. A., Lewis, H. B., Hertzman, M., Machover, K., Meissner, P. B., & Karp, S. A. (1954). *Personality through perception*. New York: Harper.

Wolf, A. (1978). Gods, ghosts and ancestors. In A. Wolf (Ed.), *Studies in Chinese society*. Stanford, CA: Stanford University Press.

Woodward, A. L. (1998). Infants selectively encode the goal object of an actor's reach. *Cognition, 69*(1), 1–34.

Woodworth, R. S., & Sells, S. B. (1935). An atmosphere effect in formal syllogistic reasoning. *Journal of Experimental Psychology, 18*, 459–82.

Zahavi, D. (2001). Beyond empathy: Phenomenological approaches to intersubjectivity. *Journal of Consciousness Studies, 8*, 151–67.

Zajonc, R. B. (1998). Emotions. In D. Gilbert, S. Fiske, & G. Lindzey (Eds.), *The handbook of social psychology* (pp. 591–632). New York: Oxford University Press.

Zak, P., Kurzban, R., & Matzner, W. (2003). *Oxytocin is associated with interpersonal trust in humans*. Working paper, Claremont Graduate School Department of Economics.

Zamagni, S. (2005). L'economia civile e i beni relazionali. In R. Viale (Ed.), *Le nuove Economie. Dall'economia evolutiva a quella cognitiva: oltre i fallimenti della teoria neoclassica*. Milano: Editrice Il Sole 24 Ore.

Zeman, A. (2001). Consciousness. *Brain, 124*, 1263–1289.

Index

R. Viale, *Methodological Cognitivism*,
DOI 10.1007/978-3-642-24743-9,

About the Author

Riccardo Viale is Professor of Epistemology of Social Sciences at the University of Milano-Bicocca. He is Editor-in-Chief of *Mind & Society* (Springer) and the author or editor of many books such as *Modelling the Mind* (with K.A. Moyeldin Said, H. Newton Smith and K.V. Wilkes, Clarendon Press, 1990); *Economics, Bounded Rationality and the Cognitive Revolution* (with H. Simon, M. Egidi and R. Marris, Elgar, 1992, second edition 2008), *Knowledge and Politics* (Physica-Verlag, 2001), *Biological and Cultural Bases of Human Inferences* (with D. Andler and L. Hirschfeld, Erlbaum, 2006), *The Capitalization of Knowledge* (with H. Etzkowitz, Elgar, 2010). His research interests are the cognitive foundation of social action, the cognitive theory of economic rationality, cognitive approaches in philosophy of science and social epistemology, tacit knowledge and science policy.

R. Viale, *Methodological Cognitivism*,
DOI 10.1007/978-3-642-24743-9, © Springer-Verlag Berlin Heidelberg 2012

MIX
Papier aus verantwortungsvollen Quellen
Paper from responsible sources
FSC® C105338

If you have any concerns about our products,
you can contact us on
ProductSafety@springernature.com

In case Publisher is established outside the EU,
the EU authorized representative is:
Springer Nature Customer Service Center GmbH
Europaplatz 3, 69115 Heidelberg, Germany

Printed by Libri Plureos GmbH
in Hamburg, Germany